Probation and Justice

Reconsideration of Mission

Edited by

Patrick D. McAnany

Doug Thomson

David Fogel

OG Oelgeschlager, Gunn & Hain, Publishers, Inc.
&H Cambridge, Massachusetts

International Standard Book Number: 0–89946–176–x

Library of Congress Catalog Card Number: 83–12195

Printed in the U.S.A.

Library of Congress Cataloging in Publication Data

Main entry under title
    Probation and Justice

    Bibliography: p. –
    Includes index.
    1. Probation—United States—Addresses, essays, lectures. 2. Criminal justice, Administration of— United States—Addresses, essays, lectures.   I. McAnany, Patrick D. II. Thomson, Doug. III. Fogel, David, 1925–
HV9278.P69 1983   364.6'3'0973   83–12195
ISBN 0–89946–176–X

Prepared under Grant Numbers AN 9 and AN 9 Supplement #1 from the National Institute of Corrections, U.S. Department of Justice. Points of view or opinions stated in this document are those of the authors and do not necessarily represent the official position or policies of the U.S. Department of Justice.

The National Institute of Corrections reserves the right to reproduce, publish, translate, or otherwise use, and to authorize others to publish and use all or any part of the copyrighted material contained in this publication, chapters 5, 7 and 13 excepted.

Quotations on pages 142-155 are reprinted by permission of Lexington Books, D.C. Heath and Company

In Memoriam
Richard A. McGee

Contents

Foreword

The decade of the 1980s has been a time of challenge for probation. Some departments have been challenged to maintain their position with other criminal justice agencies; others have been challenged merely to survive. A rare few have been challenged to accept new roles and a variety of responsibilities heretofore foreign to a traditional probation operation. These challenges have arisen from a larger social context characterized by serious economic problems and skepticism about government's capabilities in the area of criminal justice as well as elsewhere.

Recognizing the opportunity presented by such a climate to rethink how a poorly understood but important part of the criminal justice system—probation—should be conceived and presented, the National Institute of Corrections funded the project from which much of this book derives.

The chapters herein represent the thinking of persons who encourage the probation professional to be creative and centered in positively confronting the issues of the day. The chapters are not intended as light reading. They are intended to challenge you; not merely to accept the written thoughts, but instead to provide the framework within which you can shape your own thoughts. The challenge is to develop and put in place community based corrections programs that the community can both understand and accept while furthering the pursuit of justice.

Probation is at least 100 years old and yet its purpose has never been adequately examined, nor have basic contradictions in practice and tradition been squarely confronted. As a part of the ongoing debate in sentencing, probation is now challenged to rethink its mission within the wider context of the criminal justice system. This book attempts such an examination from a variety of perspectives. As a leading contender for the primary sentencing and correction rationale, retribution or just deserts adds significantly to an understanding of what the system can and cannot do within the parameters of both democratic jurisprudence and resource management. The authors hardly agree on a solution to a host of problems confronting probation, but all agree on the need to stop accepting current explanations and justifications at face value and to rethink the implications of the basic notions. This rethinking may lead to contrary results, as several authors evidence in their writings. But from the dialogue developed among them in this book, a solution by professional leaders will hopefully emerge.

This book also has a secondary theme which the National Institute of Corrections has promoted over the years: correctional leadership roles. Whether stated directly, as in the Fitzharris and Fogel chapters, or indirectly as in other chapters, this book drums in the theme that probation professionals must become responsible to themselves and their field, as well as to the community, for an assessment and response to the problems of probation. The reach of the problem is wider than just the United States as the Bottoms and McWilliams chapter testifies in the context of British probation. Nor is it merely a matter of dusting off some old ideas and updating them in more efficient fashion. As Part I illustrates, rethinking of probation is a work for professionals who are willing to put aside traditional perspectives and think anew about tasks they have done for years in the groove of received tradition. This will require, as the McAnany chapter suggests, major legislative reworking and will penetrate even to the juvenile courts as Thomson and McAnany aptly suggest. But the theme is that the work at hand begs for active participation by probation practitioners to ensure that other actors, closely or loosely associated with the field, pay adequate attention to implications for probation practice, as suggested by Thomson, for example.

Finally, the book illustrates as few other pieces on probation have done, that probation is the work of localities. Despite the overview of the field which most of the chapters take, all, or nearly all, acknowledge the fact that probation is essentially what the locality requires of convicted but unimprisoned offenders. Duffee's chapter on "The Community Context of Probation" brings the point most clearly to the surface. It is not possible to have a single blueprint of probation for every community. Each community has unique goals and resources and each will require a probation that conforms to its mandates. This theme will make the adjustment of any universal principles, including just deserts, a creative task for local leaders, as the Harlow chapter so brilliantly suggests.

In the end, this book can do little to implement its ideas if the people who work in probation fail to act upon its dictates for whatever cause. Its purpose is to stir and focus debate among probation professionals, other corrections and criminal justice actors and in the community at large. But debate, however well rehearsed and intriguing, will only become reality if the hands on the levers of political power are moved to move. It is a call to the field that we fervently hope will be heard.

Allen Breed
Director, National Institute of Corrections
U.S. Department of Justice

Introduction

Doug Thomson, Patrick D. McAnany, and David Fogel

Fifty years ago Sheldon Glueck edited a volume of essays on probation. "In the barren soil of penology," he remarked, "probation gives promise of developing into the flower among the weeds" (Glueck, 1933). We have waited patiently for the flowers to grow. The present volume does not purport to offer a grand bouquet, but it will contribute to the sparse literature on probation a group of original essays on a topic of obvious salience to our present dilmemmas of penology.

Looking back over the fifty years since Glueck's *Probation and Criminal Justice*, one cannot help but wonder what went wrong with the hopes of an earlier generation. David Rothman (1980) has argued that probation was never intended as a realistic alternative to prisons. Rather, it offered a paper solution to a system built upon the central reality of processing cases through the courts. For prosecutors, judges, and even defense attorneys, the alternative of "doing something" (probation) added to the settlement process by which cases were handled. While this offers a partial explanation of how probation survived during decades of public unrest over lack of protection against crime, it throws little light on what the "something" was that constituted the work of probation. Granted that the courtroom work group saw probation as an added chip in the bargaining process, still other levels of reality existed beyond this abstract moment in a long chain of events called criminal justice.

Reviewing the empirical and theoretical output on probation as a major institution of criminal justice leaves the impression that perhaps the cynical views of the courtroom group are correct. The past five decades have produced few contributions of any moment.

The Attorney General's Survey of Release Procedures (1939) devoted a whole volume to probation, setting forth a wealth of empirical and legal data. Prominent scholars contributed to the work of this national commission and made the portrait of probation a well delineated study of what went into the field. The work embodies certain contradictions, sharpened in later years, between a libertarian concern for defendants' rights and a social casework concern for mandated therapy; still it remains relevant today. Considerable time elapsed before another significant contribution to data or theory was made.

As Carey points out in Chapter 9 of this volume, probation as a field seemed available to all sorts of explanations without ever settling on a single one for very long. Social casework has persistently been the single most common paradigm for professional practice. Dressler's *Practice and Theory of Probation and Parole* (1959) is one summary of this tradition of training. Yet it also represents an opening to a renewed interest in the importance of law to the field. Two independent legal reform groups developed during the 1950s which produced model codes in the early years of the next decade. The first was the National Council on Crime and Delinquency, a successor group to the original professional membership agency for probation, the National Probation and Parole Association. NCCD's *Model Sentencing Act* (1963) never achieved the significance of its rival, the *Model Penal Code* (1962) of the American Law Institute. But it offered probation a prominence and clarity in the law which it had lacked up to that point. Sol Rubin, the legal advisor to NCCD for many years, became a champion of defendants' rights in later years (1973), and in many respects the concept of civil rights for prisoners grew out of the libertarian roots of probation.

The *Model Penal Code* has become the central document for all criminal law reform of the past two decades in the United States. Its views of sentencing may have become suspect in an era of just deserts (von Hirsch, 1981), but the centrality it gives to probation has not been gainsayed by the critics. For the first time in American law, the *Code* gave probation a legal status as a sentence and made that sentence a preferred choice for all but the most serious felonies (McAnany, 1976). The implications of such a change have not been well worked out in legal theory, but the impetus for bringing probation into full legal citizenship is the ongoing work of the courts. (See Chapter 2 of this volume.)

The President's Crime Commission volume on *Corrections* (1967) added some empirical data and an overview of a renewed probation working within a criminal justice system devoted to law abidance—not for defendants, but for officials. There were suggestions that probation had other roles to fulfill than social casework. Advocacy and brokerage became common terms in later literature on probation's tasks. It was just as well that counseling and other treatment technologies were de-emphasized. In the mid-seventies, a major work (Lipton et al., 1975) gave detailed evidence of the failure of a rehabilitative approach to corrections in general, including probation. Despite the ongoing debate about the efficacy of treatment, probation appears to have ignored the bad news.

In the past twenty years California has been the site of several major studies focusing on probation and probation-related experiments. The State's Probation Subsidy Project was a massive effort to divert convicted persons from state institutions into local probation case loads. Lemert and Dill's (1978) examination of this effort showed a good deal about how probation agencies organize their work and their relations with their constituencies. They describe how different departments react to a common policy and how some succeed and some falter in their efforts to absorb new clients, deal with judges, and create new roles for probation personnel. Nelson and Harlow (1980) also look at probation as an organization as they examine California departments reacting to budget cuts in the late 1970s. Another California experiment was more traditional in perspective. It sought to determine whether juveniles who were committed to the Youth Authority could be safely supervised in the community using a psychologically based typology matching youth and parole officers (Warren, 1976). While the results were mixed in terms of recidivism outcomes, they suggested that some treatment worked for some offenders—probably the watchword for future rehabilitation efforts.

This survey of some of the more significant contributions to probation over the past five decades suggests that Glueck and his colleagues in the 1930s were overly optimistic. Yet probation has, in a sense, been the flower in the weed garden of penology. Its basic premise of humanitarianism has been affirmed by the fact that it has received primacy in the law reform of the past two decades, as well as continuing to be the single largest correctional experience.

ORIGINS OF THE BOOK

The last decade has seen the decline of the rehabilitative ideal and the rise of the justice ideal (American Friends Service Committee, 1971; Frankel, 1972; McGee, 1974; Fogel, 1975; von Hirsch, 1976; Twentieth Century Fund, 1976; Singer, 1979; Allen, 1981). The major policy expression of this process has been primarily in sentencing and secondarily in institutional corrections. Probation and other forms of community corrections have largely been ignored.

Proponents of desert-based or retributive sentencing and of the justice model for corrections focused on limiting discretion as to incarcerative sentences and experiences. In so doing, they contributed to the perception of probation as something less than, or other than, a penalty. Meanwhile, proponents of rehabilitation were fighting a rearguard action on behalf of probation. Unfortunately, many of these proponents were using soggy ammunition, continuing to portray probation as 1) a rehabilitative or reintegrative enterprise, i.e., one serving the probationer as "client," and 2) a means of reducing crime and protecting local communities. Overwhelmingly, they failed to seize the opportunity to highlight probation's status as a penal sanction. By the end of the 1970s, however, probation's restitutive capabilities and potential were receiving more attention, as symbolized by the Americn Probation and Parole Association's project on Improving Victim Services Through Probation.

In the meantime, the National Institute of Corrections (NIC) was beginning to direct more scrutiny and resources toward probation. As part of this effort, they awarded a grant (AN 9) in 1978 to the University of Illinois at Chicago (UIC) to study the training needs of small probation agencies. Testimony received from around the nation as part of its hearings for developing the annual plan had convinced the NIC that there was considerable concern that program models developed for urban and large probation agencies could be inappropriate for rural and medium or small agencies or systems. Hence, NIC authorized UIC to do the small agency study and the University of Minnesota to do a companion study of the training needs of administrators in mid-sized systems.

The findings of the UIC Staff Training for Small Probation Agencies project were published and given limited circulation (Thomson and Fogel, 1980). That report noted that training appeared to be provided in greater measure than one might have expected, but that there were significant gaps in delivery of training. The authors proposed ways to correct these deficiencies. They also described at some length what probation officers in small agencies were doing and the constraints under which these agencies were operating.

Apart from the study's specific findings and recommendations regarding training, the authors recognized the desirability of clarifying probation's mission in a time of changing conceptions of sentencing and corrections. This recognition was shaped by the principal investigator's involvement in facilitating this transformation of thought and action (Fogel, 1975). Joined by their colleague Patrick D. McAnany, and supported by a further NIC grant (AN 9 Supplement #1), Fogel and Thomson subsequently contracted with several prominent analysts of probation to address various questions related to its mission. On the way to producing the final report (McAnany et al., 1982), the principals presented progress reports on the Probation Mission Project to several meetings of practitioner associations such as the American Probation and Parole Association (APPA), the American Correctional Association, the New York State Probation Officers Association, and the New Jersey Probation Officers Association, as well as to the National Forum on Criminal Justice and the American Society of Criminology. Such presentations provided the opportunity for critical comments from practitioners and scholars of probation.

The final report of the project was submitted to NIC in January 1982. Following reviews and comment, several chapters were revised and three new ones were added. This book is the result.

ACKNOWLEDGMENTS

In developing this book, we have been indulged by thousands of probation officers throughout the nation. We appreciate their time and consideration and the willingness frequently displayed to reflect critically on their work, their occupation, and the context within which they operate.

We are particularly grateful for the efforts of John Ackermann (New York State Division of Probation and past president of the APPA) and Scotia Knouff (Project Director of the APPA Improving Victim Services through Probation Project and formerly a probation manager in Nassau County, New York). They served as consultants to the project, thoughtfully reviewing and commenting on earlier drafts of many of the chapters in the book.

Many others helped, some with extensive comments or conversation, some with helpful criticism, some by providing us with resources or comparative materials. Among these, we recall the following: Donald Cochran (Massachusetts Probation Services), Robert Nunz (New York State Probation Officers Association), Robert Joe Lee and William Burrell (New Jersey Administrative Office of the Courts), Norm Helber (Gloucester County, New Jersey, Probation Department), Sidney Dwoskin (Los Angeles Probation Department), Thomas Frady (Plumas County, California, Probation Department), Andrew R. Klein (Quincy, Massachusetts, Probation Department), Nancy Lick (Philadelphia Probation Department), Anthony Czarnecki (Westchester County, New York, Probation Department), Richard Brice (Nagodoches, Texas, Probation Department), Gerry Waldron (National Office for Social Responsibility), Jay Purcell (Federal Probation System, Philadelphia), Keith Couse (University of Regina), LaMar T. Empey (University of Southern California), John Harding (Birmingham, England, Probation and Aftercare Services), Larry Solomon and Chris Baird (National Institute of Corrections), Raymond Parnas (University of California at Davis), Robert Weber (Eastern Carolina University) and Robert Compton (Federal Probation, Chicago).

We are also particularly appreciative of the support the National Institute of Corrections provided for our investigation of probation's changing mission. Special mention should be made of the role played by Marian Hyler, the project monitor. She not only critically reviewed our work, but was ever alert for pertinent connections—to literature, current research, and developments in probation practice. Allen Breed, director of NIC, has fittingly closed the circle by contributing the foreword to this volume.

Finally, we would like to note the devoted efforts of the staff of the Center for Research in Law and Justice under the direction of Joseph L. Peterson. In particular, we appreciate the proofreading and typing services of F. Desirèe Boyd, Carol Gielarowski, Theresa Johnson McKelphin, and Yvonne Smith as well as the administrative assistance of Mary Pallen and Bobbie Dunbar. Special thanks are due Steven Mihajlovic for helping out as needed. Computing services provided by the University of Illinois at Chicago Computer Center are also appreciated.

PREVIEW

The fourteen chapters that follow, all but one of which are original essays prepared for this volume, are organized into three parts. The first part, "The Justice Model and Probation," introduces the elements of the justice model and explores their relation to probation. In contrast to some other contributors to this volume, the four represented in this section are clearly advocates of the justice model.

In Chapter 1, M. Kay Harris, explores the role of the probation sanction within the justice model. She points out the problems, from a justice model perspective, with traditional conceptualizations of probation, articulates some principles that should apply to sanctions generally in a desert-based sentencing system, and concludes by indicating how such principles could be applied to probation.

Patrick D. McAnany follows with an analysis in Chapter 2 of probation's legal foundations. Beginning with the proposition that "probation as a penal sanction must conform to the principles of due process of law," he delineates how the development of criminal law and sentencing law is tending to cast probation as a justice enterprise.

David Fogel, in Chapter 3, examines structural difficulties of the probation occupation and flaws of the "needs deprivation model" for probation practice. After formulating the problem in these terms, he proposes some principles for justice model probation and makes explicit recommendations for how it might be structured, with particular emphasis on victims as clients of probation and public safety as its goal. He concludes by outlining a ten-year plan by which the probation field could move in this direction.

Chapter 4, by Doug Thomson, draws out the implications for organization and practice of justice model probation. These implications touch on probations's public safety role and its marginality, the place of offender services and of victim services, restitution, and community services orders, and the skills and activities required of probation officers. After pondering the receptivitiy of the probation field to the justice model, the chapter concludes, as it began, with cautions regarding the need for appropriate implementation of the reform with full cognizance of probation's system context and difficulties with the concept of punishment.

Part I concludes with Thomson and McAnany's chapter on the justice model and the juvenile court. They emphasize elements of juvenile court practice and ideology—in particular, blaming and responsibility—that link traditional conceptions of the juvenile court and commensurate desert principles. Their approach is to present a theory of blaming and punishment, to analyze the historical development of the juvenile court and its probation service, draw the dimensions of juvenile probation practice under a desert-based sentencing system, and indicate how larger social justice concerns can be accommodated by a reconceptualization of the juvenile court's child welfare responsibilities.

Part II, "Probation Ideology and Structure," consists of five chapters exploring how probation practice is shaped by normative and social organizational factors. Chapters 6, 9, and 10 identify considerations that should be taken into account in any attempt at probation reform. Chapters 7 and 8 propose designs more attuned to justice model reforms.

In Chapter 6, David E. Duffee puts a new light on the traditional conception of the probation officer's role as a manifestation of tensions between control and assistance, or between surveillance and service. He comprehensively describes and critiques a range of existing models which he classifies as either single (goal) dimensional or two (goal) dimensional. Then, he assesses the extent to which the various models improve our understanding of probation supervision, identifies their weaknesses, and suggests that theoretical development and research testing of more complex models can help us better articulate probation's mission.

A. E. Bottoms and William McWilliams argue in Chapter 7, which appeared first in 1979 as an article in the *British Journal of Social Work*, that while empirical and theoretical critiques of treatment are compelling, probation can still honor its traditional central values of respect for persons and hope for the future. In particular, they show how a non-treatment paradigm for probation practice permits pursuit of four traditional aims:

helping offenders, supervising offenders, diverting offenders from incarceration, and reducing crime.

Chapter 8 presents John P. Conrad's proposals for reallocating probation's traditional functions among several agencies and integrating them into a more rational correctional system. He asks what organizational auspices will most facilitate the effective discharge of the functions associated with the *status* of probation. In answering the question, he first locates probation among the six principal elements of the current criminal justice crisis, then argues that improvements in correctional services must take place in the community and that efficiency requirements here demand the redistribution of functions, and suggests a form that such reorganization might take.

In Chapter 9, James T. Carey brings empirical evidence to bear on the issue of probation's professionalization. In particular, he analyzes the diffusion and acceptance among probation practitioners of various explanations of crime and delinquency. By way of a content analysis of the *Federal Probation* journal from 1937 through 1978, he identifies six academic perspectives—social pathology, social disorganization, differential association, opportunity theory, labeling, and justice model—and analyzes how their popularity has varied over time and how they were introduced and propagated.

In the concluding chapter of Part II, David E. Duffee investigates a neglected point of view on probation reforms and goal clarification attempts —that of the client, or probationer. He observes that providing clients with organizational membership constrains organizational behavior. Hence, the client model takes into account the extent and degree of interaction between client and organization in contrast to the emphasis of the goal model on role content. Duffee uses the client biography model to compare probation with other penal sanctions and to distinguish among kinds of probation experiences. The chapter concludes with a discussion of the implications of the client biography model for reconsiderations of probation's mission.

Part III, "Prospects for Probation Reform," examines various contingencies in implementing a justice model rform or any major reform, in this field; the authors are not justice model advocates. Chapter 11, by Robert C. Cushman, presents a public administration viewpoint on probation's development in the 1980s. After noting probation's current goal confusion and other problems and discussing its precarious status despite its growing workload and responsibilities, he proposes a course of action by which probation can pragmatically influence its destiny.

David E. Duffee returns in Chapter 12 to analyze the effects of community context on probation operations and mission. He addresses community structure in terms of vertical relations and horizontal articulation, and describes four types of community—fragmented, interdependent, disorganized, and solidary—produced by the interplay of these variables. He then contemplates how probation organization might vary by community structure. The chapter concludes with a discussion of the need to consider external constraints in attempts to direct probation's future.

Nora Harlow continues this theme in Chapter 13, which focuses on impediments to justice model reform. She begins by observing the vagaries of criminal justice reform in general and the ambiguities and lack of consensus in justice model expositions. Hawlow draws on her earlier research to identify current trends in probation, then relates them to the question of the justice model's viability as a potential reform. She finds that the fit is close but incomplete, and that implementation will depend on how probation in a given jurisdiction has adapted to its environment. The chapter's conclusion is that the most satisfying future for the model lies in full but selective implementation rather than in attempts at hegemony by acommodation.

The final chapter, by Timothy L. Fitzharris, argues that effective corrective responses to probation's current troubles require national leadership. He analyzes why such leadership is lacking and describes how the stage has been set for the National Institute of Corrections to fill this role. After conceding that such a position seems contrary to recent federal policy, Fitzharris traces the history of the federal role in policy-making during the past half century and concludes that a modified advocacy/policy-making role is an appropriate and desirable consequence at this time in our history. To provide a form for such activity, he suggests a "flexible leadership" model for which he finds NIC well suited.

This book presents a variety of conclusions, some more tentative than others, emerging from a collective dialogue of several years' duration. We believe that it fills an important gap in analysis of sentencing and correctional reforms and suggests some positive directions for the development of probation. That this material is new and preliminary highlights the need for research and policy analysis efforts to test the positions advanced. Perhaps the most important message of this book is that the justice model must be thoughtfully, faithfully, and cautiously implemented if it is to achieve the desired advances in the pursuit of justice and avoid the harms inflicted or perpetuated that are the frequent legacy of superficial reforms.

REFERENCES

American Friends Service Committee (1971). *Struggle for Justice*. New York: Hill and Wang.

American Law Institute (1962). *Model Penal Code*. Philadelphia: American Law Institute.

Allen, Francis A. (1981). *The Decline of the Rehabilitative Ideal: Penal Policy and Social Purpose*. New Haven: Yale.

Carey, James T. (1983). "The Professionalization of Probation: An Analysis of the Diffusion of Ideas." Chapter 9 in this volume.

Dressler, David (1958). *Practice and Theory of Probation and Parole*. New York: Columbia.

Fogel, David (1975). ". . . *We Are the Living Proof* . . . " The Justice Model for Corrections. Cincinnati: Anderson.

Frankel, Marvin E. (1972). *Criminal Sentences: Law Without Order*. New York: Hill and Wang.

Glueck, Sheldon (ed.) (1933). *Probation and Criminal Justice*. New York: Macmillan.

Lemert, Edwin M., and Forrest Dill (1978). *Offenders in the Community: The Probation Subsidy in California*. Lexington, Massachusetts: D. C. Heath.

Lerman, Paul (1975). *Community Treatment and Social Control: A Critical Analysis of Juvenile Correctional Policy*. Chicago: University of Chicago Press.

Lipton, Douglas, Robert Martinson, and Judith Wilks (1975). *The Effectiveness of Correctional Treatment: A Survey of Treatment Evaluation Studies*. New York: Praeger.

McAnany, Patrick D. (1976). "Recommendations for Improving the Ailing Probation System." In Rudolph J. Gerber (ed.), *Contemporary Issues in Criminal Justice*. Port Washington, New York: Kennikat.

McAnany, Patrick D., Doug Thomson, and David Fogel (1982). *Probation and Justice: Surfacing a Hidden Mission*. Chicago: Center for Research in Law and Justice, University of Illinois at Chicago.

McGee, Richard A. (1974). "A New Look at Sentencing" (Parts I and II). *Federal Probation* 38 (2) and (3).

National Council on Crime and Delinquency, Advisory Council of Judge (1963). *Model Sentencing Act*. New York: National Council on Crime and Delinquency.

Nelson, E. Kim, Jr., and Nora Harlow (1980). *Responses to Diminishing Resources in Probation: The California Experience*. Report to the National Institute of Corrections. Berkeley: University of Southern California.

The President's Commission on Law Enforcement and Administration of Justice (1967). *Task Force Report: Corrections*. Washington, D.C.: U.S. Government Printing Office.

Rothman, David J. (1971). *The Discovery of the Asylum*. Boston: Little, Brown.

———(1980). *Conscience and Convenience: The Asylum and its Alternatives in Progressive America*. Boston: Little, Brown.

Rubin, Sol (1973). *The Law of Criminal Correction*. Second edition. St. Paul: West.

Singer, Richard G. (1979). *Just Deserts: Sentencing Based on Equality and Desert*. Cambridge, MA: Ballinger.

Thomson, Doug, and David Fogel (1980). *Probation Work in Small Agencies: A National Study of Training Provisions and Needs*. Chicago: Center for Research in Law and Justice, University of Illinois at Chicago.

Twentieth Century Fund (1976). *Task Force Report on Sentencing: Fair and Certain Punishment*. New York: McGraw-Hill.

U.S. Attorney General (1939). *The Attorney General's Survey of Release Procedures. Volume II: Probation*. Washington, D.C.: U.S. Government Printing Office.

von Hirsch, Andrew, (1976). *Doing Justice: The Choice of Punishments*. New York: Hill and Wang.

——— (1981). "Utilitarian Sentencing Resuscitated: The American Bar Association's Second Report on Criminal Sentencing." *Rutgers Law Review* 33:772–89.

Warren, Marguerite Q. (1976). "Intervention with Juvenile Delinquents." In Margaret Rosenheim (ed.), *Pursuing Justice for the Child*. Chicago: University of Chicago.

PART I

The Justice Model and Probation

Chapter 1

Rethinking Probation in the Context of a Justice Model

*M. Kay Harris**

Philosophers and criminologists have long debated the proper goals of criminal sanctioning systems. In recent years, most of the debate has centered on whether sanctions should be based solely or primarily on desert (i.e., retributive interests) or on utilitarian aims (e.g., rehabilitation, deterrence, and incapacitation). Other voices propose strikingly different models for responding to unlawful behavior, preferring Marxian or Maoist conceptions of redistribution of power and re-education to socialist values, or Judeo-Christian conceptions of redemption, restoration, and the building of community. We are far from consensus in this country, much less internationally. To clarify the issues involved in debates about criminal sanctioning systems, it may be useful to set forth explicitly the values, principles, and implications of the models being discussed. This chapter represents such an undertaking. Specifically, it is designed to explore the implications of adopting a justice model for the common criminal sanction of probation. This effort requires some elaboration of what a justice model is or might be, but the primary focus will be on rethinking one existing sanction in a new context.

*Department of Criminal Justice, Temple University

The term justice model as used here is drawn from the work of David Fogel and some of his colleagues. In *We Are the Living Proof* (1975), Fogel set forth a rationale and the major principles of a justice model. That work, however, considered applications of the model primarily in terms of the sanction of imprisonment. It is important to explore the implications of the model for other sanctions as well.

In many respects Fogel's work on the justice model resembles work done over the last few years under the general rubric of a "just deserts" model. *Doing Justice: The Report of the Committee for the Study of Incarceration* (1976), by Andrew von Hirsch, was a leader in laying out the arguments for and some of the implications of a model based on just or commensurate deserts. Richard G. Singer's *Just Deserts: Sentencing Based on Equality and Desert* (1979) further clarifies the issues within such a model. The justice model discussed in this chapter builds on the work set forth in these and other statements, but that does not imply that any of the other writers would necessarily subscribe to the principles or analysis that follow.

A comprehensive discussion of how to make a justice model operational would have to address a number of critical and complex issues in some detail. It would be necessary, for example, to offer specific proposals as to how criminal offenses should be defined and categorized and how serious various crimes or crime categories should be considered. It would be important to decide whether a particular approach should govern the choice of sanctions for individual offenders (such as a sentencing guidelines scheme), how discretion should be controlled at various points of the justice process, and what factors should be taken into account in assessing the blameworthiness of an offender's conduct. The works mentioned above offer general overviews, additional sources of information, and some recommendations with respect to such issues. Greater explication of how each of these important issues should be resolved still is needed, but that is a task beyond the scope of this paper.

PROBLEMS WITH THE TRADITIONAL CONCEPTUALIZATION OF PROBATION AS VIEWED FROM A JUSTICE MODEL PERSPECTIVE

Probation traditionally has been oriented toward the immediate present or the future. The stated goal has been to reduce the likelihood of crime by supervising or providing services to offenders, with the possibility of revocation as a back-up if other preventive tactics seem to be failing. Under conventional probation, wide variation in the requirements placed on offenders has been not only possible but expected. Individualization of the sanction has been regarded as necessary to take into account the backgrounds, problems, and propensities of different offenders. Thus, probation has been tied more strongly to the individual offender—what he or she might think, do, or need—than to the crime that occasioned the punishment.

Problems with Individualization of Sanctions

The conventional model of probation certainly seemed attractive on a number of counts. The likelihood of future crime would be reduced through personal attention and surveillance at the same time that the offender was being supplied with whatever skills or assistance might be needed. Several major problems, however, are not far beneath the surface of that formulation. A major issue concerns the fairness or justice of tailoring criminal sanctions to individuals, to changing circumstances, and to predictions and beliefs rather than to past acts. Is it fair to sentence one offender to three years of probation with the requirement that she abstain from alcohol, earn a high school equivalency diploma, and obtain employment, while another better-situated offender guilty of the same offense is given a shorter term with no special conditions? The special instructions or conditions that may be applied can have very different meanings or consequences for different people. Exhortations involving various forms of "good conduct" imply different things to different people. Such obligations can be unrealistic, since it may be difficult to obtain what is prescribed, such as employment or medical treatment. Another concern relates to the effectiveness of the individualistic, predictive approach. Is there good reason to believe that getting a high school education is related to the goal of reducing future crime?

The problems of reconciling a predictive, individualistic penalty with the requirements of a justice model are complicated by the fact that the variation that occurs in standard probation does not simply reflect perceived differences among offenders. The nature of a probation sentence also depends on the views of the sentencing judge, the nature of any special conditions, the orientation of the probation officer and his or her stance toward revocation, the policies of the probation office involved, and many other such variables. It makes quite a difference whether an offender appears before a judge who views probation simply as "another chance" and only hopes to see no more of the offender, or one who takes seriously the rehabilitative or restrictive aspects of the penalty and imposes detailed requirements accordingly. Variation also can occur with respect to practices such as requiring property offenders to make restitution to victims; this is a common condition of probation in some jurisdictions, but exceptional in others.

The orientation of the supervising probation officer and the office with which he or she is associated also can have strikingly differing impacts on probationers. The variation in philosophy and approach employed by probation officers is wide. Some officers take a rather paternalistic stance, expecting probationers to share problems which the officer then will "solve." Others take a more laissez-faire attitude, assuming that no news is good news. Still other probation personnel, viewing themselves primarily as law enforcement officers charged with protecting the public from any possible criminal acts, will conscientiously monitor probationers' activities. For the offender, the probation experience can vary widely. Some will feel compelled to recite their personal concerns to a paternalistic officer; those assigned to a laissez-faire officer may feel virtually no accountability; and probationers who report to a law-enforcement-oriented officer may be afraid to spit on the sidewalk.

Problems with Indefiniteness in Sanctions

When the underlying offense is not one that warrants incarcerative punishment, it seems clear that the system should not permit revocation of probation and subsequent incarceration. In current practice, however, revocation can stem from matters not even alleged to constitute crimes, regardless of the seriousness of the original conviction offense. A wide variety of behaviors—from leaving the county, to marrying, to showing lack of remorse—may be held to violate conditions of probation, possibly leading to revocation. Although revocation for such trivial problems is rare, the very possibility that they could be used to determine an individual's liberty is inconsistent with a justice model. Even if willful failure to comply with such conditions constituted a crime, incarceration would clearly be too harsh a punishment for such insignificant failings. Similarly, it seems unacceptable to punish minor infractions by modifying probation conditions to make the sanction significantly more severe.

Revocation proceedings typically employ less stringent standards of proof than are applied in criminal proceedings, threatening the principle that sanctions should be tied to proven criminal acts. This difficulty has been described well by von Hirsch and Hanrahan:

> The high standard of proof in criminal proceedings is a fundamental require-ment of fairness; it is designed to keep to a minimum the risk of punishing the innocent. . . . This principle has as much applicability to persons charged with crimes who were previously convicted and imprisoned, as it does to persons accused for the first time. It is no less unfair to punish a parolee for an alleged new offense which he may, in fact, not have committed, than to punish an alleged first offender who may be innocent. [footnotes omitted] (1978:18)

Thus there are several possible sources of variation in the content and quality of the probation sanction, and chances are good that similarly situated offenders will have dissimilar experiences. The discretionary nature of the penalty can produce continuing uncertainty and anxiety for offenders, as well as feelings of inability to control what happens to them. The variability described also undermines the clarity of sanction in the public eye.

Problems with the Treatment Model

Much has been written in recent years about the problems surrounding the treatment model in corrections. The fundamental flaw in the treatment model is that it leads us to deal with persons as if they were objects. Whereas the justice model sees punishment as a kind of debt owed by offenders because of crimes they have committed, the treatment model sees it as a means of influencing offenders' future behavior. When our response to law violators does not depend on the nature and quality of their acts, but on our notions as to what they or others might do in the future without our intervention, we are using the offenders as means of attaining social goals. When penalties are shaped to serve utilitarian interests, the concept of desert is overshadowed.

> . . . But the concept of desert is the only connecting link between punishment and justice. . . . There is no sense in talking about a "just deterrent" or a "just cure." We demand of a cure not whether it is just but whether it succeeds. Thus when we cease to consider what the criminal deserves and consider only what will cure him or deter others, we have tacitly removed him from the sphere of justice altogether; instead of a person, a subject of rights, we now have a mere object, a patient, a "case." (Lewis, 1972:43–44)

This is one of the fundamental concerns of a justice model. It is vitally important that the law and its agents treat offenders as persons rather than as means to an end. Conviction of a criminal act is no excuse for treating the offender as less than a person.

Concern for the danger of treating offenders as less than responsible persons has been reflected in such practices as having offenders "consent" to a probation order before it is imposed. But because it is virtually impossible for offenders to know what they are consenting to, this device too fails to give them adequate respect as persons. As the American Friends Service Committee asserted in *Struggle for Justice*, in critiquing parole supervision, the essential features of the probation model tend to undermine the possibility of dealing with offenders except as means to an end:

The paradigm of the system . . . is the role of the parole officer, whose job is simultaneously to help the parolee under his supervision and to protect society from that parolee. The resulting role conflict of having to serve two masters—the client and the state—corrodes the mutual trust necessary for therapy and invites the pollution of service by reducing it to a manipulative device whereby the officer's control/police function can be facilitated. (1971:28)

Proposals for Remedying the Problems with a Treatment Model

Those who have reached the conclusion that it is inappropriate to determine sanctions on the basis of rehabilitative interests generally have recommended one of two courses: restructuring or reconceptualizing the service function toward a nonmedical model; or separating the functions of service and control so that different staff members would be responsible for each function.

One model of the first sort is the non-treatment paradigm for probation developed in England by Bottoms and McWilliams (1979), as described in Chapter 7. In addition to discussing three other aims they see as central to a new model for probation, they suggest moving from the traditional assistance role, which was based on a medical model of treatment and characterized by "objectification," to a role of providing appropriate help for offenders. In its pure form, they observe, the treatment model "begins with a diagnosis by the caseworker of the client's malfunctioning; then the treater decides upon the appropriate treatment with little or no advice from the client. The client is not offered choices about the form of the appropriate treatment; he is assumed to be dependent and in need of expert attention" (1979:172).

With respect to objectification, Bottoms and McWilliams concur with the Oxford philosopher P. F. Strawson, who wrote:

To adopt the objective attitude to another human being is to see him, perhaps, as an object of social policy; as a subject for what, in a wide range of sense, might be called treatment . . . to be managed or handled or cured or trained. . . . The objective attitude . . . cannot include the range of reactive feelings and attitudes which belong to involvement or participation with others in inter-personal human relationships. [footnotes and emphasis omitted] (Quoted in Bottoms and McWilliams, 1979:170)

In the helping model proposed by Bottoms and McWilliams, (1979:171) "both overt moral correctionalism and 'the objective attitude' are to be eschewed" in favor of achieving "an adequate understanding of clients as real people" and offering unconditional help with client-defined tasks (within defined boundaries). If the offer of help is accepted, there is to be a

collaborative effort between worker and client to define the problem requiring help and to work out jointly a set of possible alternative strategies,
with the client then being free to make the choices for himself or herself.

In a paper prepared for the Probation Mission Project and included as
Chapter 8 of this volume, Conrad (1983) takes the second course mentioned,
arguing for the separation of the service and control functions into different
units. He recommends that the control/surveillance function be performed
by the police and the assistance function by a restructured probation
department. This Division of Service and Liaison would carry out all
services "needed to assist probationers toward satisfactory completion of
probation," but would have no responsibility for surveillance. Probationers
who needed no assistance would have no contact with the Division.

Unfortunately, neither of the proposed means of dealing with the problems of concern presents a fully adequate model for restructuring probation within a justice model framework. The reconceptualization proposed
by Bottoms and McWilliams seems to focus on the wrong villain. They
attack a vision of a powerful treatment-oriented caseworker who deter-
mines what an offender needs and prescribes it. They offer as a replace-
ment a vision of a helper involved in a meaningful and equal working
relationship devoted to problem solving on the basis of the offender's
perceptions of problems and the offender's definition of appropriate help.

Arrogant treaters have long been under attack, and a variety of innovations have already been tried to rid the field of them. Community resource
management teams, for example, have been instituted in probation offices
to allow officers to specialize in the various forms of assistance—employment, housing, and the like—that probationers often need and to serve as
"brokers" in procuring services the offenders say they need and want. In
such a model, the probation officer functions more as an advocate than as a
therapist. For the most part, however, such schemes have not been
completely divorced from the courts. Utilization of services still is seen as a
reason for sentencing an offender to probation, and courts expect (or
require) that the offender will accept assistance and perhaps employ it in a
particular way. Simply offering helping services to probationers who wish
to use them is unlikely to be a workable plan if such activities remain within
the purview of the court. There is a risk that offenders who do not avail
themselves of offered services would be at a disadvantage in court reports.
In any event, offenders are likely to believe that utilization or nonutiliza-
tion of services will influence the court. Moreover, as long as such services
remain attached to the courts in any way, there will probably be pressure
to use the provision of services as a means of trying to bring about
conformity to prevailing norms.

Conrad's proposed Division of Service and Liaison is to be asked to carry
out "all contact services needed to assist probationers toward satisfactory

completion of probation." Perhaps it is unfair to single out this phrase in his description, but the language suggests a lingering connection between the assistance role and the sanctioning of the offender. What will be the charge to the personnel of the Division? Would their mission be to try to provide any and all kinds of assistance requested, even if there is no plausible connection between such assistance and the state's interests? Or would their duty be linked more closely to achieving compliance with the sanction? There is also an implication, at least in Fogel, Thomson, and McAnany's restatement of Conrad's proposal, that offenders who took advantage of services would not be subject to supervision by the police unit. The authors state that probationers who did not wish to use services would be referred to the Division of Supervision. Does this mean that for some probationers utilization of services would be in lieu of supervision? These questions suggest the difficulty of fully divorcing services from the sanction if it is in the context of the sanction that the services become available.

Neither of the proposed models adequately considers why an agency of government ought to be in the business of offering help to criminal offenders (and presumably *only* criminal offenders), or why offenders would be inclined to use assistance from this source. If the goal were to rehabilitate offenders and prevent crime, provision of services and help for offenders would be a logical, indeed necessary, part of probation. But if those interests are supplanted by a justice orientation, why should such services be offered? Perhaps more to the point, why would government wish to provide the resources necessary to support them?

This last concern is mostly of a practical, political nature. If a way can be found to make utilization of services truly voluntary on the part of offenders, we will substantially reduce the major problems associated with providing help in the context of probation—the unfairness of varying the penalty according to presumed needs, the role conflict in staff trying to serve as both cops and helpers, and so on. Nonetheless, the difficulty of completely severing the sanction from services is so great that it may be wiser to pursue other avenues in trying to see that people can obtain services they want.

Problems with the Surveillance Function

Remarkably little effort seems to have been made to subject the surveillance/control role of probation to the same kinds of scrutiny that the treatment/service role has undergone. But at a minimum the control function poses the same problem of treating people as objects that we noted in the service role.

Perhaps even more directly than the helping function, the control function is oriented toward regulating the day-to-day behavior of probationers.

Supervision is primarily preventive in intent; it focuses on what might happen in the future rather than on past criminal behavior. Although offenders undoubtedly dislike being subjected to surveillance, the punitive elements of supervision are by-products rather than aims.

The control side of conventional probation aims to protect the community from criminal behavior through incapacitation and specific deterrence. The motive for incapacitation—or preventive restraint—is to reduce the likelihood of future crime by restricting the offender's behavior during the probation period. Preventive restraint can take many forms. In the context of probation, typical restraints include limitations on residence, leisure pursuits, drinking or drug use, associations, and the use of personal funds. In addition, probationers usually are required to work regularly and to report at specified intervals to a probation officer. Furthermore, probation officers are expected to investigate reports or indications of behavior by probationers that would amount to violations of the conditions imposed and to initiate revocation procedures if they seem necessary to protect the community.

Specific or individual deterrence attempts to reduce the likelihood that an offender will commit another crime by threatening him or her with unpleasant consequences. Along with reporting requirements, restrictions on a probationer's movements and activities are aimed in part at convincing him or her that deviations will be detected; similarly, the power to initiate revocation proceedings is designed to assure the probationer that deviations will not go unpunished.

To fulfill its crime prevention functions effectively, probation supervision would have to be tailored to the varying traits, histories, patterns, and problems of individual offenders. Probation officers would need substantial discretion to modify their supervisory practices according to changing assessments of an offender's progress or predictions of impending difficulties. In theory, perhaps the ideal extreme of probation supervision would be to create the impression that "big brother is watching." The reality of probation supervision, however, is ordinarily quite different. Supervision most frequently takes the form of a series of required contacts, varying in frequency and detail depending on how the probationer is classified and the policies of the department. Sometimes probationers are required to report to a probation office at specified intervals. In other cases, contact may be made simply by phone or even postcard. Unannounced visits to the homes or workplaces of probationers are employed far less frequently than other kinds of checks. Probation officers are less likely to discover their charges' problems personally than to learn of them indirectly—for example, from an employer's report that a probationer has not been showing up or from a probationer's arrrest.

Although probation supervision may be far less intrusive than the theory behind it would suggest, it is difficult to find much in either theory or practice that is consistent with a justice model. The control function is concerned with what a probationer might do next, not with administering a punishment commensurate with the seriousness of the crime for which the individual was convicted. Classification and variations in supervision are determined on the basis of perceived need or predicted risk. Probationers are warned to expect spying and prying. The most mundane of their activities, where they go, with whom, and why, may be regulated or constrained by a probation officer. Restrictions may be imposed on the basis of unsubstantiated theories as to what behaviors or associations are conducive to criminality. The manipulative, variable, predictive, individualized, and discretionary aspects of the supervision function are subject to virtually all of the criticisms leveled at probation generally and its service side in particular. If any part of probation is to be retained in a justice model, its control function needs to be reassessed just as thoroughly as its service role.

Proposals for Remedying the Problems with a Surveillance Model

Proponents of a just deserts or justice model have emphasized that the penalty imposed should be based on the crime committed. Since their function is punishment, penalties should not be selected for utilitarian reasons. The implications of this stance for probation supervision have not been discussed in much detail.

The basic idea of probation is to release offenders for a trial period to see how well they adjust; the focus is on improving their future behavior rather than on the character of the past offense. Thus, as von Hirsch notes in *Doing Justice*, the concept of probation is somewhat at odds with the Committee for the Study of Incarceration's conception of alternatives to incarceration appropriate to a just deserts model (1976:122). Von Hirsch also criticizes the discretionary features of probation, especially the facts that it may be lenient or onerous, depending on the conditions imposed, and that it is a status subject to being revoked if the conditions are violated. His only other comment on probation is that it "is sometimes used to impose certain restrictions on the offender while he is in the community; he may, for example, be required to limit his travels or observe a curfew. Conceivably, these restrictions could expressly be prescribed as the penalty for certain offenses, detached from the discretionary features and treatment objectives of probation" (1976).

Richard Singer has argued that, within a just deserts model, nonincarcerative sanctions must be viewed as punishments:

> Probationers should be put to community service, or required to live in halfway houses, make restitution to their victims, or accept other similar

conditions on their liberty. . . . Conditions that require the assent of a probation officer to marry, get a driver's license, leave the state, and so forth,
would be unnecessary and inconsistent with the desert model . . . Instead,
the conditions of a desert model probation would require the probationer to
perform some affirmative act, perhaps utilitarian, but in any event arduous
and punitive. Creativity and ingenuity by the agency that sets the possible
penalties are clearly necessary here. (1979:47–48)

This passage seems to imply that any nonincarcerative sanctions will be
administered within the general framework of probation, although many
of the traditional elements of that sanction will have been removed.

Singer does not explain exactly which elements would be inappropriate
nor does he provide explicit rationales for the exclusions he suggests. He
remarks that current conditions of probation are based on the notion that
the probation officer must have "constant power over the probationer to
assure that he does not recidivate"—seemingly suggesting that the surveillance function, with its crime prevention role, is inappropriate to
probation within a desert model. Yet Singer accepts that the conditions of
probation may serve other utilitarian ends, such as making restitution to
victims or performing work of value to the community. It is not obvious
why surveillance or reporting requirements would be less appropriate
than restitution, community service, or other penalties that have side
benefits as well as a punishment function.

Singer does not elaborate on his suggestion that a probationer should be
required to perform "some affirmative act" of an "arduous and punitive"
nature, but it seems likely that this notion grows out of his conviction that
nonincarcerative sanctions must not be seen as nonpunishments, lest they
fail to receive public support or to approach incarceration in their severity.
It should be noted, however, that incarceration is a passive sanction; it
does not require any affirmative act on the part of the one being confined.

Perhaps another concept influenced Singer to make a distinction between
active and passive sanctions. A preference for active sanctions may reflect
concern with other objectives, such as restoring a balance or harmony
among the offender, the victim, and the community. Such concepts as
"righting the wrong" or "making amends" imply that the one who committed the wrong will take action to make up for it. In contrast, concepts
like "getting even" or retaliation imply that those who were wronged (or
their representatives in the form of the state) will take action to see that
the offender will not get away with impunity. It is unfortunate that Singer
offered no rationale for this stance, since it is not obvious that a system
focused primarily on meting out punishments for past wrongs should favor
active sanctions.

NEED FOR BETTER GUIDING PRINCIPLES

We are still far from having a solid set of principles, rules, or guidelines by which to develop an array of sanctions consistent with a justice model. Some theorists, such as Norval Morris, argue that desert should be regarded as a limiting, rather than a determining principle for the selection of punishments: utilitarian concerns may dictate the selection of sanctions as long as the total weight of the sanctions is not greater than that justified by the offense (Morris, 1974). Morris regards equality as a guiding rather than a limiting principle, arguing that like cases should be treated alike unless there are substantial utilitarian reasons to support differential treatment. There are a number of difficulties with such a stance, not the least of which is that it seems to invite back the devils we have been trying to dismiss. To illustrate his view that principles such as parsimony and likely deterrent effects should be allowed to overshadow the interests of equality, Morris discusses a hypothetical case of six doctors in one city who have engaged in equal amounts of tax fraud. He suggests that all six must pay tax on the income they have failed to declare, high interest on that tax, and substantial financial penalties and that this can be arranged without formal prosecution. But sending all six to prison, Morris argues, would be inappropriate:"The extra increment of deterrence would be bought at too high a cost. It would be wasteful of the court's time and, what is perhaps also in point, it would inflict unnecessary suffering on those doctors whose punishment did not substantially increase the deterrent impact we would gain by the imprisonment of, say, two of their number. The principle of parsimony overcomes the principle of equality (Morris, 1981:265)."This form of decision-making, which Morris applauds as an expression of parsimony, has been viewed quite differently by others. Caleb Foote argues that the basic function of discretion is

> to adjust an impossible penal code to the reality of severe limitations in punishmnt resources. . . . What we have evolved is a system of symbolic punishment in which each inmate stands for half a dozen or a dozen other convicted felons who are by any standards equally eligible to be there but for whom there are no beds. This system is efficient in court administration, for the threat of being the symbol keeps the guilty pleas flowing smoothly. It is economical by cost-benefit standards, for it probably maximizes the return in general deterrence for dollars expended. It is politically expedient, at least in the short run, because it dupes and pacifies an otherwise potentially rebellious public. It is also, in my opinion, profoundly immoral, violates the spirit of due process and equal protection, turns our criminal courts into sausage factories and breeds disrespect for law in most of those whom it touches. (Foote, 1978:138)

To achieve equality in punishments, we must reexamine the way we now allocate the limited resources available for punishment.

Since the invention of the penitentiary, the United States has tended to employ long terms of imprisonment to punish serious offenses, including many property crimes as well as crimes against persons. Although we already employ some of the longest prison sentences in the world, a rather steady escalation of punishments recently has been in vogue. More and more jurisdictions are adopting death penalty provisions for more and more offenses. A growing number of offenders are being sentenced to terms of life in prison without possibility of parole. Maximum permissible prison terms are being extended and backed by mandatory minimum terms, exclusions from parole eligibility for certain offenses, or abolition of parole altogether. Behind this trend are various pressures linked to public perceptions of growing crimes rates, increasing fear of crime, and the futures of elected officials. For several reasons, however, the trend should be reversed as we develop a new penalty scale in the context of a justice model.

A Justice Model Requires Scaling Down the Severity of sanctions

A harsh sentencing system is inappropriate in America today and may undermine some of the interests of a justice model. As Rosett and Cressey put it, harshness has to do with

> a sense of proportionality of punishment to crime. . . . [I]t is difficult to accept the fact that a man may be sentenced to ten years imprisonment if he, for example, steals fifty dollars worth of apples or the carcass of a jackass, or forges a federal income tax check for $2.98. This is harshness. In more or less dramatic form, this harshness permeates American criminal codes and significantly deadens society's sense of proportionality.
>
> Harshness breeds harshness as everyone involved, including the potential criminal, becomes accustomed to the idea that crime is punishable by a ridiculously long prison term. Penalties escalate as sensibilities to the consequences become deadened. Proposals to reduce penalties across the board to a more reasonable level are seen as depriving the punishment of any impact. Yet it is only because society, like drug addicts, has built up high tolerance through habitual overdose, that it needs such increasingly massive injections to get the desired jolt. . . . [footnotes omitted] (Rosett and Cressey, 1976: 153–4)

As this writer has suggested in an earlier article, gross violations of prisoners' rights are apparently so widespread in American prisons that it is a serious question whether prisons can be reformed sufficiently to accord with our evolving standards of decency (Harris and Dunbaugh, 1979). That article also argued that imprisonment as we know it is so severe that it is unlikely to be imposed equitably; there is considerable evidence that this harsh penalty is reserved almost exclusively for minorities, the poor, and otherwise less powerful segments of our society. If, as a justice model would require, white-collar and street-crime offenders are to be sentenced to comparable punishments for crimes of similar seriousness, punishments across the board may have to be less severe than imprisonment.

Practical considerations also lend support to a dramatic reduction in reliance on imprisonment. The number of prisoners already substantially exceeds the spaces built in prisons to house them. Yet the costs of adding one additional space range up to $200,000 when costs of financing are considered. Operating costs are growing far more dramatically than the overall budgets of most jurisdictions. Furthermore, there is considerable evidence that harsh sentences undermine the certainty of punishment. Offenders plead guilty to lesser crimes, juries refuse to convict, or other avoidance mechanisms come into operation in the justice process when penalties are too severe. As Rosett and Cressey have pointed out, such circumvention or avoidance of harsh penalties is virtually a necessity in light of bureaucratic interests (not enough prison beds are available to punish everyone convicted in the way the law requires), the interests of justice (the prescribed penalty may be simply too severe in a particular case), or the desirability of gaining acquiescence (the costs of criminal trials can be avoided if defendants plead guilty to lesser offenses). They note that "contemporary American law is so harsh that its full application in all but an occasional aggravated case would be unthinkably cruel, expensive and socially destructive." (Rosett and Cressey, 1976: 153–4) Thus, humanitarian, legal, and policy-related criteria all point to the need to de-escalate our punishment practices.

If the upper limits of the penalty range are to be lowered substantially, it will be important to refine the array of sanctions that would be appropriate to a justice model. Many penalties not now in use might be considered.

A pure punishment perspective could lead to consideration of a variety of infringements, restrictions, and deprivations with no redeeming characteristics other than their ability to impose pain and suffering. We could, for example, prohibit offenders from using motorized vehicles, require them to make cross country hikes, carry heavy burdens on their backs or be blindfolded whenever they left their homes. We could impose any number of annoying, uncomfortable, or painful requirements or restrictions.

The fact is, of course, that there are a variety of constraints traditional to our legal system as well as a variety of public policy considerations that should be applied to the selection of criminal punishments. There are strong and legitimate concerns attached to allowing utilitarian considerations determine the nature, duration, and essential features of sanctions; yet few persons are prepared to determine the sanctions that should be employed solely on the basis of their punishment value.

The Distinction between Justifying a System and Justifying Individual Sanctions

This author previously has suggested one approach that may offer a way out of the dilemma posed by the dangers associated with shaping sanctions to serve utilitarian purposes on the one hand and the reluctance to disclaim any interest in utilitarian purposes on the other. It was suggested that it may be useful to make a distinction between justifying a practice or a system of rules and justifying a particular action falling within that practice or system. More specifically, it was proposed that

> . . . utilitarian arguments are appropriate with regard to questions about the purposes of a criminal sanctioning *system*, while punitive or retributive arguments should be used to apply particular rules to particular cases within that system. Thus, we might decide to develop a system of laws and sanctions because we thought it would have the consequence of furthering the interests of society. Our criminal laws and penalties for violations thereof would be developed for utilitarian reasons: to condemn actions that injure or impose hardships on others, to deter crime, to protect society, and so forth. Furthermore, in designing a system of sanctions, we would want to consider the consequence or effects of the sanctions selected. Thus, we would not wish to establish sanctions that involved unnecessary suffering, misery, degradation, or death—unnecessary in the sense that other, less drastic practices would serve as well. Nor would we want to establish sanctions that were unduly expensive . . . or that . . . required creating facilities or bureaucracies that would be resistant to change should more attractive alternatives come to light. We would also be concerned, in developing a system of sanctions, with compensation or restitution for harm done.
>
> On the other hand, once . . . we were faced with an individual who had been convicted of a criminal act, it would be appropriate only to impose a sanction for what had been done, as predetermined by the structure of our sanctioning system. No assessment of the benefit to be derived from the sanctioning of this individual would be appropriate. We could not punish whenever or in whatever way some official thought would benefit society. This would prohibit us from considering predictions of future criminality or potential for rehabilitation. In summary, in *designing* a system of laws and sanctions for their violation, we should look forward to the future effects upon

society. In *imposing* a particular sanction, however, we should look only backward, to the act committed. (Harris, 1975:286–1287)

Unbridled utilitarian motives, when applied to individuals, easily lead to injustice. On the other hand, criminal sanctioning systems do not simply punish blameworthy or criminal acts, but serve other important societal interests as well. Thus, while it may be unjust to deprive individuals of liberty or otherwise enhance penalties on the basis of what might happen in the future, it would be foolish to assert that a criminal sanctioning system should be designed with no attention to future consequences. Using this framework and the principles important to the operation of a justice model should allow progress in defining the features of the model.

One further caveat should be inserted here. In spelling out some implications of a justice model, we are not setting forth goals and principles to guide all of society or protect all interests of government; we are concerned with the narrower issues involved in one model for a criminal sanctioning system, a system of punishments. Too often this distinction gets lost amidst rhetoric about protecting society and reducing crime. If we were to focus primarily on the goals of increasing the safety of our citizens and our communities, much of the discussion should center on broader economic and social policies, on racism, interpersonal relationships, and spiritual and moral values. As Rothman has suggested, perhaps we would be wise to recognize our inability to achieve such grandiose goals as eliminating crime and transforming offenders, and try more simply to assuage the harm resulting from crime and to avoid exacerbating social harm through the ways we respond to convicted offenders (Rothman, 1981:382–385).

Summary of Principles that Should Apply to Sanctions in a Justice Model

Fundamental to a justice model is the concept that sanctions should be based on past, proven criminal behavior. It is unfair to tailor criminal sanctions to individuals, to changing circumstances, or to predictions and beliefs rather than to past acts. A justice model thus requires a backward-looking perspective in applying sanctions.

Under a justice model, sanctions should be proportional to the offense. No one should be subjected to a greater amount of punishment than is deserved for the crime committed. The concept of desert is critical in that it links punishment to justice; punishment, if undeserved, is unjust. The concept of desert also establishes limits on the amount or severity of punishment; it is unjust to punish a person more than is deserved.

Similarly situated offenders should be treated similarly. Equity is a major element of a justice model and utilitarian interests should not be allowed to create significant disparities in the nature or duration of sanctions.

Sanctions should be clear, explicit, and if not completely definite at the point of sentencing, at least highly predictable in nature. The requirements involved in a particular sanction should be clearly stated at the outset, and they should be easily understandable. They also should be of a nature that allows reasonably objective determinations of whether compliance has occurred, and that makes it easy to ascertain when the requirements have been satisfied or completed. Thus, the duration, nature, and essential features of the punishment should not be subject to variation over the course of the sanction.

Sanctions should be definite punishments and not "revocable." If failure to comply with the conditions of a sanction occurs, legal measures consistent with the nature and severity of the noncompliance should be undertaken.

Sanctions should be recognized as punishments and the punitive elements made clear. At the same time, sanctions should not be harsh or brutal. Harshness undermines proportionality, certainty, and equity and runs counter to the basic respect for persons embodied in the justice model.

The justice model rests on a view of offenders as responsible actors capable of responsible choice. Offenders should not be subject to manipulation as means to an end nor should they be unable to control what happens to them.

Discretion in the application and administration of sanctions should be carefully limited and controlled and subject to review.

In addition to these principles, the issues discussed in this chapter suggest a number of policy considerations and values that should be taken into account in designing a sanctioning system, including:

Economy—less costly sanctions are to be preferred to more costly ones.

Restraint—the criminal process should be avoided when suitable alternatives exist.

Deference to individual rights—interventions that will intrude least on individual rights and autonomy are to be preferred to more drastic interventions.

Impartiality—sanctions should be applied without bias.

Humanity and decency—continuing efforts should be made to enhance the decency of the system and to reduce harm.

Rationality—approaches should be selected that are reasonably connected to attainment of goals.

Democracy—there should be strong, democratic surveillance of the operation of the sanctioning system.

The Implications for Probation

The development of a sentencing scheme involving a range of punishments consistent with the values and principles outlined here would have fairly dramatic implications for the future of probation. Government employees would still be needed to implement and administer such a range of sanctions, but penalties congruent with a justice model would bear little resemblance to probation as now conceived. Probation has been conceived and operated primarily on utilitarian grounds; the role of such interests would be significantly downgraded in a justice model.

The traditional service/helping/assistance function of probation would have no place within a justice model—most importantly because of the grave risk of interfering with the offender's autonomy. It is unreasonable and unfair for sanctions to be based on presumed needs for treatment, skills, or tangible assistance. It is also unfair to extend or adjust a penalty on the basis of such needs.

The helping elements now attached to probation also are inappropriate in that they require too much individualization in application. It would make no sense to require probationers who never take a drink to participate in an alcohol abuse program. But if one robber were required to participate in such a program because of drinking problems and another robber who had no such problems were not, equity would be endangered. Even if certain requirements, such as abstaining from alcohol use, applied to all offenders, such a restriction would clearly prove much more burdensome to some than to others. Of course any penalty may prove more painful to some than to others, but requirements that stem from trying to predict what may lead offenders to crime seem especially subject to the problem of imposing unequal burdens. The proposition advanced here is that it is fair to exact a penalty for what an offender did—for the criminal act committed —but it is *not* fair to exact a penalty for what a person is like or seems to need.

The helping or service role is also inappropriate to sanctions within a justice model because that model is concerned with punishments. There is something perverse in trying to turn services commonly regarded as benefits into penalties, or even in creating entitlements to benefits on the basis of past criminal acts. Education should be a privilege and a joy and, at least to some extent, a right. Social casework can be of real assistance to people with problems, if undertaken voluntarily and in pursuit of goals the participant has chosen. Vocational training, housing assistance, securing a job—all the elements of the assistance role now encompassed within probation are services that many people would like to have available to them. How will offenders respond when such services are offered to them within the scope of a penalty for breaking the law? They may well perceive those "benefits" as deprivations, burdens, and tools of social conformity.

A justice model is not opposed to treatment, help, and various kinds of services. But meeting people's needs has more to do with the rights and entitlements of all citizens than with the fact of being sentenced for an offense. Many people convicted of crimes need education, vocational training, medical care, and housing. Jurisdictions may agree that it makes sense to try to meet those needs. Such services, however, should be provided completely apart from the sanctioning system and thus really are not germane to a discussion of the role of probation within such a system. If it is acknowledged that sanctions involve deprivations, inconvenience, and burdens, it is easier to see why it is important to set clear limits on the sanctions. Furthermore, only if the punitive aspects of nonincarcerative penalties are fully recognized can we expect them to be employed as real alternatives to the extremely punitive sanction of incarceration.

The supervision or community control function within conventional probation is also problematic from the perspective of a justice model. The dominant motive in supervision has historically been to prevent the probationer from engaging in crime or to catch him or her quickly if crimes are committed. This orientation would have to be changed if the individualized and predictive elements of probation are removed. One could legitimately impose regular reporting requirements or restrictions on movement as a penalty for all offenders guilty of certain classes of crimes, but it would not be appropriate to vary the penalty on the basis of the other behavior or attitudes of offenders during the term of the punishment.

Probation personnel currently help administer and monitor a variety of nonincarcerative sanctions. Many offenders sentenced to probation are also ordered to make restitution to victims or to perform unpaid labor of value to private nonprofit or public agencies. Probationers often are liable for the payment of various fines and fees, and probation agencies often are involved in monitoring and collection functions. There are also a variety of sanctions in which probation is combined with some form of residential assignment; perhaps placement in a community residential facility; confinement on weekends, at night, or during vacations; or a jail term as a condition of probation (Parisi, 1980). In a survey conducted by the National Council on Crime and Delinquency's National Probation Reporting Study, 94 percent of the 1,304 responding state and local probation offices reported the use of some form of sentencing combining incarceration and probation by the courts they served (Galvin, et al. 1981). The role now played by probation officers in arranging for community service, restitution, fines, and other conditions to be fulfilled by offenders may be the one most appropriately transferred to a justice model. However, the use of such sanctions will require more careful shaping of policies and conditions in order to satisfy the principles of the model.

In the context of a justice model, probation could move in one of three directions.

1) Probation could be abolished. This option has the merit of making it clear that there will no longer be a sanction of the kind now connoted by the term probation. It would also offer the opportunity of starting fresh in recruiting, training, and assigning personnel to the new roles and rules envisioned in a justice model, thus avoiding the effort and inevitable problems inherent in trying to move any existing system away from established practices. On the other hand, abolition of probation would generate considerable personal and organizational turmoil, disruption, and anxiety, and would make it difficult for the new system to take full advantage of existing skills, knowledge, and relationships. Probation personnel already have working ties with the court system. They already play roles in compliance monitoring, reporting, and enforcement. Many probation officers already are engaged in administering community service and restitution orders, as well as other nonincarcerative sanctions. This option may not be politically viable since it would be strenuously opposed by strong forces. The current interest in reducing the size of governments, however, might make the abolition of probation appear more desirable than it would have in the past.

2) Probation could be reconceptualized and reorganized to administer a new array of nonincarcerative sanctions. As noted above, full implementation of a justice-model sanctioning system would require a variety of punishment options, with the attendant need for personnel to administer the penalties imposed. This option would build on the existing personnel and structures of probation agencies, albeit necessitating substantial retraining and restructuring of duties. Because fundamental changes in policy and practice would be required, considerable trauma and dissatisfaction could be expected among probation personnel and other criminal justice officials. The field of probation has long been torn between factions that view themselves as part of the helping professions and factions more oriented toward law enforcement. Both groups, however, have shared a common perception of probation as a weapon in the war on crime; both have seen their mission as trying to prevent their probationers from committing future crimes. This option would require a virtual revolution in conceptions of mission and role, demanding shifts in thinking and practice far more fundamental than those advocated at either end of the treatment-versus-control spectrum. It is hard to know whether such a complete transformation could be accomplished effectively and whether it would result in any less disruption than the option of simply abolishing probation.

3) Probation could be dissociated from the sanctioning system and rededicated to a role of providing help and assistance to offenders in the community. Probation officers in Holland have taken this course. Their task, as they understand it, is to help see their role as serving their clients in obtaining services and assistance desired by the clients. They play no

law enforcement or monitoring role, even refusing to give the police information concerning alleged criminal incidents. They regard themselves as professional helpers and advocates and believe these roles can be of particular benefit when made available to criminal offenders. As discussed above in the context of John Conrad's proposal for separating the probation service role from the law enforcement supervision role, the principal drawback of this approach may center on the question of feasibility. If additional personnel were needed to implement a full array of sanctions, some new funding would be required, and additional money to provide voluntary services might not be forthcoming.

Assessing the Likely Impact of a Justice Model Perspective on Probation

It is unlikely that any of the options outlined above will be adopted in the near future. It would be astonishing indeed if the many probation workers were to agree that their mission is so flawed that the best course would be to eliminate probation as a sanction and a field, eliminating their jobs as well. Furthermore, because probation is currently the most common sanction, and roughly 60 percent of persons under correctional supervision are on probation, practical considerations are likely to support continuation of probation well into the future. And while many probation personnel might find a shift to a pure client advocacy role intriguing, such a move would probably be perceived as quaintly out of step with the current public and political climate and dominant resource allocation priorities.

Some reconceptualization and restructuring of probation is likely in the near future, but the changes made will probably not be as fundamental as those suggested above in the second option. Current trends away from an individual treatment model are likely to continue, and probation agencies will increasingly be asked to administer a variety of penalties. It is highly unlikely, however, that the crime prevention orientation will give way to the far less grandiose role of administering noninstitutional sanctions in a fair and just manner. Despite all of the practical and philosophical problems associated with utilitarian orientations to criminal sanctions, we will not easily relinquish the hope of reducing crime by what we do to convicted offenders.

Thus none of the options that would flow logically from adoption of a justice model perspective is likely to be adopted soon. In some respects, this is a reassuring conclusion. Reflection on the negative impact of some of the rethinking about crime and punishment set forth by a rather small set of reformers in the last decade or so should give pause to anyone considering formulation of additional models or greater explication of those already advanced. But if too hasty adoption or misguided application of new sanctioning schemes is a danger, the remedy is not to stop offering new formulations. Rather, the best protection lies in vigorous debate, more careful consideration of pitfalls and implications, and advancement of still other models.

Probation is currently under attack from many quarters, with critics from a variety of perspectives focusing on a range of philosophical and operational concerns. Modifications in theory and practice certainly will be made. Those who must decide on the nature and purpose of change can learn much from an exposition of the dominant features and implications of a variety of alternative courses. This chapter is offered in that spirit. Those who reject the justice model, or would interpret it differently, now have the opportunity to offer alternative ideas.

REFERENCES

American Friends Service Committee (1971). *Struggle for Justice*. New York: Hill and Wang.

Bottoms, Anthony E., and William McWilliams (1979). "A Non-Treatment Paradigm for Probation Practice." *British Journal of Social Work*, 9:159–202.

Conrad, John (1984). "The Re-Definition of Probation: Drastic Proposals to Solve an Urgent Problem." Chapter 8 in this book.

Fogel, David (1975). *We Are the Living Proof*. Cincinnati: Anderson.

Foote, Caleb (1978). "Deceptive Determinate Sentencing." In *Determinate Sentencing—Reform or Regression?* Washington, D.C.: National Institute of Law Enforcement and Criminal Justice.

Galvin, James, Jane Maxwell and Frank Hellum (1981). "Shock Probation and More." Draft report from the National Probation Reporting Study, National Council on Crime and Delinquency, June 16.

Harris, M. Kay (1975). "Disquisition on the Need for a New Model for Criminal Sanctioning System," *West Virginia Law Review* 77:263.

Harris, M. Kay and Frank Dunbaugh (1979). "Premise for a Sensible Sentencing Debate: Giving Up Imprisonment." *Hofstra Law Review*, Vol. 7:417.

Lewis, C. S. (1971). "The Humanitarian Theory of Punishment." In *Crime and Justice*, ed. Radzinowicz and Wolfgang, Vol. 2. New York: Oxford.

Morris, Norval (1974). *The Future of Imprisonment*. Chicago: University of Chicago.

Morris, Norval (1981). "Punishment, Desert, and Rehabilitation." In Gross and von Hirsch (eds.), *Sentencing*. New York: Oxford.

Parisi, Nicolette (1980). "Combining Incarceration and Probation." *Federal Probation*, 44:1–12.

Rosett, Arthur and Donald Cressey (1976). *Justice by Consent: Plea Bargaining in the American Courthouse*. Philadelphia: Lippincott.

Rothman, David (1981). "Doing Time: Days, Months and Years in the Criminal System." In Gross and von Hirsch (eds.) *Sentencing*. New York: Oxford.

Singer, Richard G. (1979). *Just Deserts: Sentencing Based on Equality and Desert.* Cambridge, Mass.: Ballinger.

von Hirsch, Andrew (1976). *Doing Justice: The Report of the Committee for the Study of Incarceration.* New York: Hill and Wang.

von Hirsch, Andrew and Kathleen J. Hanrahan. (September 1978). *Abolish Parole?* Summary Report. Washington, D.C.: National Institute of Law Enforcement and Criminal Justice.

Chapter 2

Mission and Justice: Clarifying Probation's Legal Context

Patrick D. McAnany*

The justice approach to probation can be stated simply: *probation as a penal sanction must conform to the principles of due process of law.* Consequently, the structure and application of probation must reflect the general purposes served by the criminal law. This view is a major departure from the traditional conception of probation. Probation has been seen as a program of treatment rather than a penal sentence. If probation is to take its place within a criminal justice system whose basic nature is increasingly acknowleged to be coercive, and therefore limited by due process, we must look at its mission in the context of that system.

The following analysis sees criminal law as a centrally defining element of the criminal justice system. It examines first the recent debate and present compromise on the goals that criminal law should serve in our democratic society. Second, it looks at the structural changes in sentencing brought about by the goals debate. Finally it asks how probation as a just sentence might fit within that altered structure.

*Department of Criminal Justice, University of Illinois at Chicago.

GOALS AND CRIMINAL LAW

Public Expectations

The complaint that probation is "soft on crime" is only an indirect way of saying that the criminal law is soft on crime. The public attitude toward the institution of law as it applies to crime has undergone a thorough exorcising over the past two decades. It began with the growing attention given by the Supreme Court to the requirements of due process of law for defendants. It was reinforced by the President's Crime Commission project, which examined the "crime problem" in detail and then expended billions of dollars on its eradication. As society became aware of this massive professional effort, it also noticed that crime rates continued to rise rather than decline. Eventually, this trend caused the public to turn hostile rather than attentive. The criminal law, after all, was supposed to do something about crime. That "something" was to reduce it (Wilson, 1975).

The expectation that the institutional apparatus of criminal law could affect crime rates was deeply engrained in public attitudes. The statements of many professional groups had also ascribed a crime-reduction purpose to the criminal law. But until the 1970s there had been little public interest in examining exactly what the criminal law was supposed to do. It was thought that the law existed to protect the community and that any failures in this goal could be attributed to lack of funds. After the criminal law had been subjected to careful analysis through the thousands of court appeals on a variety of topics, and after the tax support for criminal law had been vastly increased to meet the problem of failures, the public frustration gave way to anger, and anger in turn to simplicity. If the law could not, or would not, give protection, at least it could give punishment. The issue then became whether what the public wanted and what the law was created to give were the same thing.

Preventive Punishment

Until 1970 or so, penologists were in general agreement as to the rationale for criminal law and punishment. Criminal law was seen as a preventive effort by society against antisocial actors. The purpose of the law was to identify the antisocial persons and to intervene so as to prevent further harm. This general purpose was expressed in three subgoals somewhat, but not entirely, independent of each other: deterrence, incapacitation, and rehabilitation. Deterrence proceeded by means of threats against individual offenders, but with the purpose of reaching other potentially antisocial individuals as well, to dissuade them from committing criminal acts. Incapacitation meant physical restraint of identified criminals thought to pose a danger to society. In contrast to deterrence, which induced self-control by the threat of punishment, incapacitation provided an external physical control of individuals. Prison was the typical means of incapacitating an offender. Rehabilitation was directed to identified individuals whose antisocial acts were caused by unmet needs that could be diagnosed and treated. Although rehabilitation proceeded through treatment rather than punishment, a certain element of incapacitation was involved to coerce unwilling clients.

While these three subgoals of criminal law differed slightly in the audience they reached and the means they used, they all shared the *preventive perspective*. In each case, the kind and amount of remedies applied depended on anticipated acts of crime. This was the penology of Positivism, which grew up in the middle decades of the nineteenth century and represented a compromise between the utilitarian school (deterrence) and the positivist school (rehabilitation and incapacitation). (Radzinowicz, 1966).

Over the past century and a quarter, these ideas were communicated to the American public through various means and incorporated into the ideology of criminal sentencing and corrections. Lawyers were not in the forefront of this development, which centered on what the law should do with those it had already judged guilty. The formal reach of the law at this time was considered to have ended before sentencing. Lawyers and judges who kept watch over the front end (adjudication) of the criminal law apparatus had little interest in what purpose the sentence served and how it was carried out. This is why the articulation of goals of criminal law raised so little controversy in the adoption of the American Law Institute's *Model Penal Code* in 1962 and the National Council on Crime and Delinquency's *Model Sentencing Act* in 1963. While the more correctionally oriented NCCD *Act* favored rehabilitation and incapacitation over deterrence, it followed the ALI *Code* in stating goals in terms of the preventive purposes of the criminal law (Rubin, 1960; Weschler, 1961). Where there was disagreement over the issue of goals, the drafters considered the disputes "philosophical" and beyond the scope of lawmaking (Gerber and McAnany, 1967). As the law of sentencing was structured, there was no great pressure to resolve these abstract problems, since the judge and parole board had wide latitude to assign time and conditions as they saw fit. This latitude was based on the principle of individualizing sentences—that is, making the sentence fit the offender and his or her personal and social circumstances. Thus, questions about goals were either not raised at all, or were discussed only among a narrow group of experts interested in corrections.

The Disparity Problem and the Rise of Justice Model

In less than fifteen years, the goals issue moved from professional journals to the front pages of newspapers. Whether the public mood led or followed this change of attitude is less important than the fact that the rationale for criminal law has become a matter of considerable public discussion.

The issue of goals for criminal law was raised for the first time in recent American history by several critics in the late 1950s and early 1960s. They challenged the official explanation of why certain inmates were held in institutions or were held there longer than others. According to the correctional rationale of the time, these inmates needed rehabilitation which was available only in an institutional setting. If they were placed on probation, for instance, they would probably commit new offenses and would certainly not get the treatment they needed. Francis Allen was the first major critic to see through this convenient rationalization (Allen, 1959). Rejecting the false equivalence between rehabilitation and incarceration, he insisted that, however benevolent the intention of the jailer, loss of liberty through the coercion of the criminal law *was punishment itself*. But punishment, Allen said, required the same careful controls with which we surround the criminal trial. Norval Morris continued this demystification of imprisonment as correctional treatment. He suggested that no more time could legitimately be taken from an offender than was warranted by the seriousness of his offense (Morris, 1966). Neither Allen nor Morris rejected the ideal of a rehabilitative purpose in criminal law; rather, they wished to retain it, but subordinate it to the limits of the punitive reality by which it was carried out.

The extension of this insight (that any impairment of liberty is punishment) to formal principles of criminal law was made by Herbert Packer in his influential *Limits of the Criminal Sanction* (1968). Packer discovered that critical values of criminal law were being undermined by people who interpreted its purposes solely in terms of treatment or incapacitation. For these preventionists, the object of the law was to identify the dangerous and intervene before they could commit (further) crime. Forgetting the principles on which the substantive criminal law is based—responsibility, liability, guilt, and blame—they imposed long prison terms in the name of future crimes not yet committed. Such sentencing, which amounts to punishing the innocent, undermines the legitimacy of the criminal law and weakens its moral potency.

Packer only indirectly posits a retributive goal for criminal law. Rather than say that the purpose of law is to punish the guilty, he offered the principle that criminal law pursues the general goal of preventing crimes, but is restrained in this effort by the principle that only the guilty can be punished. This may seem a small advance toward rejecting the prevailing ideology of preventive justice, but because the context was a very thorough analysis of substantive criminal law purposes, it opened the eyes of the ordinary reader to the basic contradiction in our law system. Responsibility and blame are the foundation stones of criminal liability, but these concepts are flouted when sentencing "punishes" offenders for being bad risks.

The first attack on the preventive goals of criminal law directed to the general public was made by the Quakers in the early 1970s. The American Friends Service Committee's report, *Struggle for Justice* (1971), detailed how the widely distributed discretion of the sentencing and correction structure in American law provided opportunities for repression of lower-class criminals. Judges, wardens, and parole board members could each make decisions prolonging the term of inmates without the least account-ability to any legal principles, much less to principles that recognized incarceration as punishment. The report called for the reinstitution of determinate sentences among other means of controlling this widespread discretion, which assumed a technology for controlling dangerous offenders which did not exist.

Once moved into the public arena by the Quaker's report, the goals issue quickly focused on the practical problem of disparity in sentencing. Several individuals and groups published books on this issue during the mid-seventies. Frankel (1973) accused his fellow jurists of presiding over a lawless process under the indeterminate sentencing structure. Professors Morris (1974) and Fogel (1975) found that a preventive philosophy in sentencing bred a whole series of disparity problems for prison wardens and inmates. The Committee on Incarceration (von Hirsch, 1976) and the Twentieth Century Fund's Task Force on Sentencing (1976) both made proposals for restricting judicial discretion in imposing sentences. Finally, Professor Singer (1979) gave a more detailed analysis of what such a reformed sentencing system might actually look like and what some jurisdictions had already adopted by the late years of the decade (Singer, 1979).

Disparity in sentencing was discovered to relate directly to the goals problem as it had been stated by Packer in the 1960s. Preventive goals for criminal law were predictive in nature. If the purpose was to prevent future crime, then the system had to be able to predict who would commit such crime. Attention was not limited to the crime of which the individual had been convicted. Rather, offenders would be detained for a period based on what they *might do* in the future. If the danger was great and the future harm significant, then the sentence could be greater to ensure prevention. The problem with this system, as Packer hinted and the Quakers asserted, was that we do not have the technical competence to predict with any accuracy. Morris and Dershowitz both underscored this weakness in the legal system by statistical arguments based on the evidence then available (Morris, 1974; Dershowitz, 1976).

A preventive approach to sentencing also assumed that the system could accomplish rehabilitation. A series of research evaluations, however, uniformly indicated that various correctional treatment programs had little or no impact on future criminal behavior (e.g., Lipton et al., 1975). If the legal system could neither predict who would recidivate nor diagnose and treat crimogenic conditions, then the preventive goals were reduced to the claims of general deterrence.

The broad concept of deterrence is simply common sense—if you punish illegal parking severely enough, it will diminish. At least in theory, however, it should be possible to test empirically for deterrence effects. But general deterrence research was so new and complicated that studies could establish no more than the possibility that certain sanctions work under certain conditions (Zimring and Hawkins, 1973; Cook, 1980). While some still insisted that deterrence was a legitimate basis for imposing the death penalty (Erlich, 1975), other scholars argued that the effect was unproven (Zeisel, 1977). At any rate, deterrence at least recognized the punitive nature of sentencing and was open to certain limiting principles of law suggested by Packer and others.

Retribution and its Critics

Debate then focused on a goal that had been repudiated throughout the hundred years of preventive utilitarianism. That goal was called variously retribution, desert, or vengeance. In their aroused mood of the 1970s, the public seemed to be looking primarily for vengeance. That principle insisted on inflicting pain for pain and was based on the instinctive urge to retaliate against a wrongdoer. Essentially a principle without limit, unrestrained vengeance would often inflict injury out of all proportion to the initial harm. It is personal in nature, based on identity with the victim and seeking damage personally on the victimizer. It is ugly when viewed objectively and has been officially rejected by contemporary society. It is wholly negative in character and is not based on desert, reform, or any of the other justifying rationales for punishment. Yet it is based on instinct and consequently latent in all societies. Vengeance is the element that has given retributive punishment its bad name.

Some have seen the retributive principle as "vengeance dressed up" (e.g., Zilboorg, 1968). There is a half-truth in this view. Retribution is the principle that it is just to punish the criminal for his offense because he deserves it. An equally important principle of retribution is that the punishment must fit the offense committed. A corollary of this principle of proportionality is the principle of equity, which states that like cases must be treated (punished) alike. Retribution is easily understood in several catch phrases, such as "Let the punishment fit the crime," or "Treat like cases alike," or "A man must pay his debt to society." People use these phrases and appear to understand them and agree with their salience to ordinary affairs among men. Yet the justification of criminal sanctions based on retribution has raised profound doubts among most modern commentators. (Honderich, 1969).

To say that we punish because the defendant deserves it leaves unanswered the prior question of why we use punishment at all in a systematic way, not just for a specific individual. Most modern commentators see retribution as an assertion of the value behind the use of punishment, not an exploration of what it is. Many would see retributive punishment as reductively justified by a type of vengeance. We punish criminals to give satisfaction to victims and other law-abiding citizens. It makes them feel justified in obeying the law (Honderich, 1969).

Punishment as a social institution is more convincingly justified from the utilitarian perspective, which argues in terms of an aggregate balance of social good resulting from punishment. For example, the utilitarian would say that the only justification for a punishment system is its net gain of social good for all (reduced offending) over the suffering inflicted on a few (punishment) (Benn, 1958). But as we have seen, this position then opens up the possibility of punishing innocent persons to gain some greater social good. It also underscores the weakness of a justification that subordinates the individual to the good of society as a whole. It denies moral worth to the individual as an "end in himself," as Kant puts it (Murphy, 1979).

The problem of justifying punishment as a system, as well as retributive punishment's corrupting slide toward popular vengeance, has kept most commentators from adopting retribution in any complete sense (e.g., von Hirsch, 1976). But a retributive framework offers very considerable advantages in explaining criminal law. For one thing, it directly answers the question of disparity. If sentences are intended to punish, then they must be proportionate to the offense. Further, all offenders guilty of the same offense(s) must be treated alike. Thus, proportionality and equity became watchwords for reform proposals. Finally, a retributive perspective connects the substantive criminal law, with its principles of responsibility, guilt, and blame, with a sentencing law based on just deserts. It does all of this by an appeal to justice, that virtue on which all law is purportedly grounded.

And the principle of retribution appealed to the public in its hostility toward the flaws of the current system. For the vulgar sentiments of "lock 'em up and throw away the key," the justice model approach to criminal sentencing substituted a principle that was firmly grounded in justice yet open to vengeance. The problem with using public opinion to support your case is that the support may be too strong. The fear, confirmed now in several states, was that legislatures supposedly pursuing a just deserts reform, might pass draconian sentences more in line with public vengeance (Singer, 1979:57–58).

Several problems remain to complicate a justice approach to criminal law goals. First, those responsible for the reforms in sentencing have made little effort to analyze the meaning of retribution/just deserts. They have left the goal without fully exploring what retribution means in itself. Philosophers, lawyers, and others have tried to fill this gap, (e.g., Christie, 1981; Murphy, 1979; Gross, 1979; Strawson, 1974), but a contribution is needed from corrections and judicial professionals, people most closely acquainted with the operationalization of punishment. If this work is not done, then the reforms undertaken appear likely to produce the bitter fruit of either a popular vengeance or a charade of public justice which conceals the real working of the system, whatever it might be (e.g., Rosett and Cressey, 1976).

While most critics have come to accept the place of desert and punishment in sentencing, they continue to want *both* just deserts *and* the other socially attractive goals of preventive criminal law. This wish to have all possible justifications at work at once is not a misunderstanding of punishment, which is a complex, many-sided social institution. Different cultures emphasize different sides from time to time in their formal systems (Newman, 1978). Further, there is no way a social system of law administered by human beings could ever get rid of discretion entirely without producing chaos. (Davis, 1969). Therefore, there must be an accommodation of principles. Since several of the goals conflict in most circumstances—e.g., good rehabilitation is bad deterrence, or good incapacitation is bad justice—priorities must be set. In the contemporary sentencing reform effort, retribution/just deserts must be accorded the primary place, and the other goals may be invoked as appropriate, as long as they do no substantial damage to proportionality and equity. Defining "substantial damage" is a practical problem for drafters of sentencing legislation. As discussed in the rest of this chapter and elsewhere (Chapters 1–5; Chapter 14), there is no pure system that serves only just desert goals, though they are always given primary place in deciding what sentence to impose.

A retributive system appears open to abuse because it rides uneasily on the back of popular opinion. Law is always in this position of borrowing from the community, yet standing against it. Nonet and Selznick (1978) make this point in their analysis of law as both repressive (justice responding to political reality) and autonomous (justice self-consistent and objective) during various times and in different communities. The legitimacy of the law rests on the consent of people who find the reasons of the law acceptable and thus obey it. Law then cannot be too far removed from this basic source of its power. For criminal law the antinomy between peoples' lives and legal principle is all the stronger. On the other hand, the criminal law is worthless unless it can win the support of people on moral grounds. Anything less must resort to bald coercive force of the state and turn law into a power charade. But legitimacy cannot depend on the popularity of the offender. For instance, law and order groups draw deeply on the reserves of hatred toward minority and poor criminals to support their petitions to crack down on crime. Public hostility bridles at the "technicalities" of due process.

A retributive purpose for criminal law, as we have mentioned, does open it to the suggestion of mob rule, because legislators and judges may impose harsh sentences in the name of proportionality. As we will see below, principles like culpability and proportionality do not alone provide complete controls for evenhanded justice. But we do not believe a retributive law need fit the mailed fist of public vengeance like a glove. More than any other rationale for criminal law, retribution is grounded on principles of objectivity and restraint. "Treat like cases alike" makes a good brake on the impulse to give in to the crowd. The essence of the new criminal justice system would be greater accountability to law.

Since punishment in the retributive sense is based on desert and blame, the ultimate justification—indeed the ultimate understanding—of punishment derives from the moral values sustaining criminal law. It is these same central values that bond people into a community in the first place. People give punishment meaning insofar as they share common values and denounce violations of those values. Only by passing through this blame-punishment crucible can violators return to the community. Thus even those who otherwise eschew retribution like the plague will accept the punishment of children in families (cf. Griffiths, 1970). By implication, punishment done totally outside of a community context would make little retributive sense, serving only those external values of protecting strangers from one another. Thus it seems peculiarly appropriate for probation to explore the meaning of community punishment and how the law serves it.

JUSTICE AND SENTENCING

Principles for Justice-Based Sentencing

The new justice orientation for criminal law goals has been expressed in various reforms of sentencing and corrections codes throughout the United States. Singer (1979) and von Hirsch and Hanrahan (1981) provide useful summaries. Here we will lay out the main legal principles underlying these reforms and give examples of the statutory structures that embody these principles. We will then examine what probation might look like as a sentencing option in this reformed sentencing law. The latter will necessarily be largely conjecture, since current legislation reforms have not taken probation seriously in enacting new justice goals.

The following set of legal principles for justice-based sentencing is drawn from several sources, but especially Harris (1983); Singer (1979); von Hirsch (1976); Fogel (1975); and Morris (1974):

1. Criminal law is directed toward the punishment of persons properly convicted of its violation; whatever else the criminal law achieves, it primarily punishes offenders.
2. Because criminal law is punitive in nature, it cannot be used against legally innocent persons however great the social gains for others may be.
3. Criminal punishment is based on the principle of responsibility, i.e., that under ordinary circumstances the individual can make choices of committing crimes or not.
4. While not all conduct prohibited by law is immoral in itself, all crimes are immoral insofar as society through its legislative authority condemns them; choice of crime is choice of social wrongdoing.
5. Blame based on free choice of social wrongdoing is the basis for imposing punishment in criminal law and consists of the judgment of condemnation rendered by the court in the community's name, the stigma attached to it, and the sentence to carry out this judgment.
6. Punishment should be distributed in accord with the seriousness of the offense and the culpability of the offender; prior convictions may increase offender culpability.
7. Offenders who commit offenses similar in seriousness should be punished similarly, without distinctions based on fear of future offending or on the needs of society to deter others.
8. Similar sentences need not be exactly alike in nature but should be alike in the basic quantum of punishment; thus "alternatives" should not be disguised leniency which violates the principle of equality.
9. All dispositional choices, whether by plea, sentence, or parole release decision, should be governed by these basic principles of distributive justice, which should be incorporated into criteria of selection, whether in the form of guidelines, statutory criteria, or the like.
10. Maximum limits on the most serious sentences should be established, based on community sense of social condemnation but limited by constitutional principles; lesser sentences should be ranged from this upper limit in accord with gradations of seriousness.
11. Other purposes of criminal law, such as incapacitation, protection of the public, deterrence of future offending, and treatment and change of offenders, may be pursued within the limits of these principles, but only insofar as they do not undercut these primary principles.

As suggested by this summary of principles, the reforming drives of the 1970s went far beyond a simple remedy for disparity in sentencing. They reexamined the basis for criminal law and tried to create a consistency of criminal liability and punishment across both substantive and sentencing law. The reformers recognized that, whatever we call it, convicting and controlling a person on the basis of crime is punishment, and punishment requires both proportion and evenhandedness. The implications for sentencing and corrections are only now being worked out in the courts in individual cases.

These principles produced three sets of interlocking mechanisms in the reformed codes: classification of offenses, gradation of penalties, and control of discretion in applying penalties to offenses. The hope was that these structures would give society a sentencing system that is just, equal, and fair.

Classification of Offenses

Most sentencing reform since the 1960s has involved classification of offenses. Both the Model Penal Code and the American Bar Association Criminal Justice Standards required it (ALI, 1962; ABA, 1980b). The purpose was to give a rough order of seriousness to codes which had been originally constructed piecemeal by legislatures, where each newly defined penalty for one offense was typically unrelated to the punishment level of other offenses. Under justice goals, this drive to classify offenses became much more urgent. The method was to divide all offenses into a series of felony and misdemeanor classes, usually from six to ten in number. Offenses were assigned to various levels by looking at the maximum sentences assigned by prior law and ranking them. This approach had the advantage of leaving criminal codes mostly undisturbed and avoided a major political problem of trying to determine, by some legitimate means, which crimes were more serious for contemporary society. Seriousness itself was based on two components: harm intended by the offense, and degree of culpability by the offender. Thus while homicides all involve the most serious harm (taking of human life), they may fall into several categories depending on whether the criminal intent of the offender reflects purpose, recklessness, conscious disregard of risk, or negligence.

Many classification problems remain to be worked out in most codes. Relatively little attempt has been made to change ranking from current levels, most of which have been inherited from earlier times. Many offense definitions are unsatisfactory because they do not recognize factors that would change the degree of seriousness. For example, a burglary with a weapon appears much more serious than one done unarmed. But attempts to draft all or many of such factors into statutory definitions of offenses would make those definitions terribly cumbersome. Zimring (1976) noted this in critiquing just such an attempt by the Twentieth Century Fund Task Force (1976). Further, no attempt has yet been made to measure culpability more precisely than the Model Penal Code's terms of purpose, knowledge, recklessness, and negligence. Thus we are likely to see a good deal of continued "individualizing" as judges try to adjust sentences to personal culpability of offenders (Gardner, 1976).

Gradation of Penalties

Having classified offenses into levels of seriousness, a just deserts code then provides matching levels of penalties. Sentencing under the reformed codes is not mandatory, however. Most codes have avoided the problems assocated with mandatory sentencing by giving judges some leeway to determine both length and type of sentence within a certain narrow range. The usual mode is to mandate prison sentences for the top felonies with limited variation of length according to aggravating or mitigating factors, and then to offer the alternative of probation at a lower level. The use of lesser penalties, such as fines and restitution, is generally left up to the judge, whether to supplement or to replace the jail-probation choice.

In most jurisdictions the penalties available to courts include imprisonment, periodic imprisonment, probation, conditional discharge (unsupervised probation), fines, restitution, community service, and others. Nowhere does the law attempt a direct definition of their differential penal impact. Indirectly, of course, imprisonment and probation are differentiated by making the more serious felonies ineligible for a probation sentence. But when imprisonment and probation are both available choices, there is little evident concern that one sanction is much more severe than the other. This same reluctance to pin down the penalties appropriate to various levels of seriousness is reflected in the courts' freedom to determine the length of probation or the amount of a fine, limited only by a very high maximum. Thus for the top felonies some proportion is generated by elimination of probation and setting of limited ranges of length of incarceration; but for the rest of the criminal calendar of offenses all sorts of obvious contradictions prevail. One remedy, discussed below, is procedural controls on judges' sentencing. But the problem of alternatives which are not at all equivalent remains.

Some attempt must be made to regularize the penalty system. First, incarceration should be recognized as a very severe sanction, used only for the most serious crimes. Second, a formula should be established to control the comparative penal impact on offenders of probation, imprisonment and other alternatives. Third, a single-sanction system should be established so that courts would not be free to add on penalties such as fines without factoring them into proportional outcomes. The task will not be easy, because alternative sentences have been created with the very purpose of defeating the rigid demands of mandatory sentences. But unless we retreat to a true single-sanction system in which incarceration, money fine, the stocks, or some other penalty is the *only* choice, we will have to work toward a system of comparative penalties.

Procedural Controls

A third means of controlling disparity in sentencing is to govern the discretion exercised by judges and others.

The appellate courts have given defendants certain controls through their interpretation of various constitutional rights: representation at sentencing; a formal sentencing hearing; presentation of evidence in behalf of the defendant; some access to the evidence that the court uses in its decision; the right to enforce a plea bargain against the prosecutor (Schulhofer, 1980). A well-represented defendant can demand an accounting of how the system makes its decisions.

In addition, legislative reforms have added structural elements to the sentencing process that limit discretion: Judges must order a presentence report covering certain elements pertinent to proportionality (ABA, 1908: 18–5.1); judges must select the least restrictive alternative (id. 18–2.2), and must state their reasons for choice of a sentence, at least where it involves incarceration (id. 18–6.4) or falls outside the presumptive sentencing range (ULC 1979:Sec. 207–3(c)); sentences are subject to review by appellate courts (ABA, 1980B). Each of these structural changes purportedly makes judges subject to challenge on grounds that they are not honoring the purposes of sentencing and the general goals of punishment.

A third set of controls applies directly to the amount of punishment. Because the penalty ranges continue to allow some flexibility, courts are guided by aggravating and mitigating criteria set out in the statutes (e.g., Illinois, ch. 38, 1005–5–3.1 and 3.2) or by sentencing guidelines that provide a "presumptive" sentence depending on some adjustment for particular circumstance (e.g., *Minn.*, *Stat. Ann.* Sec. 244 app. (West Supp. 1982)).

These control devices make it possible to attune sentences to the values of proportionality and equity.

The present changes in sentencing codes are all consistent with the goal shift described above. Attempting consistently, if incompletely, to serve justice values, they have won the general support of both the legislators and the judges. Corrections officials are less enthusiastic about the changes, partly because the revised codes generally involve more mandatory prison sentences, creating serious overcrowding in state prison systems. But corrections personnel do not oppose the concept of a justice-based corrections system. While they may have some reservations about the meaning of just deserts or retributive punishment and its primacy in the reformed order, they do not sense a major change of practice with which they could

not live. Fogel (1975) has pointed out the advantages for prison administrators under a justice model system.

PROBATION AS A JUST SENTENCE

Principles for a Sentence of Probation

In the rapid change over the past decade, and in the attendant discussion of
rehabilitation, punishment, proportionality and the like, probation has
been an oddly neglected subject. Most reformers were concerned about
the deep end of the system—prison—and the injustice of unequal sentences
there. Considered a mild punishment at best, probation was not a subject
to stir debate. Yet one side of the dispartiy question is undue leniency.
Probation needs to be discussed as a central feature of today's sentencing
and corrections from the perspective of a just deserts law.

Our analysis will rest on several propositions about the role of probation
in a reformed, justice-oriented criminal law. These propositions are based
on earlier research (Thomson and Fogel, 1980; McAnany and Thomson,
1982), as well as Chapters 1 and 4 of this book.

1. Probation is a penal sanction whose main characteristic is punitive.
2. Probation should be a sentence, not a substitute for the real sentence
   threatened after future violations; as such it should not be subject to
   reduction or addition.
3. Probation should be part of a single graduated range of penal sanctions
   and should be available as the sentence for all levels of crime, except
   perhaps the most serious felonies.
4. The gravity of the probation sentence should be determined both by
   the length of the term and the quality and quantity of conditions;
   restitution, community services, and other conditions compatible
   with community release should be considered in determining the
   amount of punishment a particular sentence involves.
5. Neither the length of term nor any condition should be subject to
   change during the sentence, except as noted in #7 below.
6. Conditions should be justified in terms of seriousness of the offense,
   though other purposes may be served by such conditions, such as
   incapacitation.
7. Where conditions are violated, the courts should assess additive
   penalties through "show cause" hearings; new offenses should be
   tried separately and a single sentence imposed which would incorporate any remaining punishment under the old sentence; full credit for
   time served under the prior sentence of probation should be given in
   any new sentence.

These principles may seem to signal a radical shift in our present understanding and use of probation. Certainly the move from a rehabilitation purpose to a punishment one is major in every respect. But so is the conception of probation as a sentence in and of itself, rather than as a delay of, or substitution for, the real sentence (McAnany, 1976). Moreover, viewing probation as a determinate sentence not directly subject to alteration or revocation departs sharply from present understanding. All of these divergencies from our settled notions of probation are probably the best explanation of why probation has been omitted from the debate over sentencing and goals. Probation just did not lend itself to an easy fit with the terms of the reform agenda: punishment, proportionality, and equity. Here we will explore what a reformed probation would look like within the renewed context of criminal law as we have described it. We will also suggest, however, that the probation recommended is both possible and less radically different from the probation of the past.

Probation History: To Escape the (Shortcomings of) Law

Although the historical evidence is sparse, the practice of probation appears to have arisen as a technical means of avoiding the full impact of conviction. At common law, once a sentence had been imposed, courts lost most, if not all, of their ability to alter the penalty. Even when clear proof of a mistaken conviction was offered, courts were helpless to alter what they had done. It was thought that sentences finalized jurisdiction. Barring an appeal—which only recently became possible for criminal cases and then frequently not on the basis of the sentence itself—the only remedy for such injustice as a mistaken conviction was pardon by the executive. The courts enjoyed no direct powers of pardon nor could they even reduce sentences in a system of mandatory sanctions. Thus they found a way to delay finality. They suspended proceedings between conviction and sentence, creating an opportunity for the parties to explore other remedies to prevent injustice being done by fixing the sentence. Originally, this delay could not extend beyond the end of the court term, at which point the judge had to impose the sentence before he lost jurisdiction. Later interpretation allowed proceedings to be suspended beyond the term, thus allowing courts to prolong indefinitely the interruption in the case. The motive for this extension was the desire to avoid the harsh injustice of a prison term for offenses whose circumstances dictated a far less punitive response (Rubin, 1973:181–84; Attorney General's Survey, 1939:3–10; 15–21).

The later history of probation is better known. As proceedings were suspended and sentencing delayed, the convicted offender was released on good behavior. There was no real attempt to detail conditions or place the probationer, as he came to be called, under official supervision. but people in the community served as a sort of surety for his law abidance. This practice of probation grew from a few exceptional cases to more general use. At that point legislatures were asked to approve the practice and give it more suitable legal foundations—and to provide for officials to monitor the released convicts in their community status (Rubin, 1973:205–206).

Probation has historically served several important functions for the criminal law system. If a reformed justice-style probation cannot fulfill all these functions, other means will have to be found.

1. Probation practice was a statement that judges are always called on to do justice in individual cases. A completely rigid system that excludes this equity feature from courts will be intolerable and will breed its own extralegal remedies.
2. Probation was an expression of the need for intermediate sanctions. Even if the sentencing system had not been mandatory in nature, courts needed a sanctioning system that had penalties less severe than prison, but more than mere fines.
3. Probation also offered courts a chance to give a positive value to punishment by exacting good behavior, instead of only imposing pain. This was similar to the good time devices that prisons were then instituting, but was broader in nature.
4. Probation drew attention to the community as the real setting for corrections. If punishment was paying one's debt to society, doing so in society made a good deal more sense. Prisons had extinguished community sanctions by their growth during the 1830s and '40s.
5. Probation was sensitive to the problem of past criminal record and its destructive effects, and frequently made it possible to extinguish the conviction on successful completion of the sentence.

Probation as just deserts can still serve the system in many of these ameliorative ways; others, however, may be byond its reach because of the demands of proportionality and equity.

Recommended Changes

A justice-oriented probation would differ from current practice in several respects: the goal served, the nature of the penal status, and the noncondi-tional nature of probation.

Under a just deserts system all sentences are conceived as punitive in nature. This may or may not change perceptions of incarceration, fines, and other sentences. But in many jurisdictions the interpretation of proba-tion has not only posited a rehabilitative intent but explicitly excluded the notion of punishment. The Florida Supreme Court, for example, recently wrote:

> A sentence and probation are discrete concepts which serve wholly different functions. Imposed as a sentence, imprisonment serves as a penalty, as a payment of defendant's "debt to society." Imposed as an incident of probation, imprisonment serves as a rehabilitative device to give the defendant a taste of prison." *Villery* v. *Florida Parole and Probation Commission* (Fla. Sup. Ct., 1981).

Under this interpretation, probation was exclusively a rehabilitative tool and could not tolerate a punitive intent, however indirect or subordinate. Probation was not a sentence under the law, but a suspension of the sentence. As such it was cut loose from the requirements of criminal law and opposed to its purposes. It was seen as a substitute for the punishment which the law intended. As conceived by John Augustus at its inception in the 1840s, probation came to be seen as an extralegal device seeking leniency and rehabilitation.

While *Villery* represents the more extreme version of probation's goals, all courts have interpreted probation as *primarily* serving rehabilitative ends (McAnany, 1976). Because rehabilitation cannot be easily reconciled with a proportional punishment system, can probation survive? Of course it can. From the outset, probation served punitive goals. Rubin notes that probation never denied the guilt of the convicted party; its purpose was to *moderate* the sanction, not deny the appropriateness of sanctioning altogether (Rubin, 1973:184). The imposition of restrictive conditions on probationers could hardly be totally explained in a rehabilitative light. Judges knew that what they did in probation was punitive, though what they *might do* (imprison) was more punitive. Nor did the courts have to wait for a new offense and a new conviction before acting. Any failure to conform would do for revocation and imprisonment.

There is plenty of evidence, then, that probation has always served punitive purposes. The issue remaining is whether one can *exclude* rehabilitation as a goal of probation and still have probation.

The critics of the 1970s all remarked on rehabilitation's ill effects on justice and proportionality (e.g., von Hirsch, 1976; Fogel, 1975:50–62). If the goal of sentencing is to rehabilitate, then each sentence must be individualized on the basis of the defendant's personal needs, not what he or she has done. Thus, all groups rejected rehabilitation as the primary goal of sentencing. All went on to say, however, that rehabilitation was a legitimate goal of corrections, as long as it was not directly tied to the amount of punishment assigned. Thus, each of the reform plans would permit services to be offered to convicted persons on a voluntary basis (e.g., Fogel, 1975:293).

This might suffice as an answer for probation, too. Services would be offered to probationers, but they would not be required to accept them. This practice would accord with the brokerage role modern probation has come to adopt (President's Crime Commission, Corrections, 1967). There is a fuller notion of rehabilitation, however, that fits nicely with both a justice approach and the traditional view of the probation officer's counseling role. This is the notion of the requital basis of punishment. Under this approach, an evil deed deserves punishment, just as a good deed deserves a reward. The evil is requited through the moral denunciation of the evil deed. Society can make the criminal perform the sentence as symbolic of requital. Performance can be mechanical, with no effect on the person of the sufferer. But the moral nature of deserved punishment being inflicted is a call to the individual to return to the community of values impugned by the crime. In this sense punishment does not *guarantee* reform, but it *calls for* reform (Kidder, 1975; Moberly, 1968).

The second major shift for probation would be to make it a sentence. Probation is the most commonly imposed sanction under criminal law. As Cushman (1983) indicates, as many as 65 percent of all sentences are probationary. Yet in 1978 only three jurisdictions defined probation as a sentence: Illinois, Delaware, and Nebraska (Critical Issues, 1978). Although the *Model Penal Code* and ABA *Standards* treat probation as a sentence, reform codes have followed tradition in refusing to give it a formal sanctioning status. This choice reflects both the common law understanding of what a sentence is and probation's development as an alternative to the restraints of sentencing so conceived.

In common law a criminal sentence was penal, determinate, and final. Each of these features was contradicted in probation, which was rehabilitative, indeterminate, and conditional. Probation allowed the courts a means of keeping a conviction open—a grave concern in view of their inability, discussed above, to undo anything that had gone before once sentence has been imposed. In many jurisdictions (e.g., Georgia and Minnesota) probationary sentences explicitly permit the removal of the record of criminal conviction if probation is successfully completed; other jurisdictions, such as Massachusetts, provide for an expedited expunction of the record in similar circumstances (Critical Issues, 1978). An ordinary sentence, in contrast, sealed the conviction into finality and prevented its removal except by a pardoning process which was both arduous and uncertain. Probation literally gave the offender a second chance to have a clean record.

Common law sentences were also determinate. Because sentencing involved punishment, no later official could change what the court had imposed without risking a violation of the *ex post facto* prohibition, or more germanely, the double jeopardy principle which was active in common law before its enactment as part of the fifth amendment to the Constitution, *Ralston* v. *Robinson* (U.S. Sup. Ct. 1981). The only legitimate principle of alteration was executive clemency. Parole was justified on this basis. Because the executive could relieve the burden of punishment at any time, such authority could be delegated to the administrator of the executive agency, the prison. Legislation was passed early to relieve this delegated authority theory of any legal problems. Legislatures considered themselves able to create sentences that had variable outcomes dependent on conditions subsequent because they did not *add to* the imposed sentences but only provided *reductions from* them through good behavior. In effect, however, parole created highly discrepant sentence outcome for the same offense where some inmates served all or most of their sentences while others were released early. Probation represented an essentially indeterminate sentence. Its length, its conditions, and changes in both length and conditions were entirely within the discretion of the judge, at least before *Morrissey* v. *Brewer* 408 U.S. 471 (1972) made it clear that the contractual nature of the arrangement bound the state to honor some of its terms.

It was because of their penal nature that the law made criminal sentences rigid and unalterable. This offered protection to the individual, and also protected society from corrupt judges who might change the law to suit their own purposes. It even protected society from the judge who undertook the clemency task reserved to the executive.

Probation developed as a means of evading the determinacy and finality of sentencing. Making probation a sentence amounts to reversing history. But unless we are to sacrifice probation entirely, we must try to put it back into the mold it was created to break.

PROBATION AS PRACTICE: CAN JUSTICE WORK?

A just desert probation sentence would have all the features required to conform to the criminal law as we described it above. It would have to be a sanction imposed to punish convicted persons for their offense. To fulfill the requirement of proportionality and equity, it would have to be determinate. It would have to be final, not subject to later change, to conform to the requirements of *ex post facto* and double jeopardy.

Probation already is penal in nature; it appears nonpunitive only in comparison with incarceration. The lack of intermediate sanctions has been a matter of great concern for years. One way to adjust the penal grades is to shorten incarceratory sentences to bring them more into line with probation. The other way would be to increase the restrictions of probation. In fact, both elements need to be considered in creating a single graded scale of penalties that does not have obvious gaps between grades. Once probation stops being used as an *alternative to* prison and is seen as imposing a just sentence itself, the idea that probation is penal will quickly clarify. Whether there should be legitimate alternative sentences for the same offense is one that need not be decided now; there is no problem with alternatives if they are equal in penal impact. The need is to create some common measure that assures the public and defendants that they are receiving equal punishment.

Can the penal side of probation support any other goals than just deserts? The principles we have set out suggest only that the amount of punishment be proportioned to the seriousness of the offense. They do not in themselves exclude other goals. We believe, however, that direct pursuit of other goals may well undercut the justice features of the system. It might be possible, for example, to agree on the penal impact of certain conditions of probation—for example, mandatory attendance at alcoholic counseling. But we think that would undercut just deserts and that the only way to ensure that justice remains the primary goal is to make it clear that rehabilitation is only a goal for the individual (voluntary), and not the system (coercive). So too with incapacitation. Surveillance that is constant, or attendance at a community center, may be a punitive condition of probation. But if its real purpose is to control, then the inevitable tendency will be to assign it only to those who really "need" it—the dangerous. The result will be lopsided conditions that do not depend on past criminal behavior but are adjusted on the basis of other criteria. Thus, we think the system must be very clear in preestablishing rules that can resist the pull of very natural impulses toward social betterment and social control. Laudable in themselves, these impulses cannot determine the amount of punishment imposed.

Making probation a determinate sentence must be separated from making it final. We tend to confuse these concepts. The basic indeterminacy of probation today is the vague nature of the conditions imposed. Probation officers all know that they have wide authority within the stated conditions imposed, because of differences in the attitudes of the judges monitoring the process and in the resources available to support conditions imposed. Both conditions and the length of the term can change, virtually without control by the probationer. If the conditions had some objective content and probationers knew in advance exactly what was expected of them, then probation would come closer to the ideal of a determinate sentence. Determinacy is perhaps the attractiveness of restitution orders, because they can be objectively measured in dollars or hours of work. Further, repayment is extended over a definite period of time. Restitution may violate the principle of equity, however, if defendants' resources are vastly different (McAnany, 1978), and the rich pay and the poor stay (in jail). *Bearden* v. *Georgia* (U.S. Supreme Court, 1983).

We believe that, with some hard work and imagination, it would be possible to design a just desert probation that would be penal and determinate in nature. The third criterion of finality, however, presents a major practical problem in enforcement. A sentence of probation should be an unconditional order. It is imposed by the court and, apart from any indeterminacy that may mar its absoluteness, it is owed to the community and must be paid. In this sense indeterminate prison terms are final in nature but not determinate. They can be lengthened or shortened, but they cannot be changed into a death penalty or fines at some later date. Probation has traditionally been conditional, nonfinal. It might go on for five, ten, or more years and then, in theory at least, suddenly be changed into a prison term that did not recognize anything that went before.

The practical difference between a probationary sentence and a prison sentence is that the latter can be readily enforced against resisting offenders. Prison takes time passively by simply having the inmate present. It has its own enforcement problems, of course, but they are minimal compared with those of probation, even if we suppose probation with a few, precise penal conditions. Persons on probation enjoy freedom in the community which must be voluntarily given up to fulfill the sentence. The traditional probation enforcement mechanism has been the threat of imprisonment for the slightest deviation from the agreed-upon conditions. When these conditions were many and vague, the probationer never knew whether he had violated them and thus was always subject to summary placement in prison. Despite the due process protections of *Morrissey*, the least rule infraction *can* prompt a revocation (e.g., *People* v. *McCaster*, Ill. App. Ct., 1974). Even when backed by the threat of prison, however, probation has not worked well; how can it ever be expected to work if the sentence is final and not conditional on good behavior? That is the ultimate problem for a just deserts approach.

An examination of present practice on revocation suggests why the threat works so poorly (McAnany and Thomson, 1982). Once a court decides that the convicted offender does not deserve to go to prison and places him on probation, then a violation of some condition other than a new offense offers little incentive for the court to change its mind. It is left up to the probation officer to "work with" his client to gain conformity. Probation officers employ many tactics to this end, the most extreme of which is a revocation hearing whose purpose is to expose the probationer to the wrath and threats of the judge. There is some evidence that noncompliance may cause the court to extend the term or to add to the conditions. Certainly courts often extend terms to induce payment of restitution. But the overall sense is one of threats, threats, and more (and better) threats without delivery of an actual penalty. The ultimate threat of a revocation hearing, if it is seriously staged, can require significant judicial resources in the time and energy of probation staff, prosecutor, public defender, and the judge. Prosecutors are particularly uninterested in spending time on an already convicted offender. The net result appears to be an interpretation of probation conditions as really nonrevocable unless a new offense is committed. Ironically, this in turn contributes to probation's lack of meaning as a penal sanction.

We suggest that probation can be enforced if the sentence is clear and precise in what it penally demands of the offender (McAnany, 1981). One mechanism involves the arrest powers of the probation officer. If a requirement of the sentence is to perform certain public work, a probationer who fails to show up can be physically brought to the site. This immediate and direct remedy would be backed up by the administrative device of additive penalties set on a schedule to fit the violation. Thus, for example, for each day late in performing a public work project, a day would be added. For each failure to report, a fixed time would be added to the sentence. The probationer would have the opportunity to contest these added penalties in an administrative hearing. Involving minor penalties and proof by record, such hearings would be much simpler than *Morrissey* hearings. Other penalties with more immediate impact could be devised, such as detention, but care would have to be taken to avoid opening up too convenient a return to the use of incarceration. A third means of strengthening enforcement could be to create an offense of probation violation for which a jail sentence could be imposed. But there the state would have to prove the offense elements at a criminal trial. Canada has such a criminal statute (*Criminal Code*, Sec. 666 (1981)). Finally, certain cases of acute disregard of the court order over a period of time—such as fleeing the jurisdiction— might call for formal revocation. In those circumstances, a full hearing with all of the due process protections except jury trial should be offered, and credit for time actually served on probation should be given against a new sentence. But we sense that such cases would be rare if the system suggested here were seriously implemented.

REFERENCES

Allen, Francis A. (1959). "Criminal Justice, Legal Values, and the Rehabilitative Ideal." *Journal of Criminal Law, Criminology and Police Science* 50:226

American Bar Association (1980a). "Appellate Review of Sentences." In *ABA Standards for Criminal Justice*, rev. ed., vol. 4: ch. 21. Boston: Little, Brown.

———— (1980b). "Sentencing Alternatives and Procedures." In *ABA Standards for Criminal Justice*, rev. ed., vol. 3: ch. 18. Boston: Little, Brown.

American Friends Service Committee (1971). *Struggle for Justice*. New York: Hill and Wang.

American Law Institute (1962). *Model Penal Code*. Philadelphia: American Law Institute.

Benn, Stanley I. (1958). "An Approach to the Problem of Punishment." *Philosophy* 33:321–341.

Carey, James T. (1983). "The Professionalization of Probation." Chapter 4 in this volume.

Christie, Nils (1981). *Limits to Pain*. Oxford: Martin Robertson.

Commission on Accreditation (1977). *Standards for Adult Probation*. Silver Springs, MD: American Correctional Association.

Conrad, John P. (1984). "The Redefinition of Probation: Drastic Proposals to Solve An Urgent Problem." Chapter 8 in this volume.

Cook, Phillip (1980). "Research in Criminal Deterrence: Laying the Groundwork for the Second Decade." in Norval Morris and Michael Tonry (eds.), *Crime and Justice*, vol. 2:211–268. Chicago: University of Chicago Press.

Critical Issues in Adult Probation (1978). *Technical Issue Paper on Legal Issues in Adult Probation*. Columbus, OH: Program for the Study of Crime and Delinquency, Ohio State University.

Cullen, Francis T., and Karen E. Gilbert (1982). *Reaffirming Rehabilitation*. Cincinnati, OH: Anderson.

Cushman, Robert C. (1984). "Probation in the 1980s—A Public Administration Viewpoint." Chapter 11 in this volume.

Davis, Kenneth C. (1969). *Discretionary Justice*. Baton Rouge: Louisiana State University Press.

Dershowitz, Alan A. (1976). "Background Paper on Sentencing." In 20th Century Fund Task Force on Sentencing, *Fair and Certain Punishment*. New York: McGraw-Hill.

Duffee, David E. (1984). "The Community Context of Probation." Chapter 12 in this volume.

Erhlich, Isaac (1975). "The Deterrent Effect of Capital Punishment: A Question of Life and Death." *American Economics Review* 65:397–432.

Fitzharris, Timothy L. (1984). "The Federal Role in Probation Reform." Chapter 14 in this volume.

Fogel, David (1975). *We Are The Living Proof . . .* Cincinnati, OH: Anderson.

Frankel, Marvin E. (1973). *Criminal Sentences: Law Without Order*. New York: Hill and Wang.

Gardner, Martin (1976). "The Renaissance of Retribution—An Examination of Doing Justice." *Wisconsin Law Review* 1976:781–815.

Gerber, Rudolph J., and Patrick D. McAnany (1967). "Punishment: A Current Survey of Law and Philosophy." *St. Louis University Law Journal* 11:491–535.

Griffiths, John (1970). "Ideology in Criminal Procedures or a Third 'Model' of the Criminal Process." *Yale Law Journal* 79:359–417.

Gross, Hyman (1979). *A Theory of Criminal Justice*. New York: Oxford.

Harris, M. Kay (1984). "Rethinking Probation in the Context of a Justice Model." Chapter 1 in this volume.

Honderich, Ted (1969). *Punishment: The Supposed Justifications*. London: Hutchinson.

Kidder, Joel (1975). "Requital and Criminal Justice." *International Philosophical Quarterly* 15:255–278.

Lipton, Douglas, Robert Martinson, and Judith Wilks (1975). *The Effectiveness of Correctional Treatment*. New York: Praeger.

McAnany, Patrick D. (1976). "Recommendations for an Ailing Probation System," in R. Gerber (ed.), *Contemporary Issues in Criminal Justice*. Port Washington, NY: Kennikat Press.

McAnany, Patrick D. (1978). "Restitution As Idea and Practice: The Retributive Prospect." In Galloway and Hudson (eds.), *Offender Restitution in Theory and Practice*. Lexington, MA: Heath.

McAnany, Patrick D. (1981). "Probation Revocation: Fairness and Equity." Paper presented at the 6th Annual Meeting of the American Probation and Parole Association, Montreal, Canada, Oct. 19.

McAnany, Patrick D., and Doug Thomson (1982). *Equitable Responses to Probation Violations: A Guide for Managers*. Chicago: Center for Research in Law and Justice, University of Illinois at Chicago.

Moberly, Sir Walter (1968). *The Ethics of Punishment*. London: Faber and Faber.

Morris, Norval (1966). "Impediments to Penal Reform." *University of Chicago Law Review* 33:627–656.

Morris, Norval (1974). *The Future of Imprisonment*. Chicago: University of Chicago Press.

Murphy, Jeffrie G. (1979). *Retribution, Justice and Therapy: Essays in the Philosophy of Law*. Dordrecht: D. Reidel.

National Council on Crime and Delinquency (1963). *Model Sentencing Act*. New York: NCCD.

Nelson, E. Kim, and Nora Harlow (1980). *Responses to Diminishing Resources in Probation: The California Experience*. Berkeley, CA: University of Southern California.

Newman, Graeme (1978). *The Punishment Response*. Philaelphia: Lippincott.

Nonet, Phillip, and Phillip Selznick (1978). *Law and Society in Transition*. New York: Octagon Books.

Packer, Herbert L. (1968). *The Limits of the Criminal Sanction*. Stanford, CA: Stanford University Press.

President's Crime Commission (1967). *Task Force Report: Corrections*. Washington, D.C.: U.S. Government Printing Office.

Radzinowicz, Leon (1966). *Ideology and Crime*. New York: Columbia University Press.

Rosett, Arthur, and Donald R. Cressey (1976). *Justice by Consent*. Philadelphia: Lippincott.

Rothman, David J. (1980). *Conscience and Convenience: The Asylum and Its Alternatives*. Boston: Little Brown.

Rubin, Sol (1960). "Sentencing and Correctionl Treatment Under the Law Institute's Model Penal Code." *American Bar Association Journal* 46:994–998.

Rubin, Sol (1973). *Law of Criminal Correction*, 2d ed. St. Paul, MN: West.

Schulhofer, Stephen J. (1980). "Due Process of Sentencing." *University of Pennsylvania Law Review* 128:733–828.

Singer, Richard G. (1979). *Just Deserts: Sentencing Based on Equality and Desert*. Cambridge, MA: Ballinger.

Strawson, Phillip F. (1974). *Freedom and Resentment and Other Essays*. London: Methuen.

Thomson, Doug, and David Fogel (1980). *Probation Work in Small Agencies: A*

National Study of Training Provisions and Needs. Chicago: Center for Research in Law and Justice, University of Illinois at Chicago.

Twentieth Century Fund Task Force on Sentencing (1976). *Fair and Certain Punishment*. New York: McGraw-Hill.

Uniform Law Commissioners (1979). *Model Sentencing and Corrections Act*. Washington, D.C.: Government Printing Office.

United States Government (1939). *Attorney General's Survey of Release Procedures*, vol. 2, *Probation*. Washington, D.C.: Government Printing Office.

von Hirsch, Andrew (1976). *Doing Justice: The Choice of Punishments*. New York: Hill and Wang.

von Hirsch, Andrew, and Kathleen J. Hanrahan (1981). "Determinate Penalty Systems in America: An Overview." *Crime and Delinquency* (July 1981):289–316.

Wechsler, Herbert (1961). "Sentencing, Correction, and the Model Penal Code." *University of Pennsylvania Law Review* 109:465–501.

Wilson, James Q. (1975). *Thinking About Crime*. New York: Basic Books.

Zeisel, Hans (1977). "The Deterrent Effect of the Death Penalty: Facts v. Faith." *Supreme Court Review* 1977:317–343.

Zilboorg, Gregory (1968). *The Psychology of the Criminal Act and Punishment*. New York: Greenwood Press.

Zimring, Franklin E., and Gordon Hawkins (1973). *Deterrence*. Chicago: University of Chicago Press.

Zimring, Franklin E. (1976). "Making the Punishment Fit the Crime: A Consumer's Guide to Sentencing Reform." *Hastings Center Report* 6:13–17.

Cases

Bearden v. *Georgia, No. 81–6633, Decided May 24, 1983, United States Supreme Court*.

Morrissey v. *Brewer*, 408 U.S. 471 (1972).

People v. *McCaster*, 19 Ill. App. 3d 824 (1974).

Ralston v. *Robinson*, 454 U.S. 201 (1981).

Villery v. *Florida Probation and Parole Board*, Criminal Law Reporter 29:2178 (1981).

Chapter 3

The Emergence of Probation as a Profession in the Service of Public Safety: the Next Ten Years

*David Fogel**

Over the years, probation practice has varied considerably. This variation should not be surprising, since it is an occupation that has not yet clearly delineated its claims to professional status. Without such clarity many, perhaps too many, directions have been available in probation work, and it has lacked the coherent identity of the more traditional professions.

In more than a century of practice, probation has debated, organized, and reorganized itself to match models current in any given era along a continuum from pathology to justice (Carey, 1983). The vigor and rapid expansion of probation is remarkable when one considers the lack of agreement concerning the minimum education necessary for a probation professional; the educational discipline upon which to base entry requirements for practice (there are no schools of probation),[1] the theory of practice, the methodology of practice, and the mission of the occupation. Lack of agreement has perhaps been a spur to growth, rather than a con-

*Department of Criminal Justice, University of Illinois at Chicago

straint, given the prevailing anomie in probation from state to state, between departments within a state, between the same departments under different incumbent directors, and indeed among practitioners within the same department at any given time.

Given uneven levels of development, probation did not grow as a solid body but rather as so many appendages without a central nervous system to coordinate and channel its development. This analysis may serve as a partial explanation of why a philosophy or central mission, driven by a paradigm, has yet to quicken in the field of probation. While the pages of *Federal Probation* yield an intellectual history of sorts (the play of ideas reflected by the more articulate), it is less instructive about actual practice. The ideas of authors may not have been clearly and effectively translated among the thousands of noncommunicating probation agencies across the land. Given the historically fragmented development of probation services and despite their explosive growth (Rothman, 1980:44), there is little evidence that probation's direction has been purposive, its leadership unified, or its practitioners confident about either their purpose or unity.

In the beginning probation was heavily police-oriented, with some lay participation (Rothman, 1980:243). The historical record suggests that probation moved from this shaky start to paid workers, finally displacing Augustus and the original small bands of volunteers who pioneered the field (Rothman, 1980:84). Although the case method rapidly caught the hearts and minds of the professionals, the strain between policing and counseling has never been fully resolved. The field was able to operationalize new concepts in management, surveillance, and casework methods and even find theoretical underpinnings for these changing paradigms. We will explore how probation managed to accommodate these concepts and yet remain in a police-casework dilemma.

As a result of the noncommunicating, fragmented growth, some departments accommodated new ideas under a casework umbrella; others (probably more *adult* agencies) were able to maintain a quasi-police posture while incorporating other new ideas offered in the literature. There were, after all, no professional standards with accompanying sanctions insisting upon a particular direction from chief probation officers or their superiors. The judiciary, with a few notable exceptions, has not shown an abiding interest in shaping the future of probation.

In sum, we have a hundred-year-old field that has been marked by piecemeal growth and showered with ideas that may or may not be reflected in practice. Thousands of probation agencies are manned by practitioners who vary considerably in education, philosophy, and commitment to a method. They lack professional leadership and are currently under attack for a variety of reasons.

The current search for a firmer identity is, however, driven by historically unique forces. Earlier innovation came from academe and elite practitioners. Probation's concerns, during an earlier growth period, were more oriented toward refinement of practice. Since the issue is no longer "survival at any cost," the current debate has a distinguishable moral flavor. The concerns are, as conceptualized by Lubove (1965), as much a matter of *cause* as of *function*.

Kay Harris (1980)[2] suggests there are at least three primary reasons why probation as a sanction and probation as an occupation need fresh articulation.

> One reason is that the field of probation is suffering from role confusion and conflict and a poor public image. Thus it needs a new model around which to rally or focus debate. A second reason is that as the variety of incarcerative sentencing alternatives has increased in use, it has become clear that there is a need to consider more fully how these various options relate to probation, how they should be structured and how they can best fulfill their potential to reduce jail and prison populations. The third reason is that probation as traditionally conceived and operated does not fit well within the more attractive theoretical frameworks for punishment and sentencing now receiving active consideration, especially in relation to a just deserts or justice model. (Harris, 1980:1–2)

Historically, we are at a crossroads. We need to emerge from this debate with at least a minimal agenda identifying the needs for the future development of the field or be consigned to another generation of fragmented noncommunication. But there are some encouraging signs. In earlier days, when probation concerns centered on operational questions, those seeking a debate about the future of probation could hardly muster a quorum. Currently, the question of the future of probation is perceived by practitioners and academics alike to be one of overarching concern. Though the reasons for the urgency of the concern may differ, there is now an indisputably wider constituency for reexamining the future than has heretofore been available. Some question the philosophic bases for current probation practice. Others see probation as an endangered species in an era that combines law and order rhetoric with the passage of Proposition 13 and similar referenda and statutes. Still others see probation as an even larger growth industry than prisons. (In point of fact, when considering client head count, probation has for some time been the largest component of corrections, yet the least expensive, and staffed by its best educated personnel.) Thus as Dickens observed of eighteenth-century revolutionary Paris, and as we conclude about the field of probation at the beginning of the 1980s., "It was the best of times; it was the worst of times . . . "

Whether out of intellectual calculation, financial despair, or professional optimism, probation's leading thinkers and practitioners are subjecting the field to a self-evaluation of historic rigor. It is in the spirit of constructive optimism that this work and its authors are dedicated to advancing the debate.

THE NEEDS DEPRIVATION MODEL

The case method (sometimes referred to as the treatment or rehabilitation model) has been extensively discussed and analyzed in the literature. Even when recent innovative ideas (community resource management, intensive supervision, and newer risk assessments and classification techniques) are taken into consideration, the case method theory remains essentially a "needs deprivation" model. Whatever the resources available, this conception deploys them in a fashion that centers on the offender (client) and sees the probation officer (therapist) as responsible for developing, through a referral or the probation officer's own direct service efforts, the resources necessary to meet the client's needs to assure his or her future lawful behavior. In this view, offenders are driven to their crimes because of some intrapsychic imbalance or environmental deficiency/pathology. Convicted offenders may be shown leniency because the diagnosis (presentence report) is optimistic about their prognosis for law-abiding citizenship provided a treatment plan (the Rx) is implemented. It is therefore a theory that centers on the *offender*, rather than the *offense*. The offender is somehow not whole but can be made whole again with the skillful assistance of a probation officer, trained in the case method (borrowed directly from psychiatry and social casework). The presenting crime, some theorists suggest, is a "cry for help." Presumably, the offender might have lived lawfully, albeit in conflict, had the cry for help (the unlawful act) not emerged from the subconscious. Some thirty years ago proponents of this point of view suggested that we treat offenders "as sick people, which in every respect they are. [some day] . . . the jailer will be replaced by the nurse, and the judge by the psychiatrist . . . " (Sutherland and Cressey, 1974:605). Such enthusiasm has moderated in more recent times.

Almost all one-to-one and even group methods in probation proceed from a needs deprivation starting point. Different technologies for reaching the client abound, but all attempt to patch up gaps in the client's psyche. Sometimes the answer lies in obtaining a high school education, sometimes in taking a vocational training course, sometimes in intensive psychotherapy, and often in monthly chats between client and counselor, usually about the former's unverifiable experiences.

Implicit in this arrangement is the utilitarian assumption that the probation officer can enhance the public safety by providing "help" to the offender-client. Indeed, if the client is not adhering to the treatment plan (sometimes dimly captured in a court order specifying the conditions of probation), the officer may want to talk about revocation and prison as an alternative to help. Herein lies the central flaw in the model. Despite the rhetoric of rehabilitation (now frequently, particularly in parole circles, referred to as "reintegration" or "reentry" as in space technology), coercive treatment emerges because the client is not accorded *volition*. In the last analysis, all strains between treatment and public safety in probation (as in prison) are invariably settled in favor of public safety, which in effect means controlling offenders because of guesses about their future behavior based on observations of their conformity with the prescribed court ordered regimen.

The convicted person placed on probation undergoes several transformations in the criminal justice system: initially a *suspect*, he or she then becomes an *alleged offender*, next a *defendant* and upon conviction an *offender*, and finally, depending upon the sentence, either a *prisoner* (*resident* or *convict*, and later potentially a *parolee*) or a *probationer*. In the latter status he or she becomes a *client* with the probation officer cast as the *therapist* (helper, treater, counselor)—though the officers's prior training might have been in animal husbandry or art. Official perceptions of the client's volitional capacity shift considerably along the way. In court a crime must be proven to be a function of the act *and* intent of the actor—that is, responsible and volitional behavior by an offender. Once found guilty of the commission of a volitional act (or the omission of a legal duty to act), the criminal is transformed into an object, not a responsible actor, and dealt with as one who needs to carry out a self-improvement plan rather than being simply punished for the wrong committed. The person wronged receives scant attention—a problem to which we will return shortly.

It is in the construction of the presentence investigation that the probation officer first learns of the biography of the offender. The more psychosocial material requested, the more complex the offender becomes. Increasing complexity inexorably leads to extenuation and overidentification with the client (Fogel, 1969). It is interesting to speculate whether the same process would occur for victims; if so, the natural outcome might well be greater punitiveness, rather than greater leniency toward the offender.

All of this assumes a professional ability to develop independent objective data on the client. As one works in the field and reads the literature, something less than ideal practice appears to be the norm, though the rhetoric of the ideal remains.

A JUSTICE MODEL FOR PROBATION: RECONCEPTUALIZING

Before proceeding to the discussion of an alternative model for probation practice, we urge a frank acknowledgment of the place of probation on the continuum of criminal sanctions. Over all counseling sessions between a probation officer and probationer (or a parole officer and parolee) falls the shadow of prison; the threat may or may not be acknowledged by the participants but is plainly known to both. Whatever the rhetoric of rehabilitation may be on the surface, the deeper force at work in probation is the *centrality of coercion*. Just as probation may operate well because of the looming specter of a jail, the minimum custody correctional facility can operate because a maximum custody penitentiary also exists. Although few social work and counseling curricula may admit to the centrality of coercion as a driving force in rehabilitation-oriented agencies, we believe its presence must be acknowledged if we are to unravel the convoluted ideology and conflicting roles presently abroad in the field of probation. Straight talk is frequently the best medicine for confusing images.

More to the point, however, we must recognize that probation itself is a penalty, both ceremonially and, depending on the conditions imposed, behaviorally, since it restricts liberty. Moreover, for normative as well as pragmatic reasons, we think it essential to reaffirm, emphasize, and elaborate this reality of probation as a sentence and process. This is central to the approach proposed (McAnany, 1983).

The field of probation is derivative. Procedural law gives vitality to other elements of the criminal law system—police, prosecution, defense, and the prison—but probation is by and large a discretionary arm of the courts. None of the other agencies is likely to decline or decisively alter its basic mission, although there may be room for modification and modernization. Probation, like parole, could be drastically altered or even abolished without causing a fatal dislocation in the basic operation of the criminal justice system. In this period of drift, probation must reassert itself and identify what it does and what it intends to offer in the future. Mission is the problem.

A mission must be based on a relatively unambiguous view of human behavior and the criminal law. Despite some similarities, probation operations are not social work agencies, but arms of the court—criminal law agencies. Very few people engage the probation agency as voluntary clients seeking services (although they may come to accept such services).

It has been argued elsewhere (Fogel, 1975) that corrections can be operationalized around a justice model that does not exclude social services but does not see them as the prison's raison d'être. A number of postulates for correction were offered (based upon the work of Stephen Schafer) to guide mission setting for prisons. We paraphrase them here for application to probation:

1. The criminal law is the command of the sovereign.
2. The threat of punishment is necessary to implement the criminal law.
3. People are socialized to respond to the command and expectations of the ruling social-political power.
4. The criminal law and its agencies protect the power of the dominant prescribed morality.
5. In the absence of an absolute system of justice or "natural law," no accurate etiological theory of crime is possible nor is the definition of crime itself stable.
6. Although perfect free will may not exist, the criminal law is largely based upon its presumed vitality and forms the only foundation for criminal sanctions.
7. A criminal sentence represents a punishment embodied in a statute, invoked by a judge (constrained by procedural law) upon a person adjudged responsible for his or her unlawful behavior.
8. Although a sentence may have several intended purposes (deterrence, retaliation, rehabilitation), it is specifically a measured punishment proportionate to the harm inflicted by the criminal.
9. Probation is a criminal sentence and should not be represented as an abstention from punishment. The guiding principle is that there is no punishment without a crime and no crime without punishment.
10. The entire process of criminal justice must be played out in a milieu of justice. Justice-as-fairness represents the superordinate goal of all agencies of the criminal law.
11. When probation becomes mired in the dismal swamp of treating its clients, it is in danger of becoming dysfunctional as an agency of justice. Probation officers should engage probationers as the law otherwise dictates—as responsible and volitional human beings.
12. Justice-as-fairness is not a *program*; it is an *aspiration* which insists that all agencies of the criminal law perform their assigned roles with non-law-abiders lawfully. While individual probationers may need specialized intensive services, probation officers should not be responsible for providing them nor should probationers be judged (for revocation purposes) on their success or lack of success in completing such treatments.
13. William Pitt warned that "where the law ends, tyranny begins"; so too does discretion. Discretion is inevitable, but unbridled discretion undermines the rule of law. While discretion (or professional judgment) cannot be eliminated, the justice perspective seeks to narrow and control it and make it reviewable.

14. Probation as a sentence must be made explicit. At present it suffers as an indefinite legal sanction which invests wide discretionary powers in a probation officer while offering vague or largely unexplicated purposes for its imposition.

15. The presentence investigation should be treated as a legal document and should be discoverable by the defendant. Its focus should be on the victim and the extent of the harm done. Since the offender's legal culpability was established by the court, the presentence report now turns to the broader issue of how the offender may assist in restoring the offended to the pre-crime status quo.

16. While the judge should decide upon the sentence of probation, he should have flexibility in determining the individual conditions of the probation order. At this point it is relevant to consider what assistance the offender may furnish the victim. An order permitting the offender to remain in the community has to be balanced against the question of whether nonincarceration would suggest disrespect for the law.

17. Probation is a summary sentence; it is not leniency, it does not replace another sentence and it contains explicated conditions. The court should have statutory authority to sentence to probation and set unambiguous conditions. The offender and probation officer's continuing relationship is undertaken in the context of the conditions of the probation order. The conditions are made explicit so that allegations of violation may be more objectively determined by the court.[3]

18. Central to a justice model approach is the voluntary acceptance by the probationer of social treatment, if treatment is to be provided at all. When treatments are ordered, two problems arise: coercion by the officer and manipulation by the probationer.[4]

19. Revocation of probation represents a greater intrusion into the offender's life and an interruption of assistance to the victim (where such was ordered); therefore, the standard of proof for revocation should be at least as high as for the original finding that occasioned the sentence of probation (i.e., beyond a reasonable doubt) and should not be grounded upon nebulous assessments of attitudes.

20. The needs of the victim, whether an individual or a community, should be explicitly taken into consideration in any sentence and specifically reflected in court-ordered conditions of probation. The probation officer's mandate from the court should be as weighted with concern for making the victim whole as it is with the offender. Restitution (financial or moral) and community service should be ordered when feasible as a component of the conditions of probation.

With these propositions in mind, we may now illustrate the incompatibility of traditional probation premises and practices with the justice model.

A further caution is necessary before proceeding. This work is concerned with probation sentencing and practices. We have deliberately excluded unconditional discharges and all other lesser penalties from this discussion although we are mindful of their validity as sanctions.

Kay Harris has written:

> Chief among the features that are inconsistent with a justice model are that [probation] has been highly discretionary, individualized, linked to prediction, and based on a conception of probationers as less than fully rational. By way of contrast, a justice model requires that the sanction be reasonably clear and predictable, that the penalty be based on past, proved behavior, and that probationers be assumed to be capable of responsible choice. . . . the requirements involved in a particular sanction should be spelled out in advance and easily understandable. They also should be of a nature that allows reasonably objective determinations to be made as to whether or not compliance occurred (Harris, 1980:17).

The wide variation in requirements currently placed on probationers is a natural outcome of the principle of *individualization*, which emphasizes attention to offenders' varied backgrounds. Although the rhetoric of the conventional model may be attractive, in practice it does not fulfill its promise to personalize attention and surveillance and simultaneously offer whatever skills and assistance might be necessary.

> A major issue concerns the fairness or justice of tailoring criminal sanctions to individuals, to changing circumstances, and to predictions and beliefs rather than to past acts. Is it fair to give one offender three years of probation with the requirement that he abstain from alcohol, earn a G.E.D. and obtain employment and give another offender guilty of the same offense but who is well-situated a shorter term with no special conditions? Another concern relates to the effectiveness of the individualistic, predictive approach. Is there good reason to believe that getting a high school education is in fact reasonably related to the goal of reducing further crime? Also, the special instructions or conditions that can be used have very different meaning or consequences for different people. Exhortations involving various forms of "good conduct" imply different things to different people. Such obligations can also be completely unrealistic since it may be difficult to obtain what is prescribed, such as employment or medical treatment (Harris, 1980:17).

There may also be discrepancies between how a judge views a special condition of probation, the world-view of the probation officer, the administrative and ideological bent of the probation department involved, and other variables. One judge might view probation as a "second chance" and wish only to see no more of the offender. (Channel 7 in Chicago entitled an "exposé" of the local adult probation department *"Crime's* Second Chance.") Another judge, truly believing in either rehabilitation or surveillance, might impose minutely detailed orders to accomplish that objective. Other variations see restitution widely ordered for property offenders in some jurisdictions, but rarely in others. "Too often," Harris reminds us, "the punitive effects of the penalty (special conditions) are disregarded when the stated intent is rehabilitative" (Harris, 1980:19–20).

Variations in supervision and treatment are not only a managerial problem, but raise questions of discretion and equity.

> The number of opportunities for introducing variation means that there is a good chance that similarly situated offenders will have dissimilar experiences. The discretionary nature of the penalty also can produce continuing uncertainty and anxiety for offenders, as well as feelings of inability to control what happens to them. The variability described also undermines the clarity of the sanction in the public eye.
>
> A justice model for criminal sanctions holds that it is undesirable for such broad powers to be exercised over individuals with respect to the duration, nature, and essential features of the punishment that can be expected for a crime. This is not to imply endorsement of the notion that the only way to be fair is to treat all offenders guilty of the same crime in identical fashion. The point is that variation in penalties should be tied to reasoned decisions derived from clear goals and standards (Harris, 1980:20.)

Finally, probation-as-punishment stirs the emotions and conjures up an imagery of repression. Repression is foreign to our perspective of justice-as-fairness. The search for explicated reasons for sentencing and specificity in probation conditions is intended to limit an offender's liability while engaging his or her volition. This is an offender empowerment model. We subscribe to the notion of punishment as a *limiting principle* in a system of justice.

PROBATION AND PUBLIC SAFETY

Viewing public safety as the raison d'être for the criminal law is the first step in probation mission building. We do not here mean the assessment of risks to the public's *future* safety (i.e., predicting the offender's future unlawfulness). Rather we focus on the jeopardy, the degree of harm caused by the offender and suffered by the community. In this perspective public safety is the satisfaction and confidence the public sense in having justice done for the present offense. Practitioners and administrators should see public safety as the overriding reason for the establishment of criminal justice agencies. In a real sense public safety is perhaps the one unifying theme that brings police, courts, and corrections under ths same umbrella. While debate continues within each of these criminal justice subsystems about how best to "insure domestic tranquillity," it is generally accepted that domestic tranquillity is at the core of all their efforts.

In comparison with other subsystems in justice, the police have probably struggled harder with the question of how to "serve and protect" and have moved more dramatically to reform the delivery of their services over the last two decades. The reforms have reached into deeply entrenched and heretofore inviolate assumptions and practices. Nor has the debate leading to change been always polite, reasoned, or even consensual. The pace of change in police practices has been indisputably rapid, and frequently uneven, but changes in practice and attitudes are so quickly institutionalized that new officers today are operating with constraints and opportunities quite unanticipated by their brethren a short generation ago. Probation has yet to undergo a comparable practice revolution.

Change in police practice has been forced from the outside, (Supreme Court, public clamor, legislation), innovated from within, and reached through reason and compromise with the public, particularly minority communities wishing to play a role in crime prevention (community relation and beat representative programs, crime prevention education and the rapid, if uneven, rise in opportunity for minorities and women to become police officers). The police have gone through reform efforts that were initially thought to require simply larger numbers, then more selective recruitment, followed by a reliance (perhaps dependence) upon improved technology and better deployment of personnel. Of more recent vintage is the police effort to build alliances with citizens of the communities with highest crime rates (which also contain the majority of victims) to improve the quality and efficiency of their protective services. Whatever the agenda of police reform has been, no major objection has been raised to the centrality of public safety as the mission.

As noted, the revolution in police practice has not been a quiet one carried out in an orderly manner. The crucibles of change have been in the courtroom, on the streets, in referenda, in union halls, in squad rooms, and in the academies. The debate has been rancorous, heated, and freqently confrontational in style. The old station house fiefdom is passing into history. When the history of policing in the 1960–1980 era is written, it will give prominence to the efforts of leading charismatics who questioned old styles, developed new ones, and constantly challenged their colleagues to modernize. The Police Evaluation and Research Forum (PERF) under the leadership of Patrick Murphy is a leading case in point.

While institutional correctional service is now at a middle phase of such a revolution, probation's counterpart effort has barely begun. The most significant accomplishment of the police transformation has been to conduct debate and change in the context of *policing in a democratic society.* Perhaps of equal importance for the future of any occupation or profession (since any change in practice takes place within an ephemeral, historical, and developmental context) is the broader gain achieved in flexibility, accommodation, and self-confident emergence following soul-searching criticism.

We are confident that we in the field of probation can also debate and emerge renewed. But having learned from the police debate, we urge that the rancor, at least, be muted in our reassessment. The binding force begins with our unchallenged common allegiance to the goal of achieving public safety in a democratic society. The debate will revolve about the question of *how to increase the probability* of enhancing the public safety within the context of improving the quality of justice and avoiding repression. We now proceed under the assumption that form should follow purpose.

Our resources—human, fiscal, and legal—are limited. The legal resources establish a context for *practice*, fiscal resources limit the extensiveness and perhaps the *quality of practice*, while the human resources (personnel) affect the quality and context of the *delivery of probation services.*

It may be unkind, but probably fundamentally true, to say that in the quarter-century before 1970, probation was basically an offender-based interview technology. The question was how to reach the client. The most radical suggestion in more recent years has been a division of labor approach (community resource management) and even more recently the technology of classification probably born out of the ideology of behavior management. Probation's earliest mission (to focus upon offender needs) remained challenged. The offender, as previously noted, has been at the core of practice. We have linked the profession's worthiness to the offender's lawfulness. Very few commentators (Conrad, 1983) have pointed out that probation has had an unfair natural advantage over ex-prisoner agencies such as parole simply because of the halo effect of *being selected* and occupying *the status of probationer.* We start out with the most law-abiding of the non-law-abiding. Having largely selected our own clientele, we have been busy developing a technology that protects probation from its major critics. Most unkindly we are dealing with the boy scouts, both misdemeanants and felons. The technology, such as it is, has not advanced probation as an alternative for use with "higher level risk" clients. Rather the technical changes have settled practitioners in comfortable niches with a basically "safe" clientele.

PROBATION AND THE VICTIM

It would be unfair to single out probation for its singular inattention to the victim. The whole of criminal justice, since our English forebears decided that all crimes were breaches of the King's Peace, has systematically excluded the victim's weal. We are mindful of the expansion of victim compensation, offender restitution, victim assistance, and witness protection programs, but here we are concerned with *probation's* focus on the victim. Consider a system of criminal justice that rightfully reaches its majesty in protecting the rights of the accused and insists upon constitutional standards for the care of the convicted but leaves its victims few options for redress.[5] Consider further that in our Malthusian criminal processes we produce victims in geometric proportions to criminals and organize our ameliorative services (probation, institutions, and parole) to serve, however imperfectly, the convicted criminal. Herein lies a constituency-building dilemma and opportunity of major proportions for probation. An enormous potential constituency of victims remains untouched, uninvolved, and largely forgotten. Although this constituency may be a natural one, there was no intrinsic reason for probation to have tapped it when the prevailing practice ethos called for a focus on the offender. We dangle the potential of this political base but it is not our major argument for urging a change of focus from the offender to the offended.

Our major argument is that a shift of concern to the victim is *right*, in the sense of *fair*, in a democratic society that asks its criminal justice agencies to operate from the justice perspective. The resources of the state, from the justice perspective, are rightly deployed to protect its citizenry from internal enemies (criminals). When such efforts at public safety fail, the second line of defense should be no less concerned with the citizen as victim. When a family is the victim of a 2 a.m. burglary, why do we not routinely provide needed services (which might include repairing a broken window pane in freezing weather, reassurance for trauma, bilingual communication if necessary, and so on). We are not necessarily suggesting that probation provide such services, although a case might be made for collapsing all victim assistance services now offered sporadically and infrequently by various justice agencies into the probation service. Even victim protective services might be offered by probation, justified by its particularly strategic position as an arm of the courts and the courts' proprietary interest in the flow of unobstructed information.

The current confining role of probation is an anachronism linked to its earlier definition as an alternative to prison. Historically the probation service centered on exploring the offender's candidacy for a nonincarcerative sentence. When such a sentence was ordered by the court, it became incumbent upon probation to mobilize its efforts with the offender as the focus, to fulfill its earlier promise (as contained in the presentence investigation). Restitution might have been ordered, and the victim might have testified as to his or her loss and might even have been consulted about the sentence, but the victim's involvement was primarily concerned with how the offender should ultimately be treated.

At this point we are not yet ready to offer policy choices for restructuring probation departments to emphasize victim services. We need, however, to discuss the probation officer in relation to the victim since the officer will eventually have to transform rhetoric into service.

Chief among the reasons probation officers feel directionless has been their growing awareness of the dysfunction of integrating social control and social assistance roles in a single individual. Conrad suggests a structure that creates a path out of this moral thicket. Its guiding principle is to divide probation's many services into functionally discrete areas, thereby eliminating role confusion and conflict (Conrad, 1983). Conrad's first discrete area is social investigation. Within this division we may envision a presentence investigation that begins with the harm done by the offender, the nature of the loss to the offended person(s) or community (has it caused a continuous impairment?), a mandatory statement by the victim, and a plan for participation in making the victim whole.

The investigating probation officer will therefore have to become proactively involved with the individual victim or the community-as-victim. The presentence investigation should begin with such harm and restoration analyses, augmented by the police report. If a community sentence is to be considered, then a community perspective should guide the next section of the presentence investigation, which will consider the offender's potential to fulfill his or her obligations to the offended. When this kind of social investigation is routinely done, the investigator has in effect become a victim advocate in the sentencing process. No longer exclusively preoccupied with the offender, the investigating probation officer now becomes an advocate for equity. The presentence investigation thus essentially captures the victim's perspective and in turn largely forms the basis for the conditions of the sentence of probation.

Since this research was undertaken the federal government has indeed adopted the victim perspective. Among other things, the Omnibus Victim Protection Act of 1982 provides (Title I, Section 101) for a Victim Impact Statement by amending Rule 32 of the Federal Rules of Criminal Procedure to read:

> The [presentence] report shall also contain verified information stated in a nonargumentative style assessing the financial, social, psychological, and medical impact upon and cost to any person who was the victim of the offense committed by the defendant. The [presentence] report shall also include a

statement of any need of the victim for restitution and any such information as may be required by the court.

A powerful implementation resource (Title V), known as the Federal Accountability Section of the Act, was unfortunately deleted before it became law; it would have required the attorney general to provide guidelines for a full range of victim and witness services.

We will need a mild revolution in our thinking about sentencing itself to attain the victim perspective notion we advance. Mandatory prison sentencing based upon the presumption of incarceration will have to yield to the *presumption of nonincarceration*—the presumption of probation (Gradess, 1978:5).

As many have pointed out, it is at the point of the state's greatest potential intrusion into citizens' lives that the rule of law has yet to be firmly applied in most U.S. jurisdictions. Jonathan E. Gradess unambiguously states:

> when our government, as sovereign, exercises its police power, it may do so only to protect the health, welfare and safety of the community. . . . Community protection is the compelling state interest underlying the criminal justice system and it is the compelling state interest underlying sentencing.
>
> It is not permissible for government to further this compelling state interest by a choice of means which unnecessarily burdens the exercise of a fundamental right (Gradess, 1978:6–7).

When the choice of means is the presumption of incarceration, the fundamental right of liberty is automatically placed in jeopardy. Gradess finds current sentencing practices to be standardless:

> In sentencing, despite the desperately important nature of the inquiry, we provide no real means for challenging governmental action against the individual because we have no procedures which facilitate such a challenge. . . . The inquiry at sentence concentrates not on whether a sanction will protect the community but rather on the individual predilections of probation officers and jurists. We will never develop a common law of sentencing until we treat the process by which sentences are imposed in the same way the adversarial system treats far less important questions. When we determine whether governmental sanctions may permissibly be applied to infringe upon other fundamental rights, we hold hearings to determine whether the means chosen by government to fulfill its mission *under a statute* are permissible or whether they are overbroad; whether they are purposeful or fanciful (Gradess, 1978:7–8).

Central to the Gradess argument is the presumption of nonincarceration. The state should have to establish, beyond a reasonable doubt, that a particular sanction is justified. The sentencing hearing thus takes on a new significance:

> Witnesses should be sworn, testify, and be subjected to confrontation and cross examination; parties should be permitted to file memoranda of law and briefs with the court; a stenographic record should be kept, and written findings of fact and conclusions of law should be required delineating the evidence specifically relied upon for the sentence. The stenographic minutes of the sentencing hearing should constitute part of the record on appeal and the defendant should have the right to appellate review of the sentence imposed.
>
> This process will improve sentencing procedures: It will require judges to become accountable, to find facts, to make records, and to develop a consistent body of legal principle. It will, by appellate review, create sentencing guidelines. It will provide for the development of widespread alternatives to incarceration and will facilitate innovative and imaginative non-incarcerative limitations on freedom. Such hearings will require prosecutors to determine in advance which offenders they *truly* believe require incarcerative sentencing and which do not. Hearings will also give both prosecutors and defense lawyers the opportunity to advocate at the only truly important stage of the criminal process. Such hearings will structure, rather than eliminate, judicial discretion and they will provide a process where the offenders, victims, and society can be brought into reasonably acceptable mutual relationships (Gradess, 1978:7–8).

If a victim emphasis in community-supervised sentences is to be successfully implemented, the offender must be both a prudent public safety risk and a good candidate to assist in the victim's restoration. This means the offender's active participation in the sentence. Supervision of the offender now passes, in Conrad's plan, to another unit of the probation.

The supervising probation officer is exclusively concerned with compliance with the sentence of probation. The order (conditions of probation) is partly a product of the presentence investigation and explicitly spells out the offender's responsibility to the victim and/or community. The offender may or may not need social treatment. If he or she does require and want it, the supervising probation officer should play the advocate's role in obtaining such services. But social treatment should be voluntarily entered into and its success should not be made a requirement of the order. "Failure" in treatment should not be made a basis for revocation. Kay Harris's analysis of the service aspect of probation is instructive:

> We have gotten accustomed to the notion that it is reasonable to prescribe *help as part of a punishment*. Indeed, unless utilization of proffered help is

voluntary, it must be considered a part of punishment. It is unreasonable and unfair for criminal penalties to be based on presumed need for treatment, skills, or services. It is also unfair to extend or increase a penalty on the basis of such needs. The proposition advanced *here is that it is fair to exact a penalty for what an offender did, for the criminal act committed, but it is not fair to exact a penalty for what a person is like or seems to need. If meeting offender needs on a voluntary basis were truly conceptualized as a central mission of probation, much more imagination and effort might be expended to make the help offered more attractive and relevant.* (Harris, 1980)

If after mutual exploration with the supervising probation officer, the probationer does not wish to accept specialized social service or if such services are not indicated, the probationer is moved to another unit of the department which operates under a regimen of strict surveillance and compliance. John Conrad's recommendation is that this unit be a police bureau even for those who do not voluntarily opt for services.

The current pursuit of a modernized probation mission is not wholly a local matter. Western European nations have been struggling with this problem as well. Chapter 7 of this volume attests to the United Kingdom's debate. A reading of *Probation in/en Europe* (Cartledge et al., 1981) is convincing evidence of historic changes in Western systems. The struggle to disentangle help from control is ubiquitous in western Europe.

Closest to our thinking are the developments in Finland and Sweden. The Finns are considering a *mandatory reporting* type of probation which involves the police. It is not unlike John Conrad's idea for splitting off social services from surveillance. In Sweden the search for a new mission for probation began in the mid-1970s. By 1978 the Swedish Working Group for Criminal Policy reported a proposal for a three-tiered noncustodial sanctioning system. Treatment in the conventional clinical sense was not abandoned by the Working Group but was made a right which the offender under sentence could voluntarily claim. The *New Penal System* (National Swedish Council for Crime Prevention, 1978:29–30) defined the following purposes for criminal sentences:

The criminalization of an act implies a pointing out of that act and is an attempt to prevent the act that is criminalized. There must be a relation between the reasons for criminalizing and the character of the sanction system.

Punishment should not be motivated by the fact that the offender needs punishment. It is not in the interest of the offender to be punished. Punishment is for what one has done and not for who one is.

The limit for the severity of a penalty for a criminal act should be determined by the punishment value of the act. This is to set a value upon how serious the crime is deemed to be. This is a matter for a political decision. Here lie possibilities for reform—if the political will for them exists.

When assessing the punishment value of any particular offence, circumstances related to the offender's personal situation can also be given consideration.

Within the general frame of the punishment the offender's various needs should be met. The working group is *not* against treatment, help, and various kinds of social service but only against justifying or legitimating the intervention by an alleged need of treatment. Treatment and service are to be offered during the sentence as a right that the offender can claim if he wishes.

The conclusions of the working group do not imply any reinforcement of general preventive grounds for punishment measures in absolute terms. It is rather the case that certain reasons for punishment, those of individual prevention, are peeled away so that the reasons that have always existed, and always must exist, stand out more clearly.

The Swedish proposal closely parallels ideas by several authors in this volume. It can be imported, and its groundwork is already widely under discussion in North America and the United Kingdom. In capsule form it restricts liberty to the following three community-based sanctions (National Swedish Council for Crime Prevention, 1978:49–52):

1. *Conditional sentences* are more a warning than a penal sanction since no prison sentence is established. A trial period of two unsupervised years is set in motion. A fresh offense may lead to revocation and a new sanction imposed for the old offense, the new one, or both. In addition, a day fine may be imposed. The requirement of a "good prognosis" is dropped and even those "living under socially unsatisfactory conditions could thus be sentenced to this sanction."

2. *Supervision* is the next step up on the ladder of severity. It is similar to probation but with tighter requirements for contacts with supervising lay or professional probation officers. Weekly or semiweekly contact is recommended. If weekly supervision is ordered, then the sentence to supervision might be from a minimum of two months to one or two years. The probation department would have no authority to increase or reduce the sentence: only a court could modify its own order.

3. *Intensive supervision* is the severest noncustodial sentence. It is imposed on more serious offenders (and recidivists) after other milder measures have failed. It is particularly designed to avoid imprisonment. To remain a credible alternative to incarceration, it needs to be a measure that is more intrusive in restricting liberty. The Swedes intend it to "entail more intensive control and more inconvenience than present-day probation."

The nucleus of the new sanction would be a requirement for very frequent contacts with either the police or correctional authorities. This contact whould occur several times a week. The court would govern the length of the sentence, deciding how long this intensive supervision should continue.

We have, with some detail, fleshed out our proposal for a new type of probation service. Thus far we have proposed that probation's mission is justice-as-fairness and its objective is equity. Victim restoration is to be a central concern. Probation will provide discrete investigation and social treatment on an advocacy and brokerage basis when voluntarily accepted by the probationer; for those refusing or not requiring service, it will provide surveillance.

Probation officers need not fear that by dropping the mantle of rehabilitation they will somehow be left with a purely punishment role. The pursuit of justice is a quite legitimate, even lofty goal, but perhaps more important is that it is manageable. Further, the pursuit of justice holds promise of unifying the fragmentation of current practice and the several reform formats now being advanced. Meeting the probationer as a truly responsible volitional actor may produce some initial anxiety since it requires some unlearning, but we reiterate Harris's notion that under such a voluntary regimen "much more imagination and effort might be expended [by probation officers] to make the help offered more attractive and relevant."

ORGANIZING FOR JUSTICE: A TEN-YEAR PLAN FOR PROBATION

Before we recommend a national organizational format for institutionalizing and sustaining the probation mission as we understand it, we should first be clear about our identity. Probation is a criminal justice system response to crime that represents three-fourths of the entire U.S. caseload. Over 1,500,000 adults were under probation and parole supervision in 1982, according to the U.S. Department of Justice. About a third of that number were under sentence to correctional facilities. Probation is thus, by far, this nation's major response to crime. Why then the problems of lack of direction, low status, and lack of public confidence?

For answers to these nagging questions we turn to the analyses of Timothy Fitzharris (1983) and Robert Cushman (1983).

Problems

Probation is only half as old as the American correctional system. The first probation law was enacted in 1878, barely 100 years ago (Cushman, 1983).

Probation's greatest advances have occurred since 1950, and its future great leap forward promises to take place before this century ends. The budding national consciousness necessary to drive that promise is now, *literally now*, developing. We are still the new kid on the block. Although 75–90 percent of probation cases are successful (in this and other nations), probation still suffers from an image of leniency (Fitzharris, 1983). At a minimum, we are effective with three out of four and send the fourth to prison (Cushman, 1983). Half of those incarcerated do not show up again as criminals within five years after discharge (Cushman, 1983). Probation costs less than prisons in both dollars and social harm, but it is widely understood as a nonsentence. The data available indicate that a probationer is statistically more likely than a prisoner to remain law-abiding in the future. Yet the public doubts the efficacy of probation. Public confidence probably can be strengthened, but it is not simply a question of increasing the public relations budget.

Probation is uniquely subject to local pressures that discourage venturesomeness. Most frequently probation is directly under the supervision of the judiciary. By their training and the nature of their role in the criminal justice system, judges are and must remain judges—not advocates (Cushman, 1983). (So rare are the exceptions that such judges become historic figures.) But it is of small comfort to an aspiring profession to have the reflected prestige of the court at the expense of being submerged and submissive. Where then might local probation executives look for support and a constituency? The fact is that probation has no obvious local or national constituency or spokesman. Further, we have neither a powerful national reference group (professional) nor obvious advocates (political). Few elected officials run with probation issues on their platforms. Those who do either have "safe" districts or they lose. The American Correctional Association (ACA) is still largely dominated by prison, not probation officials, though as we have shown, prisons serve only a minority of America's correctional clientele.

Our experience with national probation organizations is not encouraging. The American Probation and Parole Association is still in its infancy and seems at the moment to have a largely eastern constituency. Several states have probation and parole associations and chief probation officer organizations. A new organization called The National Association of Probation Executives is currently forming. There is also a well-organized association for federal probation and parole officers. But politicians can still disregard all of these associations with impunity. At the local level probation lacks a natural reference group (no PTA, no health association, no counterparts to the county bar or medical association). There are no local chapters of the ACA, though recently state chapters have been formed. Ex-offender groups, church groups, minority-oriented groups, and other professional groups such as the National Association of Social Workers and the American Psychological Association might become "coalition" groups for particular issues but rarely engage themselves in probation issues. (We will return to this problem shortly.)

The lack of constituency certainly impedes professional development and also makes probation particularly vulnerable in times of diminishing resources. Probation has fared worse than other components of the criminal justice system at the hands of politicians in Proposition 13-like jurisdictions (Cushman, 1983). Probation, as the elected official frequently sees it, serves the "undeserving," the offender. Further, probation is not a front-line agency protecting the public; rather it is still all too often seen as "Crime's Second Chance." Probation lacks the forceful imagery that other occupations in criminal jsutice can claim; police catch criminals, prosecutors try to get them locked up, judges put them in prisons, guards and wardens keep them there, but what do probation officers do?

Internally probation lacks a professional identity. There is no widely recognized professional school to prepare leaders for probation. Fordham University's pioneering program is essentially concerned with issues of practice. There are as yet no nationally recognized scholars, practitioners, or administrators who can be called eminent leaders in probation (Cushman, 1983) Every important journalist has a reference list of experts in a variety of fields to call upon for information and advice when an issue emerges. Legislators, who have to worry about the effects of their actions as they affect finances and services, also keep lists of potential allies or foes. Is probation yet a significant enough force to appear on either list? Major new legislation in the fields of medicine and criminal justice cannot be passed without winning the support, or neutralizing the opposition, of the AMA and the IACP (or the ABA) respectively; probation lacks a professional organization with equivalent clout.

Probation is uneasy about what it actually produces in the way of measurable results. While a certain amount of residual anxiety is probably a healthy sign—even a sign of incipient professionalism—too much anxiety is stultifying and demoralizing. Having enjoyed a good track record, certainly better than the "clearance rate" measure commonly used in police evaluations of effectiveness, we now find ourselves in a time of public frustration with rising crime, apt to lose resources just when the demand for service will probably increase. This may or may not hurt our effectiveness but it will be demoralizing unless we enter this era fully conscious of the strains involved.

First Tasks

There are no quick fixes available. We need to subject the field of probation to an intellectual and organizational modernization process that has no historical antecedents. We will need to apply the best tested principles of public administration and organization to ourselves. We will need to be wary of finding *the solution* before we have examined many future scenarios. But some steps in the *process* of reemergence are not so fuzzy. Cushman (1983) identifies three:

1. *We need to establish a clear mission.*

   In an era of limited resources, probation leaders at both state and local levels must now decide upon probation's mission and goals at their own organizational levels, articulate that mission to the public and policy makers more effectively than ever before and explain what they do and, more importantly, why they do it.

2. *Knowledge building should guide our efforts to upgrade probation.*

   During the last few decades there have been numerous studies of probation programs and services. . . . Despite the cumulative body of research reports that have been produced, we still seem to be asking the same question: "What works?" The answers will probably continue to elude us until we admit that "it all depends" and begin to isolate the factors that influence success or failure, as well as the reasons those conditions exist in some settings and not in others. Only then will we be able to offer the kind of empirically derived administrative knowledge needed to guide probation leaders and policy makers toward a clear definition of mission and the management knowledge needed to accomplish that mission.

3. *Steps toward professionalism.*

   Probation professionals should be required to meet and maintain specific personal and professional qualifications. These standards should be known and supported by the public and probation clients. They should be accompanied by a professional code of ethics and sanctioning of professional membership organizations.

   Once these three steps are accomplished, probation will be guided by a clearer, understandable and more unifying philosophy . . . These actions must build on the pervasive force of political power and influence in the criminal justice system. Professionalism should not mean isolation or insularity. To solve the "probation problem" one must go far beyond the bounds of the probation service to engage the police, the courts, and generally elected officials of state and local governments (Cushman, 1983).

These three first tasks, if widely shared in the field, could produce at least a common reference point. Our next step is to state some assumptions that we believe every probation agency should understand, and respond to through self-study:

1. Probation is a sanction and a part of the criminal justice system that is here to stay.
2. Probation's share of the correctional load will not decrease, given the growing numbers in prison and the costs of institutionalization and the strong advocacy of alternative community-based correctional programs.
3. It is possible to interpret probation services to the public in a positive manner.
4. Consistent with the movements to reorganize correctional services, attempts will continue to seek better ways to finance probation services, however organized.
5. There will be continuing pressures for more consistent and rational ways of organizing correctional services, including probation.
6. There is probably no one best organizational structure for all states. Structures are important only if they contribute to the achievement of the organization's goals and purposes. (Cushman, 1983.)

The Improvability of Probation

The American mystique favors the underdog and believes in giving the errant a second chance. At the same time we are intolerant of the recidivist and downright hostile toward the miscreant. We are severe with the criminal but support decent living for the convict when we become aware of atrocious prison conditions. Our Judeo-Christian heritage presses us to impose the least restrictive punishment and to seek redemption as an ultimate goal for most criminals. The tolerance for nonincarceration rises for children, women, and the nonviolent and ebbs for young male adults who are recidivists, armed, and/or violent criminals. For the foreseeable future (95 percent of crime is nonviolent), probation can be projected as America's first line of defense against repetitive crime. There is not even much of a debate about severely limiting probation for the nonviolent (Cushman, 1983).

Earlier we pointed to the lack of a constituency as a problem—but not an insurmountable one. Of all the subsystems in criminal justice, probation probably enjoys the longest and most intensive *positive* relationship with the public despite its apparent low esteem. Probation has used volunteers more extensively and meaningfully than other subsystems. An unscientific conservative estimate suggests that there are some 100,000 adult citizens who know something of probation services from their involvement as volunteers. Millions of the estimated 40–50 million living adult Americans who have at some time been sentenced for a criminal act have also been on probation. Three-quarters of this group successfully completed their terms. This represents a large untapped potential constituency whose members have received services that assisted them in avoiding deeper penetration into the criminal justice system. Adding their families swells the potential considerably. It is these groups that can, if mobilized, capture the attention of legislators and opinion molders, or least assure that policy changes sought by these publics cannot be summarily dismissed.

Other natural constituencies also exist: employers, trade unions, the Veterans Administration and the American Legion, and professional organizations (mentioned earlier).[6] There is a growing movement to broker out many of the direct services traditionally attempted by probation. This trend opens the door to constituency building with other public and private social service agencies, their boards of directors, staffs, and volunteers (Cushman, 1983).

The more the public sees probation as a front-line service, the better we can compete for scarce resources. It appears to us to be a question not so much of sharpening our ability to predict risk or recidivism as of just plain talk about what we can do and actually do do with the resources available.

Although probation as a sentence might theoretically be a presumption for any class of *crime*, it is obviously not going to granted, nor should it be sought, for any sort of *criminal*. Probation is more lenient than prison but it is a summary sentence responsive to a harm done and more than 75 percent of probationers respond with no further criminal involvement. This heroic effort is largely unrecognized. The media usually report failures and correctly so, at least in regard to some admittedly bizarre cases.[7] Failure to get the overwhelmingly positive side of the story into the media can only be attributed to unimaginative thinking, neglect, and/or timidity on the part of the criminal justice system. The judiciary's natural inclination to put some distance between themselves and the press may also be a factor in some jurisdictions.

In the last analysis, we will need to project a tough (not the opportunistic "get tough") public safety image. If we have oriented our practice too much toward the client, we have done so at the peril of losing public confidence. This can be remedied by thoughtful victim-oriented programs and accompanying public information efforts.

The Search for New Political and Organizational Structures

The sanctity of local government in the United States is politically axiomatic; we need to explore its implications for administering and financing probation. We are not suggesting that probation should be an independent entity outside of the judiciary. Rather, we are urging that the problems associated with operating probation at the local level be recognized and dealt with.

Judges are local. They are appointed or elected in local districts. Even when operating expenses come from the state, they look to the local taxpayer for sustenance. Pressure to move local burdens to the next higher level of government causes disparities in sentencing outcomes. This is especially true in the choice between probation and prison.

A not so obvious shift to the states in the last few years has been the deliberate policy of the U.S. attorney general to decline prosecution on offenses below a certain level. The population of the federal prison system fell dramatically for a few years while that of most state prison systems continued to rise. Thus the states have been called upon to receive clientele from both directions (federal and local). This escape hatch now seems exhausted as the federal prison system population is slowing rising again.

Since strings will inevitably attach to subsidization and since probation will remain largely wedded to the local level of government, a mature accommodation must be thought through and negotiated. Cushman offers some initial guidance.

> First, a statement of the obvious—each jurisdiction with a unique set of laws, practices, and needs must start from where it is. Ideas and principles can be adapted from elsewhere but rarely can someone else's system be transplanted and superimposed on another without modification. Second, in looking for appropriate models, one should not limit the field to other criminal justice or correctional systems. There are far more mature experiences in parallel systems such as the public school systems in our fifty states and thousands of local districts. It might also be useful to examine the manner in which the British home office helps to support and maintain quality in its local and metropolitan police districts. There are other parallels, though not precise analogues, in mental health, public welfare, water districts, and so on (Cushman, 1983).

It is easier to identify problems than to propose solutions. Probation is clearly in trouble. But the very nature of the trouble also provides opportunities that may be seized. There is no one best solution but our system of federalism permits experimentation with different organizational and funding formats. We need now to depart from our Rip Van Winkle heritage and be consciously aware that we can affect the development of probation. We can be agents in our future. We are not without resources. On this generation of probation leadership falls the task of engaging the more than 35,000 employees in some 4,000 probation departments in a dialogue about the future of the profession dealing with America's largest correctional caseload.

A Vehicle for a National Forum.

Probation has no spiritual parent agency at the national level. Without national leadership or even continual concern, how will the thousands of probation officers engage in a dialogue about their future? Fitzharris has said:

> What we now have has been characterized as a "non-system," resulting from resurgent growth, entangled jurisdictions, conflicting goals, and too little articulation and coordination. Probation may or may not add to the confusion, depending upon whether its basic objectives can be clarified, its functions defined and operationalized, and criticisms of it (valid or not) responded to constructively—and in time (Fitzharris, 1979:30).

At present there is no recognized national voice for probation. We believe that none will be forthcoming for a while. But where should it be sought? Can employee or professional organization play such a role? At the moment, these prospects are dim. Employee groups, whether state associations or nationally affiliated unions, have concentrated on narrower issues of self-aggrandizement—as they probably should. Professional associations, in the few states in which they exist, are a bit more expansive. The APPA is the only national professional group (and it recently voted to affiliate with the prison-oriented ACA). But even these professional associations' efforts have been limited to standards development and some research and conference convening (Fitzharris, 1983). The probability of sustained leadership from academia and/or the courts is quite low.

Without a proactive probation leadership (or even an effective reactive one), developments in the field are likely to be shaped by political pressures responding to perceived crises. Repressive measures invariably ensue. The outcome of weak leadership (or its complete absence) was succinctly described by Allen Breed.

> As long as correctional decision-makers remain moral neuters on criminal justice issues facing the field, as long as we expect to operate without any clear cut public policy, it is understandable that the public attitude will be shaped by fear, misunderstanding, and understandable revenge. Correction then becomes a repressive, warehouse operation with limited resources placed in those community programs which are most hopeful but which are also potentially the most dangerous. (Breed, 1979:10)

We are in full agreement with Breed and propose that the National Institute of Corrections is the most suitable (and perhaps only) national group that can logically become probation's national advocate for the next decade. We are not suggesting a regulatory relationship; rather a facilitating role for a decade of development.

National Institute of Corrections.

The NIC was created by Senate Bill 821, which eventually became the Juvenile Justice and Delinquency Prevention Act of 1974. Its sponsors said:

> The provision for a national institute of corrections in this bill is intended to establish a center in the nation to which the multitude of correctional agencies and programs of the states and localities can look for the many kinds of assistance they require. The institute would serve as a center of correctional knowledge. It would identify and study the many problems that beset the correction field. *With the advice and active participation of state and local correctional personnel, it would develop national policies for the guidance and coordination of correctional agencies.* The projected scope of activities covering both adult and juvenile offenders and the full range of correctional problems, programs and needs—*with due emphasis on community corrections as opposed to institutional corrections*—would establish the institute as *the focal point* for *a long-belated national* drive to bring about vitally needed improvements and reform in corrections. . . . the state of correctional activities in the United States amounts to a national problem of such moment that *only this course can yield the results which we hope to achieve.* (emphasis added, 93rd Congress; 1974:49–54).

The legislative intent is unequivocal and clear, and was uncontested. The NIC was launched to develop a national policy for the guidance and coordination of correctional agencies with the active participation of the latter. It was charged to place a due emphasis on community corrections to serve as a focal point for reform. The March 1981 reorganization of the NIC established a Community Corrections Center of equal weight with its Jail Center. Only an influential national agency, it was thought, could deal with the nation's multijurisdictional, local, and fragmented correctional sprawl. Why then should there be any doubt that Congress specifically intended the NIC to lead probation out of the wilderness?

No responsible correctional leader denies the existence of a national correctional problem; the only question is whether it is of such Congressional moment as to warrant a proactive stance by the NIC. There is some evidence that Congress and other federal agencies view corrections as a severe national problem. The continuing explosion of Section 1983 civil rights actions in the federal courts, resulting in some 60 percent the states' having a part or all of their prison systems under court order, should testify to the national nature of the crisis. Ironically, probably the most persistent, prestigious, and outspoken advocate for American corrections had been the chief justice of the U.S. Supreme Court. Justice Burger's 1969 Dallas speech gave birth to the ABA Commission on Correctional Facilities and Services. His 1971 Williamsburg speech before the National Conference on Corrections (itself initiated by the federal government) helped speed the NIC into existence. His most recent Houston speech (1981) may assist in the development of a greater federal presence at the local level. In August 1981 the Bell-Thompson Presidential Commission recommended to the U.S. Attorney General the allocation of two billion dollars to speed state prison construction. Finally, on January 2, 1983, Chief Justice Burger called for a national policy for corrections, stating that the doubling of the population in the last decade threatens to overwhelm the efforts of state prison authorities to cope with resultant problems.

The Crime Control Act of 1976 specifically mandated a study of "existing and future needs in correctional facilities in the nation and the adequacy of *Federal,* state and local programs to meet such needs" (NILE, 1977:1). The Director of the National Institute of Law Enforcement was specifically directed by statute to involve other federal, state, and local agencies in making this study.

The U.S. Department of Justice, after much controversy and opposition by the ACA, issued federal standards governing its own prison practice. This set of standards spanned two administrations. Before Congress at this writing is the most momentous federal intervention yet devised by a legislator. Senator Robert Dole of Kansas has proposed a $6.5 billion law enforcement construction program. The NIC assists states in emergency situations through timely consultation either before federal courts or in the aftermath of a state prison riot. Finally, the Congressionally mandated prison study mentioned earlier found that although the American correctional system is not monolithic, "the unifying characteristic is that most jurisdictions are in trouble" (NILE, 1977:254).

Clearly Congress and federal agencies are trying to come to grips with the problems in corrections. What role can the NIC play? The statute that created the organization (Sect. 521, Title 18, USC) called upon it to

> Conduct, encourage, and coordinate research on corrections.
> Evaluate the effectiveness of new programs techniques, or devices.
> Encourage and assist efforts to develop and implement improved corrections programs.
> *Formulate and disseminate correctional policy goals, standards, and recommendations for federal, state, and local correctional agencies, organizations, institutions and personnel.* (Fitzharris, 1983)

There was a three-year hiatus between NIC's birth and its first appropriation (1974–1977). To give more specificity to the law, the NIC developed its own mission statement for itself which should erase any ambiguity about its national advocacy role. It identifies corrections as "long having been the weakest component of the Criminal Justice System," recognizes a need for "Federal leadership to assist state and local government in improving correctional practice" and identifies itself as the agency that serves as the primary national advocate for Federal correctional policy affecting state and local correctional programs" (NIC 1980:3).

Fitzharris, in an attempt to understand the NIC's current reluctance to assert its national advocacy role, suggests that the federal government, since the Kennedy presidency, has been moving along a continuum from centralization to decentralization. Thus, in its relationship with state governments, the federal role in federalism is diminishing. Fitzharris documents each phase of the withdrawal from the heyday of the 1960s grants-in-aid programs to the Reagan election based in part upon the slogan of getting the government off the backs of its citizens. But rhetoric aside, the debate does not seriously anticipate the elimination of federalism, rather a redefinition of how it will operate in the future. Increasingly, federal and state officials will have to have a better understanding of the totality of conditions surrounding their relationship. Nelson, Cushman, and Harlow have suggested that in the field of community corrections, intergovernmental relationships should be based upon shared understandings of the problem, the strategies for change, and the resources to be committed (Nelson et al., 1980) Futher, they provide a checklist of questions that intergovernmental collaborators should ask themselves: Where does the impetus for change originate? What are the objectives of the change in policy? What is entailed in the scope of policy change? What intergovernmental relationships help to shape the policy change? What revenue sources will be used to support the policy change? What are the existing and necessary new linkages between the correctional organization and its surrounding community? What is the impact of the policy change on future service delivery?

In sum, Fitzharris concludes that if NIC is to become the advocate, it must be able to gain the trust and commitment of the local participants. Fitzharris lists the elements that he believes will help assure the local trust and commitment necessary for a fruitful partnership:

Flexible Leadership Model

1. *An intermediation system, including peer networking.*
2. *A mechanism to channel local and state thinking to federal level.*
3. *A means for developing shared understanding of problems, strategies payoffs, and resource commitments.*
4. *A vehicle for assessing the field of forces in each situation.*
5. *A recognition of the time needed for consensus to develop around change.*
   (Fitzharris, 1983)

By its commission, by Congressional mandate, by its own mission statement, and by its experience, the NIC is, among all federal agencies known to us, *the ideal candidate* to carry out this flexible leadership role. Prime among its attributes is that it does not have much money. It is highly respected in all local correctional quarters. It is located in an apparently inappropriate but sheltered organizational setting: the Federal Prison System, which is also part of the U.S. Department of Justice, both of which report to the attorney general. It is thus not associated with ephemeral political movements (wars on crime.) Ten of the fifteen members of its advisory board are not federal officials. It holds hearings nationwide before programs are organized and takes its board's input seriously. The present incumbent NIC leadership come from long and distinguished careers in state government. They bring the local perspective with them, the locals know this and are apt to be more trusting of them than of the usual agency staffed by federal career employees where all too often the underlying tone is of one-way largesse.

NIC and its Leadership Obligations to Probation.

The NIC itself will have to decide if it has a national advocacy role to play in corrections. We urge the new "Flexible Leadership Model." NIC has not solicited this role. Indeed, its director has seriously questioned whether a federal agency should have a strong role in developing public policy in corrections. *But he eschewed only a "strong role," not any role.* Similarly the assistant director doubted that a federal agency could accomplish what the professional association could not, or that a higher level of government could do what a lower could not. *But he did not suggest that a cooperative venture should not be undertaken or that the federal agency could not assist other entities* committed to pursuing a particular direction.

We have described the present model as a federal-state relationship based upon local impetus and mutuality to which we believe NIC could and indeed should accommodate. The NIC's files of regional hearings include scores of suggestions as to how it might play a larger role in improving both institutional and probation correctional services. The Fitzharris chapter in this volume lists some two dozen possible roles, all of which are worthy of consideration. Yet both sets of documents may suffer from a lack of thematic unity and sequential impact. NIC leaders have challenged the field of corrections to present its ideas, commit financial resources, and perhaps join in a planning partnership with NIC. We now identify a narrower issue, that of probation development to be undertaken over a ten-year period.

A Ten-Year Probation Developmental Plan

The Probation Mission Study represents the first phase of the Ten-Year Plan. It is itself an extension of an earlier (1977) double-pronged NIC initiative to survey probation agencies of a size up to 100 staff to determine training needs (Thomson and Fogel, 1980; Seltzer and Clugston, 1981).[8] The present study was commissioned as an attempt to define probation's mission. In fulfilling the goals of this study we have involved significant numbers of the field's intellectual and practice-based leadership. We have presented interim reports to all major probation forums in the United States and Canada.[9] We have had continual feedback and review from the field, and our efforts have been closely monitored by NIC itself. We now recommend what we believe to be a modest plan that builds upon past efforts widely known in this nation and Canada; thus these endeavors may serve to instituionalize the thrust begun by NIC. But the responsibility still remains dependent largely upon the field itself for its substantive continuation.

The Plan as a Symbol. The announcement of a development plan, its dissemination, debate, and the local participation inherent in such a process will in itself build morale among practitioners and scholars throughout the nation. It will deliver a message of historic importance to the field and public. We expect that a sense of solidarity and cohesiveness will emerge that will help create a common purpose and direction. This will not assure unity of direction, but it will create the conditions necessary for an orderly national debate concerning the direction.

The debate will need focus but not necessarily a fixed agenda. We are reluctant to define a few narrow points as key parmeters of the dialogue. Our shopping list of discussion topics will probably be no better than a list prepared by others. What is *not* necessary now is still another rhetorical leap forward in probation (by the few) while most practitioners sit on their hands or applaud lightly from a distance. Instead we must involve the field itself in this process.

Pre-Plan Planning. The developmental plan projected ultimately cannot be based solely upon academic thinking. While this project has roots in the field, they are not now deep enough. We can therefore only outline a plan to be brought before leading figures in probation and support agencies for further modification and refinement. Perhaps all our ideas will be adopted, but it is the process of involvement that we wish to advance rather than a finished product.

To foster a process of sustained local involvement, we urge the adoption of a Ten-Year Development Plan. The first message to be delivered is that the United States government, through the NIC, is willing to join in a focused developmental effort.

Second, we suggest that a select group of leaders be invited to make extensive comment on this study and that they hold a retreat to plan refinements, funding, and monitoring of this ten-year effort. The group should include individuals from the National Institute of Corrections; NCCD; Ford Foundation; Edna McConnell Clark Foundation; American Probation and Parole Association; the California Probation, Parole and Correctional Association; the New York State Probation Officers Association; the Probation Executive Association; the National Sheriff's Association; the American Correctional Association; the Federal Probation Officers Association; leading state jucicial councils; National Association of County Organizations; chairpersons and vice chairpersons of judiciary committees from some leading state legislatures, staff from both sides of the aisle from relevant Congressional committees, and public members representing minority groups and correctional citizens' action groups. The group need to be no larger than sixty persons.

Having read this report and any available critiques of it, this working conference would be prepared to further critique it and with temporary staffing (arranged by NIC) would be responsible for the finished product. The latter includes a nine-year funding plan. The target date for completion of the plan of action would be one year from its inception.

Fiscal Resources to Support the Plan.   We recommend the involvement of NIC, a major private foundation, ACA, and APPA as the principals. The APPA should serve as the administration for the project with an agreed-upon step-down funding plan. A detailed plan has been presented to the NIC and the APPA; it relies upon substantial public (NIC) and private (APPA, ACA, and foundation) support initially, with NIC, ACA, and foundation support gradually withdrawn as APPA membership grows and establishes its pre-eminence in the field of probation. After a decade of development we anticipate a membership organization of 10,000, a presence in Washington, D.C., and a self-sustaining organization ready to plan the next decade of development. We believe that such a plan meets the crucial test of what the new federal agency role might be in relation to advocacy. It combines local initiative (APPA and ACA), supplementary (foundation) support, and the faciliative support of a federal agency (NIC) in a partnership that envisions step-down funding by the support agencies and step-up funding (thus responsibility for its own future) on the part of the lead professional organization representing the field of probation—the APPA.

If the Ten-Year Plan is successful we would expect the following accomplishments, among others, by the early years of the 1990s:

A training program for probation leadership, on the model of West Point.

A strong professional membership group for probation officers.

A full-time lobbyist and national presence for the membership organization in Washington, D.C.

A mission statement with a method for its updating.

A probation journal.

A clearinghouse for probation information.

A variety of model community correction legislative packages.

A model uniform probation law.

A professional association that offers technical assistance to local agencies.

A full-time partnership of the field (through its association) with the NIC toward the end of planning the next generation of development.

A plausible path toward professional development has been recorded. The question remains: In 1983, was the will present to accomplish the task?

NOTES

1. We are aware of the distinguished pioneer effort at Fordham University.
2. M. Kay Harris, "Rethinking Probation as a Sanction" (unpublished paper, 1980).
3. Harris recommends

   . . . that the limits for the severity of any . . . intervention . . . be determined by the punishment value of the crime. . . . [proposing further] . . . that less responsibility and discretion for determining the nature and duration of probation sanctions should rest with the authorities responsible for implementing the sanctions. Insofar as feasible, the essential elements of each penalty should be clearly spelled out as applicable to all who are sentenced to them. . . .the punitive elements of sanctions should be delineated clearly and highlighted. This is not to increase the harshness of sanction. On the contrary, this recommendation is related to a belief that sanctions currently are far harsher than is generally recognized. If it is acknowledged that sanctions are disagreeable, it is easier to see why it is important to set clear limits on them. In addition, only through full recognition of the punitive aspects of non-incarcerative sanctions can they be expected to increase in use as real alternatives to the extremely punitive sanctions of incarceration (Harris, 1980:25).

4. Harris notes that voluntarism in such a relationship may protect the integrity of the relationship:

   It is proposed that under most circumstances, rehabilitative interests should be approached by voluntary means rather than as a part of the sanction. This does not suggest opposition to treatment, help, and various kinds of services. The concern involves the dangers connected with attempting to justify or modify a penalty on the basis of presumed needs for treatment. The content of probation should be constructed around a simple framework that explains what is required of the offender. General rules requiring good conduct and special instructions concerning the offender's way of living should be avoided as both vague and unrealistic. What is suggested here is that meeting people's needs has more to do with the rights and entitlements of all citizens than with the facts of being sentenced for an offense (Harris, 1980:23–24).

5. While these services may be available in part in discrete jurisdictions, we are here referring to the expansion and routinization of such services.

6. Both management and labor have organized offender and ex-offender services (The National Alliance of Businessmen, AFL-CIO Community Services). The Veterans Administration has extended itself into prisons through the G.I. Bill and other services and the American Legion has established prison chapters in several states.

7. For example, a person who was placed on probation *ad seriatum* for three different crimes at three different times. Admittedly, this is difficult to explain or understand—especially if the subsequent crimes appear to be increasingly serious.

8. The University of Illinois at Chicago and the University of Minnesota were contracted to complete these surveys.

9. The following represents a partial listing of presentations:

P. McAnany, "Probation and Equity: A Justice Model Approach," American Correctional Association, August 1980, San Diego.;

D. Thomson, P. McAnany, and D. Fogel, "Probation as a Pursuit of Justice: A Preliminary Report to the Filed on a Reconsideration of Mission," International Seminar on Community Corrections, October 1980, Niagara Falls, N.Y.;

P. McAnany, "Probation and Community Service Orders," National Conference on Community Service Orders, Rutgers University-NCC, Newark, N.J., December 1980;

D. Fogel, "Probation in Search of an Advocate," 13th Annual John Jay Criminal Justice Institute, New York, May 1980.;

P. McAnany, D. Thomson, and D. Fogel, "Probation Mission: Practice in Search of Principle," National Forum on Criminal Justice, Cherry Hill, N.J., June 1981.; and

D. Thomson, "Probation History and the Contemporary Retributive Justice Movement," 6th Annual APPA Institute, Montreal, Canada, October 1981.

REFERENCES

Breed, Allen (1979). Speech to the 49th Annual CPPCA Institute. Reported in *California Correctional News* 33 (7–8):12–xx.

Carey, James (1984). "The Professionalization of Probation: An Analysis of the Diffusion of Ideas." Chapter 9 in this volume.

Cartledge, C. G., P. J. P. Tak and M. Tomic-Malic (1981). *Probation in/en Europe.* Hertogenbosh, Holland: The European Assembly for Probation and After-care.

Conrad, John (1984). "The Re-Definition of Probation: Drastic Proposals to Solve an Urgent Problem." Chapter 8 in this volume.

Cushman, Robert (1984). "Probation in the 1980s: A Public Administration Viewpoint." Chapter 11 in this volume.

Fitzharris, Timothy (1979). *The Future of Probation.* Sacramento, CA: CPPCA.

——— (1984). "The Federal Role in Probation Reform," Chapter 14 in this volume.

Fogel, David (1969). "Fate of the Rehabilitative Ideal in California Youth Authority Dispositions." *Journal of Crime and Delinquency* 5(4 October).

——— (1975). *We Are the Living Proof.* Cincinnati, OH: Anderson.

Gradess, Jonathan (1978). Testimony Given Before the New York State Executive Advisory Commission on Sentencing, Nov. 15 (mimeo).

Lubove, Roy (1965). *The Professional Altruist.* Cambridge, Mass: Harvard University Press.

McAnany, Patrick (1983). "Mission and Justice: Clarifying Probation's Legal Context." Chapter 2 in this volume.

National Institute of Corrections (1980) *Mission for the '80s.* Washington, D.C.: NIC.

National Institute of Law Enforcement, (1977). *Prison Population and Policy Choices.* Cambridge, Mass.: ABT Books.

Nelson, E. Kim, Robert Cushman, and Nora Harlow (1980) *Unification of Community Corrections.* Washington, D.C.: U.S. Government Printing Office.

The National Swedish Council for Crime Prevention's Working Group for Criminal Policy (1978). "New Penal System—Ideas and Proposals" (English Summary of Report No. 5). Stockholm, Sweden: The National Swedish Council for Crime Prevention.

Rothman, David (1980). *Conscience and Convenience.* Boston: Little, Brown.

Schafer, Stephen (1974). *The Political Criminal.* New York: The Free Press.

Seltzer, Miriam, and Richard Clugston (1981). *Training Needs of Administrators of Probation and Parole Systems in the United States.* St. Paul: University of Minnesota.

Sutherland, Edwin, and Donald Cressey (1974). *The Principles of Criminology,* 9th ed. Philadelphia: Lippincott.

Thomson, Doug, and David Fogel (1980). *Probation Work in Small Agencies: A National Study of Training Provisions and Needs.* Chicago: University of Illinois at Chicago.

United States 93rd Congress, Senate Committee on Juvenile Justice and Delinquency. Prevention Act of 1974 Report. Washington, D.C.: U.S. Government Printing Office.

Chapter 4

Prospects for Justice
Model Probation

*Doug Thomson**

A model advancing a particular mission for probation should help the field by stimulating consideration of the challenges facing it and providing some conceptual and analytic tools for the task. In addition, the justice model can be a reasonable guide for policy since it is flexible in the same sense that the law is flexible, i.e., individual circumstances of a case can be accommodated within the general norms and principles of the model or the law. This chapter will consider the value and flexibility of the justice model for probation and suggest its implications for organization and practice. Along the way, we shall consider some of the criticisms that have been directed at the model and examine its limitations.

VALUE, FLEXIBILITY, AND LIMITATIONS
OF JUSTICE MODEL PROBATION

The two central features of a justice model approach to sentencing and corrections are *retrospectivity*, a focus on present, not future, criminal

*Center for Research in Law and Justice, University of Illinois at Chicago

behavior, and *proportionality* of sanctions to crime committed. The former principle implies that law is a given and requires determination of culpability as well as the particular facts of the crime. The latter principle implies a range of graduated sanctions.

These two principles have several important corollaries. First, punishment is conceived to have only modest value and individuals, whether offenders or victims, are accorded a high degree of respect and dignity. Hence, while sanctions recognize the breach of public law, they must be moderate and must be administered in a way that requites the wrong (Kidder, 1975), i.e., accepts the offender back into the community after the sanction is experienced and restores the victim. Second, the limited appropriateness of incarceration, particularly long-term incarceration, is recognized. Hence, incarcerative sanctions are avoided except for the most heinous and harmful crimes (American Friends Service Committee, 1971; von Hirsch, 1976). Third, it is acknowledged that the justice model—as well as any extant alternative approach to sentencing—is tangential to social justice. The best the justice model can offer is to serve as a learning model, within the area of formal justice, for the pursuit of substantive justice. Hence, the radical critique of the justice model as epiphenomenal is accepted (Wright, 1973). But within the context of what is possible in the field of criminal justice, it seems that the small advances offered by a correctly implemented justice model would be an improvement on the "healthy hypocrises" (Cressey, 1982:xxiii) characterizing current operations.

These principles of proportionality and retrospectivity share a concern with fairness or evenhandedness in the determination, imposition, and administration of criminal sanctions. The proportionality principle demands that society respond in like manner to like events (i.e., crimes that are equivalent in terms of harm done). The retrospectivity principle demands that the response be based fundamentally on what has happened. The first principle prohibits responses tailored to characteristics of the offender. The second principle prohibits sanctions based on predictions of their consequences for the offender—or for the community.

To the extent that individualization is permitted by this approach, it must refer to the circumstances of the offense and the capabilities of the offender to serve an appropriate sentence. For example, existing work and family responsibilities may be factors in determining the form and the duration of a particular sentence such as restitution, community service, or reporting to the probation officer. Circumstances of the event include the perspectives of the victim and the community as well as the offender. Some may want to call this individualization. But any such classification scheme requires comparative references to similar and dissimilar events of various kinds so that the "individualized" sentence/response makes sense

—is fair—in terms of precedents (cf. Wilkins, 1969:22–29 on a related theme, the uniqueness of individuals).

The retrospectivity goal is to return the situation, as much as is possible, to what it was before the violation. There is correction, but of the situation rather than the offender. Here the justice model contrasts with approaches that make it a preeminent goal to improve the offender or to make the offender or others less harmful in the future. Only in this peculiar sense, is it fair to style the justice model for probation a conservative approach; it seeks to return circumstances to what they were before the harm was done.

As these two principles, proportionality and retrospectivity, suggest, justice model advocates do not propose a monolithic model for the organization and operations of probation nor do they posit a prefabricated way of doing probation work that would be everywhere the same, ignoring community context and jurisdictional law. The variety of probation policies and practices advanced in this volume by justice model proponents (e.g., Harris, McAnany, Fogel, Conrad, and Thomson) should demonstrate that the justice model can accommodate diversity. This recognition follows von Hirsch (1976) in his proposal of both a just deserts and a modified just deserts model for sentencing.

THE NEED FOR SYSTEM COMPATIBILITY IN IMPLEMENTING JUSTICE MODEL PROBATION

A justice model for probation makes little sense if the model is not more widely applied. If we have learned anything about criminal justice operations in the past twenty years it is that, despite problems of coordination, our crime control apparatus is a system of interdependent agencies functioning as a loosely coupled system (Remington et al., 1969; Gottfredson and Gottfredson, 1980). No one would claim that probation agencies are sufficiently strong and independent to declare their emancipation from the rest of the criminal justice system and establish their own policies. To demand that probation agencies do justice without considering the larger issues that constrain probation would be absurd. We need to explore how probation as a penal sanction should fit within a desert-based criminal justice system.

Probation's Identity Within the Criminal Justice System

In contemplating whether a justice model for probation is reasonable, it would be well to consider probation's origins and emergence. Probation developed historically as a default option, a means by which judges avoided punishments they deemed too harsh, i.e., ones that failed the proportionality test (Rubin, 1973). In this sense, probation has its origins in a justice model context, albeit a quasi-legal one providing a negative or residual definition for probation. Over the years, probation began to be defined more in terms of rehabilitation and special deterrence as it was opportunistically adopted by larger social movements and ideologies (Rothman, 1980; Allen, 1981). Contemporary justice model proposals suggest that 1) probation should return to its source, but 2) those quasi-legal origins should be corrected by explicit recognition and affirmation of probation's grounding in the law, and 3) the ad hoc rationalizations for probation that emerged over the centuries should be de-emphasized.

Probation has often been justified in terms of its status as an alternative to incarceration. That is, it has been defined in negative terms, as an entity whose identity is based on and justified in terms of another entity (Schlossman, 1977). Further, this identity and its justification have required an emphasis on the unattractive features of the basic entity (incarceration) and a depiction of the other entity (probation) as less unattractive. Thus, it has conventionally been argued that probation is cheaper and more humane than incarceration (Fitzharris, 1981). It has rarely been argued that probation has value in itself, except by those arguing from a rehabilitation perspective. Research of recent years (Lipton et al., 1975; Greenberg, 1977) has raised serious empirical questions about such claims. While subsequent research (Martinson, 1979; Gendreau and Ross, 1979; Ross and Gendreau, 1980; Andrews, 1980) has lent support to the rehabilitation claims, it is far from clear that probation in general produces positive rehabilitative outcomes—or if it does, that this has much to do with reducing crime rates. Paradoxically, then, the most cogent argument for rehabilitation is, like the justice model's, a non-utilitarian one, i.e., it is a good thing to do in itself (Cressey, 1982; Cullen and Gilbert, 1982).

Probation, with its rehabilitative goals, is implicitly recognized as disjunctive with other criminal justice agencies; its objectives fit uneasily with those of its sibling agencies. When the ideology of rehabilitation and individualization was predominant, one could argue that probation agencies and prisons shared a rehabilitative intent (Rothman, 1980). The demise of that ideology with respect to prisons (Allen, 1981), and the recognition that such institutions instead serve retributive, deterrent, or incapacitative purposes, left probation holding the rehabilitation bag (Thomson, 1981b).

It will be difficult for probation to become a public service occupation if it continues to be construed legislatively as an alternative to a sentence, if judges grant and administer probation as leniency, if prosecutors continue to use it as a bargaining chip in plea bargaining, and if defense attorneys present it to their clients as a good deal. Probation officers cannot be expected to pursue justice by themselves; probation officers are not the key actors in criminal sentencing and consequently are left with a seriously atrophied correctional role. Many probationers and former probationers believe that they have not been convicted of a criminal offense. This is the public perception of probation; it is not punishment because it exacts no penalty, or certainly no penalty to compare with the pains of incarceration. Statutes, case decisions, and the opinions and actions of legal professionals reinforce this public perception.

To the extent that probation administrators and officers share this view and act accordingly, they too contribute to this perception. But it is critical to recognize that probation is severely constrained by its legal and organizational environment (McAnany and Thomson, 1982). Probation officers cannot act from a just deserts frame of reference if judges treat probation as an endeavor aimed at rehabilitating the offender and prosecutors use it as a convenient way of processing the court's caseload. If probation is truly to be a public service occupation, "a jurisdiction of justice" (McAnany, 1976:81), and a legal mechanism of community and victim rehabilitation, it must be so recognized in statutes, case decisions, court rules, and judicial training and by the actions of judges, prosecutors, and defense counsel.

Probation can fit well with other elements of the system when it is recognized that the goals of the system are justice and retribution. In such a system, probation is part of a set of sanctions ranging from arrest, conviction, and conditional discharge, at one extreme, through fines, straight probation, monetary restitution, community service orders, home confinement, and split sentences to incarceration as the most severe measure (Harris, 1983; Thomson et al., 1980; McAnany et al., 1981). For reasons stated at length throughout this book, such a conceptualization of probation is quite compelling. It also harbors potential dangers, however. We turn now to a consideration of these dangers and ways of dealing with them.

Punishment's Limitations and Social Justice's Requirements

Notions of retributive justice and just deserts have not enjoyed great favor in probation circles in recent decades (Rubin, 1973; Gettinger, 1981) although they have experienced a renascence of some magnitude in areas of more general concern, such as sentencing and the goals of criminal justice (von Hirsch, 1976; Twentieth Century Fund, 1976; Singer, 1979; Sechrest et al., 1979). There is a tendency to confuse retribution with vengeance. This fallacy has been skillfully disputed in the jurisprudential literature (Gerber and McAnany, 1976; McAnany, 1978; Singer, 1979) but the popular misunderstanding persists. Consequently, there is some concern that a

justice model for probation will lead to vengeful punishment of probationers. While I disavow any notion of retribution as vengeance, and
instead conceive of retribution as, among other things, an avenue to and an
and an opportunity for requital (McAnany, 1978: 22; Kidder, 1975), I do
recognize the danger that, as practice and policy, a justice model for
probation will be abused. (See Sieber (1981) and Doleschal (1982) for
trenchant analyses of recent examples of perverse consequences of well-
intended reforms.) Indeed, the arguments and fundamental appeal of the
justice model have already been used in perverse ways in pernicious
sentencing reforms (Greenberg and Humphries, 1980; Reiman and Headlee, 1981; Cullen and Gilbert, 1982).

There are two major concerns: 1) a net-widening effect and 2) excessive
punishment and harassment of probationers. Net widening has been a
generally recognized negative consequence of the proliferation of diversion programs in the 1960s and 1970s (Blomberg, 1980). Rothman (1980)
has pointed to the same phenomenon in the development of probation in
the Progressive era (1900 to 1965); this reform had the effect of expanding
state control rather than reducing the use of incarceration. The present
fear is that justice model probation will be used to bring minor offenders
onto the probation rolls, rather than to reduce institutional populations.
Similarly there is a danger that probation as sanction may be used to
harass and unduly punish probationers. Unsettling prospects of such a
development can be found in the use and enforcement of restitution orders,
for example. Throughout the land, unskilled, illiterate, and unemployed
probationers are periodically hauled into court for revocation hearings,
degraded, reprimanded, and ordered to serve an extended probation
sentence so that, in a faltering economy, they can make restitution for a
window they broke or dog food they stole several years ago. Such practices
are antithetical to the idea of probation as a pursuit of justice.

Both types of abuse can be forestalled if policymakers, probation practitioners, and community residents show a prior concern with proportionality
and fairness. Glib rhetoric about getting tough on criminals must give way
to thoughtful consideration of liberty issues. Deprivations of liberty inherent in probation sentences must be recognized as penalties sufficient for
some harms. This assessment should be a part of a more general recognition
of the limitations of punishment, and of an appreciation of the existential
realities of punishment, including both probation and incarceration.

There are also controls, both active and passive, that can be placed on
the abuse of justice model probation. In transforming proportionality and
fairness from philosophy into policy and practice, and designing a reasonable range of escalating penalties tied to degree of harm done and culpability of the offender, policymakers would have to focus on the consequences
of their decisions for probation and institutional populations. One could

establish thresholds of severity such that net widening will not occur and institutional populations will be reduced, other things being equal. Valuable precedents are provided by the development of sentencing guidelines in Minnesota and Pennsylvania (von Hirsch and Hanrahan, 1981) and the development of the subsidy formula for the Minnesota Community Corrections Act.

More passive controls might help also. Limited availability of "punishment resources" (Foote, 1978) means that they must be used judiciously and that there are systemic constraints on abuses of retributive justice approaches to probation. A more compelling and longer-term control is related to the value of punishment. Although it is extremely difficult to exclude utilitarian purposes from considerations of correctional policies (Harris, 1983), de-emphasizing these purposes can lead to an appreciation of the intrinsic value of punishment as a simple matter of doing right by victim, offender, and community. Punishment as retribution is valuable in itself apart from any utilitarian consequences, e.g., deterrence, incapacitation, or moral reformation. If proportionate and fair punishment, monitored by autonomous law (Nonet and Selznick, 1978), is administered for the sake of doing justice, a great deal has been accomplished, namely, the affirmation of law with regard to satisfying victim claims for retribution and to protecting the rights of the sentenced offender.

If being candid about the punitive purposes of probation helps to reveal the limitations of punishment as social policy, then we may be freed to be more realistic about building a just society. In this connection, it should be noted that probation is and will generally be only a modest punishment—but many crimes deserve no more. Nevertheless, justice model probation would probably lead to a significant increase in the punitive content of a small proportion of probation sentences. If the justice model for sentencing is taken seriously and understood correctly, there will be substantial decreases in institutional populations as incarceration comes to be seen as a punishment reserved for those who commit acts of major violence against persons and those who frequently are convicted of other serious crimes. With increasing numbers of armed robbers, for example, sentenced to probation rather than to prison, probation must become more punitive in content in recognition of the harm caused by the offense.

Yet implementation of the justice model, like the implementation of any other model, must contend with centripetal tendencies of people-processing organizations. In addition to tendencies such as organizational expansion, maintenance, and inertia, there are the dynamics of typification, normalization, and routinization (Sudnow, 1965; Skolnick, 1966; Scheff, 1965; McCleary, 1978). Hence, as probation comes to be viewed more widely as a sentence and is more extensively used as a punitive measure for those who would otherwise have been incarcerated, it will probably still often consist of token conditions such as monthly reporting to the probation office. The sheer press of time and numbers, the limits of "punishment resources" (Foote, 1978), and the tendency of large organizations to routinize outcomes will inhibit the individualization of penal justice, just as the individualization of rehabilitative treatment has been inhibited and found wanting as a policy.

The difference will lie in the value of ritual in itself in a justice model context. The emphasis on liberty threats, understood as a continuum ranging from the indignities and ceremonial punishments of arrests, court appearances, and convictions through more extended behavioral and symbolic constraints on freedom in probation, community services, restitution, fines, and incarcerative sentences, should lead to a public appreciation that punishment does not have to mean incarceration and that community disapproval, even routinely expressed, should be a potent enough sanction for a great many crimes. Hence, the organizational ritual processing problem is not a major one. Moreover, the justice model is intended to unmask the limitations of punishment as a policy tool for ensuring justice. Thus, the paradox is that by emphasizing punishment, less will come to be expected of it as it loses its image as magic and comes to be recognized as a commonplace, with attention ultimately being focused on the need for finding more central routes to social justice than are offered by the bypaths of rehabilitative services or just deserts punishments.

JUSTICE MODEL IMPLICATIONS FOR PROBATION ORGANIZATION AND PRACTICE

During the last few years, much has been said and written about aplication of the justice model to probation. Much of this discussion and debate has focused on questions of philosophical or ideological fit and occupatieceptivity. The following section turns to largely uncharted territory, examining how justice-based probation would be organized, what role probation officers would play, and what they would do. First, we shall consider how the identity of the probation occupation might be altered, and then next how community context is likely to shape the implementation of justice model probation. Following this is a discussion of the marginality of probation at system, organization, and officer levels. The place of offender services in justice-based probation is then assessed at some length, and guidelines are proposed. The next section makes the case for probation involvment in supervising victim services, restitution, and community service orders by analyzing the work elements involved and the skills and capabilities of probation officers and agencies. Finally, we examine ways in which current probation officer roles are congruent with justice-based probation and the differential importance for reform application of conventional skill areas.

Probation as a Public Service Occupation

A justice model probation is likely to be seen as a public service occupation, rather than a human services occupation. This would have both advantages and disadvantages for individual probation officers. Whether advantages will outweigh disadvantages is a complex issue depending greatly on local circumstances (cf. Harlow, 1983) and on the role orientations and capabilities of probation officers affected. From a public policy perspective, however, it is important to consider whether such a shift constitutes a net advantage to the public.

Blau and Scott (1962) observe that formal organizations can be usefully classified in terms of their beneficiaries. They suggest that there are four types of organizational beneficiaries: members, owners, clients, and the general public. Mutual protection associations and unions are examples of organizations that exist primarily to benefit the membership, while businesses are typically designed to benefit owners of the enterprise. As prototypes of organizations that primarily benefit their clients and the public, Blau and Scott cite social work agencies and police departments respectively.

The selection of these examples of service and commonweal organizations is particularly striking in the current context because probation has long been seen as an occupation torn between police and social work roles (Glaser, 1964; Ohlin et al., 1956; Klockars, 1972). We suggest that to the extent probation is perceived as a human service organization, it is more closely aligned with social work and other client service organizations. This concept of probation is premised on assumptions of client needs or deficits and provision of services to clients that will lead to their rehabilitation. Such a formulation plays down concerns about justice, community norm reinforcement, and victim rehabilitation. If instead probation is perceived as a public service (commonweal) organization, its primary beneficiary would be the general public and such concerns would come to the fore.

The public should gain from this type of redirection of probation by receiving better service. Probation officers should gain from a more widespread recognition and appreciation of the work they do. Probation officers might suffer the loss of some prestige within the hierarchy of professions. In return they could gain a more generous share of public resources. To the extent, then, that probation officers are doing publicly beneficial work, they could gain from the greater visibility and altered identity suggested.

Community Context

While much of the literature on police work focuses on the link with the community, relatively little attention has been paid to this connection in the probation literature. Probation officers recognize the importance of their knowledge of local community networks and of the availability of community resources, and much work has been done on community resource management approaches to probation work (Dell'Apa et al., 1976). But, until recently, there has been little analytic work concerning the fit between different types of probation departments and types of communities. There has been nothing comparable, for example, to Wilson's (1968) and Banton's (1964) analyses of how police department operations reflect the communities they serve.

Two explanations are apparent. First, probation has not been considered as intrinsically interesting as policing either for research or for policy analysis. Second, because the police agency has been much more clearly identified as a commonweal organization, the community congruence issue has seemed much more salient there than with regard to probation.

Recent years have seen some change, however, as a few social scientists have begun to take probation seriously as a topic for research. Hagan (1977), for example, has examined urban-rural differences in the way probation officers develop presentence investigation recommendations. Even more notably, finer-grained analyses of the community-probation agency congruence question have recently been produced by Nelson, Cushman, and Harlow (1980), Nelson and Harlow (1980), Duffee (1983a) and Harlow (1983).

Clearly there should be, and there is, some congruence between types of communities and types of probation agencies. Nevertheless, to the extent that probation is a law system, some guidance mechanism, such as a justice model, is needed to ensure a minimum level of conformity across jurisdictions to prevent injustices and inequities. Beyond this baseline, there is considerable room for variations within justice model probation operations, variations which should and will reflect the needs, capabilities, and experiences of local communities.

Hence, the justice model provides considerable latitude for probation agencies in the extent to which they emphasize utilitarian by-products. In some communities, the probation department may be content to monitor reporting and restitution conditions, while in others it may take a more active role facilitating reconciliation between victim and offender. Still other communities may place greater emphasis on the public safety functions of various sanctions, and there the probation department's presentence investigations may recommend extensive use of periodic confinement, home confinement, daily reporting, and other conditions that temporarily incapacitate the probationer or provide for easier surveillance in the course of punishment. Similarly, local economic conditions may help determine the relative use of restitution and day fines as opposed to community service orders, victim service orders, and other nonmonetary sanctions.

For justice model probation to maintain its identity (Harlow, 1983) and its corrective potential, however, utilitarian considerations must be subordinated to desert principles. Incapacitation, for example, can only be considered if it is an appropriate punishment for a given level of harm and culpability. Thus, if three weekends in jail is an equivalent sanction to six months of weekly reporting to a probation officer, and each is proportionate for given circumstances of a certain offense, say aggravated assault, some communities could legitimately choose the former on public safety grounds while others could legitimately choose the latter on cost grounds. In either case, utilitarian outcomes are incidental to desert purposes.

Further, justice model probation requires a special emphasis on its community context. As discussed in several chapters of this book, punishment is essential to justice model probation. But the legitimation of punishment rests on the extent to which it comes from and is administered by the community whose law has been breached (Moberly, 1968). Without community, punishment can be gratuitous and vengeful. The need for community to provide the link between punishment and justice is perhaps the justice model's most vulnerable point. Curiously, this fundamental problem seems to have been ignored by critics who have focused instead on some consequences of the problem such as harsh sentencing schemes, increased prison populations, declining humanitarianism, and objectification of the offender. The probation department, through its presentence investigation and mediation roles, can make a significant contribution to facing this problem. It should be recognized, however, that the problem of the community's legitimation of punishment and reward structures is one that extends far beyond sentencing. Hence, we find in this problem a common source of inequities in criminal and social justice.

Probation's Marginality

Probation work is a clear example of a marginal occupation. Probation officers are in an ambiguous position with regard to two systems of control: the legal and the social services. Each system claims the allegiance of probation officers, who are also subjected to cross-pressures at more micro levels. The probation officer is frequently caught among the wishes and demands of probationer, judge, department administrator, police, social service agencies, and influential members of the community. Klockars (1972) has examined the consequences of such dynamics for probation supervision. Emerson (1969) has analyzed how the local political ecology of enforcement and treatment agencies constrains the case decision options available to probation officers. Thomson (1980) has suggested some of the accountability implications of such collective cross-pressures. Probation officers are uncomfortably caught between law enforcement officers, who see them as too lenient, and human services workers, who find them too strict, punitive, and capricious (Thomson and Fogel, 1980:121–55).

At the same time, the probation officer has lower status in the court-house than the legal professionals, i.e., judges, prosecutors, and defense attorneys, who are popularly viewed as the principal actors, are better paid, and enjoy greater prestige. Similarly, at the organizational level the probation agency has relatively low status.

This situation would not have such serious consequences if probation officers enjoyed a strong occupational reference group. Historically, no such group has existed, but as probation shows promise of emerging as an occupation in itself, we have seen some encouraging signs in the develop-ment of the American Probation and Parole Association, the founding of the National Association of Probation Executives, and the increased atten-tion paid by the National Institute of Corrections to probation technical assistance, professional development, and policy analysis.

Although a justice model approach could assist probation's development as an occupation, it would greatly increase the probation officer's marginal-ity. The probation officer would be principally and clearly an agent of the legal system rather than of the social services system, but organizational marginality would remain. The probation officer would still be a person very much in the middle of the local organizational environment. Most importantly, marginality would be increased by the imperative that proba-tion officers approach their work from multiple perspectives, playing a mediator's role. The probation officer would not be the client's advocate or the prosecutor's investigator or the judge's bailiff or the police's informant or the human services agency's referral source or the victim's sympathetic ear. Instead, he or she would be committed to a commonweal function, serving the public, which includes victim *and* witness *and* offender *and* legal representatives *and* community agencies *and* general citizenry. The probation officer would have to be able to listen to each of several parties in conflict or competition, appreciate the perspectives of each while remain-ing impartial, evaluate the evidence, reach a disinterested conclusion and offer a just recommendation, and mediate the divergent interests of the parties involved.

This is hardly a simple task. Demanding and frustrating, the probation officer's role could also be an extremely important and rewarding one. It may even suggest a legitimate and publicly attractive argument for the professionalization of probation. It calls for great investigative and mediating skills, knowledge of the law and legal instruments, an ideal of service to the public, a high standard of ethics in matters of great public concern, and work which while not necessarily dangerous would be emotionally, intellectually, and physically draining. Probation officers may for good reason be reticent to accept such a role—although many probably believe they have already done so—but it suggests the significance of probation work in a justice model framework.

Organizational marginality also implies a positive function which should be augmented by the mediating role being advocated here. That function is buffering. There is some evidence that probation officers and agencies, by virtue of their marginality, actually aid in the operations of local systems of justice by serving as buffer between parties actually or potentially in conflict (Thomson, 1982b). This buffering function would be more explicitly required and formulated by the mediator role.

As Bennett (1981) has observed in his study of oral history in delinquency research, marginality can be a significant force in social change. Viewed from this perspective, probation's marginality can be understood as a potentially useful resource in the generation of authentic desert-based sentencing reforms. That probation has been ignored and virtually untouched by previous sentencing reforms may be an indication of why those reforms have gone awry. Viewed from the other direction (i.e., examining the effects of justice model initiatives on probation), the preceding analysis suggests that a comprehensive desert-based sentencing system would increase the role marginality of probation officers and decrease the marginality of the probation agency as part of a law system while its marginality within its local organizational environment would remain steady.

Offender Services in Justice Model Probation

Strictly constructed, the justice model is conceptually incompatible with rehabilitative efforts as traditionally conceived. For this reason, the allowance for such activities within the framework of an earlier, preliminary version of the justice model for probation (Thomson and Fogel, 1980:16) may appear inconsistent. Several arguments can be made, however, for accepting a rehabilitation/reintegration component within the parameters of a justice model for probation.

The first argument is strictly humanitarian. Most would agree that it is good in itself to address human needs wherever they are found. Disagreement typically focuses on who should do the addressing, to what end, at whose initiation, under what circumstances, and at whose expense. Ideally, the wisest course, for reasons of justice, equity, and sensibility, would be to ensure minimum levels of well-being generally rather than making commission of a crime a condition for receiving remedial—or basic—

services, a point Chapter 5 discusses in the juvenile court context. This pursuit of social and economic justice goes far beyond what any reform of epiphenomenal superstructures, such as criminal justice systems, can ever accomplish. It is to these more modest concerns that our attention must now be directed, however, since social and economic injustices do not excuse smaller injustices nor relieve us of our responsibility for dealing with them (Greenberg, 1981).

Given the desirability of responding affirmatively to human needs, does it make sense for criminal justice agencies to provide such ameliorative services? We would say yes, for several reasons. One is that conventional human services agencies frequently refuse to deal with offenders and those who "present too many problems," are "difficult to work with," or are "resistant to services." To a very real extent, the criminal justice system is a last resort for providing human services. Significantly, as David Fogel emphasizes in Chapter 3, justice model probation creates the possibility of a broader role for probation officers in providing a similar array of services for victims as well as offenders.

A second argument for offering voluntary services to offenders is that such efforts apparently can diminish the probability of future crimes (Andrews, 1980; Gendreau and Ross, 1980). While the effect may not be as great as some claimed in the heyday of the rehabilitative ideal (Allen, 1981), it should not be ignored—particularly since so much attention has been given in recent years to the opposite conclusion, frequently buttressed by reference to the early work of Lipton, Martinson, and Wilks (1975). Particularly if monitoring ensures that services are provided either voluntarily or under conditions of detailed-offense-based[1] prediction (Clarke, 1979), probation services could legitimately play a limited role with the goal of reducing recidivism, i.e., a public safety function. Moreover, as Bottoms and McWilliams (1979) imply, a justice model context improves the chances of rehabilitative success by honoring the autonomy of the subject and refusing to treat him or her as an object for manipulation, treatment, or servicing. Again, however, remember that utilitarian efforts must be governed by and be incidental to desert purposes. Otherwise, equity gains offered by the justice model would be quickly eroded and overcome by safety and service considerations.

Finally, there are some very pragmatic reasons for providing probation services. Many probation officers are oriented toward counseling and helping efforts, and appear to derive intrinsic job rewards from such activities (McCleary, 1978; Lemert and Dill, 1978; Sullivan et al., 1977). Moreover, while probation work as pursuit of justice can be a very rewarding and exciting occupation, many will continue to be motivated by the pursuit of rehabilitation and reintegration. And to the extent that a trust relationship between probation officer and probationer is a useful means of ensuring compliance with the conditions of probation, and is a probable outcome of the socio-emotional commitment of probation officers as persons who enjoy developing amicable relationships with others, it is inevitable that services will be another outcome of the relationship, whether they are encouraged, discouraged, or prohibited. Thus, since services will be provided, it behooves us to ensure that probation officers are skilled in human services, at least to ensure they do not have a harmful effect. This requirement, however, will probably become less important over time as rehabilitation-oriented probation officers are replaced by justice-oriented probation officers in jurisdictions that pursue justice model applications.

In allowing a place for services within a justice model design for probation, we must be careful to avoid the abuses associated with earlier "rehabilitative" efforts. An earlier report argued that services could legitimately be provided "*if* the offender is so inclined and *if* the probation officer is so trained" (Thomson and Fogel, 1980:16). Continuing economic crisis and its effects on probation operations (Nelson and Harlow, 1980; Harlow and Nelson, 1982; Nelson, Segal, and Harlow, 1982; Fitzharris, 1979; Waldron, 1982) suggest an additional requirement: offender services should be offered only if the agency's available resources are adequate.

It is very important to understand that the position outlined above prohibits offender services except under limited circumstances; in particular, the principles of proportionality, retrospectivity, and voluntary participation must be honored. Again, utilitarian aims are permitted only when the resulting state exercise of coercive power is no greater than that prescribed by desert. Mabbott made this point lucidly more than four decades ago:

> The truth is that while punishing a man and punishing him justly, it is possible to deter others, and also to attempt to reform him, and if these additional goods are achieved the total state of affairs is better than it would be with the just punishment alone. . . . But reform and deterence are not modifications of the punishment, still less reasons for it. A parallel may be found in the case of tact and truth. If you have to tell a friend an unpleasant truth you may do all you can to put him at his ease and spare his feelings as much as possible, while still making sure that he understands your meaning. In such a case no one would say that your offer of a cigarette beforehand or your apology afterwards are modifications of the truth still less reasons for telling it. You do not tell the truth in order to spare his feelings, but having to tell the truth you also spare his feelings. . . . Prison authorities may make it possible that a convict may become physically or morally better. They cannot ensure either result; and the punishment would still be just if the criminal took no advantage of their arrangements and their efforts failed. Some moralists see this and exclude these "extra" arrangements for deterrence and reform.

They say it must be the punishment *itself* which reforms and deters. But it is just my point that the punishment *itself* seldom reforms the criminal and never deters others. It is only "extra" arrangements which have any chance of achieving either result. (Mabbott, [1939] 1961:40–41)

This analysis suggests the following definition of allowable probation services for offenders:

Measures to help the probationer comply with the conditions of probation.

Measures to which the probationer voluntarily consents, preferably by initiating the request; i.e., offender participation in such measures is not mandated by court order or coerced by probation staff.

Measures that the probation officer is capable of providing directly or arranging.

Measures that do not divert agency resources from other responsibilities to the court for ensuring equitable treatment.

Since the probation officer's principal responsibility as officer of the court is to see that the sentence of probation is successfully served, i.e., a coercive function, involvement in probation services should be kept to a minimum. Whenever possible, the probationer should be referred elsewhere, so that the probation officer's role is not compromised and the possibility of coercive treatment is minimized.

The alternative to permitting offender services constrained by desert principles is bizarre and unrealistic. Categorically prohibiting such services would require probation officers to be rigid legalistic bureaucrats. The justice model proposes instead that they play an important role as mediators in their communities in the pursuit of reparative justice, a role with which limited offender services responsibilities are congruent. Mediation necessitates flexibility and the ability to provide something of value.

Moreover, offender services can improve the odds that the probation sentence will be successfully completed. It should be remembered that life conditions are frequently less than comfortable for many probationers. A probationer who has lost his job, whose home and marriage are falling apart, and who is drinking heavily may find it difficult to report to the probation office four times a week as required by the probation order. If probation officers are told to view such matters narrowly and to ignore probationers' requests for help with such problems, the cause of justice is not served. (Neither, of course, is the cause of justice served if probationers are coerced into accepting services.) The ability and willingness of probation officers to respond, in legally acceptable ways, to such calls for help can be critical to community well-being, particularly in rural areas (Thomson and Fogel, 1980), and hence to the legitimation of punishment as a community function (Moberly, 1968).

In conclusion, there are at least five areas in which it is reasonable and appropriate for probation officers to provide services. The first area is victim services. This responsibility is a consequence of the expanded notion of client implicit in the justice model for probation (Fogel, 1983). The second area is compliance with conditions of probation, a corollary of the responsibility of the probation officer for monitoring and facilitating compliance. The third area is victim-offender reconciliation. This responsibility devolves from the reparative goal of retribution and will be most likely to become a reality in communities that choose to deal with their crime rather than ignore it. The fourth area is defined by situations in which the probationer states a desire for probation services that the probation officer is capable of providing. This is the basic constraining principle of service provision under any justice model. The fifth area is requital (Kidder, 1975; McAnany, 1978). Here the service is provided in the sentence and must be actualized by the probationer.

Victim Services, Restitution, and Community Service Orders

Contemporary rethinking of probation's purposes and forms mirrors the development of other nonincarcerative sentencing arrangements (e.g., restitution and community service orders) and ameliorative responses to individuals other than the offender (e.g., victim services). This section considers the implications of a justice model approach to probation for other community sentences that emphasize functions other than services to—or human services control over—probationers.

The focus in recent years on victim services reflects public restiveness with official concern for rights of the accused, more visible human services efforts on behalf of offenders, continuing neglect and even official abuse of victims, and increased academic interests in the characteristics and behavior of victims (victimology). One effort has been the Improving Victim Services through Probation project funded by the National Instiute of Corrections and the Law Enforcement Assistance Administration and sponsored by the American Probation and Parole Association under the leadership of Scotia B. Knouff. As the newsletters of this project attest, victim services through probation is a diversified enterprise.

While efforts to consider victims are welcome developments, justice model conceptions of probation caution against exchanging an inappropriate preoccupation with offenders for an inappropriate preoccupation with victims. Instead, the role suggested for probation officers would be more complex than either of thse emphases would demand. Probation officers would be required to be responsive to the rights of victims and of offenders, but would also be required to serve a broader public interest that goes beyond the particular interests of victims and offenders.

Restitution is an area in which innovative community sentences and consideration of victims potentially come together (Galaway and Hudson, 1978; Hudson, et al., 1980). Restitution is an ancient penal response (Armstrong, 1981) revived in recent years, a revival heralded by implementation of restitutive measures in Minnesota (Neier, 1975:170). Inasmuch as restitution focuses on making victim and community whole again, it is eminently compatible with a justice model formulation (Hudson and Galaway, 1981).

Other justice model issues concerning restitutive community sentences are discussed by David Fogel in Chapter 3. Here we shall consider the extent to which probation agencies can be considered proper organizational homes for other community sentences. In particular, we examine a variant on restitution, community service work orders (Harris, 1979), or as they are sometimes known, moral restitution. The analysis and conclusions are substantially transferable to the case of financial restitution and, to a lesser degree, to victim services.

One approach to considering the proper organizational home for the management of community service work orders is to define the work elements required of the managing agency and agent and examine the capabilities of prospective organizations and occupations for adequately discharging these responsibilities. Eleven work elements can be identified: 1) fact-finding investigation, 2) assessment and matching, 3) recommendation, 4) resource mobilization, 5) assignment and linkage, 6) monitoring, 7) adjustment, 8) reporting, 9) closure, 10) follow-up, and 11) evaluation. (It should be noted at the outset that I view most of these activities as clearly within the province of probation. A more difficult question is the appropriate organizational locus for victim services.)

The first three elements are activities to be carried out during the presentence investigation period and should logically be conducted by the party responsible for such investigation and reporting. *Fact-finding investigation* means assessing the amount of harm done and the degree of culpability of the offender, e.g., in a plea-bargained case where detailed facts of the case are not entered into the court record. Judgments of this type, and skills required to make them, would be critical components of probation work in a justice model framework. *Assessment and matching* means determination of offender capabilities and constraints with regard to work assignments and identification of prospective work situations, employers, and supervisors that would fit the offender's situation, both legally (i.e., the debt required by sentence to be repaid) and behaviorally (i.e., the ability to comply with the conditions of sentence as realized in a given work setting). The *recommendation* of appropriate community service should be part of the presentence investigation report and thus falls logically to the probation officer. Consideration of the appropriateness of such a sentence within the legal arena is also critical as a means of ensuring compliance and establishing precedents.

One could argue that although the probation officer should be responsible for such presentencing activities, some other party should be responsible for actual management. In support of this approach, one could cite examples of and arguments for the division of probation labor into investigative and supervisory responsibilities. Such divisions, however, have retained both functions within the probation department, and in any case, cogent arguments can also be made against such disassembly. Again, there are compelling reasons to assign management of community service orders to probation officers. Elements four through seven, i.e., *resource mobilization, assignment and linkage, monitoring,* and *adjustment,* are the heart of the popular and promising community resource management approach to probation work. In a recent national survey of 1105 probation officers in small agencies, 44 percent (481) saw their primary role as managing community resources for probationers (Thomas and Fogel, 1980). In addition, ability to deal with questions of employer liability, which is sometimes cited as an obstacle to the use of community service orders, will be an important skill in convincing prospective employers/supervisors to assume the risk of harm to or by probationers serving community service order sentences. To the degree that probation officers are challenged by this kind of problem, community service orders are an appropriate area for them to tackle.

Community service order assignments must sometimes be modified in response to developing problems, e.g., a probationer's lack of compliance with the order, or supervisory deficiencies in the employment situation. It makes sense to assign this adjustment responsibility to probation officers, since it is similar to other adaptive adjustments they make in their supervisory relationship with probationers. Moreover, to the extent that adjustment requires taking a case back into court for modification of conditions, revocation proceedings, contempt proceedings, resentencing, or termination, it makes sense to assign the responsibility to those experienced in such matters, i.e., to probation officers.

Reporting, element eight, is again a function already performed by probation officers, who must report in writing and orally, to the court on case progress. Elements nine and ten, *closure* and *follow-up,* require skills and ways of being associated with social work and human services. Although desert-based probation recommends de-emphasis of such capabilities, or more precisely of the ideology associated with them, it does not proscribe them. As discussed above, they will inevitably continue to be important to probation officers and to be valued technologies within probation work. The final work element, *evaluation*, is an extension of monitoring and requires analytic abilities that presumably are being fostered in prospective probation officers in schools of criminal justice.

Finally, recognizing the perniciousness of establishing single-purpose organizations that consume resources for administration and become committed to self-perpetuation, why would one want to establish a new organization when we already have one whose staff members have the appropriate training, experience, and role orientation, and whose current functions are compatible with the proposed new responsibilities? The argument is bolstered further by the observation that multiple-purpose organizations are more effective than single-purpose organizations (Etzioni, 1964:13–14).

Role Definitions, Core Skill Areas, and Presentence Investigations

We have already considered briefly how probation officers are perceived by others and analyzed the role of offender services and victim services in justice model probation. It remains to examine some key role definitions and skills of probation work, and their relation to a justice model framework.

Commitment to the human services role of probation officers may be principally rhetorical for a large proportion of those in the probation occupation (Duffee, 1983b). Or this commitment may be overstated, perhaps because advocates of the social services role have controlled the means of communication, e.g., journals, associations, training units, and programs of higher education. Either possibility suggests the wisdom of considering those for whom the application of social services technologies is not a preeminent concern. We can identify at least six other definitions of the probation worker's role:

1. Legal agent.
2. Bureaucrat.
3. Aide to the judge.
4. Mediator.
5. Punitive agent of the community, of some more limited constituency within it (e.g., office holders, buisness elite, professional elite, moneyed interests), or of self.
6. No role definition—i.e., passive agent, payroller, or short-termer.

These roles are not necessarily incompatible with each other or with the social services role. Yet they are useful as analytic constructs. From a justice model point of view, types one (legal agent) and four (mediator) are attractive; probation officers who define what they do in such terms should find themselves quite comfortable with the proposed formulation of probation. Moreover, if their capabilities measure up to their role conception, such probation officers already have skills required by our model.

The role types identified here are quite broad; no doubt many probation practitioners could elaborate at considerable length about the richness of variations in probation officer behavior, opinions, and attitudes within single categories. Such elaboration could be quite helpful, both in improving our understanding of probation as work and in guiding staff development efforts. For now, however, we will concentrate on some subtypes within the legal agent and mediator roles, the two most compatible with the mission suggested for probation.

The reader may wonder why we have not mentioned a police role for probation officers, since so many earlier analyses of this subject have focused on the "cop/social worker" polarity (Crow, 1974; Dembo, 1972; Glaser, 1964; Ohlin et al., 1956). The law enforcement-oriented probation officer is in fact one of the subtypes within the legal agent category, which also includes the presentence investigator and the role of ensuring compliance with the conditions of probation. Note that particularly in the last role, social service skills may be very useful in service of the law even though the formal role type is defined in other terms.

Not even these subtypes capture the attributes congruent with or inimical to a justice model of probation. Reference to a police subtype is not terribly enlightening, since there is a wide range of behavior among law enforcement officers (Muir, 1977) and presumably among probation officers identifying with such a role. To the extent, however, that such a role orientation reflects a commitment to the rule of law and internalized norms of accountability, there is support for a justice model formulation.

The mediator role also embraces considerable variation with regard to the parties to mediation, and the emphasis given to advocacy, brokerage, resource management, resource mobilization, and liaison. Some of these variants have customarily been more closely identified with the social services role orientation (i.e., those that emphasize brokerage, resource management, and resource mobilization), while others are more obviously compatible with justice model probation (advocacy, liaison). The former skills can be accommodated within a justice model, but we will require a broader conception of who is served by the probation agency and officer.

A useful means of assessing what would be required of probation officers working in a justice model context is to consider the core skills of probation. Lubove (1965) has argued that occupational control of a core skill area is necessary for successful professionalization efforts. James T. Carey's research, presented in Chapter 9 of this volume, highlights the absence of a core skill in probation work.

It seems reasonable to say, however, that there are five potential core skill areas in probation. Listed roughly in order of their compatibility with a justice model approach, from most to least compatible, they are:

1. Investigation.
2. Mediation.
3. Liaison and resource mobilization.
4. Surveillance/supervision.
5. Casework/counseling.

Of these five, the one with the strongest claim to being a core skill is investigation (for the purposes of the presentence investigation report). It is a prototypical probation officer activity rarely done by anyone other than a member of this occupation,[2] although its quality is susceptible to monitoring and its utility to control by other occupational groups, notably judges, prosecutors, and defense counsel (Hagan et al., 1979).

Of greater significance for present purposes is the fact that in a justice model probation agency, the role of the presentence investigation should become much more important. The court will need 1) detailed information regarding circumstances and consequences of the offense and the degree of offender culpability, and 2) realistic, appropriate, and sometimes creative recommendations regarding the content of proposed probation sentences. For a justice model to work, the presentence investigation report must be taken with the utmost seriousness, in contrast to some current practices (Hagan et al., 1979), or another means of systematic sentence determination tied to details of the offense must be found.[3]

One may wonder at this emphasis on the presentence investigation under a determinate sentencing system. But while previous determinate sentencing schemes have fixed sentences in terms of the general offense (von Hirsch and Hanrahan, 1981), presumptive sentencing recognizes variations in circumstances within an offense category, and allows for aggravating and mitigating factors. More importantly, justice model approaches stress the primacy of nonincarcerative sentences (Singer, 1979), but legislation to date has tended to define proportionate sentences in terms of length of incarceration, leaving the probation sentence undifferentiated. While there are good reasons to conclude that legislation is not the place to spell out the details of allowable probation sentences (Zimring, 1976), proportionality in probation sentences must be taken more seriously than it has in previous sentencing reforms (Cullen and Gilbert, 1982). For this reason, presentence investigation fact-finding and recommendations, as well as judicial reasons for passing probation sentences of various types, should be a matter of readily accessible record. Moreover, this information should be compiled and reviewed at frequent intervals by a sentence review commission with resources adequate to the task. These reviews should be used as the basis for assessing proportionality and equity in probation and other sentences. In this way, a justice model approach to probation, properly implemented with due concern for system context, can contribute to the control of plea bargaining (Ryan and Alfini, 1979; Nimmer and Krauthaus, 1977; Yale Law Journal, 1972), a point to which we return at the end of this chapter.

RECEPTIVITY OF PROBATION FIELD
TO JUSTICE MODEL

Here and in the preceding chapters of this volume, we have presented principles and law system justifications for a justice model for probation and suggested some of its implications for probation work. We should now consider a question of great moment for justice model prospects: how receptive will probation officers be to such a formulation?

Survey data can supplement the significant but unsystematic evidence regarding justice model acceptability gathered from probation conferences and other communications with probation officers during the Probation Mission Project. These data were collected in 1979 in a large-scale survey of 1105 local, state, and federal probation officers working in 551 agencies throughout the United States (Thomson and Fogel, 1980). These data were collected for the purposes of the Staff Training for Small Probation Agencies (STSPA) project rather than for estimating the acceptability of justice model approaches to probation; the sample is limited to officers working in small agencies (i.e., offices with nine or fewer officers). Nevertheless, secondary analysis of this data set for present purposes is appropriate because of the size of the sample, its national scope, and the pertinence of some of the questions asked.

Two items from the STSPA data set are of particular interest for estimating the acceptability to contemporary officers of a justice model for probation. One would expect such an approach to be more acceptable to probation officers who stress the role of law in probation work than to probation officers whose priorities lie elsewhere. Accordingly, our indicators of justice model acceptability are related to probation officers' opinions regarding the importance of law for probation work. The first indicator is derived from a question asking what five subjects should be included in a training program for experienced probation officers. A respondent who includes one or more law or legal issues topics among these subjects will be considered amenable to a justice model for probation. The second indicator is derived from an item requesting a rank ordering of the four most important types of information for inclusion in the presentence investigation report. Mention of any subject pertaining to current offense or prior record as the most important information type will be considered evidence of a law-oriented approach to probation work.

Table 4.1 documents the significant law orientation of probation officers in small agencies dealing with adult offenders. Almost half mention law

Table 4.1. Probation Officer Opinions Regarding Importance of Law in Probation Work (N = 1105)

A. Ideal Training Curriculum for Experienced Probation Officers		
One or More Law Subjects Mentioned	464	(45%)
No Law Subjects Mentioned	577	(55%)
Total	1041 [a]	(100%)
B. Most Important Item of Information for Presentence Investigation Report		
Current Offense	335	(32%)
Prior Record	438	(41%)
Other	283	(27%)
Total	1056 [b]	(100%)

Source: STSPA Survey of Probation Officers, 1979.
[a]64 missing cases.
[b]49 missing cases.

subjects as a topic for inclusion in a curriculum for experienced probation officers, and almost three-quarters report that current offense or prior record data are of greatest importance for inclusion in the presentence investigation report. These simple frequency distributions, while providing only imperfect and rudimentary measures of the degree of law orientation among probation officers, do suggest that the field may be receptive to justice model approaches.

In subsequent analysis, we will focus on the presentence investigation indicator of law orientation. The other indicator is more ambiguous, since some law-oriented probation officers might not have mentioned a law subject for inclusion in a curriculum for experienced personnel, reasoning that legal issues are so important that they should have been mastered during entry-level training. The presentence investigation item is also more useful because it allows differentiation among legal factors identified, i.e., between those suggesting a retributive orientation (current offense) and those suggesting a deterrence orientation (prior record).

Von Hirsch (1981), in his continuing monitoring and analysis of the determinate sentencing movement, delineates the difference between relying on previous record and on current offense information in determining penal sanctions. He notes that reliance on previous record suggests a deterrence orientation, since such an approach is premised on a utilitarian purpose, i.e., predicting dangerousness and tailoring sentences accordingly. In contrast, sentence determination based on current offense suggests a retributive intent: offenders will be punished for the harm for which they are culpable, not for previous offenses or for social condition or for estimates of potential dangerousness. While an emphasis on current offense is the more consistent with a justice model approach, emphasis on prior record is closer to a justice model position than is emphasis on social factors. In fact, prior record can be seen as consistent with a just deserts position if the prior record is related to offender's culpability. Nevertheless, since it appears that empirical reliance on prior record in sentencing tends to be predictive, the present analysis will follow von Hirsch's position and interpret the mention of current offense as an indicator of a retributive orientation, prior record as an indicator of a deterrence orientation, and the "other" category as an indicator of a rehabilitative orientation. This last category includes information such as offender's personal and family history; physical, interpersonal, religious, leisure, and financial environments; available resources; evaluation, prognosis, treatment plan, and recommendation.

Table 4.2 reveals a striking relationship between level of government and jurisprudential orientation. A majority of federal officers take a retributive position on the presentence investigation information question, half of the state system officers take a deterrence position, and local systems officers are fairly evenly distributed among rehabilitative, deterrence, and retributive orientations. A previous analysis (Thomson, 1982a) suggested that retributive orientation tends to increase with age, experience, and education. When level of government was introduced as a test factor, however, these relationshps disappeared, indicating that they are mediated through the level of government-jurisprudential orientation relationship. To the extent that federal probation officers exert particular leadership in their chosen occupation (Carey, 1983), the predominance of retributive thinking in this segment of the field may improve the prospects for justice model approaches. Much primary research must be done, however, before we have a clear understanding of the receptivity of probation officers to justice model proposals, both philosophically and in terms of their expected impact on probation work.

Even if this research is done, questions will remain regarding the receptivity of probation agencies and communities to justice model proposals. Fortunately, these important issues have begun to be addressed by Duffee (1983a) and Harlow (1983).

Table 4.2. Jurisprudential Orientation by Level of Government

Level of Government	Jurisprudential Orientation			
	Retributive	Rehabilitative	Deterrence	Total
Local	115 (27%)	160 (38%)	150 (35%)	426 (100%)
State	113 (26%)	102 (24%)	215 (50%)	430 (100%)
Federal	105 (53%)	21 (11%)	72 (36%)	198 (100%)
Total	334 (32%)	283 (27%)	437 (41%)	1054 (100%)

Source: STSPA Survey of Officers, 1979.

$\chi^2 = 87.1$, d.f. $= 4$, $\pi < .0001$.

$\gamma = .07$ (asymmetric with jurisprudential orientation dependent).

MISCONCEPTIONS OF PUNISHMENT AND REFORMS GONE WRONG

A major obstacle to acceptance of the justice model is general misunderstanding of the uses and abuses of punishment and of how the latter can be controlled. Thus, some critics of the justice model offer a highly malevolent view of punishment (e.g., Empey, 1979; Cressey, 1982; Cullen and Gilbert, 1982). Indeed the justice model can be, and has been, misappropriated by those with utilitarian aims and nonhumanitarian attitudes. Just deserts imagery has been used to support sentencing reforms that are overly punitive, i.e., fail the justice model's proportionality test. Such reforms have also tended, at least formally, to constrain discretion in ways inconsistent with attempts to pursue justice (Rosett, 1979).

In this sense, critics of the justice model (e.g., Reiman and Headlee, 1981, and Cullen and Gilbert, 1982) are correct in suggesting that, in some empirical instances, less social harm would probably result from maintaining the current situation than from misguided sentencing reforms in which justice model arguments are used rhetorically for inauthentic purposes. That is, if justice model reforms are not initiated correctly, they may not be worth establishing at all (cf. Sieber, 1981 and Doleschal, 1982 for more general considerations on this point). Indeed, this was a key point of some of the earlier justice model proposals (American Friends Service Committee, 1971) as Cullen and Gilbert (1982) have observed. To implement the justice model appropriately, it is not enough to honor the proportionality and retrospectivity principles; an appreciation of the humanitarian, egalitarian, and reparative possibilities of punishment is also needed, along with a recognition of the limited appropriateness of incarceration, and the preferability of community sanctions (American Friends Service Committee, 1971; von Hirsch, 1976), and the need for moderation in punishment (Rothman, 1981).

Two major questions are raised by this analysis: what would a correct justice model sentencing scheme look like, and how can it be achieved? The first question, already addressed in Chapter 1, can now be examined in slightly different form by presenting a hypothetical justice model sentencing matrix consistent with the five principles enunciated above. To place the matrix in perspective, Table 4.3 also shows applicable penalties from Illinois's current sentencing schedule, and gives examples of offenses from each class.

Four characteristics of this schedule should be noted. First, incarcerative penalties are generally greatly scaled down from current prescriptions and practices in the United States, although they resemble those imposed in some other countries (Wade and Paulson, 1980). Second, probation penalties are systematized. Third, penalties are measured in days to foster

Table 4.3. A Justice Model Sentencing Schedule Compared with the Current Illinois Sentencing Schedule

Justice Model Offense Class	Justice Model Offense Examples	Current Illinois Sentence	Justice Model Sentence
F1	Murder	Death or 7305 to 14,610 days incarceration	4000 to 18,000 days incarceration
F2	Aggravated kidnapping for ransom; rape; deviate sexual assault	2191 to 10,957 days incarceration	750 to 3000 days incarceration
	Aggravated arson; voluntary manslaughter	1461 to 5478 days incarceration, or probation up to 1461 days	750 to 3000 days incarceration
F3	Aggravated kidnapping other than for ransom	Probation up to 1461 days, or 1461 to 5478 days incarceration	Probation Type A or 60 to 750 days incarceration
	Involuntary manslaughter	Probation up to 913 days, or 730 to 1826 days incarceration	Probation Type A or 60 to 750 days incarceration
	Reckless homicide	Probation up to 913 days, or 365 to 1095 days incarceration	Probation Type A or 60 to 750 days incarceration
F4	Home invasion	2191 to 10,957 days incarceration	Probation Type B or A or 10 to 200 days incarceration
	Indecent liberties with a child	Probation up to 1461 days or 1461 to 5478 days incarceration	Probation Type B or A or 10 to 200 days incarceration
	Kidnapping; forcible detention; arson; bribery	Probation up to 1461 days or 1095 to 2556 days incarceration	Probation Type B or A or 10 to 200 days incarceration
F5	Armed robbery	2197 to 10,957 days incarceration	Probation Type B or A or 1 to 120 days incarceration
	Intimidation; perjury; official misconduct	Probation up to 913 days, or 730 to 1826 days incarceration	Probation Type B or A or 1 to 120 days incarceration
	Unlawful restraint	Probation up to 913 days, or 365 to 1095 days incarceration	Probation Type B or A or 1 to 120 days incarceration

Table 4.3. *(Continued)*

Justice Model Offense Class	Justice Model Offense Examples	Current Illinois Sentence	Justice Model Sentence
F6	Residential burglary	1461 to 5478 days incarceration	Probation Type C or B or 1 to 100 days incarceration
	Robbery	Probation up to 1461 days, or 1095 to 2556 days incarceration	Probation Type C or B or 1 to 100 days incarceration
	Grand theft; forgery; eavesdropping (subsequent offense)	Probation up to 913 days, or 730 to 1826 days incarceration	Probation Type C or B or 1 to 100 days incarceration
	Unlawful use of recorded sounds; obstructing justice; tampering with public records	Probation up to 913 days, or 365 to 1095 days incarceration	Probation Type C or B or 1 to 100 days incarceration
F7	Burglary (nonresidential)	Probation up to 1461 days, or 1095 to 2556 days incarceration	Probation Type C or B or 1 to 40 days incarceration
	Eavesdropping (first offense); criminal damage to property (over $300)	Probation up to 913 days, or 365 to 1095 days incarceration	Probation Type C or B or 1 to 40 days incarceration
M1	Aggravated assault; battery; reckless conduct	probation up to 365 days, or incarceration up to 365 days	Probation Type C or B or 1 to 30 days incarceration
M2	Contributing to the sexual delinquency of a child; unlawful sale of firearms; resisting peace officer; petty theft; criminal damage to property (less than $300)	Probation up to 365 days, or incarceration up to 365 days	Probation Type C or B or 1 to 10 days incarceration
	Assault	Probation up to 365 days, or incarceration up to 30 days	Probation Type C or B or 1 to 10 days incarceration
M3	Public indecency; criminal trespass to vehicle; unlawful possession of weapons	Probation up to 365 days, or incarceration up to 365 days	Probation type C or 1 to 5 days incarceration

Table 4.3. *(Continued)*

Justice Model Offense Class	Justice Model Offense Examples	Current Illinois Sentence	Justice Model Sentence
	Disorderly conduct (false reporting or voyeurism)	Probation up to 365 days, or incarceration up to 182 days	Probation Type C or 1 to 5 days incarceration
	Criminal trespass to land; false personation	Probation up to 365 days, or incarceration up to 30 days	Probation Type C or 1 to 5 days incarceration

Note: Probation types are defined as follows:
   A. Weekly reporting for 24 to 36 months plus up to 800 hours of community service.
   B. Monthly to weekly reporting for 12 to 24 months plus up to 200 hours of community service.
   C. Quarterly to monthly reporting for 6 to 12 months plus up to 50 hours of community service.
Restitution or victim services could also be imposed as additional penalties in conjunction with those listed above.

thinking of punishment in more modest terms. Fourth, relative to each other, crimes against persons and against the public trust are considered more serious and crimes against property less serious in the justice model schedule than in the current Illinois schedule.

In addition, this schedule—or any other constructed with reference to our five criteria for justice-based sentencing—might resist erosion by plea bargaining, since the modest penalty structure reduces incentives for bargaining (cf. Feeley, 1979, and Ryan, 1980). Also, ideal enabling legislation would guide judicial discretion in terms of imposing sentences based on desert and would require recording of sentencing rationales and a means of reviewing sentencing practices.

Current sentencing practices seem to take account of the offender's perceived moral character in determining punishments (Rosett and Cressey, 1976). This raises two questions, one ethical (should it be this way?) and one empirical (must it be this way?). The proposed system assumes a negative answer to each question. The ethical issue is discussed at length in several chapters of this book as well as elsewhere in the just deserts or justice·model literature. The empirical question can only be answered hypothetically pending empirical reform and testing. Our belief that desert-based sentencing is practical rests on the following expectations: 1) reduction in penalty structure, 2) normalization based on offense as functional equivalent for normalization based on combination of offense and offender's moral character (Sudnow, 1965), 3) provisions for judicial discretion based on culpability and harm assessments (including enhanced presentence investigation role for probation officer), and 4) an effective sentence review mechanism. The justice model does not seek to eliminate discretion—a task both impossible and undesirable—but rather to regulate it. Subsequent chapters of this book should shed some light on the remaining question of how to implement a justice model correctly.

NOTES

1. The phrase "detailed-offense-based" is used in lieu of Morris's (1974) medical term "anamnestic," adapted by Clarke (1979).
2. Note, however, the recent development of private presentence investigations by parties with whom defense counsel contracts, e.g., Thomas Gitchoff of San Diego, California, and Jerome G. Miller of Washington, D.C.
3. The approach proposed by Gradess (1978) and discussed by David Fogel (1983) in Chapter 3 is one possible alternative. However, the presentence investigation approach is largely in place and probation officers are trained for it, although there would have to be major changes in many jurisdictions in perceptions of the functions and value of the report as well as in how it is developed. Also, it should be less expensive than, for example, the Gradess approach.

REFERENCES

American Friends Service Committee (1971). *Struggle for Justice*. New York: Hill and Wang.

Allen, Francis A. (1981). *The Decline of the Rehabilitative Ideal: Penal Policy and Social Purpose*. New Haven: Yale.

Andrews, D. A. (1980). "Some Experimental Investigations of the Principles of Differential Association Through Deliberate Manipulations of the Structure of Service Systems." *American Sociological Review* 45:448–62.

Armstrong, Troy L. (1981). *Restitution in Juvenile Justice: Issues in the Evolution and Application of the Concept*. Chicago: National Center for the Assessment of Alternatives to Juvenile Justice Processing, School of Social Services Administration, University of Chicago.

Banton, Michael (1964). *The Policeman in the Community*. London: Tavistock.

Bennett, James (1981). *Oral History and Delinquency: the Rhetoric of Criminology*. Chicago: University of Chicago.

Blau, Peter M., and Richard Scott (1962). *Formal Organizations*. San Francisco: Chandler.

Blomberg, Thomas G. (1980). "Widening the Net: An Anomaly in the Evaluation of Diversion Programs." In Malcolm W. Klein and Katherine S. Teilmann (eds.), *Handbook of Criminal Justice Evaluation*. Beverly Hills: Sage.

Bottoms, A. E., and William McWilliams (1979). "A Non-treatment Paradigm for Probation Practice." *British Journal of Social Work* 9:159–202. Reprinted as Chapter 7 in this book.

Carey, James T. (1984). "The Professionalization of Probation: An Analysis of the Diffusion of Ideas." Chapter 9 in this volume.

Clarke, Stevens H. (1979). "What is the Purpose of Probation and Why Do We Revoke It?" *Crime and Delinquency* 25:409–24.

Conrad, John P. (1984). "The Re-definition of Probation: Drastic Proposals to Solve an Urgent Problem." Chapter 8 in this volume.

Cressey, Donald R. (1982). "Foreword" to Cullen and Gilbert (1982).

Crow, Richard T. (1974). *The Perceptions of Training Needs of Adult Probation and Parole Officers in Colorado*. Ann Arbor, Michigan: University Microfilms.

Cullen, Francis T., and Karen E. Gilbert (1982). *Reaffirming Rehabilitation*. Cincinnati: Anderson.

Cushman, Robert C. (1984). "Probation in the 1980s: A Public Administration Viewpoint," Chapter 11 in this volume.

Dell'Appa, Frank, W. Tom Adams, James D. Jorgenson, and Herbert R. Sigurdson (1976). "Advocacy, Brokerage, Community: The ABC's of Probation and Parole." *Federal Probation* 40.

Dembo, Richard (1972). "Orientation and Activities of the Parole Officer." *Criminology* 10:193–215.

Doleschal, Eugene (1982). "The Dangers of Criminal Justice Reform." *Criminal Justice Abstracts* 14:133–52.

Duffee, David E. (1984a). "The Community Context of Probation." Chapter 12 in this volume.

——— (1984b). "Models of Probation Supervision." Chapter 6 in this volume.

Emerson, Robert M. (1969). *Judging Delinquents: Context and Process in Juvenile Court*. Chicago: Aldine.

Empey, LaMar T. (1979). "From Optimism to Despair: New Doctrines in Juvenile Justice." In Charles A. Murray and Louis A. Cox, Jr. (eds.), *Beyond Probation: Juvenile Corrections and the Chronic Delinquent*. Beverly Hills: Sage.

Etzioni, Amitai (1964). *Modern Organizations*. Englewood Cliffs, NJ: Prentice-Hall.

Feeley, Malcolm M. (1979). *Probation in an Era of Diminishing Resources*. Sacramento: Foundation for Continuing Education in Corrections.

——— (1981). *Economic Strategies in Probation: A Handbook for Managers*. Sacramento: California Probation, Parole and Correctional Association.

Fogel, David (1984). "The Emergence of Probation as a Profession in the Service of Public Safety: The Next Ten Years." Chapter 3 in this volume.

Foote, Caleb (1978). "Deceptive Determinate Sentencing." In *Determinate Sentencing: Reform or Regression?* Washington, D.C.: U.S. Department of Justice.

Galaway, Burt, and Joe Hudson, eds. (1978). *Offender Restitution in Theory and Action*. Lexington, MA: Heath.

Gendreau, Paul, and Robert R. Ross (1979). "Effective Correctional Treatment: Bibliotherapy for Cynics." *Crime and Delinquency* 25:463–89.

Gerber, Rudolph J., and Patrick D. McAnany (1967). "Punishment: Current Survey of Philosophy and Law." *Saint Louis University Law Journal* 11:502–35. Reprinted as "The Philosophy of Punishment" in Norman Johnston, Leonard Savitz, and Marvin E. Wolfgang (eds.), *The Sociology of Punishment and Corrections*. New York: Wiley, 1970.

Gettinger, Stephen (1981). "Rx from Dr. Karl: 'Eliminate Punishment.'" *Corrections Magazine* 7:17–23.

Glaser, Daniel T. (1964). *The Effectiveness of a Prison and Parole System.* Indianapolis: Bobbs-Merrill.

Gottfredson, Michael R., and Don M. Gottfredson (1980). *Decisionmaking in Criminal Justice: Toward the Rational Exercise of Discretion.* Cambridge, MA: Ballinger.

Gradess, Jonathan E. (1978). Testimony before the New York State Advisory Committee on Sentencing, November 15.

Greenberg, David F. (1977). "The Correctional Effects of Corrections: A Survey of Evaluations." In David F. Greenberg (ed.), *Corrections and Punishment.* Beverly Hills: Sage.

——— (1981). "Praxis and Marxian Criminology." In David F. Greenberg (ed.), *Crime and Capitalism: Readings in Marxist Criminology.* Palo Alto, CA: Mayfield.

Greenberg, David F., and Drew Humphries (1980). "The Cooptation of Fixed Sentencing Reform." *Crime and Delinquency* 26:206–25.

Hagan, John (1977). "Criminal Justice in Rural and Urban Communities: A Study of the Bureaucratization of Justice." *Social Forces* 55:597–612.

Hagan, John, J. D. Hewitt, and D. F. Alwin (1979). "Ceremonial Justice—Crime and Punishment in a Loosely Coupled System." *Social Forces* 58:506–27.

Harlow, Nora (1984). "Implementing the Justice Model in Probation." Chapter 13 in this volume.

Harlow, Nora, and E. Kim Nelson (1982). *Managment Strategies for Probation in an Era of Limits.* Washington, D.C.: National Institute of Corrections.

Harris, M. Kay (1979). *Community Service by Offenders.* Washington, D.C.: National Institute of Corrections.

——— (1984). "Rethinking Probation in the Context of a Justice Model." Chapter 1 in this volume.

Hudson, Joe, and Burt Galaway (1981). "Restitution and the Justice Model." In David Fogel and Joe Hudson (eds.), *Justice as Fairness: Perspectives on the Justice Model.* Cincinnati: Anderson.

Hudson, Joe, Burt Galaway, and Steve Novack (1980). *National Assessment of Adult Restitution Programs—Final Report.* Duluth: School of Social Development, University of Minesota.

Kidder, Joel (1975). "Requital and Criminal Justice." *International Philosophical Quarterly* 15:255–78.

Klockars, Carl B., Jr. (1972). "A Theory of Probation Supervision." *Journal of Criminal Law, Criminology and Police Science* 63:550–7. Reprinted in Robert M. Carter and Leslie T. Wilkins (eds.), *Probation, Parole, and Community Corrections,* 2nd ed. New York: Wiley (1976).

Lemert, Edwin M., and Forrest Dill (1978). *Offenders in the Community: the Probation Subsidy in California.* Lexington, MA: Ballinger.

Lipton, Douglas, Robert Martinson, and Judith Wilks (1975). *The Effectiveness of Correctional Treatment: A Survey of Treatment Evaluation Studies.* New York: Praeger.

Lubove, Roy (1965). *The Professional Altruist: The Emergence of Social Work as a Career, 1880–1930.* New York: Atheneum.

Mabbott, J. D. (1939). "Punishment." In Frederick A. Olafson (ed.), (1961) *Justice and Social Policy.* Englewood Cliffs, NJ: Prentice-Hall. Reprinted from *Mind 48.*

Martinson, Robert (1979). "New Findings, New Views: A Note of Caution Regarding Sentencing Reform." *Hofstra Law Review* 7:244–52.

McAnany, Patrick D. (1976). "Recommendations for Improving the Ailing Probation System." In Rudolph J. Gerber (ed.), *Contemporary Issues in Criminal Justice.* Port Washington, NY: Kennikat.

———— (1978). "Restitution as Ideal and Practice: The Retributive Prospect." In Burt Galaway and Joe Hudson (eds.), *Offender Restitution in Theory and Action.* Lexington, MA: Heath.

McAnany, Patrick D., and Doug Thomson (1982). *Equitable Responses to Probation Violations: A Guide for Managers.* Chicago: Center for Research in Law and Justice, University of Illinois at Chicago.

McAnany, Patrick D., Doug Thomson, and David Fogel (1981). "Probation Mission: Practice in Search of Principle." Paper presented at the National Forum on Criminal Justice, Cherry Hill, New Jersey.

McCleary, Richard (1978). *Dangerous Men: the Sociology of Parole.* Beverly Hills: Sage.

Moberly, Walter (1968). *The Ethics of Punishment.* Hamden, CT: Archon.

Morris, Norval (1974). *The Future of Imprisonment.* Chicago: University of Chicago.

Muir, William K. (1977). *Police: Street Corner Politicians.* Chicago: University of Chicago.

Neier, Aryeh (1975). *Crime and Punishment: A Radical Solution.* New York: Stein and Day.

Nelson, E. Kim, Robert C. Cushman, and Nora Harlow (1980). *Unification of Community Corrections.* Washington, D.C.: National Institute of Justice.

Nelson, E. Kim, Jr., and Nora Harlow (1980). *Responses to Diminishing Resources in Probation: The California Experience.* Report to the National Institute of Corrections. Berkeley: University of Southern California.

Nelson, E. Kim, Lenora Segal, and Nora Harlow (1982). *Probation Under Fiscal Constraints.* Washington, D.C.: National Institute of Justice.

Nimmer, Raymond T., and Patricia Ann Krauthaus (1977). "Plea Bargaining: Reform in Two Cities." *Justice System Journal* 3.

Nonet, Phillipe, and Philip Selznick (1978). *Law and Society in Transition.* New York: Octagon.

Ohlin, Lloyd, Herman Piven, and Donnell Pappenfort (1956). "Major Dilemmas of the Social Worker in Probation and Parole." *National Probation and Parole Association Journal* 2:211–25.

Reiman, Jeffrey H., and Sue Headlee (1981). "Marxism and Criminal Justice Policy." *Crime and Delinquency* 27:24–47.

Remington, Frank J., Donald J. Newman, Edward L. Kimball, Marygold Melli, and Herman Goldstein (1969). *Criminal Justice Administration.* Indianapolis: Bobbs-Merrill.

Rosett, Arthur (1979). "Connotations of Discretion." In *Criminology Review Year-book*, Vol. 1. Sheldon L. Messinger and Egon Bittner (eds.). Beverly Hills: Sage.

Rosett, Arthur, and Donald R. Cressey (1976). *Justice by Consent: Plea Bargains in the American Courthouse*. Philadelphia: Lippincott.

Ross, Robert R., and Paul Gendreau (1980). *Effective Correctional Treatment*. Toronto: Butterworths.

Rothman, David J. (1980). *Conscience and Convenience: the Asylum and Its Alternatives in Progressive America*. Boston: Little, Brown.

——— (1981). "Doing Time: Days, Months and Years in the Criminal Justice System." In Hyman Gross and Andrew von Hirsch (eds.), *Sentencing*. New York: Oxford.

Rubin, Sol (1973). *The Law of Criminal Correction*, 2nd ed. St. Paul: West.

Ryan, John Paul (1980). "Adjudication and Sentencing in a Misdemeanor Court: The Outcome Is the Punishment." *Law and Society Review* 15:79–108.

Ryan, John Paul, and James J. Alfini (1979). "Trial Judges' Participation in Plea Bargaining: An Empirical Perspective." *Law and Society Review* 13:479–507.

Scheff, Thomas (1965). "Typification in the Diagnostic Practices of Rehabilitation Agencies." In Marvin B. Sussman (ed.), *Sociology and Rehabilitation*. Washington, D.C.: American Sociological Association.

Schlossman, Steven L. (1977). *Love and the American Delinquent: The Theory and Practice of "Progressive" Juvenile Justice, 1825–1920*. Chicago: University of Chicago.

Sechrest, Lee, Susan O. White, and Elizabeth D. Brown, eds. (1979). *The Rehabilitation of Criminal Offenders: Problems and Prospects*. Washington, D.C.: National Academy of Sciences.

Sieber, Sam D. (1981). *Fatal Remedies: the Ironies of Social Intervention*. New York: Plenum.

Singer, Richard G. (1979). *Just Deserts: Sentencing Based on Equality and Desert*. Cambridge, MA: Ballinger.

Skolnick, Jerome H. (1966). *Justice Without Trial: Law Enforcement in Democratic Society*. New York: Wiley.

Sudnow, David (1965). "Normal Crimes: Sociological Features of the Penal Code in a Public Defender's Office." *Social Problems* 12:255–76.

Sullivan, Dennis C., Elizabeth Elwin, and Thomas Dexter (1977). *Probation as a Workplace: a Qualitative Analysis of the Job of a Probation Officer*. Albany: New York State Division of Probation.

Thomson, Doug (1980). "Accountability in Small Probation Agencies." *Journal of Probation and Parole* 12:1–17.

——— (1981a). "Estimate of Number of Probation Officers." Unpublished.

——— (1981b). "Probation History and the Contemporary Retributive Justice Movement." Paper presented at the American Probation and Parole Association 6th Institute, Montreal, Quebec, October 19.

——— (1982a). "Practicing Probation as Justice Pursuit." In Patrick D. McAnany, Doug Thomson, and David Fogel (eds.), *Probation and Justice: Surfacing a Hidden Mission*. Chicago: Center for Research in Law and Justice: University of Illinois at Chicago.

—— (1982b). *The Social Organization of Enforcement Behaviors in Probation Work*. Ann Arbor, MI: University Microfilms.

Thomson, Doug, and David Fogel (1980). *Probation Work in Small Agencies: a National Study of Training Provisions and Needs*. Chicago: Center for Research in Law and Justice, University of Illinois at Chicago.

Thomson, Doug, Patrick D. McAnany, and David Fogel (1980). "Probation as Pursuit of Justice: A Preliminary Report to the Field on a Reconsideration of Mission." Paper presented at the American Probation and Parole Association International Seminar on Community Corrections, Niagara Falls, New York and Ontario.

Twentieth Century Fund (1976). *Fair and Certain Punishment*. New York: McGraw-Hill.

von Hirsch, Andrew (1976). *Doing Justice: the Choice of Punishments*. New York: Hill and Wang.

—— (1981). "Desert and Previous Convictions in Sentencing." *Minnesota Law Review* 65:591–634.

von Hirsch, Andrew, and Kathleen Hanrahan (1981). "Determinate Penalty Systems in America: An Overview." *Crime and Delinquency* 27:289–316.

Wade, Steve, and Laurel Paulson (1980). "Crime and Incarceration in Holland: The Lesson for US." *frying pan* (February):22–7.

Waldon, Gerald (1982). "Los Angeles County Probation Department: An Overview," in *Rethinking Probation*, compiled by National Office for Social Responsibility, Alexandria, Virginia.

Wilkins, Leslie T. (1969). *Evaluation of Penal Measures*. New York: Random House.

Wilson, James Q. (1968). *Varieties of Police Behavior: The Management of Law and Order in Eight Communities*. Cambridge, MA: Harvard.

Wright, Erik Olin (1973). *The Politics of Punishment: A Critical Analysis of Prisons in America*. New York: Harper and Row.

Yale Law Journal (1972). "Comment: Restructuring the Plea Bargain." *Yale Law Journal* 82:286–312.

Zimring, Franklin E. (1976). "Making the Punishment Fit the Crime." *Hastings Center Report* 6:13–17.

Chapter 5

Punishment and Responsibility in Juvenile Court: Desert-Based Probation for Delinquents

Doug Thomson* and Patrick D. McAnany**

Juvenile court is a major institution of justice currently under strong pressures for reform. Its probation function is a major component of the system and will reflect the philosophy and structure taken on by the system as a whole. There are many indications that the juvenile court is moving toward a model more nearly reflecting adult court goals, while still retaining certain unique features. Thus, there is need to anticipate changes and direct attention toward issues raised by these changes.

We should begin by stating several assumptions that underlie the present dicussion. Since this chapter cannot do justice to each of them and still get on to its central purpose of discussing what a desert-based juvenile law and probation system would look like, we seek the reader's indulgence in acceptng them for the sake of convenience.

*Center for Research in Law and Justice, University of Illinois at Chicago
**Department of Criminal Justice, University of Illinois at Chicago

McAnany is primarily responsible for the first and third sections of this chapter, Thomson for the other three sections.

1. Desert has become the major norm for adult sentencing during the past decade and will remain central to sentencing for the foreseeable future; probation as the major sentencing option will increasingly become desert-oriented.
2. Juvenile court has undergone extensive procedural reforms since *Gault* (1967) and will continue to assimilate adult court due process changes.
3. Pressures from the general public for a more punishment-oriented justice system apply to juvenile courts as well as to adult courts.
4. Institutional mutuality, which in the past has caused changes to move from the juvenile justice system to adult (e.g., rehabilitation), will cause juvenile court to adopt sentencing reforms of adult courts.
5. The juvenile court will remain a separate and unique institution, but will adapt to the demands of society and due process to produce general changes in goals and structure for itself.

The next two sections will examine the present juvenile law/probation system as it is in transition from a pre-*Gault* interventionist court of treatment to a post-*Gault* one of due process and justice for the child. The main section of the chapter will then be devoted to an examination of the central features of a desert-based juvenile court, and the implications such a system would have for juvenile probation.

JUVENILE COURT IN TRANSITION: WHITHER AND HOW QUICKLY?

In this chapter we are using the juvenile court as a symbol for the whole range of institutions and agencies dealing with the problem of juvenile crime. We intend to exclude from our discussion the extensive and important powers of the court to deal with in-need-of-supervision youngsters, as well as neglected and dependent ones. We focus on the court because it both summarizes the central function of the system—to determine jurisdiction and assign status—and serves as its law-guardian. Probation is a distinct institution, but its role in current juvenile justice practice is essentially tied up with the court's function and, as we see it, any role it has in the future will remain closely tied to the judicial work effort.

However one characterizes pre-*Gault* courts, they shared certain features that have undergone major modifications. They were informal in procedure, oriented to dispositions and not fact-finding, dependent on official discretion largely controlled or influenced by the probation officer, but within a court dominated by the figure of the judge. Schultz and Cohen

(1976) observe that even *Gault* did not change juvenile court process as significantly as many of the pre-*Gault* proponents argued because the holdings of that case were cautious on detail and continued to rcognize the validity of the social welfare goals of the past. Sarri and Hasenfeld (1976) make a related point. In a national survey conducted in 1974 they found that many precedents of the Supreme Court were honored in name only by the juvenile courts they examined. On the other hand, one cannot examine current practice without recognizing that juvenile courts are becoming ever more closely assimilated to adult courts in procedure (Davis, 1980).

Thus, the major court reform efforts of the recent past have assumed procedural regularity as a given and have moved on to more radical areas, such as dispositions, corrections, and even goals. These current reform agendas are significant in number as well as auspices, representing all the major interest groups of juvenile justice. Since 1976, four major task forces have contributed reform proposals: the National Advisory Commission on Criminal Justice Standards and Goals, sponsored by the Law Enforcement Assistance Administration (LEAA) (1976); the Institute of Judicial Administration and the American Bar Association (IJA-ABA) (1977); the Task Force on Youth Crime of the Twentieth Century Fund (1978); and the Committee on Juvenile Justice and Delinquency Prevention of the Office of Juvenile Justice and Delinquency Prevention (1980). All produced thick, detailed plans for renovation of the venerable institutions of juvenile justice. Despite the scope and detail of these formulations, there is a great deal of harmony between them which makes the reform proposed a distinct probability.

The critics have focused on certain central weaknesses of the juvenile law: discretion, over-intrusiveness, ambiguity of goals. The reforms they propose to meet these deficiencies are a departure from the traditional justification for juvenile court. For instance, all reformers would more clearly separate the delinquency jurisdiction of the court from its in-need-of-supervision, dependency, and neglect powers. Further, they would confine delinquency to behaviors made criminal for adults. While not rejecting broad discretionary powers to divert cases from the court, each reform proposal narrows the scope of discretion by developing criteria for making such choices and managing remaining discretion. In the area of dispositions, departures from the past are sharpest. Judges would no longer enjoy an essentially untrammeled choice of dispositions to fit the needs of youth. Rather, under proposals of the task forces, sanctions are tied to the seriousness of offenses on a scale roughly paralleling adult law classification. The court must fix the length of time the juvenile must serve at the time of imposition. Most services to meet the needs of the youth are voluntary and are not tied to the kind and length of the disposition. The goals to be served by the juvenile court are recast to include community protection and getting juveniles to accept responsibility for their offense. (Carey and McAnany, 1983, Chapter 15)

How many of these reforms will be enacted and how soon? No state has yet enacted wholesale the reform agenda of any of these national groups. There is evidence, however, that juvenile courts are moving in the direction of the reforms.

Procedure

As a measure of due process protection, the presence of attorneys may suggest the extent of reform. A recent national survey of the 150 largest juvenile courts indicates that notice of the right to be represented in delinquency matters is given 86 percent of the time at intake and 94 percent of the time on first appearance; more important, counsel are assigned to indigents 100 percent of the time (NCSC, 1981:125–128). Granted that these data depend on the veracity and knowledge of court personnel, still they indicate a high degree of attorney presence and coincide with other data to the same effect (Carey and McAnany, 1983, Chapter 12). One may suppose that attorneys will be aware of the procedural rights of clients and active in pursuit of them without forgetting that attorneys might also serve the convenience of the system. The point here is that much has changed since pre-*Gault* days when attorneys were rarities in juvenile courts. Whatever discretion remains in court officials, and we concede it is extensive, cannot be exercised without potential resistance from counsel.

Dispositions

There has not yet been a widespread move toward determinacy of juvenile dispositions. Several states have introduced guidelines that promise greater determinacy (Minnesota, 1981; Washington, 1981), but the detailed mechanisms suggested in the IJA-ABA Standards are clearly lacking. Nevertheless, dispositions are subject to some control by rules in present juvenile court acts, such as the principle of "least restrictive alternative" (Sussman, 1978), *Morrissey* hearings for revocation of probation and parole, and rules that limit commitments to training schools to behavior that is criminal for adults (e.g., *Illinois Revised Statutes*, ch. 37, sec. 705–2(1)(a)(5) (1981)). The punitiveness of juvenile dispositions has also been changing. In many states, transfers to adult court have been expanded and facilitated (Sussman, 1978; *Ill. Rev. Stat.*, ch. 37, sec. 702–7(6) (1982)), fines and short-term detention added as appropriate dispositional alternatives, and habitual offender statutes grafted onto juvenile court acts (e.g., *Ill. Rev. Stat.*, ch. 37, sec. 705–12 (1981)).

Goals

As the courts have become more formal and punitive, goal statements have tended to change, at least in their emphasis. First, courts more frequently invoke the language found in most acts to the effect that one of the purposes to be served is the "interests of the community." These courts say, if the statute itself does not do so, that community interest is protection against criminal behavior. Other courts and legislatures go even further and state the purpose as a punitive one, as did the Illinois Supreme Court in interpreting the Illinois Juvenile Habitual Offender Act (*People ex. rel. Carey* v. *Chrastka*, 83 Ill. 3d. 67 (1980)). Courts have also interpreted such penalties as restitution and fines in terms of repayment and justice to victim and community, rather than as rehabilitative only. Finally, Washington's Juvenile Justice Act of 1977 has been applied and interpreted as allowing punishment outright—but not yet with all associated adult criminal rights (*State* v. *Lawley*, 91 Wash. 2d 654 (1979)). While the courts were careful to refrain from saying that juveniles deserved to be punished for their misdeeds, they clearly opened up the goals issue to several alternate meanings not made explicit before.

PROBATION IN TRANSITION: SHRINKING BUT NOT CHANGING?

Given the scarcity of empirical data on what juvenile probation officers do and what they think about the mission of the juvenile court, our comments in this section must be guarded. We offer some tentative conclusions regarding the nature and directions of juvenile probation work. These conclusions are based on our personal familiarity with this occupation gained through reading, research, conversation, and work (as probation officer and as trainer).

Early Progressive Era (Beginning of the Twentieth Century)

Useful historical research has been done on the nature of probation work during the early years of the juvenile court (Schlossman, 1977; Rothman, 1980; Platt, 1969). Hence, the origins of the juvenile court probation service as a volunteer effort is well known, as is the rapid shift to a paid staff. Moreover, we know that these early officers were an aggressive component of the larger Progressive movement toward reforming the poor. Thus, Schlossman concludes his analysis of juvenile probation practice during the early years of this century in this fashion:

> The sponsors of the juvenile court . . . conceived of the modern city much as a seventeenth-century "little commonwealth," where moral boundaries were known by all and were easily enforceable. Then they cast the probation officer in the role of a Puritan tithingman, or moral inspector, who was to canvass individual households and assure uniformity in behavior and thought (along middle-class lines, of course). Together with truant officers, visiting teachers, visiting nurses, visiting home economists, public health inspectors, and a variety of other private voluntary organizations, probation officers were to be part of a new civic phalanx devoted to standardizing socialization practices in the modern urban community—the new tithingmen. (Schlossman, 1977:190)

Such historical research on the Progressive period is similar to much of the research on subsequent and contemporary probation in its focus on probation's philosophy, its relationship to larger movements and more central crime response agencies, and its investigative and court presentation practices. In the process, supervision practices have tended to be ignored.

Of course, supervision is much more difficult to observe than court performances. But we suspect that the scholarly neglect of supervision reflects a presumption that it is less consequential than court activities, a presumption probably shared by probation officers whose work product is most visible in the court (Czajoski, 1969). But if probation officers spend the bulk of their time in supervision-related activities (Carlson and Parks, 1979:311–47), and if "probation is reporting" (Thomson 1982: 205), and if probation as a status means something, then some attention must be given to all phases of juvenile probation work, supervision as well as intake and investigation (Lemert and Dill, 1978).

End of the Progressive Era (Mid-Century)

Perhaps the most comprehensive research treatments of juvenile probation work are the pre-*Gault* ethnographic studies of Cicourel (1968) and Emerson (1969). Since the due process initiatives in juvenile court heralded by the *Gault* decision in 1967, research has focused more on the impacts of these decisions on courtroom practices and outcomes (Stapleton and Teitelbaum, 1972; Ito and Stapleton, 1981), the structure and organization of juvenile courts (Sarri and Hasenfeld, 1976), and a variety of supplements to regular probation (Coates et al., 1978). Again, probation practice as an entity in itself has not been very visible. The following description of juvenile probation work in the years immediately preceding *Gault* is based primarily on Cicourel and Emerson.

By the 1960s, juvenile probation work had become much more routinized than in its early volunteer days, and much more integrated into the governmental network of legal enforcement agencies. Whereas the bulk of the juvenile court's referrals in its first decades came from social agencies, by the middle of the century, most referrals were coming from the police. Probation intake became part of the political economy of enforcement, with probation officers adopting decision-making criteria compatible with the primary source of the court's referrals. In the absence of a due process imperative, probation officers lacked the legal resources to do anything but acquiesce in what was generally perceived as a utilitarian control enterprise.

In the investigation function, probation officers, like police juvenile officers, attempted to elicit information from youth but employed an ersatz version of the social work interview and lacked the juvenile officer's network of intelligence (Cicourel, 1968:69). Like their predecessors, 1960s probation officers were more interested in getting at "underlying problems" than in the delinquent act itself. This focus gave the probation officer great latitude both in directing the investigations and in arriving at conclusions and recommendations. Hence, the investigating probation officer could generate organizationally desirable conclusions by steering the interview toward superficially explanatory topics while omitting other topics (Cicourel, 1968:297–301). The process, as observed in one interview, consisted largely of "searching questions to document the P.O.'s theories about 'what happened' and the juvenile's motivations for her actions. Thus each question was not a probe searching for basic information, but a follow-up of unstated assumptions about what 'really happened', calculated to elicit the documentary evidence to support the preestablished theories" (Cicourel, 1968:300). Consistent with this investigative stance was an official presentation of probation suprvision as a device to help delinquent children solve their problems (Cicourel, 1968:299).

In practice, however, cases were "dealt with in a highly routinized, bureaucratic manner" (Emerson, 1969:229). At worst, probation supervision was "decidedly short-term and negative," relying on a "disciplinarian regime directed toward deterring and inhibiting troublesome conduct" (Emerson, 1969:219). At best, it was passive and noninterventionist with the probation officer's assistance limited to referrals to other agencies (Emerson, 1969:227–228). Control was implemented via "stereotypical rules" applied on the basis of whether a youth's character was assessed as normal or troublesome. As a case became more difficult to control, the probation officer increased involvement and augmented legal power by imposing additional burdens backed by the capability to "surrender" the youth for violating probation, with incarceration functioning as the ultimate threat (Emerson, 1969:220–221). Since probation officers relied on a well-developed surveillance network including school, police, and parents to make such threats credible, youths tended to become suspicious of adults and distrust was a hallmark of the relationship between probationer and probation officer. And because it had been successfully integrated into the network of conventional institutions, probation failed to assume responsibility for advocacy on behalf of juvenile probationers vis-a-vis such institutions.

In this context—and we make no claim that such a description is representative of 1960s juvenile probate work, only that it illustrates some of the abuses possible in an overripe rehabilitation-justified control system—*Gault* and the due process revolution can be seen as a liberating force for probation work as well as for alleged delinquents. Unfortunately, the implications for the occupation have not been articulated nearly so well as the implications for its clients.

Early Equitable Era (1967 to 1975)*:
Juggling Due Process, Deinstitutionalization,
Diversion, and Dollars

Following *Gault*, the most valuable ethnographic studies of correctional field services have focused on adult parole (Studt, 1973, and McCleary, 1978). While there are many similarities in the ways in which adult parole and juvenile probation officers work their caseloads, for present purposes we must rely for information regarding post-*Gault* juvenile probation work practices on fragmentary evidence from studies of California corrections in the 1970s (Lerman, 1975; Lemert and Dill, 1978). Supplementary material at the national level, derived primarily from a survey, is available from Sarri (1976).

Lerman found that in the Community Treatment Project, initiated in 1960, juvenile parole agents, functioning in a role very much like one required in intensive probation work, tended over time to rely heavily on temporary detention as a social control device. While agents frequently justified this practice in therapeutic language, their agency appeared to move away from the I-level classification system which had been heralded as the technological vehicle for effective treatment (Lerman, 1975:72–77). During the course of this innovation, justified as a program of deinstitutionalization through intensive treatment (Lerman, 1975:19), social control efforts apparently predominated but were justified with the rhetoric of treatment, as a result of several organizational factors (Lerman, 1975:90–104).

---

*The term "Equitable Era" is our own. It is meant to capture the positive aspects of what has transpired in sentencing and correction in the past two decades with the advent of the due process revolution. The year of 1967, marks an approximate beginning for this era. Another convenient point of demarcation is 1975, which saw the publication of influential books by Lipton, Martinson, and Wilks and by Fogel. Soon afterward came the National Advisory Commission on Criminal Justice Standards and Goals volume on juvenile justice (1976) and the Institute of Judicial Administration and American Bar Association's draft volumes on juvenile probation (1977a, 1977b).

Probation subsidy was another California innovation, established five years after the Community Treatment Project. It provided a fiscal incentive to reduce institutional commitments while fortifying probation operations. As in the Community Treatment Project, however, professionalization was apparently associated with increased social control (Lerman, 1975:199–201). Again, this trend would be less disturbing had it not been justified as rehabilitation, i.e., as something it was not, and had adequate due process monitoring been part of the package.

Another account of the Probation Subsidy (Lemert and Dill, 1978) fills in the picture of post-*Gault* juvenile probation work. The lesson of this study seems to be that, during the early years of the Equitable Era, policy focus and availability of funds produced a superficial emphasis on human services treatment in juvenile probation along with cosmetic organizational adaptations in that direction. A new definition of the occupation also emerged, built with the rhetoric of the "treatment professional" and the image of a higher and more heroic calling.

During the California Probation Subsidy, a perception of special supervision probation work as a calling emerged (Lemert and Dill, 1978:101–2). Special supervision was to be the main vehicle by which probation departments were to justify reduced commitments to the California Youth Authority. As this reform expanded, probation officers assigned to special supervision units came to see their work and themselves in a new light. They began to demand recognition of the professional correctional knowledge required for their new role and, to the extent they were free to treat their clients, to perceive their work as professional. They based their claims to professional recognition and autonomy on the premise that dealing with small caseloads required greater resourcefulness, ability, and dedication. They characterized regular probation supervision work as routine, monotonous, and uncommitted, placing a premium on impersonality, distance, and noninvolvement with probationers, whereas commitment and involvement with clients were required when working with small caseloads.

As probation officers were recruited to the special supervision role, many of them underwent something akin to a conversion experience. Instead of minor bureaucratic functionaries, they now saw themselves as "treatment professionals" (Lemert and Dill, 1978:102).

They characterized their previous philosophy as "punitive," and rejected it. In addition to the intrinsic satisfaction of their new role, these "reborn" nonpunitive officers also benefited from such tangible rewards as autonomy, the reduced caseloads themselves, adequate secretarial support, and special training. But the perceptual transformations of occupational identity seem to have had as much an effect on relationships within the occupation as on relationships with probationers.

In some departments conflict developed between the newly defined treatment professionals and their colleagues who continued in a more conventional role (Lemert and Dill, 1978:14, 102–103). While the rewards of special supervision work produced commitment to the profession and the department, they also stimulated resistance to the organization's system of control. Special supervision probation officers wanted to participate in organizational decision making as a means of controlling the conditions of their work. The structural consequence was a severe bifurcation of supervision responsibilities, as "subsidy staff differentiated into cohesive work groupings. In essence they became a self-defined elite corps with particular notions about their responsibilities to their 'host' organizations" (Lemert and Dill, 1978:103). Thus, an emphasis on human services treatment plus adequate resources to implement it and reward participation in the program fostered intradepartmental friction by augmenting, highlighting, and differentially valuing divergent approaches to juvenile probation work.

Such tensions were manifested in accusations that special supervision probation officers were overprotective toward their clients. Such accusations were evidence that special supervison had failed to provide the kind of core technology or powerful rhetorical imagery needed to capture the field; in addition, the charges reflected the disparities in liberty infringements that can be produced by unmonitored discretion.

Curiously, despite the substantial levels of expenditures and the missionary zeal with which special supervision was received by some, the Probation Subsidy in some jurisdictions produced little in the way of a long-lasting legacy of correctional treatment. Instead, experimentation sometimes meant a half-hearted application or expansion of a variety of therapies that "did not succeed in standardizing or crystallizing a new body of specialized skills justifiable as treatment" (Lemert and Dill, 1978:183). Thus, such important outcomes as reductions in the number of youths committed to state institutions (albeit apparently purchased by increases in local incarceration (Lerman, 1975)) appeared to be more the result of expedient organizational and occupational adaptations than of long-lasting changes in attitude or in the content of juvenile probation work (Lemert and Dill, 1978:191).

Again probation was defined as an alternative to something else (incarceration) rather than as an entity in itself (Thomson, 1983). The key objective was to reduce institutional commitments; strengthening probation was at most a means to that end, and perhaps litle more than a way to justify it. There is little compelling evidence that juvenile probation supervision during this period was given much credence as either a penalty or an opportunity for teaching the importance of responsible behavior.

While the California Community Treatment Project and Probation Subsidy reforms of 1960s and 1970s were atypical in terms of both their size and their pioneer status, they highlight broader trends in juvenile probation work during the early years of the Equitable Era. Neither the extent nor the consequences of the due process revolution signaled by *Gault* had yet been appreciated.

Just as important was the attention focused on criminal justice agencies with the work of the President's Commission on Law Enforcement and the Administration of Justice in 1967. The creation of the Law Enforcement Assistance Administration and the appropriation of monies for invigorating state and local law enforcement efforts, the expansion of educational and training opportunities, and other commissions and their reports followed. While it received relatively little attention, probation did share in the wealth. Juvenile probation work became more "professionalized" as entry requirements, promotional standards, and pay scales were raised; staff size and caseloads increased; and disagreements festered between the new "treatment professionals" and their old-line colleagues.

And, in a way, probation was put on the spot. For years it had claimed that it had never been given adequate resources to do its job; now the new largesse provided "the chance of 'proving up' the claim that probation could be an effective form of treatment" (Lemert and Dill, 1978:14). The extent of contemporary skepticism and retrenchment suggests that probation did not adequately redeem this opportunity.

These California examples indicate ways in which juvenile probation practice was affected by the diversion and deinstitutionalization movements of the 1960s and 1970s. The due process movement has also had its effects, sometimes in combination with those of diversion. For example, in Cook County (Chicago) Juvenile Court, probation officer screening of delinquency complaints was discontinued in the late 1960s because of concerns about its due process propriety. In 1973 and 1974, the Court reinstituted the practice under the banner of diversion, then a fashionable movement espoused by the National Commission on Criminal Justice Standards and Goals, among others. By the early 1980s, decision-making discretion by Complaint Screening probation officers had been severely circumscribed by the prosecutor's office, both on the basis of its statutory perquisites and because of a desire to respond more forcefully to juvenile delinquency. Others (Rubin, 1979; Sagatun and Edwards, 1979) have noted the role prosecutors have assumed in areas of juvenile court operations formerly the province of probation.

Juvenile probation work has been similarly buffeted by the community corrections movement, although the influence on probation has been less obvious. The community corrections movement in the juvenile area has stressed alternatives to incarceration, deinstitutionalization, and intensive supervision of and specialized services for delinquent youth. While there has been some recognition of probation's claim to being one of the first alternatives to incarceration, the tendency has been to establish community corrections programs apart from the court and its probation service. The consequences have included greater visibility and understanding of the newer forms of community corrections, a residual function for probation (i.e., dealing with the presumably more tractable youth not referred to presumably more exciting programs), and, in political economy terms, a loss of power for probation. Consider the attention directed toward efforts such as the Community Advancement Programs (CAP), heralded as a key element in Massachusett's juvenile deinstitutionalization reform of the early 1970s:

> CAP takes youngsters who have failed in the modern version of probation and attempts to apply Augustus' original concept. They are placed in the care of counselors with case loads of no more than five, and sometimes as few as two. The counselors' most important responsibility is to know where the youths are and what they are doing twenty-four hours a day, seven days a week. They must see each of their charges four or more times a week. They are responsible for keeping them employed or in school, for their recreation, for vocational and educational counseling, for seeing that they get proper medical and dental care. If a youth gets in new trouble with the law, the counselors intervene on his behalf with the police and courts. If he has problems at school, the counselor tries to work it out with the teacher. He is expected to make frequent visits to the youth's home and talk about his progress with his parents. He often ends up being counselor not only to the child, but also to his parents, brothers, sisters, and friends. (Serrill, 1975:13)

One might ask why probation has not undertaken such "deep-end" efforts, consistent as they apparently are with John Augustus's vision for this line of work? It seems quite likely that this failure is the result of probation's expansion and institutionalization. Augustus's efforts were heroic but, by definition, the efforts of a majority of the members of an occupation will be routine, not heroic. Similarly, the efforts of organizations such as CAP are heroic and, not coincidentally, such organizations experience high rates of burnout and turnover.

The probation occupation, as an entrenched public service, presumably deals with somewhat less challenging cases in more routine ways. This is not meant to disparage probation. Such an approach is necessary if probation is to handle a large number of cases. In effect, there is an organizational division of labor, with newer community corrections entities handling small numbers of "veteran" delinquents and probation departments dealing with large numbers of presumably less risky, less needy, less troublesome youths. While the latter function may be undramatic, it is socially important unless either a majority of adjudicated delinquents are to be released unsupervised or a huge amount of resources is to be devoted to more vigorous reactions to them.

For present purposes, this division of labor is even desirable since it frees juvenile probation officers to operate as officers of the court, intent on ensuring that the law is honored and delinquent youth given the opportunity to accept responsibility for their behavior. Since probation has left some of the heavy counseling responsibilities to others, the role of the officer can be somewhat less complicated. And there is evidence that juvenile probationers appreciate the distinction between their counselors, who advise and help them, and their probation officers, who exercise influence on their behalf (Murray et al., 1978:102–103).

Yet recognition of the primacy of law in juvenile court and in its probation operations does not mean that the juvenile court should be a miniature criminal court. As we have attempted to demonstrate in the beginning pages of this chapter, there are compelling reasons why the juvenile court should maintain a distinctive identity, even within the just deserts framework we propose. The concept of culpability provides both the rationale for reduced penalties for juveniles (assumption of diminished capacity) and the justification for offering aid (assumption that errant youth should be allowed a special opportunity for help in maturing into responsibility). Such a position is not nearly as far from current practice as the notion of just deserts for juvenile court may have seemed to imply (Shireman, 1976). The major changes called for by a justice approach have to do with determinacy of sentencing and voluntariness of service receipt, as discussed below. Even here, we are not breaking entirely new ground, given Washington's and Florida's experiences with juvenile determinate sentencing and a longstanding skepticism about "enforced therapy" (Kittrie, 1971).

Recent Equitable Era (1976 to Present): From Expansiveness to Skepticism

There are some similarities between juvenile probation work and adult probation work, or even parole work. All involve investigative and supervisory activities, the need to recognize legal parameters, and tensions between the need to restrict and the desire to help. But since the general nature of correctional field services is presumably understood by most readers, and is covered by other chapters in this volume, our immediate interest is in what is distinctive about juvenile probation work today. We turn then to the same data set analyzed in the last section of the preceding chapter (Thomson, 1983).

Although that data set was limited to small probation agencies dealing with adult offenders, a sizable minority of respondents also carried juvenile probationers in their caseload. Since the proportion of such officers is small at the federal and state levels, we limit our investigation here to local officers supervising at least ten cases. Of these 414 officers, 54 percent had no juvenile probationers, 21 percent had juvenile probationers as less than half their caseload; and 25 percent had juvenile probationers as half or more of their caseload.

Juvenile and adult probation officers show some differences in their personal characteristics, as indicated in Table 5.1. Probation officers dealing with juveniles tend to be younger than those dealing with adults, and a larger proportion of the juvenile officers are women.

There appears to be a relation between probation officers' jurisprudential orientation and their assignment to juvenile or adult cases. Thomson (1983) has argued that jurisprudential orientation can be judged on the basis of the information officers consider most important to include in the presentence investigation report. An officer who stresses information pertaining to the present offense is more likely to have a retributive orientation, while those who stress prior record information are probably oriented toward deterrence, and an emphasis on social background, circumstance, or prognosis is associated with a rehabilitation orientation. Table 5.2 indicates how probation officers supervising varying proportions of juvenile probationers are classified along these dimensions.

Table 5.1. Sex and Age Distributions of Local Small Agency Probation Officers by Juvenile Probationer Share of Caseload (N = 414)

	Juvenile Probationer Share of Caseload		
	None	Less than Half	Half or More
Sex			
Male	176	61	63
	(79%)	(70%)	(61%)
Female	47	26	40
	(21%)	(30%)	(39%)
Age			
Under 30	68	27	49
	(30%)	(31%)	(48%)
30–39	80	32	37
	(36%)	(37%)	(36%)
40–49	38	11	7
	(17%)	(13%)	(7%)
50 and over	37	17	10
	(17%)	(20%)	(10%)
Mean age (based on age data not collapsed)	37.3	38.0	32.3

Source: Survey of Agencies (SA) and Survey of Probation Officers (SPO), 1979 (both under the auspices of the Staff Training for Small Probation Agencies project).

Table 5.2   Jurisprudential Orientation by Juvenile Probationer Share of Caseload (N = 391)

	Juvenile Probationer Share of Caseload		
Jurisprudential Orientation	None	Less than Half	Half or More
Retribution	61	22	23
	(29%)	(27%)	(23%)
Deterrence	91	27	23
	(43%)	(33%)	(23%)
Rehabilitation	58	32	54
	(28%)	(40%)	(54%)
Total	210	81	100
	(100%)	(100%)	(100%)

Source: SA and SPO, 1979
$\chi^2 = 21.89$ with 4 degrees of freedom.
$\pi < .001$.
$\gamma = .245$.

The larger the proportion of juvenile probationers supervised, the less likely an officer is to take a retributive or deterrence perspective. A deterrence orientation characterizes 43 percent of probation officers supervising no juvenile probationers but only 23 percent of those supervising mostly juvenile probationers; rehabilitation orientation increases from 28 percent to 54 percent. The practice in many juvenile courts of characterizing the presentence report as a social investigation or social history report reflects the same differential approach by probation officers to the sanctioning of juveniles and adults.

Another popular way of characterizing probation officers has been in terms of the extent to which they operate like law enforcement officers or like social workers (Ohlin, Piven, and Pappenfort, 1956; Glaser, 1964; Crow, 1974). A particularly dramatic indicator of a law enforcement approach is the carrying of firearms (Keve, 1979). As indicated in Table 5.3, the carrying of firearms by small agency probation officers is strongly related to supervision responsibilities.

Thus, in offices in which probation officers are authorized to carry firearms, most (55 percent) of those who do not supervise juvenile probationers do carry firearms, compared with less than a quarter (22 percent) of those supervising mostly juveniles. Again, there is evidence that contemporary juvenile probation officers are less law enforcement oriented than their colleagues supervising adult probationers.

A final indication of work orientation is the proportions of their time probation officers allocate to various work activities. Officers were asked to estimate the number of hours they spend in an average week in each of fifteen activities. Table 5.4 presents this information in standardized form,

Table 5.3   Firearms Carrying by Juvenile Probationer Share of Caseload (N = 140[a])

Carry Firearm While Working	Juvenile Probationer Share of Caseload		
	None	Less than Half	Half or More
No	35	22	21
	(45%)	(69%)	(78%)
Yes	42	10	6
	(55%)	(31%)	(22%)
Total	77	32	27
	(100%)	(100%)	(100%)

Source: SA and SPO, 1979

$\chi^2 = 10.76$ with 2 degrees of freedom.

$\pi < .01.$

$\gamma = -.489.$

[a]Includes only those officers in offices in which probation officers are authorized to carry firearms.

i.e., as percentges of the total work week rather than as numbers of hours. While one might question the reliability of self-reported data gathered through a mailed survey questionnaire, comparison with more rigorously designed time budget studies (Allen et al., 1979:80–82; Carlson and Parks, 1979:311–347) reveals a substantial degree of congruence in reported allocations of time to various activities.

Since the work week is divided into so many categories, similarities, rather than differences, among the groups are most apparent. Nevertheless, there are several modest differences of note. As juvenile supervision responsibilities increase, officers spend less time supervising or counseling clients in the office, more time doing so in the field, more time advocating on clients' behalf, working with community agencies, and traveling, and less time in investigation and report writing. In comparison with the adult probation officer, the juvenile probation officer seems somewhat less office-bound, less dominated by court and bureaucracy, and more linked to community. Such features are consistent with work traditionally identified with child welfare activities and requiring attention to the dependency needs of youth.

In sum, the time budget analysis reveals some small differences, whose size perhaps reflects the truncated nature of the sample, i.e., the exclusion of juvenile probation officers in agencies not dealing with adult offenders. Perhaps more important than the raw percentages and numbers is the reality they probably reflect, i.e., differences in qualitative importance of central work activities and responsibilities at adult and juvenile levels. These in turn reflect role differences. In comparison with their colleagues, juvenile probation officers seem to be more tied into the lives of their

Table 5.4. Percentage of Average Work Week Spent in Each of Fifteen Work Activities by Juvenile Proportion of Caseload (N = 403 to 407)

Work Activity	Juvenile Probationer Share of Caseload			Pearson's r
	None	Less than Half	Half or More	
Client supervision in office [a,b]	22.4	21.8	16.5	−.18
Client supervision in field [a,b]	7.6	9.0	10.1	.14
Client supervision by telephone or mail [a]	7.3	5.4	6.4	.04
Advocating on clients' behalf [b]	4.5	4.7	5.2	.10
Working with and making referrals to community agencies [a,b]	4.4	4.7	5.7	.17
Information gathering for presentence investigation reports [b]	10.4	9.9	8.8	−.08
Other investigative duties	4.8	4.3	4.5	−.04
Writing PSI and other reports to court [b]	9.9	9.4	8.4	−.09
Other paperwork	7.7	7.9	7.5	.00
Making presentations in court	4.2	3.6	4.7	.05
Waiting to appear in court	2.7	2.8	3.0	.05
Traveling [a,b]	4.7	8.3	7.9	.20
Staff meetings [b]	1.9	1.6	2.3	.10
Administrative duties	5.7	4.9	4.9	−.07
Other activities [b]	2.0	2.0	3.4	.11

Source: SA and SPO, 1979.

[a]Grouped differences (shown in first three columns) are statistically significant at .05 level using analysis of variance technique.

[b]Pearson's r (shown in fourth column) is statistically significant, i.e., ungrouped measure of proportion of caseload consisting of juvenile probationers is related to officer allocation of time for that activity.

clients, who are relatively dependent and offer relatively more developmental potential than adults.

Other differences can be interpreted as supportive of this role distinction. Juvenile probation officers are more concerned with rehabilitation and function less like law enforcement officers. Their age and sex distributions are consistent with a reduced social distance from youth and, in terms of traditional sex roles, more nurturance.

In some ways, then, juvenile probation officers do not appear to represent as receptive an audience for desert-based sentencing as do adult probation officers. But as we have argued, the effects of such reform on juvenile court should be different from the effects on criminal court probation operations. In fact, the mediation, advocacy, and accountability activities of juvenile probation officers may provide important antecedents for the complex version of the justice model probation officer role suggested in the preceding chapter (Thomson, 1983).

This assumes that juvenile probation officers will be able to negotiate the shift to a positive interpretation of punishment. Their close links to community networks may help them more readily realize the reparative and requital functions of punishment. If they can accomplish this transformation, juvenile probation officers seem to have the wherewithal, in terms of work socialization and attitude, to act on the integrative potential of punishment and responsibility and to avoid the negative connotations of vengeance and despair with which retribution has inaccurately been associated (Empey, 1979).

Having completed this whirlwind tour of juvenile probation work over the decades, we can now draw some tentative conclusions about where it has been and where it is going. For each of the four periods of probation examined, we can identify a dominant imagery, justification, or rationale for probation and a distinctive institutional alliance or identification.

During the early Progressive Era (1900–1920), as described by Schlossman (1977), Rothman (1980), and Platt (1969), probation officers emphasized the search for an "underlying cause" of youthful misbehavior. In Chapter 9, Carey indicates that such a perspective continued to dominate, at least in practitioner literature, into the 1930s and 1940s in the form of the social pathology perspective. With the development and expansion of the juvenile court in the first decades of this century, juvenile probation was identified with other Progressive reforms such as mothers' pensions, child labor laws, and the Sunday School movement. Like them, juvenile court and its probation service shared the mission of socializing and saving of the immigrant urban poor.

By the last years of the Progressive Era, as described by Cicourel (1968) and Emerson (1969), juvenile probation had adopted somewhat different imagery and new sources of support. As intake and investigation, probation work had an inquisitorial cast, with the probation officer serving very much as a court functionary rather than as a child welfare agent. As supervision, probation work seemed to perform harasssment and surveillance functions for the court. Officers emphasized the control trigger, relying on their power to surrender the probationer to induce compliance. As probation departments accommodated to their environment of treatment and political agencies, officers became more closely identified with law enforcement, from which quarter they now received the great majority of referrals—in sharp contrast to the situation at the turn of the century (Schlossman, 1977). A greater affinity with law enforcement emerged even as probation officers continued to pay homage to identifying "underlying problems" and used interviewing techniques modeled on those of social workers.

After *Gault*, rehabilitation ideology and terminology flowered fully, manifested in social work imagery and traditional human services technologies (Lerman, 1975; Lemert and Dill, 1978). With the support of prestigious groups such as the President's Commission on Law Enforcement and the Administration of Justice, probation evoked considerable optimism as a prototype for diversion and alternative to incarceration movements. During this period, bolstered by educational resources, probation increasingly identified with social work and sought the mantle of professionalism. The occupation was perhaps wary of law enforcement, which was embattled during the late 1960s and early 1970s and was pursuing a different course of professionalization. Steps toward the professionalization of probation were accompanied by the expansion of formal social control, justified as rehabilitation, e.g., the increased use of "therapeutic detention" in the Community Treatment Project.

In recent years, with the decline of the rehabilitative ideal (Allen, (1981)), skepticism, if not despair (Empey, 1979), has become the order of the day. Confronted with muddled directives, juvenile probation officers have retreated to eclecticism. External forces have encouraged a greater focus on due process and public safety (Sarri, 1976).

Many continuities link juvenile probation today with what it was earlier. Since it is not our objective to predict what juvenile probation will become, but to suggest how historical trends may coincide with the desert-based model advocated, we shall not analyze here the possible paths lying before probation. Rather, we note that juvenile probation's history and current situation appear compatible with an occupational identification with the court and as a public service endeavor. This recognizes the demise of juvenile probation's delinquency intake function and anticipates the focusing of investigation and supervision on harm, culpability, punishment, moral requital, reparative opportunity, and community reconciliation. In the following sections, we shall delineate the basis of such an approach and outline what it might encompass for juvenile probation work.

A DESERT-BASED JUVENILE COURT: CAN WE BLAME AND PUNISH?

Despite the significant movement of juvenile court toward a more adult criminal court model, almost no reformers have described the purpose of delinquency jurisdiction in terms of punishment. As indicated at the beginning of this chapter, the issue has been skirted. Here we will put the matter baldly: what would a retributive juvenile court look like? We do not suggest that such a juvenile court will actually evolve; we have too much respect for the accidents of reform, as well as the complexities of a cultural institution such as the court. Rather we suggest that such a court would not seriously contradict the values of the juvenile court as it has come to be shaped in present-day society.

One difficulty in such an analysis lies in the lack of clarity about what just deserts, justice model, or retribution means in the context of criminal sentencing. For sake of this analysis, we offer the following four elements: 1) *wrongdoing* by a 2) *responsible* individual for which 3) *blame* and 4) *punishment* are imposed by the court. From this definition follow other features of a desert-based sentencing system: e.g., punishment must be proportional to the wrong, and like cases must be treated (punished) equally.

Autonomous Persons: Rights and Responsibility

To grasp why a desert-based philosophy has become so popular and how its analysis fits into the wrong-blame-punishment sequence, we can invoke two levels of criticism about the administration of justice in contemporary society. At the more popular level, critics have attacked the general inefficiency and downright harm done by government intervention in the lives of troublesome citizens (e.g., Platt (juveniles), 1969; Rothman (prisons), 1971; Stone (mental health), 1975). They argue that government has created problems in tendering solutions and in the process has grown too powerful and pervasive. There is need of less protective services built on a simpler set of goals (e.g., von Hirsch, 1976). At the more abstract level, the dominant positivism that supported the interventionist approach of government has been repudiated and a new analysis of social reality is grounded on the autonomous individual (e.g., Murphy, 1979) or a contractarian government which is not subject to the defects of utilitarianism (e.g., Rawls, 1972).

Concerning juveniles, the second level of criticism has been advanced by Houlgate (1980). He argues that juveniles are subject to overcontrol by the state on the supposition that they are not autonomous persons. Rights are denied them and they are treated as objects to be controlled rather than as persons to be respected. He explores several philosophical approaches to the question of whether juveniles should be considered to enjoy the same rights as fully mature adults. His conclusion is that there should be, at some point, a presumption in favor of according rights to juveniles who manifest the capacity for self-control and direction. Zimring makes the same point in his recent analysis of the legal world of adolescence (1982).

How this analysis fits into the sentencing debate may not be immediately apparent. But to us it establishes the basis for a desert system by creating a fully responsible individual whom society can blame for his or her criminal acts. In fact, Murphy's series of essays published during the 1970s do this explicitly. He argues that by repudiating retribution, the American criminal justice establishment paved the way for a diminution of personal freedom and subjected individuals to the control of government in the worst sort of ways (Murphy, 1979). The autonomous individual should be subject to government intervention only if he has violated the criminal law, and then only by way of a punishment which he deserves because he has freely chosen his criminal behavior. It then becomes just for government to punish, but only in proportion to the degree of the crime itself. Thus, while the philosophy of autonomous rights protects persons against an overintrusive government, it also exposes them to the consequences of their own choices in the form of a just punishment.

Relatively little has been written about juveniles' "right to punishment," though an early piece by Fox (1974) raised the issue. For instance, Houlgate (1980:178) balks at drawing conclusions from his analysis of juvenile autonomy when he comes to apply it to juvenile court. But it appears to be a legitimate inference that if juveniles are autonomous persons for other rights, including the rights of formal adjudication, they are also persons who have a right to be punished.

There is the subsidiary question of how we tell when a juvenile is responsible. The easiest way is to set an age line beyond which all will be held to be responsible. With juveniles this is not easy to do. We all sense that adolescence is a period of passage from immaturity and nonresponsibility to full personhood. But not everyone makes the passage at the same rate. Some kids mature early, in both the good and bad sense; others late; some, it seems, not at all. The common law set up a scheme whereby the youngster between seven and fourteen would be presumptively nonresponsible unless the state proved otherwise. After fourteen, the presumption shifted against the youth, who now had to adduce special evidence of nonresponsibility. Further, levels of blame differed at sentencing where youthfulness was taken into consideration. Current juvenile courts obviously make adjustments in blame based on an assessment of responsibility at disposition. They also do so in most transfer hearings where issues of maturity and sophistication are proxies for responsibility. In a desert-based juvenile court, this issue of fixing the responsibility line would have to be assessed carefully.

Blame and Desert

The second consideration in a desert analysis is blame, a distinctive feature of a retributive system. Utilitarians eschew the use of blame, and incapacitationists and rehabilitationists would have nothing on which to base it. It is, however, based on a common feature of everyday living, as Strawson indicates (1974), and reflects a common element ("stigma") in penological literature. Blame follows from responsiblity and choice of wrongdoing. It is a negative reaction to the freely chosen doing of wrong and is encompassed in such words as "repudiation," "denunciation," "reprobation," and the like. We argue that blame is *deserved* because of both the nature of the wrongful action and its free choice by the doer. The blame feature of criminal justice consists of the official judgment of conviction rather than the imposition of a sentence. Relatively little effort has been made in the literature to distinguish blame from punishment, though an early piece by Feinberg (1965) establishes the importance of doing so.

Over the years, the official ideology of juvenile court has been that no one was being blamed. Instead, the court was said to be making an inquiry about the needs that might lie behind a criminal act. But practice failed to reflect this rationale. In fact, the juvenile was blamed—or asked to accept responsibility—by each person on the system's assembly line: police, intake worker, judge, probation officer. Even more so were parents held accountable. As necessary parties to a delinquency petition, parents represented both the problem and the solution. It was they who had "failed" when their child committed a criminal act. It was they who could turn the situation around by undertaking better control over the malefactor. Juvenile court never did, nor was it intended to, exclude the blame element of punishment.

The problem with blame as a systematic component of a criminal justice apparatus is that it is both ineffective and overly effective. Blame for wrongdoing tends to be based on interpersonal relations (Bennett, 1980) and as such suffers in the translation to the official and impersonal setting of a court. It is one thing for a friend to berate you for a misdeed. It means a lot and has a bite that a stranger's denunciation just does not carry. But it is also vitally dependent on the restraints personal to the denouncer. If your friend happens to be a belligerent and loudmouth sort, you are likely to be overrepaid for your wrongdoing. This feature of control and proportion is supposedly the specialty of courts. But insofar as they are *blaming* rather than *punishing*, there are few formal restraints. If the only blame is the conviction itself, then it is both controlled and somewhat indifferent as a shaming device.

But convictions—and all the added features of official action by criminal courts, called stigma—are very hard to undo. Once a person has been labeled, or blamed, it seems impossible ever to be blameless again. This is a part of the new desert-based system that very much needs exploration to determine how one's debt to society is ever really repaid.

For juvenile court, we suggest the blaming feature of punishment is relatively amenable to current practice and escapes some of the weakness of the adult system. Despite the formality of juvenile courts post-*Gault*, they still embody a personal approach on which blame might more firmly rest. Further, blame is less destructive than in criminal court because juvenile adjudications are less likely to constitute a lifelong record. Finally, juvenile court has more of a community imprint than many adult criminal courts. There is a sense that the immediate community in which the court sits has a role to play. The juvenile and his or her parents are subject to the condemnation of those with whom they live.

The foregoing remarks may not apply in metropolitan areas where life is impersonal and mass-produced. Nevertheless, the court itself has retained features that fit well with a desert approach to juvenile justice.

Punishment: Nature, Amount and Purpose

The practical salience of desert to the current operating system is its guarantees of equity and proportionality. Disparity of outcomes among offenders alike in offense seriousness was the rallying call for sentence reform along justice lines (Singer, 1979). The argument was that a preventive criminal sentencing policy could produce (and justify) very different outcomes for much the same kinds of offenses; by requiring courts to determine outcomes strictly on the basis of the past offense, we could eliminate disparity. Whether the proportionality between crime and punishment were determined by explicit legislative norms, as suggested by the Twentieth Century Fund proposals (1976), or by legislative norms applied by judges, as suggested by Fogel (1975), or by administrative guidelines as enacted in Minnesota (von Hirsch, 1982), it was to be based on the seriousness of the offense and the culpability of the offender. Proportionality was a principle derived from the punitive nature of the sentence. Blame, reactive in nature, depended on the degree of wrong, which in turn set the limits for the penalty. Some mechanism was needed for ranking offenses into an ordering that would match a scale of penalties. As von Hirsch acknowledged in his early essay (1976), it would not be enough simply to transpose current levels of offense and maximum sentences. A serious effort was needed to account for how the present system is constructed and applied, and a neutral way to reassess the gravity of an offense. Moreover, we would have to develop a single measure for penal impact so that diverse sanctions might be used without violating proportionality.

That such a system has not yet been devised for adult sentencing may tell us something of the problems of *measuring* justice in its penal sense. It is this issue that has dissuaded some sympathetic scholars who otherwise find the goals of desert admirable but who fear the results will be disastrously increased penalties (Zimring, 1976; Bedeau, 1978; Sherman and Hawkins, 1982).

But apart from its implementation problems, just deserts has had difficulty explaining its negative character. Most of its critics observe that it appears to be punishment for punishment's sake. The purpose is to make a person suffer who has caused another to suffer, without notable gain for the parties or society. While there has been some effort among philosophers to rescue just deserts from this negativism (Moberly, 1968; Kidder, 1975), there has been relatively little on the professional side (cf. McAnany, 1979). Most defenders of the reforms content themselves with a "lesser of two evils" approach, saying that desert at least limits the reach of the state into citizens' lives and makes sure the penalty is applied equitably. Perhaps the best practical answer is to point to an increasingly popular sentencing alternative, restitution, for an acceptable and "positive" penalty that even rehabilitationists can accept. Of course, such a sanction may not be retribution at all (McAnany, 1978).

Translating all this to juvenile court may be impracticable and naive in the extreme. On the other hand, a number of efforts have already been made to apply sentencing guidelines to juvenile court which suggest that it might not be too difficult to articulate proportionality for delinquents (Utah, 1982: Washington, 1981). Obviously, a first step would be to eliminate all status offenses from consideration. If we wish to punish juveniles for criminal acts, then we must create a different order for any control features we may wish to impose on them for obedience to parental and derivative authority. Crime deals with the rights of others. In addition, criminal offenses have to be scaled in degrees of seriousness and comparable penalties assigned. Here again the Utah system has come up with a reasonable facsimile of adult guidelines, as shown in Table 5.5, which assigns a certain number of points to each offense category. The point totals are scaled to the nature of four levels of intervention (institutions—long- and short-term, community corrections, and probation) and length of terms.

The major obstacle to implementing a desert system for juveniles is fashioning an acceptable rationale for the use of punishment. Juvenile training schools probably always resembled adult prisons in most of their features. As much was implied in *Gault*. But the Court there recognized

Table 5.5. Utah Juvenile Sentencing Guidelines

		Life Endangering	Property Endangering	Against Public Order
	Capital Offenses			
Felonies	First degree	95	75	50
	Second degree	90	15	12
	Third degree	80	10	8
Misdemeanors	Class A	7	6	6
	Class B	6	3	2
	Class B	6	3	2
	Class C	2	2	1
Infractions		—	1	0

Source: Juvenile Court and Youth Corrections Guidelines, State of Utah, Oct. 18, 1982, p. 10.

that the official rationale of rehabilitation had a continuing value to the work of the juvenile court, though it insisted on narrowing the discretion to select juveniles for its application. If the system were now to acknowledge that its central purpose is to punish juveniles for their offenses, how could that be reconciled with its venerable tradition of rehabilitation?

Insofar as a desert system is an accountability process, juvenile court personnel probably would have little difficulty in accepting and using it. Very much of their work is in assisting the juvenile to recognize and accept responsibility to respect the rights of others. Parents become partners in this process as well, especially where probation works with parents to create a program of change in the youngster's behavior. Further, juvenile court personnel are not above seeing virtue in imposing a little pain to make the point that an offending juvenile has violated basic rights of others by committing the crime. In the past, they have had to explain this to themselves in terms of their rehabilitative ideal, as Lerman noted in his review of California's Community Treatment Program (1975). This hypocritical distortion of language would not be necessary if desert was part of the juvenile rationale.

The problem is then to reconcile rehabilitation with a justice approach. We perceive that responsibility provides a key link between these approaches. Individuals deserve punishment for their crimes because they are responsible. But the fact that they have chosen to violate the rights of others demonstrates that they lack a strong sense of responsibility. By doing the youth the justice of blame-punishment, the goal is to return him or her to the community as a right-choosing person. Whether this will work depends ultimately on the autonomous individual, but it remains a goal sought by the justice process itself. These ideas are all familiar to juvenile court personnel. The only novelty is in casting them in terms of justice and punishment, though in fact both are present in much juvenile court activity.

To achieve such ends, juvenile court might call upon its current assets of being a community-based agency of justice with a personalized technique in assessing blame. These assets would fit well with a desert-based system in the following ways. First, in assessing responsibility, juvenile court has always striven for a personalized version of the criminal event in which the youth's role and culpability are individually assessed. Further, the victim has frequently been included in intake processes where probation mediated a solution to settle the issue of the harm done. This process has the strength of concrete details, and there is no reason why these details could not add to a particularization of culpability which desert requires.

In measuring seriousness for both blame and punishment, the juvenile court can draw upon its community context to give more detailed expression to generalized schemes of seriousness set up for the state as a whole. While it is the state law that has been violated when a criminal act is committed, it is also the community's values that have been affronted. In a juvenile court setting, the community's reaction is much more likely to be measurable than in criminal courts. This particularization of the community has value because it makes more vivid the rights assaulted by the particular offender. Further, it offers a context in which the reconciliation feature of punishment might be implemented. In an impersonal and disembodied community, the offender can never be reconciled because there is no party of the second part to be reconciled with. Juvenile court may function better by including victims more intimately in the whole process, but also needs to recognize the community to which the juvenile offender might return.

A JUSTICE-BASED JUVENILE PROBATION

Now let us imagine that in some jurisdiction, following a protracted period of intense discussion, debate, research, and analysis, a justice model approach to the juvenile court is adopted. That is, as far as the court's delinquency jurisdiction is concerned, the focus is no longer on the youth's interests or the protection of the community but on administering justice as fairness, i.e., giving the offender, the victim, and the community their just deserts in terms of the amount of harm done by a particular offense and the cupability of a particular offender. What happens to probation work in such a juvenile court?

A minor effect would be that the language of the juvenile court would become more like that of criminal court. Thus, while it would probably be desirable to retain terms such as "delinquent" and "delinquency" to recognize the presumption of reduced culpability among juvenile offenders processed at juvenile court, "defendants" rather than "respondents" would be "convicted of a delinquent offense" or "plead guilty" rather than be "found delinquent" or "enter an admission to delinquency." Likewise, youths would be "arrested" rather than "taken into police custody," and "presentence investigations" rather than "social investigations" would be undertaken by officers serving on delinquency calendars.

More importantly, each function of probation work (i.e., intake, investigation, and supervision) would become more homogeneous across officers as discretion was limited, controlled, and monitored. The intake function of probation would be transformed. Decisions about overnight detention pending a hearing and filing of delinquency petitions would be the province of the prosecutor, using legal criteria, rather than of probation, detention staff, or the police. Thus, intake of the alleged juvenile offender would be handled by the prosecutor reviewing allegations to determine that elements of crime are present, that probable cause can be shown, and that this is an offense of sufficient gravity for the state to proceed. Intake of the victim would be handled by court services staff, who would make an initial assessment of what reparative measures are indicated.

Probation's investigation function would become more important, and would focus on issues of harm, culpability, and appropriate sentence. Thus, the probation officer doing the presentence investigation for offenders found (or pleading) guilty would have to determine the degree of harm to the victim and the extent and nature of reparative services required. Some of this information could be drawn from the intake report, but a victim impact statement would be a required part of the presentence investigation. The finding of guilt will have established a minimum legal level of culpability but byond that, the investigating probation officer would try to judge how aware the youth was of right and wrong and of the consequences of the act. The probation officer would identify the role of the offender in committing the crime, e.g., if multiple offenders were involved, was this youth an initiator and active participant in the crime or was he or she less involved? The probation officer would also address issues regarding the extent of peer or family influence on the youth's commission of the crime as well as the situational factors involved. For example, if the youth had not eaten for two days before stealing food, this would probably be considered a mitigating factor. A probation officer who discovered such circumstances during the investigation could file a neglect petition in the interest of the youth, thus enabling the juvenile court to respond with appropriate services but apart from its delinquency jurisdiction. Finally, the probation officer would have to assess which types of sentence, within statutory guidelines for a given offense, seem indicated, given harm done and degree of offender culpability, and which sentence types within this range the offender is capable of serving. Thus, for example, if restitution is indicated but the youth is unable to find employment, some other type of reparative arrangement may be indicated, perhaps victim services.

In a justice model juvenile court, probation supervision would be primarily a matter of facilitating compliance with conditions of probation (i.e., the sanctions imposed), with less emphasis on providing services to probationers and attempting to reform them. But since, under a justice model, preferred penalties are those that actively engage the offender as opposed to passive penalties such as incarceration, the probation officer will have to do considerably more than maintain records of appointments kept and missed. Probation officers will still need mediation skills as they assume responsibility for correction of the situation, rather than of the offender. They will frequently be dealing not only with the offender, but with the victim and parties whose cooperation are necessary to aid the probationer in completing the sentence, e.g., prospective or actual employers. When victim-offender reconciliation is an objective, group work and dispute resolution skills could be important. Perhaps community organization capabilities would be required if we take seriously the need for community as the justification for linking punishment with justice. But generally, offender services would be greatly de-emphasized in justice model juvenile court, being limited by the following criteria: 1) voluntary participation by the offender; 2) facilitating compliance with conditions of probation; 3) within the capability of the probation officer and agency to provide; but 4) with priority given to referring the individual elsewhere for services indicated by 1) and 2) (to prevent compromising the probation officer or coercing the offender).

Given all of this, how would probation work change? That would depend on what probation officers are doing now. In some jurisdictions and for some probation officers, the proposed roles might be quite compatible with current practice. In other cases, our proposals will have little relationship to what probation officers currently do and would be viewed with some alarm.

But the juvenile law need not be changed dramatically to accommodate a desert-based system of dispositions if we are correct in our assessment of both the meaning of desert and the values and practices attached to the juvenile court as a system of justice. While what we offer may seem to contradict everything the juvenile court stands for, we believe that as an exercise in trying to anticipate and control the consequences of changes already going on in the juvenile justice sytem, it may offer food for thought—and even practical action.

We do not anticipate that probation's workload will be reduced by adoption of desert-based sentencing in juvenile court and an associated and consistent alteration of probation practices. Although less time may be spent in client contact or intake activities, more may be required at the presentence investigation stage in differentiating levels of offender culpability, determining degree of victim impairment, identifying appropriate penalties and ways of monitoring their completion, and mediating reparative arrangements. Moreover, it is quite possible that client contact time will increase rather than decrease, given 1) continued provision of or referral to ameliorative services when probationers request them, 2) the expansion of the concept of client to include victims, and 3) officer commitments frequently required in implementing active, reparative penalties such as restitution, community service work, and victim services. To be sure, we expect variations across communities (and across courtrooms and caseloads), with some opting for a minimal response model, perhaps as a means of saving money. But, in general, we expect that justice model probation at the juvenile court will not release resources for other purposes.

BEYOND RETRIBUTION: THE JUVENILE COURT AND SOCIAL JUSTICE

Like other criminal sanctioning rationales, the justice model avoids more central concerns of social justice (Thomson, 1983). This limitation is particularly acute in the case of the justice model, since critics reasonably question the possibility of just sentencing procedures embedded in unjust legal, political, social production, and economic systems. A conventional rejoinder by retributivists is that 1) penal justice should be recognized as a circumscribed area within which expectations of doing good must be modest, and 2) social justice must be pursued through action along central avenues rather than neglected bypaths.

This response is less than totally satisfying when we focus on the juvenile court, an institution that avowedly pursues social justice in terms of the welfare of youth. Obsession with desert-based sentencing for delinquents could divert the court from seriously confronting this larger mandate. In concluding this chapter, we suggest a way, consistent with both the assumptions underlying the justice model and the imperative to seek social justice, that the juvenile court might accept its responsibility in this area.

An Entitlement Approach to Juvenile Court

In many jurisdictions, broad statutory language gives the juvenile court a mandate for protecting the welfare of children in its jurisdiction. This mandate applies most appropriately to the court's neglect and dependency jurisdictions. Although the court has typically intervened on the basis of harms or deprivations inflicted within the family unit on individual children, statutory language provides more expansive posibilities. Consider, for example, the Juvenile Court Act of Illinois:

> The purpose of this Act is to secure for each minor subject hereto such care and guidance, preferably in his own home, as will serve the moral, emotional, mental, and physical welfare of the minor and the best interests of the community. . . . This Act shall be liberally construed to carry out the foregoing purpose and policy. (Article 1, Section 701-2)
>
> Those who are neglected include any minor under 18 years of age (a) who is neglected as to proper or necessary support, education as required by law, or as to medical or other remedial care recognized under State law or other care necessary for his well-being. . . . (Article 2, Section 702-5)

It is apparent, then, that its child welfare responsibilities require the juvenile court to continue to play a role distinctively different from that of the criminal court. But if the court is to fulfill its social justice mandate, rather than simply serve a palliative function, this protection-of-youth role would require action in the interest of all youth exploited in certain ways. In effect, the court would be the state's ombudsman for youth as a class, and would function in an advocacy position vis-a-vis other governmental agencies, private agencies, and private organizations.

When a condition harmful to youth came to the court's attention—by whatever means, whether social investigation, a broader fact-finding investigation by probation staff, citizen reports, police reports, investigative journalism, or otherwise—the court could, as a last resort, conduct fact-finding hearings and issue orders for corrective action. Thus, the juvenile court might issue restraining orders on racial steering by real estate agencies, enjoin insurance companies from determining home fire insurance rates by area rather than by condition of a particular house, order increased surveillance at schools where children are being victimized, or bring suit against employers discriminating in hiring or employment practices against particular classes of youth or their parents.

In a way, this approach may be considered an extension of contemporary efforts by the juvenile court to intervene more energetically and more preventively to protect youth against exploitation within the family unit, such as child abuse or incest. The proposed approach, however, is considerably broader, going beyond correcting wrongs within family units to confronting larger structural inequities thought to underlie the family and individual probems on which the juvenile court has traditionally concentrated.

What are the implications for probation officers at the juvenile level? We are suggesting an ambitious program of reform for the juvenile court. A cadre of officers will be required to investigate exploitation of youth as a class, to attempt to remedy these harmful situations short of court action, and to monitor compliance by other agencies and organizations with the conditions imposed by the court in the interest of youth. These activities would be in addition to the duties probation officers would perform in regard to adjudicated delinquents and the duties involved in assisting individually neglected and dependent children and their families. This suggests major new roles for juvenile probation officers, more consistent with those of advocacy and social reform.

Save the Children—All of Them

The proposed entitlement approach to the juvenile court is based on a set of assumptions that are either basic to the justice model for sentencing or compatible with it. First, it seems unfair to provide services to children simply because of their discovery via conventional—and haphazard—legal processes. Rather, basic services—adequate food, shelter, clothing, care, and education—should be provided as entitlements to all children, regardless of whether they are delinquents, victims of delinquents, neglected by their parents, or deprived because of the way goods and services are distributed in our society. In many situations, the most equitable and effective way of filling entitlement deficits will be to intervene on behalf of all children hurt by a given situation rather than on a case-by-case basis.

There are two reasons for guaranteeing these entitlements for children. The more important is that it is morally right to do so. A purportedly child-centered society should have no qualms about guaranteeing that all of its children are adequately cared for. Moreover, it may be in society's long-run interests to provide such entitlements. That is, net social costs may be reduced, thus meeting the traditional juvenile court objective of serving "the best interests of the community." Should this utilitarian purpose not be satisfied, however, the moral justification is sufficient in itself to support the policy.

The juvenile court, given its origins and history, legal mandate, and legal authority, is the most logical extant social institution to serve as the last-resort advocate on behalf of children for the resources to which they are entitled. This would rapidly become the court's most important function, and the determination and administration of sanctions for children legally proven to have violated the law would become residual activities. This would be an eloquent commentary on expected effectiveness of punishment and its value relative to distributional transformations in reaching for social justice.

The Entitlement Role of the Juvenile Probation Officer

What would probation officers (or more accurately, officers of the court, do in helping the juvenile court to fulfill its entitlement mandate? The role required would be a demanding one. Officers would have to be proficient in aspects of legal work, investigative journalism, applied sociology, mediation, and community organization.

The responsibilities involved and the required skills indicate that this would be a new role requiring a new title. For now, social conditions investigator (SCI) will do. SCIs would be charged with finding and documenting conditions harmful to classes of children, typically children living in certain geographic areas, e.g., police districts redlined by insurance companies, park district areas receiving inequitably small amounts of total resources, public housing projects in which the elevators do not work. SCIs would be persons trained in the social sciences and law, who would both initiate their own investigations and pursue the allegations of others to determine 1) existence of a socially harmful condition, 2) social inequalities fostered or perpetuated by the condition, 3) parties responsible for the condition, and 4) plausible links between the condition and social disadvantage of children in that area.

The SCI would then present the case to the juvenile court. It may be objected that this type of entitlement policy would exacerbate the problem of excessive litigation. SCIs, however, would attempt first to achieve correction of the situation by persuasion and mediation. Thus, the juvenile court would initially use its good offices to achieve voluntary correction of the condition. Failing that, the situation would be publicized and resources of media, civic action organizations, community groups, and professional associations would be mobilized. Only as a last resort would the juvenile court bring civil suit against the offending party, or join as *amicus curiae* in such an action.

This proposed role is reminiscent of the more active orientation of probation during the Progressive Era, when "the probation officer was anything but passive; he did not simply administer cases brought to his attention by others, but sought out potentially justiciable cases on his own" (Schlossman, 1977:252). The vast majority of juvenile court cases around the turn of the century (at least in Milwaukee, where Schlossman did much of his research) were initiated by the court. Today, however, the great majority of delinquency referrals come from the police.

While juvenile court officers investigating social conditions would share with their Progressive Era counterparts an aggressive approach to their work, the content of that work would be markedly different. Caught up in the ascendancy of the rehabilitative ideal and the emphasis on individual and family reform and early intervention which characterized the era (Allen, 1981; Schlossman, 1977), probation officers during the early years of the juvenile court sought out problem situations in families, particularly among the poor and the immigrants. Working within a desert/responsibility/social justice framework, juvenile court probation officers of the future would seek out systemic and organizational situations harmful, directly or indirectly, to entire classes of children, e.g., in a particular neighborhood or at a given school.

REFERENCES

Allen, Francis A. (1981). *The Decline of the Rehabilitative Ideal: Penal Policy and Social Purpose*. New Haven: Yale University Press.

Allen, Harry E., Eric W. Carlson, and Evalyn C. Parks (1979) *Critical Issues in Adult Probation: Summary*. Washington, D.C.: U.S. Department of Justice.

Bedau, Hugo A. (1978). "Retribution and the Theory of Punishment." *Journal of Philosophy* 75:601–13.

Bennett, Jonathan (1980). "Accountability." In Zak Van Straaten (ed.), *Philosophical Subjects: Essays Presented to P. F. Strawson*. Oxford: Clarendon Press.

Carey, James T. (1984). "The Professionalization of Probation: An Analysis of the Diffusion of Ideas." Chapter 9 in this volume.

Carey, James T., and Patrick D. McAnany (1983). *Introduction to Delinquency: Youth and the Law*. Englewood Cliffs, NJ: Prentice-Hall.

Carlson, Eric W., and Evalyn C. Parks (1979). *Critical Issues in Adult Probation: Issues in Probation Management*. Washington, D.C.: U.S. Department of Justice.

Cicourel, Aaron V. (1968). *The Social Organization of Juvenile Justice*. New York: Wiley.

Coates, Robert, Alden Miller, and Lloyd Ohlin (1978). *Diversity in a Youth Correctional System*. Cambridge, MA: Ballinger.

Crow, Richard T. (1974). *The Perceptions of Training Needs of Adult Probation and Parole Officers in Colorado*. Ann Arbor: University Microfilms.

Czajoski, Eugene H. (1969). "Functional Specializations in Probation and Parole." *Crime and Delinquency* 15:238–46.

Davis, Samuel M. (1980). *Rights of Juveniles: The Juvenile Justice System*, 2nd ed. New York: Broadman.

Emerson, Robert (1969). *Judging Delinquents: Context and Process in Juvenile Court*. Chicago: Aldine.

Empey, LaMar T. (1979). "Foreword—From Optimism to Despair: New Doctrines in Juvenile Justice." In C. A. Murray and L. A. Cox, Jr., *Beyond Probation: Juvenile Corrections and the Chronic Delinquent*. Beverly Hills: Sage.

Feinberg, Joel (1965). "The expressive function of punishment." *The Monist* 49:397–423.

Fogel, David (1975). ". . . We Are the Living Proof . . . ," *The Justice Model for Corrections*. Cincinnati: Anderson.

Fox, Sanford J. (1974). "The reform of juvenile justice: the child's right to punishment." *Juvenile Justice* 25:2–9.

Glaser, Daniel T. (1964). *The Effectiveness of a Prison and Parole System*. Indianapolis: Bobbs-Merrill.

Houlgate, Laurence D. (1980). *The Child and the State: A Normative Theory of Juvenile Rights*. Baltimore: Johns Hopkins University Press.

Illinois (1981). *Illinois Revised Statutes Annotated*. St. Paul, MN: West.

Institute of Judicial Administration and American Bar Association (1977). *Juvenile Justice Standards Project*, 23 vols. Cambridge, MA: Ballinger.

—— (1977a). Standards Relating to Corrections Administration (tentative draft). Cambridge, MA: Ballinger.

—— (1977b). Standards Relating to the Juvenile Probation Function: Intake and Predisposition Investigative Services. Cambridge, MA: Ballinger.

Ito, Jeanne A., and Vaughan Stapleton (1981). "The Role of Court Type in Juvenile Court Dispositional Outcomes." Paper presented at the Annual Meeting of the Southern Sociological Society in Louisville, Kentucky.

Keve, Paul W. (1979). "No Farewell to Arms." *Crime and Delinquency* 25:425–35.

Kidder, Joel (1975). "Requital and Criminal Punishment." *International Philosophical Quarterly* 25:255–78.

Kittrie, Nicholas N. (1971). *The Right to Be Different: Deviance and Enforced Therapy*. Baltimore: Johns Hopkins University Press.

Lemert, Edwin M., and Forrest Dill (1978). *Offenders in the Community: The Probation Subsidy in California*. Lexington, MA: D.C. Heath.

Lerman, Paul (1975). *Community Treatment and Social Control: A Critical Analysis of Juvenile Correctional Policy*. Chicago: University of Chicago Press.

Lipton, Douglas, Robert Martinson, and Judith Wilks (1975). *The Effectiveness of Correctional Treatment: A Survey of Treatment Evaluation Studies*. New York: Praeger.

McAnany, Patrick D. (1979). "Justice for the Justice Model: Exorcising Some Myths." Paper presented at American Society of Criminology meeting, San Francisco, November 1979.

——— (1978). "Restitution as Idea and Practice: The Retributive Prospect." In Burt Galloway and Joe Hudson (eds.) *Offender Restitution in Theory and Action*. Lexington, MA: D.C. Heath.

McCleary, Richard (1978). *Dangerous Men: The Sociology of Parole*. Beverly Hills: Sage.

Minnesota Department of Corrections (1981). "Release Guidelines for Juvenile Offenders." *Perspectives* 7:1–3.

Moberley, Walter (1965). *The Ethics of Punishment*. London: Faber and Faber.

Murphy, Jeffrie G. (1979). *Retribution, Justice and Therapy: Essays in the Philosophy of Law*. Dordrecht, Holland: D. Reidel.

Murray, Charles A., Doug Thomson, and Cindy B. Israel (1978). *UDIS: Deinstitutionalizing the Chronic Juvenile Offender*. Washington, D.C.: American Institutes for Research.

National Advisory Commission on Criminal Justice Standards and Goals (1976). *Juvenile Justice and Delinquency Prevention Report*. Washington, D.C.: Government Printing Office.

National Center for State Courts (1981). *Study of Structural Characteristics, Policies and Opeational Procedures in Metropolitan Juvenile Courts*. Williamsburg, Virginia.

Office of Juvenile Justice and Delinquency Prevention, National Advisory Committee (1980). *Standards for the Administration of Juvenile Justice*. Washington, D.C.: Government Printing Office.

Ohlin, Lloyd, Herman Piven, and Donnell Pappenfort (1956). "Major Dilemmas of the Social Worker in Probation and Parole." *National Probation and Parole Association Journal* 2:211–25.

Platt, Anthony (1969). *The Child Savers*. Chicago: University of Chicago Press.

President's Commission on Law Enforcement and Administration of Justice (1967). *The Challenge of Crime in a Free Society*. Washington, D.C.: U.S. Government Printing Office.

Rawls, John (1971). *A Theory of Justice*. Cambridge, MA: Harvard University Press.

Rothman, David J. (1971). *The Discovery of the Asylum*. Boston: Little, Brown.

——— (1980). *Conscience and Convenience: The Asylum and its Alternatives in Progressive America*. Boston: Little, Brown.

Rubin, Ted H. (1979). "Retain the Juvenile Court? Legislative Developments, Reform Directions, and the Call for Abolition." *Crime and Delinquency* 25:281–98.

Sagatun, Inger J., and Leonard P. Edwards (1979). "The Role of the Distict Attorney in the Juvenile Court: Is the Juvenile Court Becoming Just Like Adult Court?" *Juvenile and Family Court Journal* 30(2):17–23.

Sarri, Rosemary (1976). "Service Technologies: Diversion, Probation and Detention." In Sarri and Hasenfeld.

Sarri, Rosemary, and Yeheskel Hasenfeld, eds. *Brought to Justice? Juveniles, the Courts and the Law.* Ann Arbor, MI: National Assessment of Juvenile Corrections, University of Michigan.

Schlossman, Steven L. (1977). *Love and the American Delinquent: The Theory and Practice of "Progressive" Juvenile Justice, 1825–1920.* Chicago: University of Chicago.

Schultz, L. Laurence, and Fred Cohen (1976). "Isolationism in Juvenile Court Jurisprudence." In Margaret K. Rosenheim, (ed.), *Pursuing Justice for the Child.* Chicago: University of Chicago Press.

Serrill, Michael S. (1975). "The Community Advancement Program: Supervising Delinquents in Their Own Homes." *Corrections Magazine* 2(2):13–16.

Sherman, Michael E., and Gordon Hawkins (1981). *Imprisonment in America.* Chicago: University of Chicago Press.

Shireman, Charles (1976). "Perspectives on Juvenile Probation," in *Pursuing Justice for the Child*, (M. K. Rosenheim, ed.). Chicago: University of Chicago.

Singer, Richard G. (1979). *Just Deserts: Sentencing Based on Equality and Desert.* Cambridge, MA: Ballinger.

Stapleton, Vaughan, and Lee E. Teitelbaum (1972). *In Defense of Youth: A Study of the Role of Counsel in American Juvenile Courts.* New York: Russell Sage.

Stone, Alan A. (1975). *Mental Health and the Law: A System in Transition.* Rockville, Md.: National Institute of Mental Health.

Strawson, Peter F. (1974). *Freedom and Resentment and Other Essays.* London: Methuen.

Studt, Elliott (1973). *Surveillance and Service in Parole.* Washington, D.C.: National Institute of Corrections.

Sussman, Alan (1978). "Practitioner's Guide to Changes in Juvenile Law." *Criminal Law Bulletin* 14:311–42.

Thomson, Doug (1982). *The Social Organization of Enforcement Behaviors in Probation Work.* Ann Arbor, MI: University Microfilms.

———— (1983). "Prospects for Justice Model Probation." Chapter 4 in this volume.

Twentieth Century Fund (1976). *Task Force Report on Sentencing: Fair and Certain Punishment.* New York: McGraw-Hill.

———— (1978). *Task Force Report on Sentencing Policy Toward Young Offenders: Confronting Youth Crime.* New York: Holmes and Meier.

Utah (1982). *Juvenile Court and Youth Corrections Guidelines For Level of Restrictiveness and Length of Secure Confinement.* Salt Lake City: Department of Social Services.

von Hirsch, Andrew (1976). *Doing Justice: The Choice of Punishments.* New York: Hill and Wang.

————— (1982). "Constructing Guidelines for Sentencing: The Critical Choices for Minnesota Sentencing Guidelines Commission." *Hamline Law Review* 5:164–215.

Washington (1981). *Washington Code Annotated, Ch. 13.040.* St. Paul, Minn.: West.

Zimmerman, Mary K., and David B. Chein (1981). "Decision Making in the Juvenile Court." *Social Work Research and Abstracts* 17:14–21.

Zimring, Franklin E. (1976). "Making the Punishment Fit the Crime: A Consumer's Guide to Sentencing Reform." The Hastings Center Report 6:13–17.

————— (1982). *The Changing Legal World of Adolescence.* New York: Free Press.

PART II

Probation Ideology and Structure

Chapter 6

Models of Probation Supervision

*David E. Duffee**

Like any other aspect of organized criminal punishment, probation has had a circuitous and conflict-ridden history. Probation is both a criminal sentence and an organization for the implementation of sentences. It has been considered leniency or mercy as well as active control and intervention in the lives of persons who undergo it. It has been influenced by a variety of philosophies and ideologies, often simultaneously. Moreover, probation has been so varied in administrative structure, resources, and results—over time, from place to place, and in one place and time as it is experienced by different offenders—that for many purposes generalizations about "it" are often misleading. There are many different probation systems operating in many different contexts.

The research project that gave rise to this set of papers examined some of the variations in small and rural probation offices, and to some extent compared variations in problems, practices, and training needs of these small offices and of large, urban probation departments (Thomson and Fogel, 1980). While that project has produced helpful findings, particularly regarding staff training and training deficiencies, its greatest contribution

*Department of Criminal Justice and Public Policy, State University of New York at Albany

may well be not what it has finished but what it has begun. One of its major conclusions is simply that we know very little about the variations in probation and perhaps even less about the significance of the variations that have been observed. In some respects there is as much variation within size categories as between them for example, (Thomson and Fogel, 1980:4). Currently, we do not know many of the dimensions on which probation organizations and practices could be usefully ordered. In other cases we are even ignorant of the variations in outcomes or results that need explanation.

These deficiencies in information and understanding are important—particularly right now. For a variety of reasons, some internal, some external, probation systems face serious challenges. Recent reports of the General Accounting Office (1976, 1975) have attacked both local and federal probation, calling the former "systems in crisis" and the latter mismanaged. Some have suggested or implied that probation as it now operates should be replaced by police surveillance or a system of fines. Others have argued that the resources of probation have been seriously misplaced and should be redistributed to victims and witnesses of crime. At the same time, probation as a sentence is being used more than ever before. And to probation are being added restitution, community service, initial jail time, and other innovative conditions that may change the entire character of the sanction.

In short, probation is facing changes that will affect a large number of people. And yet we know little about the systems that are to be changed and consequently little about the feasibility of those changes or the nature of their effects.

In this situation, it is important to try to develop coherent statements about the mission or missions of probation. One initial step in the search for guiding reform is the task of modeling the systems of probation as they exist. We need more accurate, complete, and consistent models of the present if we are to achieve a planned future. This paper is a contribution to that modeling process. It presents a review and critique of some relatively well-known models of probation, parole, correctional administration, and supervision in other social service areas. Unless there is a particular reason for distinguishing probation from other activities, the discussion ranges across the entire set of programs and agencies. The stress is on the similarities and differences in the structure of the models, rather than on the differences in service areas and service roles on which the models are based.

Some pitfalls are inevitably encountered in this lumping process. Probation and parole officers do differ in important respects. Models of correctional systems do not focus on the same behavior as models that attempt to classify individual agents. The reader should keep these differences in mind. Nevertheless, all of the models *do* seem relatively similar. By and large, they focus on the goal conflict of public agencies that supervise troublesome clients, or the role conflicts experienced by agents who work in such systems. Moreover, each of these models, whether it deals with probation, parole, or public welfare, has *something* to say about probation. Hence we will reserve until the end of the paper comments on the relative applicability of these models.

All of the models discussed in this paper are relatively clumsy and unsophisticated. They are typologies—rather gross categories—of *some* aspects of client supervision, and *some* aspects of the organization of client supervision. Each of these models offers something of value: each offers some insight about significant, or allegedly significant, dimensions important to probation. Each inevitably fails to describe the full reality of operating probation systems. Typological models simply do not have sufficient variety and discriminatory power to capture all of the variation in living systems. But ironically, much of the value of such models exists in that failure—their distortions and blank spots, if appreciated and utilized, increase our powers of observation and multiply our avenues of inquiry. If their weak points and strengths are properly evaluated, these models can be used as guides for future research and future policy making.

EXISTING MODELS OF CLIENT SUPERVISION

Over the last thirty years, several writers have attempted to capture the essence of corrections, or of particular aspects such as sentencing, probation, or parole. A variety of starting points and methodologies have been used in these endeavors.

Some of these depictions have focused, allegedly, on the goals of punishment or on the mandates to criminal punishment agencies. There has been a good deal of discussion of retribution, deterrence, rehabilitation, incapacitation and the like. Many of these efforts actually focus on the justifications for punishing rather than on explaining the variety of structures and programs that may emerge in the course of implementing punishments. Consequently, some discussions are highly philosophical or jurisprudential and do not deal very directly with the public organizations that execute punishments and supervise offenders.

Some attempts to describe corrections take a somewhat closer look at what actually happens in punitive relationships. These often attempt to type or model at least parts of correctional practice. Some of these focus on decision making, others on policy making, others on supervision styles of correctional front-line staff, and others on relationships between staff and the persons under supervision.

These attempts to describe what is actually taking place *generally* differ from the goals or mandates approach in that these "models of what we have" are less likely to emphasize justifications for punishment or to stress the "right" way of doing things. While there is a link, to be sure, between justifications of punishment and the operations of punishing, operational models are more likely to accept the fact that probation, parole, prisons, jails, and other mechanisms of punishment are complex systems influenced by different ideologies, philosophies, and justifications. Because punishment is and probably will remain a heavily value-laden, politically controversial topic, the builders of operational models often explicitly or implicitly favor *one* model over another. They may offer either theoretical grounds why such and such an operation *should* be more effective or more desirable or some empirical evidence of differential effects in certain instances. Despite these tendencies, the operationalists will at least *begin* with an attempt to describe existing variety rather than to guide it.

The operational models vary significantly in methodological sophistication and level of abstraction. Some may be purely theoretical, although even these models are probably based on a good deal of observation. Other models are more inductive, in that at least some effort has been made to alter and refine initial concepts against empirical evidence. Some researchers have attempted to validate the variables used in the models against the attitudes or behavior found in real correctional settings.

Other models—often flow models or decision models—attempt to be even more inductive. They may simply attempt to describe *what* parts of the system are doing, rather than try to understand *why* the actions occur or are organized in a certain way. For example, some models may seek to count persons processed or rates at which persons are channeled in one direction or another, with little questioning of the motives, goals, policies, or objectives implied in such movement.

This paper will focus on the middle set of operational models described above. That is, we will review operational models that attempt to identify theoretical dimensions in correctional agencies or to clarify and order concepts. We limit our focus for two reasons. First, since the Probation Mission Project is concerned with policy-level developments in probation, it seems more useful to catalogue the means of describing present operations than to debate the justifications of punishment. At the same time, the Project is concerned with the potential of a developing probation mission. For that reason, models concerned with the clarification of concepts may be more useful than models that only measure directions or rates of client flows.

Single-Dimension Models of Supervision

One common approach to probation (and also to prison, parole, public welfare, and mental health) is the stipulation of a single goal dimension along which particular agencies, practices, or staff are expected to range. The opposite ends of the goal dimension are given various terms, depending on the type of human processing that is being examined. But in any case, it is argued that some agencies fall close to pole A while others fall close to pole B and that still others fall somewhere in the middle of the goal dimension, so that they display characteristics of both poles.

While the studies using a single dimension often refer to the poles as goals, the poles are probably more accurately described as cultural or political orientations (Griffiths, 1970, calls them "ideologies"), since they are never specific enough or complete enough to represent all the objectives sought by individuals or organizations. Perhaps the most widely known example in the criminal justice field is Packer's (1968) with its "Crime Control" and "Due Process" models of the criminal process. As in many other single dimension models, the poles are ideal types, which are never completely manifested in reality. Instead, it is presumed that both orientations are deeply embedded in American culture and more or less permanent values that exist in tension. Policy changes and conflicts in practice are explained as the continuing give-and-take along the dimension between the poles.

A similar approach has been taken in the analysis of prisons. In this case, discussion focuses on conflicts between "custody and treatment" or "punishment and rehabilitation." Hall et al. (1966:494) note that in individual correctional workers, "the role conflict which results from the discrepancy between protection and rehabilitation components of correctional objectives has proved to be virtually immobilizing." Halleck (1967:331) observes, "Correctional institutions have built in tendencies which undermine therapeutic progress." Likewise Cressey (1960) writes: "The fundamental organizational problem in progressive contemporary prisons arises from the directive to inflict punishment by custodianship while maintaining a program based on a new conception of the process of reformation, namely rehabilitation through treatment." Another observer, noting "that correctional institutions are conflict prone," suggests that "these conflicts arise out of the incompatible requirements of custodial and treatment goals," so that there is simultaneous pressure for "punitive control techniques . . . and permissive and close staff-inmate relations" (Zald, 1962:22). The American Friends Service Committee (1971:86) has been sharply critical of the adoption of the treatment ideal by prison administrators for the purposes of maximizing conformity among inmates and for controlling population flow. Other observers have suggested that the treatment-custody conflict not only has negative internal consequences for correctional agencies but also hampers their interaction with other organizations (Mandel, 1971).

While commentators on prisons have apparently settled on the incompatibility of punishment and rehabilitation as the key difficulty with prisons, a brief survey of other social service areas reveals that a similar emphasis on "polar orientations" is endemic in many areas of social policy. For example, it has long been argued that the public welfare system is hampered by its joint service and income maintenance functions. This joint control and service mission seems to have negative effects on individual welfare workers and on welfare organizations, in which it is difficult to reconcile the rendering of service with the watchdogging of public revenue (Ritti and Hyman, 1977). In the mental health field, conflicts are observed between goals of patient control, or maintenance of institutional order, and goals of care or service provision (Fairweather et al. 1969). Similar observations have been made about agencies caring for the mentally retarded (King and Raynes, 1968). As would be expected, the analysis of conflict in the juvenile justice system is quite similar to analysis of conflict in adult corrections. Choice between protection of community and welfare of the juvenile has been identified as a major conflict for judges in juvenile detention decisions (Gottfredson, 1968). Similar conflicts are also raised in types of social service that seem rather far afield from the administration of criminal punishment. For example, agencies for care of abused or neglected children (Koerin, 1979) and the elderly (Etzioni, 1976) seem vulnerable to similar conflicts.

In correctional field work (specifically parole), the best-known single-dimension model is probably that of Dembo (1972). Dembo argues that we need to examine three dimensions of the social-psychological orientation of parole officers: 1) conception of the parolee (as a type or as an individual); 2) view of parole purpose (protection of community or rehabilitation); and 3) belief in rule enforcement (literal, for deterrrence, or interpretive, as an aid). These three dimensions are later collapsed into two "orientations," that of punishment and that of reintegration.

In each of these social service areas, attempts have been made to reform organizations so as to reduce the conflict between polar orientations and thereby increase program effectiveness. In the welfare system, the administration of social services and income maintenance functions have been separated. This reform is supposed to free service workers from their policing role as well as to remove the client from the bind of accepting services in order to receive income supplements (Hoshino, 1972). In the mental health fields, the principal reform movement is that of deinstitutionalization. Following the work of Fairweather et al. (1969) and others, mental health systems seem to have largely abandoned their custodial duties in order to maximize treatment, in contrast to recent trends in penology. Similarly, organizations dealing with mental retardation seem to have moved toward deinstitutionalization, as has the juvenile justice system to some measure. However, we also see the reverse move in juvenile justice, where there has been some call for both more severe punishment and control (Krajick, 1978) and more secure facilities (Isabel, 1980). Systems for care of the elderly have progressively moved toward retirement communities and away from institutional settings. This change is intended to increase the self-sufficiency of the elderly and reduce the chances that the serving organization will control its clients to make service delivery efficient.

In other terms, we have been increasingly dubious about the efficacy of combining in the same agency the functions of "social control" and "mutual support" (Warren et al, 1974). Since many persons who need human services occupy a marginal status in the social structure (in terms of age, income, skill, etc.), the separation of control and support may be understandably hard to bring about.

Many attempts to resolve the conflicts between the poles appear to center on clarifications of the moral image of the client in question (Beck, 1967). Some client groups, by themselves or in association with more powerful political groups, have succeeded in reducing the moral ambiguity associated with their governance needs. The handling of mentally retarded children is a prime example. In such instances, reform has managed to distill the technology of the organization around its service core and to reduce organizational structures associated with high regimentation and routinization of clients (King and Raynes, 1968). To use Etzioni's (1961) term, the *scope* of the organization has been reduced. In other instances, reform seems to emphasize the moral undeservingness of clients, and in those instances to distill organizational technology around the question of scope or high control while reducing organizational services aimed at enabling clients to better themselves.

In other words, the single-dimension models of social organizations have led to a stress on the ineffectiveness, inefficiency, and in some cases the immorality of tying up both control and service poles in the same agency or the same set of programs. Reform has consequently stressed severing the poles somehow and thereby eliminating conflicting messages and double binds. While specific reforms use different languages and deal with different social problems, the general path of reform seems to be to take the bull by the horns—to say, for example, that while punishment may be unpleasant it is required, and it is wishful thinking to try to combine it with treatment; thus we should separate these goals or roles in different agencies.

Problems with the Single-Dimension Models

A few recent studies raise some doubt about the accuracy of analysis based on the two-pole models. Three studies will be reviewed here, one each from the areas of adult community corrections, juvenile justice, and social welfare. In each case, the researchers were examining the impact of organizational structure upon clients in agencies that had been reorganized with the explicit intent of reducing conflict in orientation. While the question asked and the methodology used are somewhat different in each study, all three investigations found that some of the problems and conflicts that had provided impetus for change reemerged in the new organizational forms.

Piliavin and Gross (1977) have provided an explicit test of the assumptions underlying the separation of services and income maintenance in public welfare. On the assumption that the separation of these two functions was intended to "provide services under nonadversary and non-demeaning conditions, . . . and to permit services to be rendered in a manner assuring recipients freedom of choice (Piliavin and Gross 1977:390), they evaluate the experience of welfare recipients randomly assigned to four different kinds of caseload. The separate treatments were devised by crossing 1) the combination or separation of income maintenance and social services with 2) worker-initiated or client-initiated service contact. If the assumptions underlying welfare reform had been accurate, then separating maintenance and service and providing service only when requested by the client would have resulted in greater effectiveness of service and greater client satisfaction. Piliavin and Gross found, however, that "recipients in the combined conditions express a stronger view that service workers are concerned with providing them with help . . . and recipients in the separated and client initiated conditions had a less positive view of their workers' helpfulness" (Piliavin and Gross, 1977:400). They also found that fewer services were requested and rendered under client-initiated conditions. The authors conclude that "separation policy was implemented without any knowledge about how social services were used by welfare recipients and what factors influenced client utilization. Thus social workers, among others, simply developed arguments consistent with the actions that had been taken" (Piliavin and Gross, 1977:404). In terms of the one-dimensional model, this study suggests either that control and service are not as incompatible as we thought, or at least that separation of these functions is not the answer.

An effort to reduce conflict in the juvenile system is described in reports concerning the deinstitutionalization of juveniles in Massachusetts (Coates et al., 1978). Deinstitutionalization was motivated by the conviction that custodial and treatment functions of large institutions were incompatible. Custody, it was argued, inevitably blunted and altered the aims of therapeutic programs (Miller and Ohlin, 1976). The most effective treatment would require that the system be reorganized to eschew the expressed intent of protecting the public from the youth. Had this hypothesis been correct, conflict between staff units should not have occurred in the new community-based programs and small residential houses for juveniles, and staff and juveniles in the new programs should have formed a more cohesive group.

Evaluation of deinstitutionalization in Massachusetts found that the same or similar conflicts among staff and between staff and juveniles arose directly out of certain types of service provision. For example, the youth rated staff most helpful when there was an emphasis upon high youth-staff interaction, as in group therapy, and when there was sufficient variety of staff that the youth were able to find at least one staff member with whom they could identify. But attempts to increase staff-youth rapport, or to increase attitude change, continued to conflict with the provision of educational programs and with efforts to increase the youths' access to or links with the community groups and resources (McEwen, 1977:48).

Allocation of youths to treatments in the new, reformed system also bore considerable resemblance to the old system. Inner city youths with the longest or poorest court records were the ones most frequently sent to intense, psychologically oriented programs that were relatively isolated from the community. Youths whose offenses were minor and whose fathers held white collar jobs were allocated to the more open programs, which gave greater attention to advocacy and community linkage (Coates et al., 1978:96). This allocation pattern occurred despite the observation that inner city youth are less amenable than others to intense psychological intervention and may be more in need than others of resource linking and advocacy activities that would help provide for their basic needs (Smith and Berlin, 1978:169–181). In terms of the one-dimensional model, the Massachusetts experience suggests either that separating control and treatment is impossible, or that separations at *one* level do not help at *another*. McEwen's work, in particular, suggests that *all* treatments exact some kinds of controls. If we stress attitudes, we may also tend to stress isolation. But neither the access emphasis nor the attitude emphasis were conceived of or organized as punishment. They both existed at the "treatment" pole on the single dimension. They just happen to conflict with each other.

Finally, Rudolph Moos provides us with some data relevant to adult correctional reform. Moos has worked for some years on the measurement of social climates in both mental health and correctional settings. His objectives have included the design of quantitative measures that would enable us to compare correctional units in terms of organizational ethos or "character." He has assumed that more accurate and replicable procedures for describing the social atmosphere or the environmental press of an organization upon its participants would make possible more sophisticated research on client behavior problems, such as violence or misconduct, as well as on the outcomes of organizational processing such as recidivism (Moos, 1968). His Correctional Institution Environmental Scale has been administered in a variety of adult and juvenile correctional organizations, to both inmates and staff. Moos later developed a similar instrument for the measurement of social climate in community correctional programs. The COPES (Community Oriented Program Environmental Scale) instrument taps similar dimensions of climate, although some variables are different because of the greater permeability of the community programs.

This classification analysis identified six clusters of programs for both the institutional and community units. The resulting social climate profiles for the institutional and community programs were so similar that Moos gave them the same names: 1) therapeutic community program; 2) relationship-oriented program; 3) action-oriented program; 4) insight-oriented program; 5) control-oriented program; and 6) disturbed behavior program (Moos 1975:246–251). In comparing institutional and community-oriented correctional units, he concludes:

> More than 30% of the community based programs have social environments that are not specifically treatment-oriented. Almost 25% of the programs are control oriented (i.e., they do not emphasize any of the Relationship or the Treatment Program dimensions). [This finding] leads to the conclusion that some institutional programs may be "better" (at least in terms of their social climate characteristics) than some community programs . . . On the whole, the movement toward community-based alternatives to regular institutional programs is clearly beneficial. However, it is impossible to classify community based programs as "treatment-oriented" and institutional programs as "control-oriented." (Moos, 1975:250–251)

A recent revision of Moos's social climate measurement by Wright (1977) calls into question some of the specific dimensions that Moos claimed to identify, but only strengthens the basic conclusion about community-institutional comparisons. Wright examined the experience of a halfway house program for adult felons that had been established specifically to combat the prison factors (such as inmate culture and inmate-staff differentiation) that are presumed to blunt the effectiveness of prison treatment. Some prison environments, it turned out, had fewer manifestations of the staff-inmate conflict and inmate culture characteristics than did some halfway houses. Ironically for prison reformers, Wright discovered that the halfway houses with the *most* prison-like environments were those that emphasized their *treatment* functions rather than custody functions (Wright, 1977:174–176). These data tend to corroborate the finding in Massachusetts that control as service, or control as an aspect of service, is not necessarily unique to programs with a manifest purpose of punishing rather than treating. Instead, certain staff-inmate dynamics and certain staff conflicts seem to be embedded in particular treatment regimes, independent of the polar orientation of the organization.

Two-Dimensional Models: Expanding the Conceptual Schemes

In response to the problems of the single-dimension approach to agencies supervising clients, a number of somewhat more complex models emerged in the 1960s. The point of departure from the one-dimensional models is the recognition that reliance on two poles does not explain a number of interesting variations among agencies and supervisory styles. Two difficulties with the single-dimension conception, in particular, made some people wonder whether polar opposites such as "rehabilitation" and "punishment" provide a satisfactory frame of reference.

One of the noted difficulties with the one-dimension framework involves the level of activity, the intensity, or perhaps the amount of commitment displayed by some agents and agencies. That is, there is substantial variation *within* as well as between the polar types. For example, among ostensibly punishment-oriented agencies, some seemed very active in the policing or surveillance activity while other agencies seemed relatively inactive. The mere failure to engage in intensive surveillance activities does not mean that an agency is treatment oriented; it may not engage in any active helping activities either. It would be impossible, some argue, to place the inactive agencies on the continuum between the poles. They "fell out." In other words, it was discovered that some agencies were so bureaucratic (in the pejorative sense) that they could not be said to have *either* of the polar orientations, nor could it be said that they fell somewhere in between the poles.

The second difficulty with the one-dimensional view concerns a somewhat more complex problem. According to the one-dimension model, agencies would either display *most* of the characteristics of *one* pole or display some, but not all, of the characteristics of both. That is, the "mixed" models, logically, existed in that tense field of comproimising values between two clear opposites. The mixing of the two poles was thought to involve a difficult give-and-take which would make them both less punitive and less therapeutic. However, observers noticed instances of actual practices in which the mix did not result in wash-out or compromise. Some agencies and some agents managed to maintain a "both" rather than an "either-or" orientation. Such cases could not be typed in the one-dimensional model. The existence of simultaneously strong orientations toward dual demands suggested that poles A and B were not necessarily contradictions.

Observing these anomalies, theorists began to play with the possibility that the presumably separate poles of a single dimension were in fact the high points on two separate dimensions. In many accounts, the first model to incorporate this recognition is that of Ohlin et al. (1956). Strictly speaking, these authors did not present a two-dimensional model of correctional casework. They spoke of "major dilmemmas" facing correctional social work and attempted to specify how caseworkers would resolve these dilemmas in different fashions. They used the most frequent solutions to these dilemmas to indicate types of caseworker orientation: the "welfare officer," the "protective officer," and the "punitive officer." The difference between their approach and single-dimension models can best be seen in their description of the protective type. This orientation, rather than compromising on punitive or welfare orientations, attempts to manifest both orientations at once by providing a good deal of active service as well as being highly active in conformity demands.

This ground-breaking typology soon led to the recognition of two dimensions underlying probation/parole officer orientations. Glaser (1964) completed the two-dimensionality of the Ohlin et al. typology by adding a fourth type: the passive agent, or the bureaucrat who was not active in either assistance nor control. In contrast to the one-dimensional approach, which apparently recognized the welfare agent (high on assistance) and the punitive agent (high on control), Glaser's model of federal probation officers' orientations allowed for agents high on both or neither dimensions. Thus, "treatment" and "punishment" (although these may not be the best names for the concepts), which originally were seen as opposite scalar values of *one* variable, were now seen as two separate variables each having its own scale.

Most two-dimensional models of probation, parole and other kinds of client supervision have followed Glaser relatively closely. The authors owing Glaser an intellectual debt include Studt (1973), Stanley (1976), Klockars (1972), O'Leary and Duffee (1971), and probably (although Glaser is not directly cited), Scheurell (1969), Hall et al. (1966), and Blake et al. (1979). There are, of course, a variety of differences among the two-dimensional models. Some are more important than others.

One difference concerns the *level* of the phenomena being explained. Most of these models (Glaser, Studt, Stanley, Klockars, Blake et al., Hall et al.) deal directly with front-line staff supervision of offenders. O'Leary and Duffee, in contrast, attempt to explain variations in correctional policy rather than face-to-face interactions at the front line. Scheurell's model seeks to combine an interest in the agent's interaction with the agency and the agent's interaction with the client.

Another difference is the terminology used for the two dimensions. The most common is assistance and control (Glaser, Stanley, Klockars). Studt makes a minor shift to surveillance and service. Scheurell speaks of agency orientation and client orientation (although Scheurell intimates that the agency orientation is demonstrated in practices that control new crime, or protect the agency from community criticism because of illegal behavior by offenders). O'Leary and Duffee identify dimensions called "concern for the individual offender" and "concern for the community," much like Scheurell. The remaining two are somewhat different from the others. Hall et al. write about an agent's displayed concern for the offender's "commitment" to a course of action and for the offender's "conformity" to a course of action. Blake and colleagues use the dimensions "concern for problem solution" and "concern for client as a person." Since concern for the client is demonstrated in the degree to which the caseworker supports and develops the client's feelings and beliefs, the concept of Blake et al. is very similar to the Hall group's "commitment" or "ownership" of the course of action to be followed.

In contrast to these relatively minor differences in terminology and level of focus, a more important distinction among two-dimensional models rests on the nature of one of the types. The two-dimensional models differ rather drastically in their representation of the "high-high" position. In some of the models (Glaser, Stanley) the officer seeking control and assistance simultaneously is a problematic figure, at least for the client and perhaps for others. This type of orientation, in their description, leads to very inconsistent behavior—helping an offender find a job one day and issuing a technical violation the next. It is this officer who wraps his client in a warm hello hug, bruising him with his gun butt as he does so. Hence, Glaser calls this type of officer "paternalistic." He has not, in fact, resolved the dilemma of competing demands but intensified it by passing it on to his clients. He cannot be trusted by clients because he is inconsistent. He can control the inconsistency to some extent—by concentrating assistance on some offenders and control on others, or by concentating on assistance one day and control the next. But Glaser makes it clear that the paternal officer has not found a consistent and coherent path incorporating both assistance and control in one new style.

In contrast, all the other authors, with the exception of Scheurell (whose models do not apply to this problem), described a high-high position that *reduces* rather than heightens conflict because it integrates rather than fragments the two demands. Studt calls this position the insider-outsider relationship between parole officer and parolee. The insider operates as a gatekeeper of opportunity, opening doors of membership and legitimacy in return for the client's conformity to the rules of the community he or she is entering. In the O'Leary and Duffee policy model, high concern for both individual offender and community yields a "Reintegration" policy that orchestrates changes in both community and offenders. Hall et al. see a high concern for both commitment and conformity manifested in the officers helping offenders find specific roles to which they are committed because they maximize their own values. Very similar is the view of Blake et al., who describe a "9,9" position (i.e., high rankings on each variable) of concern for the client as a person and for problem solution. This "mutual problem solving approach" integrates the two concerns by finding problem solutions that are mutually satisfactory to both client and agent.

The models that include this integrative type *also* seem to recognize the behavior characterized by Glaser and Stanley as paternalistic, but they do not place it in the high-high position of the two-dimensional grid. For example, Hall et al. speak of a "paternalistic swing," in which an agent behaves in a 1/9 client-centered fashion for a period of time and then, as if recognizing that conformity is also important, behaves in a 9/1 task-centered fashion for the next period of time. Similarly, Studt reports that parole agent-parolee relationships that originally focused on service can become highly concerned with surveillance after an "escalation episode." In Studt's term a guardian-ward relationship can "deteriorate" into a "prosecutor-defendant" relationship. Hence it would seem that the "paternalistic" type combination of assistance and control can be incorporated *within* the models that also allow for integration of the two concerns, while the Glaser model does not allow for the "integration" or "resolution" position. Thus the second group of models (Studt, O'Leary and Duffee, Hall, etc.) may be more complete.

In between these two camps is Klockars. While he speaks of a conflict-resolution type, his description of this "synthetic officer" suggests that the resolution he has in mind may be less complete than the integration type described by Studt, O'Leary, Hall, and Blake. According to Klockars, the synthetic officer resolves the conflicting demands of law enforcement and service provision by utilizing the "agency" as a mythical third party. The synthetic agent presents conformity demands as coming from the agency while promise of service comes directly from the agent. Scheurell's model, in which some agents protect clients from the agency, is similar on this score.

Klockars' discussion of the resolution between the demands of conformity to agency rules and the proffering of help by the agent is somewhat different from the lack of resolution presented by Glaser or the integration of concerns presented by Studt or O'Leary and Duffee. Klockars speaks of the agent using two forms of "currency," one of aid and one of law enforcement. He suggests that if the probationer conforms, there is no need to offer help. If, however, conformity is difficult (and he suggests that in most cases it will be, simply because the rules are ambiguous, all-encompassing, and demeaning), the opportunity for exchange of currencies occurs. In essence, Klockars argues that the synthetic officer develops a relationship with the offender that leads to rapport, by suggesting that what the offender cannot get directly from the department by strict conformity, he can obtain from the officer by engaging in a cooperative, counseling relationship. Some officers use two forms of power: one of formal authority, by which they perform as ministers of the department, and one of personal authority (which may be either their own charisma or their gatekeeping ability), by which they perform as mediators, standing between their clients and the law enforcement demands of formal policy.

In contrast to Glaser's paternalistic type, the synthetic officer does not use control and assistance at the same time, but instead uses different kinds of control as the agent-client relationship develops, first insisting on perfunctory rule observance, then moving to a negotiative and personal approach. Distinguished from Studt's insider-outsider relationship or O'Leary and Duffee's Reintegration policy, Klockars' synthetic officer does not "own" the rules and expectations identified as the department's, but trades in his adherence to these rules as the means of cajoling, coercing, or bargaining for a more personal and direct relationship with *some* (but not all) offenders.

There is a position, in some of the two-dimensional models, that appears to capture Klockars' version of resolution. This position is most evident in the Hall et al. and Blake et al. "grids," which allow for a fifth position as another model type of supervision strategy. Both Hall and Blake identify a "5/5" position—called by Hall "charismatic change" and by Blake "the tried-and-true orientation"—in which the officer compromises between strict adherence to the principles of client-oriented support and the principles of strict adherence to problem solving or monitoring of conformity. The description of the synthetic officer seems to conform closely to these middle-of-the-road positions. The difference, and an important one, is Klockars' emphasis on the developmental nature of the agent-offender relationship. Few agents, he suggests, are rigid adherents to any one style of supervision; many use a variety of appeals with the same offender as situations change and as the perceptions of the offender change during the course of supervision. It would be unfair to suggest that the other models do not allow for an evolution of intervention styles, but the patterns of development and sequencing remain implicit in most of the other presentations. Studt, for example, emphasizes the fragility of any particular officer-parolee relationship, and the tendency for any of the preferred styles to deteriorate into a prosecutor-defendant relationship.

A Critique of Two-Dimensional Models

These comparisons of models raise two important issues. First, it would appear that the major differences among two-dimensional models involve measurement techniques rather than basic concepts. The use of static or developmental models produces somewhat different results. And an emphasis on describing officer average proclivities yields different results from those associated with an emphasis on types of relationship between officer and offender. Officer profiles may allow us to say something about how Mr. Jones differs from Ms. Smith across entire caseloads. Relationship profiles allow us to say something about how either Mr. Jones or Ms. Smith may approach particular cases, or shift his or her approach within a single case over time. The differences among these approaches are important, and should lead eventually to an integration of the static and dynamic and the officer-centered and relationship-centered models; nevertheless, it would seem to be the similarity across the technical differences that is most noteworthy at the present time.

Second, it may be, however, that various authors cited are primarily engaged in the academic enterprise of emending each other, rather than responding to the realities of probation. (For an examination of this problem in relation to models of policing, see Hoestedler, 1980.) To put the question boldly: are assistance and control (or the other variants of these concepts) dimensions that describe supervision practice or are they simply "myths" through which analysts communicate with each other? This question recognizes a relationship between research and practice that is often highlighted as a key problem for methodologists, but is rarely controlled for in the research that attempts to describe probation. Are assistance and control valid descriptors (or generalizations of more specific descriptions) or are these concepts forced on the phenomena by the investigators? The question of validity may be more complex here than in some other forms of research because probation and parole model building is frequently conducted by persons who are very close to the field—perhaps ex-practitioners themselves—or who adopt the rhetoric of the field in their efforts to define it. (In fact, the reverse is also true. Probation, parole, and other client supervision professions, even though they have many characteristics of apprenticeships or crafts rather than more formalized professions, are composed of a relatively articulate, literate, and self-conscious group. The practitioners do contribute to the literature that in turn informs their practice. Hence in some cases, it is difficult to ascertain whether the researcher accepted the rhetoric of the field or the field accepted the rhetoric of research.)

To say that assistance and control are myths does not imply that these concepts have no real consequences. But it may be important to tease out on what level their significance applies. Both in everyday life and in the kind of research described here, it is widely understood that there are *always* discrepancies between what is done and our ability to capture that doing in communicable terms. In a field such as probation, which is undeniably rife with heartache, disappointment, conflict, and surprise, the attempt to nail down, analyze, and understand workaday problems may be quite important to the well-being of the persons experiencing the problems. Attempts to understand work problems, to come to grips with the demands of work, may have emotional benefits even if they fail to describe accurately the problems experienced or to resolve these problems by changing action. In fact, we might suppose, if only for the sake of argument, that model building in the probation field is therapeutic for those who engage in it. It provides tension relief if nothing else. But, in addition, it is likely to create a community of persons who actively trade and tinker with their models, under the assumptions that 1) it is fun and 2) "your models may be more helpful to me than mine." In other words, model building can become an integral part of the world of practice, but one that takes on a life of its own, independent of its utility in description or its steering capacity to change practice. Model building is an aspect of the practitioner's job that makes the rest tolerable; at the same time, in the researcher's world it is a means of describing how practitioners communicate with each other and with researchers. And it may have real benefits beyond tension reduction: it can yield publications, enliven conferences and workshops, and serve as a major mechanism by which newcomers are indoctrinated into the field. But it can do all of this without describing or altering supervision. (For a similar discussion on another level, see Meyer and Rowan, 1977).

If *this* description is valid, model building and development can appear to be progressing—becoming more complex and truer to the essence of probation—by continually becoming truer to the mythical descriptions rather than to the various actions taking place between agent and office or agent and offender. Face validity for the models can be and usually is obtained by "testing" the types and the dimensions against the reactions of the practitioners. The models are "valid" in this sense if they match practitioners' versions of the same myth. Content validity of instruments measuring these models can be obtained by measuring the consistency with which specific descriptors are placed in certain boxes by respondents—but again without any means of ascertaining whether the logically (or emotionally) grouped descriptors distinguish one supervisor from another or one supervision sequence from another. Since almost all of these models attempt to relate behaviors to underlying dimensions or motives, almost all of them require either the practitioner or the researcher to classify particular variations of behavior into groups consistent with the value premises manifested in the myth itself. Control and assistance, surveillance and service, concern for offender and concern for community can never be directly observed.

We could conclude that there is at least a significant possibility that these two-dimensional models really do not take us much further than the one-dimensional models. In relationship to parole-agent-parolee interaction, for example, Irwin remarked:

None of these types are especially useful in explaining the different forms of parolee adaption to the agent-parolee system. This is because these types are constructed from variables which (1) result in differences in parole-agent behavior which are not visible to the parolee and (2) are related to differences in agent behavior which though visible to the parolee are not important to him. For instance, in their actual performance in regard to the parolee it has been pointed out that persons with a "social-worker" orientation are in effect more punitive than "cop-oriented" parole agents. . . . (O)ther writers have suggested that authority can be a "treatment" tool. . . . Consequently, the treatment-punishment dichotomy does not make a meaningful division in parole-agent behavior relative to the parolee. . . .

Furthermore, these particular schemes, which are based on variables *related to ideologies of parole work and modes of adaptation to the frustrations of agent status*, are not equipped to classify a wide variety of patterns of parole work which are related to many different variables . . . (Irwin, 1970: 165–166, emphasis added).

Irwin goes on to suggest the variables of *consistency* (rightness), *tolerance*, and *intensity* are far more predictive of parolee response to supervision and outcomes of various parolee-agent interactions. But rather than focus on missing variables (and there are many of them), it is probably better to highlight the difficulties with the two-dimensional models as they stand.

First, few of the two-dimensional models attempt to account for and organize client actions into the models of supervision. (The exceptions are Blake et al., who present a client grid as well as a caseworker grid, and Studt, who discusses parolee goals and perceptions). In other words, many of these models are incomplete as models of supervision systems.

Second, the two-dimensional models present little evidence for the logical consistency of their underlying dimensions (although they do display great ideological consistency). As Irwin has very acutely observed, describing an agent's activity as assistance or control says more about our (or the agent's) attempts to condone or to justify the motivations for the activity than about the activity itself. Facilitation or the giving of help can demand just as much conformity from the aid recipient as control or surveillance does. It would be impossible to determine whether control or assistance had been provided by examining the outcomes of the interactions, since the outcomes are in many cases the same. As Studt has pointed out, it is difficult to observe surveillance or service as processes because neither term refers to specific behaviors.

It is very possible that the distinctions made between assistance and control, service and surveillance, and so on, tell us more about preferences of researchers and practitioners than about the consequences (if any) of those preferences. Any facilitative action will include its means of monitoring results and include feeding back to the recipient of our attention the extent to which he has implemented the suggestion or has capitalized on the resources called help.

There may also be some doubts about the validity of the term usually placed on the horizontal axis (control, surveillance, concern for community). We typically respond to this notion only in comparison to the Y axis concept, rather than as an empirical reality in its own right. Hence while most of these models use this term to refer to the "get tough," "monitoring," "evaluating" and "sanctioning" aspects of probation and parole work, they never ask directly what we are getting tough with or what we are monitoring against. The assumption, apparently, is that "it is not necessarily judgmental to expect individuals to employ certain kinds of behaviors" (Hall et al., 1966:321). Implicit in these models is the notion that society has a single set of standards to which offenders can be asked to conform and from which officers can draw consistent and complete criteria for evaluation. There is little evidence to support this position, either in studies of the social value of helping services (Warren et al., 1974) or in studies of community reaction to correctional policies (Duffee and Ritti, 1977).

WHERE DO WE STAND?

We have examined a number of one- and two-dimensional models of probation and related types of client supervision. The two-dimensional models appear to encompass more variation than the one-dimensional models. All of the models ignore a good deal of reality, but each captures some facet of supervision that should be considered. We now consider how the models improve our understanding of supervision, and what weaknesses need most immediate attention.

Levels of Concern in Approaching the Conceptualization of Supervision

The existing models reflect several different levels of concern about the supervision of clients. One level involves abstract goals such as punishment and treatment. These goals, in turn, apparently relate to rather broad distinctions about social institutions and generic social processes such as social control and socialization. At another level, we hear concern about public organizations and the means by which these formal systems translate public policies and mandates into organizational policies and programs. At this level considerable attention is given to the nature of organization-environment linkages and how these links constrain, alter, or channel behavior inside the organization. At still another level, these models reflect concern for particular people working in an agency. Some of the models stress roles of classes of people. Other models seem more attentive to agents' attitudes. Moving on, we find a distinction between the roles agents perform and the attitudes they hold, and a concern with the face-to-face interaction of agent and client. The focus here is on relationships among persons. Finally, a few of the models also seem attentive to another level—that of the client facing the agent or the agency.

One positive contribution of the models we have reviewed is that they can help to identify these different levels of concern. The fact that models of supervision range across a whole analytical spectrum, from societal to interactionist perspectives, underscores the point that a complete understanding of client supervision is not to be gained in one model, or one frame of reference. We will need to employ different disciplines, different methodologies, and a good deal of caution. Many different aspects of supervision will require separate analysis each in its own right. We will also need imagination in proposing how one level of this topic relates to the other levels. We can say that an adequate understanding of client supervision must deal with 1) the institutional context, 2) complex organization and relationship of organization to environment, 3) delineation of work roles in organizations and the patterns of coordination among specialities, 4) patterns of interaction among clients and agents and 5) the social psychology of role incumbents (for staff and clients).

If model development has heightened our awareness of complexity, it has unfortunately not helped us very much to clarify the issues on each level, or to sort out the relationships among levels. The models collectively embody this complexity, but each in itself seems rather cavalier about what is left out. Moreover, individual models tend to bounce from one level to another. Users need a rather good ear to identify the level on which each model is operating and to sense when the level of concern may have shifted—perhaps inadvertently.

Let's look at a few examples of the problem. The treatment-punishment dichotomies describe organizational goals in very broad strokes. The gross distinctions made may be quite useful on a societal level. Etzioni (1961) used such broad goal characterizations to compare types of organizations. For Etzioni, organizations differ because they serve different societal goals (perhaps functions is a better word). If our interest lies on this level of abstraction, this kind of goal specification may be sufficient. This notion of "goal as social function" is not very helpful, however, if we wish to make distinctions among organizations within the *same* societal function (Street et al. 1966:17–18).

Now, recall the research on organizational reform by McEwen (in Massachusetts), Moos (on institutional and community correction), and Piliavin and Gross (on separation of social service and income maintenance). These studies demonstrated that the results of reform were somewhat different, and in the welfare case quite opposite, from what the reformers expected to bring about. In each case, the reforms were conceived by persons using a societal-level model of the supervision problem. That is, in each case the model focused on the need to realign the organization in the institutional context. And perhaps such realignment took place. *But* the reformers *also* anticipated that this realignment would have immediate and unidirectional impact on both the role and interactional levels within the organizations. The data indicate that the links between the institutional and interactional levels are not direct. The institutional level models are not necessarily wrong, nor is policy that uses them inept. But experience with these and similar reforms would suggest that *if* a reformer were truly committed (say) to increasing client satisfaction with service, then it would be better to use a model that describes variables endogenous to the interaction system. If, on the other hand, the real concern were with altering the societal function of the organization in question, then the expressed concern for client satisfaction would be either a smoke screen or naivete.

Clearly Irwin's criticism of the agent attitude models is provoked by a similar concern for differing levels of analysis. He is not necessarily saying that Glaser is wrong. For many purposes, an agent's orientation toward assistance or control may be important. But, says Irwin, this concern is only tangential to an understanding of client-agent interaction or to the effects on clients of parole supervision.

In the future, we could be more careful about using the model most appropriate for a particular kind of question. Additionally, we might be more cautious about justifying change to solve problems on one level, unless we know how those changes will affect outcomes on other levels.

Before putting the level-of-analysis issue to rest, one other comment seems useful. This review of models indicates that some levels of concern have received more attention than others. It would be a happy accident if model development had stressed those levels of concern that are most important or most amenable to change. We probably have not been so lucky. In this review, the issues of concern that seem to have attracted the *least* attention are 1) the interaction of organizations with their environments, and 2) the orientation of clients to supervision. Model development on these two levels would seem important in several respects. We do not yet thoroughly understand the multiple constituencies of public organizations. For example, we hear many proposals to reform organizations to make them more effective or more humane. But we know less about how organizations take advantage of reform. We know little about how varying the environmental context of an organization is related to changes within it.

Nor do we know very much about how shifting the auspices of an activity (e.g., from county to state government) may change organizational functions. There is some evidence that state and federal auspices tend to result in greater professionalization and focus on community than local auspices. But models capable of addressing this and similar issues are lacking. At the other end, we lack models that approach supervision from the point of view of the client (although Irwin has given us a start). Such models would seem useful *regardless* of whether we see supervision as a sanction or a service. In either case, the salience of the organization for the person supervised, and the effects of that relationship, are policy-relevant variables.

Acceptance or Resolution of Conflict

We have stressed that two-dimensional models encompass greater variety, and therefore include patterns of belief or types of activity that the one-dimensional models exclude. When punishment and treatment, or surveillance and service, are conceived as separate dimensions, the conceptual framework permits discussion of types high on both dimensions or low on both dimensions. Inclusiveness is, of course, an important criterion in evaluating the merits of typologies, and therefore there is something to be said for the two-dimensional models. But now that we have introduced the notion of analytical level, perhaps we should add something to that comparison.

The two-dimensional models can be said to be an advance over the one-dimensional ones, as long as both models are concerned with the same level of the supervision problem. But the analysis of the last few pages implies that this may not always be the case. We have suggested that the dichotomous models may in fact be reflecting a rift at the institutional or societal level and, moreover, that such models may have been inappropriately used if they have been applied to the categorization of roles or interaction patterns. Perhaps at the societal level, there are conflicts between punishment and treatment, or between social control and socialization functions. Perhaps there are policy questions that arise and can be addressed only at this level, such as whether we invest in education, developmental services, income redistribution, or greater controls on those least advantaged by the current economic system.

It appears to be a characteristic of at least this society not to resolve conflicts on that level. As substitutes for societal-level decision apparatus, we invest in public organizations with multiple functions. We "resolve" by delegating. At least we have done so until now. Hence there has been tremendous concern for the hard choices at the role and interactional levels.

The one-dimensional models of supervision provide no resolutions of conflicting goals. These models—most notably Packer's rendition—merely *describe* an unending tension. The conflict is accepted as simply part of the nature of things. In contrast, all of the two-dimensional models describe personal resolutions of conflict. Glaser's welfare agent ignores control, his punitive officer ignores assistance, his passive agent simply ignores. Other models, such as those of Studt, Klockars, and Hall et al., include resolution positions that involve an integration of demands. These positions may be more aptly called solutions than resolutions. Perhaps the epitome of this solution was the description of the "collaborative prison" in the report of the President's Commission Task Force on Corrections (1967). (Parenthetically, another full-blown solution was Griffith's 1970 "family model," in which he suggested a solution to the tension between due process and crime control). The collaborative prison represented a solution of conflict at a very high level. It was not to occur in the role performance of individual agents, or in the happy interaction of some agents with some clients. Instead, it was to occur at an organizational or perhaps even a societal level. The collaborative prison, as depicted in the Commission report, manages to blend the "commonwealth" and "service" functions of prisons. Such a prison would achieve both the political, social control mandate and the social service mandate.

Even if it is feasible, such a solution has not yet occurred. Nor, for that matter, has a solution very often been found at role or interactional levels. Instead, the major policy shifts we have seen in the last decade point to a reacceptance of the one-dimensional model as best depicting the nature of things at the societal level. Corrections systems are instruments of punishment and should be pushed toward the punishment pole. Social ends associated with the treatment pole should be pursued through other organizations.

To restate the issue, as we look at how correctional policy shifts from two- or one-dimensional models, we see a corresponding shift in emphasis from conflict acceptance to conflict resolution. While we were unwilling or unable to make policy choices at higher levels, for several decades correctional models stressed how those unmade choices influenced roles and interactions. In the last six or seven years, however, we have seen a new willingness to make choices at the higher levels (Morris, 1974; Fogel, 1975). Thus while there was great emphasis in the 1960s and early 1970s on training agents to see and adopt the role-level solutions, we can predict that the 1980s will focus on reorganization. Whereas in the past concern centered on conflict *within* roles and agencies, in the future we should see more concern about conflict *between* roles and agencies.

The Difference Between Understanding and Enabling.

We began this chapter by stressing that there are different kinds of models, or different ways of understanding. Some models of supervision may allow us to understand in the sense that they provide concepts that collect many specifics in a way that makes sense. These models suggest orderliness in a rather unruly and confusing enterprise. Other models may allow us, on the basis of some information, to predict what will follow next. Or, if the model provides us with information that allows us to make choices, we may be able to achieve one outcome rather than another.

The existing models of supervision seem to fall far short of providing the latter types of understanding. They allow us to make sense of supervision, to understand it, but do not enable us to change the situation. Glaser's model, for example, offers us the understanding that officers who revoke frequently are punitive; those who find jobs are welfare agents; those who revoke frequently *and* find jobs are paternalistic; those who do neither are passive. The underlying dimensions, assistance and control, are inferred from frequencies of behavior. If these dimensions exist, they presumably exist as attitudes within the officer. If a valid instrument exists for measuring these attitudes, we may be able to predict which officers will most frequently engage in which behaviors. But if our concern is with the behavior, we are probably better off measuring it directly than trying to guess at it from an indicator of attitude.

If a manager of a probation department were attempting to shuffle people to maximize control or minimize service, he could probably do as well without the model as with it. The manager may find the model of some use as a shorthand way of referring to the behavior: he can say "Joe Doles is paternalistic" instead of "Joe Doles files lots of revocation requests but also helps people find jobs." He can also invoke the model for justificatory purposes: "control" may be easier to sell than technical violations.

But it is unlikely that even this use of the model would be attempted. As suggested in the critique of the two-dimensional models, the major use of such models is probably their heuristic value—they allow us to say, in a short and clear way, why the supervision task is so difficult. By and large, they do not incorporate the type of information that would allow us to predict how to make the job less difficult.

Seeking models that enable us to act may be asking too much. But such models have been built in other spheres of activity. Probation as a sanction, or as a profession, or as an organization, may be considerably strengthened if we invest in such an effort here. But to do so we need to get beyond our present stage of understanding. The models should be validated, or discarded, on the basis of the actions they permit, or the choices they help to make.

We have to start, naturally, where we are. But we would go forward by converting these simple models into variables and examining relationships among the variables. The initial selection of variables must be guided by existing theory. Since probation is short on theory, the initial concepts might be borrowed from other fields. But as research continues, these devices will be modified and refined. As they gain in power, theories can help us move the practice of probation.

This work has begun, certainly. Its future development apparently needs greater support than existing resources and organization of probation research have so far allowed. Advancing that effort would have much to offer the development of a mission for probation.

REFERENCES

American Friends Service Committee (1971). *Struggle for Justice.* New York: Hill and Wang.

Beck, B. (1967). "Welfare as a Moral Category." *Social Problems* 15:259–277.

Blake, R., J. Mouton, L. Tomaino, and S. Guitierrez (1979). *The Social Worker Grid.* Springfield IL: Charles Thomas.

Coates, R., A. Miller, and L. Ohlin (1978). *Diversity in a Youth Correctional System.* Cambridge MA: Ballinger.

Cressey, D. (1960) "Limitations on Organization of Treatment in the Modern Prison." In R. Cloward et al. (eds.), *Theoretical Studies in Social Organization of the Prison.* New York: Social Science Research Council.

Dembo, R. (1972). "Orientation and Activities of the Parole Officer." *Criminology* 10, 2 (August):193–215.

Duffee, D., and R. Ritti (1977). "Correctional Policy and Public Values." *Criminology* 14, 4 (February):449–460.

Etzioni, A. (1961). *Complex Organizations.* New York: Free Press.

Etzioni, A. (1976). "Old People and Public Policy." *Social Policy* 7:21–29.

Fairweather, G., D. Sanders, H. Maynard, and D. Cressler (1969). *Community Life for the Mentally Ill.* Chicago: Aldine.

Fogel, D. (1975). ". . . We are the Living Proof . . . ." Cincinnati: Anderson.

General Accounting Office of the United States (1975). *Probation and Parole Activities Need to Be Better Managed.* Washington, D.C.: General Accounting Office.

General Accounting Office of the United States (1976). *State and County Probation: Systems in Crisis.* Washington, D.C.: General Accounting Office.

Glaser, D. (1964). *The Effectiveness of a Prison and Parole System.* Indianapolis: Bobbs Merrill.

Gottfredson, D. (1968). *Measuring Attitudes Toward Juvenile Detention.* New York: National Council on Crime and Delinquency.

Griffiths, J. (1970). "Ideology in Criminal Procedure or a 'Third' Model of the Criminal Process." *Yale Law Journal* 79, 3 (January):359–417.

Hall, J., M. Williams, and L. Tomaino (1966). "The Challenge of Correctional Change: The Interface of Conformity and Commitment." *The Journal of Criminal Law, Criminology and Police Science* 57:493–503.

Halleck, S. (1967). *Psychiatry and the Dilemmas of Crime.* New York: Harper and Row.

Hoestedler, E. (1980). "Typologies of Individual Police Officers: A Test." Dissertation Prospectus, State University of New York at Albany.

Hoshino, G. (1972). "Separating Maintenance from Social Service." *Public Welfare* 30:54–61.

Irwin, J. (1970). *The Felon*. Englewood Cliffs, NJ: Prentice Hall.

Isabel, L. (1980) "Lock-ups for Youth: DYS Weighs Needs." *Boston Globe*, January 1, p. 21.

King, R., and N. Raynes (1968). "An Operational Measure of Inmate Management in Residential Institutions." *Social Science and Medicine* 2:41–53.

Klockars, C. (1972). "A Theory of Probation Supervision." *Journal of Criminal Law, Criminology and Police Science* 63, 4:550–557.

Koerin, B. (1979). "Authority in Child Protective Services." *Child Welfare* 53:660, 657.

Krajick, K. (1978). "Illinois: A Blow for the 'Get Tough' Side." *Corrections Magazine* 4:19–22.

Mandell, W. (1971). "Making Corrections A Community Agency." *Crime and Delinquency* 17:281–288.

McEwen, C. (1977). "Subcultures in Community-Based Programs." In L. Ohlin, A. Miller, and R. Coates (eds.), *Juvenile Correctional Reform in Massaschusetts*. Washington, D.C.: Law Enforcement Assistance Administration.

Meyer, J., and B. Rowan (1977). "Institutionalized Organizations: Formal Structure as Myth and Ceremony." *American Journal of Sociology* 83, 2 (September):340–363.

Miller, J., and L. Ohlin (1976). "The New Corrections: The Case of Massachusetts." In M. Rosenheim (ed.), *Pursuing Justice for the Child*. Chicago: University of Chicago Press.

Moos, Rudolph (1975). *Evaluating Correctional and Community Settings*. New York: Wiley.

——— (1968). "The Assessment of the Social Climates of Correctional Institutions." *Journal of Research in Crime and Delinquency* 17, 4 (October):373–386.

Morris, N. (1974). *The Future of Imprisonment*. Chicago: University of Chicago Press.

Ohlin, L., H. Piven, and D. Pappenfort (1956). "Major Dilemmas of the Social Worker in Probation and Parole." *National Probation and Parole Association Journal* 11 (July):211–225.

O'Leary, V., and D. Duffee (1971). "Correctional Policy—A Classification of Goals Designed for Change." *Crime and Delinquency* 17, 4 (October):373–386.

Packer, H. (1968). *Limits of the Criminal Sanction*. Stanford: Stanford University Press.

Piliavin, J., and A. Gross (1977). "The Effects of Separation of Services and Income Maintenance of AFDC Recipients." *Social Service Review* 51:389–406.

President's Commission on Law Enforcement and Administration of Justice (1967). *Task Force Report: Corrections*. Washington, D.C.: Government Printing Office.

Ritti, R., and D. Hyman (1977). "The Administration of Poverty: Lessons from the Welfare Explosion 1967–73." *Social Problems* 25:157–175.

Scheurell, Leonard P. (1969). "Decisionmaking in Correctional Social Work." *Issues in Criminology* 4:101–108.

Smith, A., and L. Berlin (1978). *Introduction to Probation and Parole*. St. Paul: West.

Stanley, D. (1976). *Prisoners Among Us*. Washington, D.C.: Brookings Institution.

Street, D., R. Vinter, and C. Perrow (1966). *Organization for Treatment*. New York: Free Press.

Studt, E. (1973). *Surveillance and Service: A Report of the Parole Action Study*. Washington, D.C.: United States Department of Justice.

Thomson, D., and D. Fogel (1980). *Probation Work in Small Agencies: A National Study of Training Provisions and Needs*, Vol. I. Chicago: Center for Research in Criminal Justice, University of Illinois at Chicago Circle.

Warren, R., S. Rose, and A. Bergunder (1974). *The Structure of Urban Reform*. Lexington, MA: Lexington Books.

Wright, K. (1977). "Correctional Effectiveness: A Case for an Organizational Approach." Doctoral dissertation, Pennsylvania State University.

Zald, M., (1962). "Power Balance and Staff Conflict in Correctional Institutions." *Administrative Science Quarterly* 6:22–49.

Chapter 7

A Non-Treatment Paradigm
for Probation Practice

A. E. Bottoms* and William McWilliams**

SUMMARY

Empirical and theoretical critiques of treatment can no longer be ignored in probation practice, but the probation service's traditional core values of respect for persons and hope for the future can be realized in a non-treatment context. Four traditonal aims of the probation service are identified, namely i) the provision of appropriate help for offenders; ii) the statutory supervision of offenders; iii) diverting appropriate offenders from custodial sentences; iv) the reduction of crime. It is argued that each of these aims remains worth pursuing, but that they need radical reconceptualization in the light of the collapse of treatment. A paradigm for practice in respect of each aim is offered for criticism and comment.

*Center for Criminological Studies, University of Sheffield and The Faculty of Law, University of Sheffield and Director-Designate, Institute of Criminology, Cambridge University

**South Yorkshire Probation Service and the Faculty of Educational Studies, University of Sheffield

Note: This chapter first appeared in the *British Journal of Social Work*, 9; 2 (1979), pp. 159–202.

If I were asked what was the most significant contribution made by this country to the new penological theory and practice which struck root in the twentieth century—*the measure which will endure,* while so many of the other methods of treatment might well fall into limbo . . .—my answer would be probation . . . *Probation is fundamentally a form of social service preventing further crime* by a readjustment of the culprit under encouraging supervision of a social worker guided by the courts of justice. (Radzinowicz[1]: italics added).

The reformation of the criminal . . . has been central to the English approach to criminal justice since the end of the nineteenth century. . . . But penological research carried out in the course of the last twenty years or so suggests that penal "treatments," as we significantly describe them, do not have any reformative effect, whatever other effects they may have. The dilemma is that a considerable investment has been made in various measures and services, of which the most obvious examples are custodial institutions for young adult offenders and probation and after-care services in the community for a wide variety of offender. *Are these services simply to be abandoned on the basis of the accumulated research evidence?* Put thus starkly, this is an unlikely proposition but one which, by being posed at all, has implications for the rehabilitative services concerned. *Will this challenge evoke a response by prison and probation officers* by the invention of new approaches and method? (Croft[2]: italics added).

These two quotations, respectively by the first Director of the Cambridge Institute of Criminology and the present Head of the Home Office Research Unit, are separated in time by only 20 years; but they seem poles apart in orientation. Radzinowicz, reflecting the accepted wisdom of the time, accords to probation the coveted prize of being the jewel in the crown of the "new penology." Croft, in the unassertive tone of the English civil service, quietly but starkly poses the possibility of the disappearance of this once-priceless gem.

In the light of what has happened in those 20 years, we believe that Croft is entirely right to pose this question. The research results do indeed cast major doubts on Radzinowicz's confident assertion that probation is "a form of social service *preventing further crime.*"

This is not the appropriate place to discuss the various research studies in detail; suffice it to say that all those who have responsibly reviewed the relevant literature (Lipton, Martinson and Wilks; Greenberg; Brody[3]) have reached the same broad conclusion—that dramatic reformative results are hard to discover and are usually absent. A few clues about differential treatment results may be found, but often these fail to reach statistical significance; a good example was the Home Office's own IMPACT study of probation effectiveness, which grew out of the equally pessimistic National Study of Probation and MESPA study (Folkard et al.[4]).

Against results like these, some will argue that the probation service is not, and never has been a crime-preventing agency. The task of the service is, they will say, limited to the classic statutory duty to "advise, assist and befriend." But we do not think that this objection cuts much ice. Most probation officers, and certainly almost all policymakers, have always tacitly assumed that the advice and assistance offered did have an effect in steering at least a proportion of their charges away from criminal acts. It is precisely because this assumption is now seen to be very doubtful that the crisis of confidence implied by Croft has arisen.

Yet in one sense Croft, radical though his stance may seem, poses only one-half of the possible critique of probation's traditonal rehabilitative practice. His critique is empirical: probation treatment does not seem to reduce recidivism. But, especially in the USA, a theoretical critique of treatment has also developed. As the American Friends Service Committee neatly put it, this criticism provides:

> compelling evidence that the individualised-treatment model, the ideal towards which reformers have been urging us for at least a century, is theoretically faulty, systematically discriminatory in application, and inconsistent with some of our most basic concepts of justice.[5]

For present purposes, the most important of these three charges are the first and the third—that the treatment model is theoretically faulty, and capable of injustice. Why theoretically faulty? The issue is complex, and any short answer potentially unsatisfactory, but essentially the fault lies in the persistent yet inappropriate analogy made with individual medical treatment. This analogy is doubtful on a number of grounds. First, in the understanding of ordinary language, most crime is voluntary and most disease is involuntary; and even if one rejects this simple ordinary language distinction at a philosophical level, one is still left with important differences in the meaning context of the events which the voluntary/involuntary appellation reflects. Second (and closely related), the assumption of the medical model is that crime is pathological, but this notion is difficult to sustain, at any rate for most crime, in the light of sociological critiques (Durkheim; Taylor, Walton and Young[6]). Third, the treatment model applied is one of individual treatment, while many of the assumed causes of crime are social; treatment-oriented criminology has never learned the lesson of social medicine that better drains may be worth scores of doctors.

Moreover, such criticisms cannot be sidestepped by trying to point to the few apparent "successes" in the treatment of offenders. As Greenberg[7] has recently argued:

The diversity of programmes showing an initially favourable effect which disappears after subjects have been released for some time suggests to me that the limited effect that programmes do have may be achieved, not through the conventionally imagined therapeutic effect of the programmes, but by increasing legitimate aspirations and commitment to the avoidance of illegal behaviour, probably as the result of social attention and in some instances, possibly through special deterrence. That this effect slowly extinguishes when offenders return to their old social worlds is exactly what we should expect; it shows the limitations of an individual approach to criminality.

In the heyday of the "rehabilitative ideal," as Allen[8] has aptly dubbed it, no one raised these kinds of empirical or theoretical doubts about treatment. And this led to treaters taking upon themselves the right to coerce offenders into accepting what was going to be "for their own good in the long run." As a report of the Principal Probation Officers Conference put it in 1968:

There is substantial evidence to show that many people with anti-social tendencies and quite pronounced behaviour problems can be helped in the long term if relationships are sustained by formal disciplines of the kind characteristic of probation orders . . . There are also positive indications that a high proportion of people currently supervised by the probation service are not strongly motivated to seek help. Intervention in these circumstances must, initially at least, *lean heavily upon a degree of coercion* to sustain contact in which change or modification becomes possible (italics added).[9]

It is precisely this ready acceptance by treatment agents of the need for coercion which raises the possibility of injustice referred to by the American Friends Service Committee. For if a probation officer ineluctably believes in his powers of treatment, and in his right to force others to submit to them, then eventually he will almost certainly reach two conclusions. First, he will decide that he has a right to take compulsory power over people's lives additional to that which is justified by the offence, in order to make the treatment "work." Second, he will tend to ignore the so-called "client's" view of the situation, and to define the situation entirely in his (the treater's) terms. It is the results of these pieces of implicit arrogance (which, to set the record straight, the authors have themselves subscribed to in the past as practising probation officers) that may be criticized as unjust.

Yet is all this criticism of treatment fully relevant? It is oten suggested that there is an important difference between theory and practice in probation work, and that probation officers are not really committed to a treatment perspective in their routine work. Rather, it is argued, that day-to-day practice is pragmatically based, and they proceed on a basis of common sense, not treatment theory. This is a plausible suggestion which has received some empirical support (Davies[10]), and we certainly would not wish to argue that all probation practice is informed by the treatment model. What we do suggest, however, is that at those points at which common sense fails and theory is required, the theory chosen tends to be that provided by the treatment model. Moreover, the points at which pragmatism fails are often precisely those at which important decisions are made or justification for action is required. For example, social inquiry practice (where important decisions about recommmendations to the courts are made) is heavily influenced by the treatment model (McWilliams, Hardiker[11]), and where practitioners are constrained to write about their work the language of treatment is usually well to the fore.[12]

In short, probation's present position is extremely problematic. It has relied heavily on the treatment model for crucial decisions and justifications, but treatment appears not to be effective. One reason why treatment appears to be ineffective is that it is probably theoretically faulty. And morally, treatment is at least sometimes questionable because it produces arrogance in the treater, leading to injustice for the offender. In the light of this indictment, there can be no doubt that Croft was right to throw down the gauntlet: "Will this challenge evoke a response by . . . probation officers by the invention of new approaches and methods?

RECENT WRITING ON THE FUTURE OF THE PROBATION SERVICE

There has recently been a spate of writing on the future of the probation service. Much of this displays an awareness of the current dilemmas of the service without, we would argue, ultimately grasping the central issues.

Both Fisher[13] and Harris[14] identify as a central problem the conflict between the court's requirement of surveillance, and the social worker's casework function. "It is . . . the element of force, of power, which is in question," says Fisher, "and its use as a justification for casework intervention." In court, she goes on, few defendants "appreciate the *social work* implications of (a probation) order: it is *not mentioned on the order that probation is 'treatment'* " (italics added). But, she believes, the situation is changing because the new generation of generically trained social workers cannot compromise their values by operating as surveillance agents or effectively 'treat' reluctant clients for their criminality.

Harris takes this position to its logical conclusion and argues for "the dissociation of the probation service from the court's sentences." Probation officers are social workers, and should offer social work skills, not carry out court orders and other penal responsibilities. They are and have been ineffective in reducing crime, but they are said to be good at providing "a highly trained, caring and effective social work service to a disadvantaged section of the community: the offender." Non-custodial court orders should continue to exist, and offenders may legitimately continue to be forced to carry out certain actions as a result of those orders. But "what they are forced to do should be punishment, with any therapeutic gains merely fortuitous spin-offs. The social work treatment should be kept distinct from the punishment."

Harris offers no details about how such a separation of functions might be achieved in practice, but his position would appear to require a wholly new non-social work based "community surveillance agency," whilst the probation service would continue to receive (at least most of) its present funds. Such a proposal can only be described as hopelessly unrealistic politically, quite apart from the obvious potential problems about the relationships between the two new agencies. The dilemma which Fisher correctly identified concerning "forced social work treatment" is certainly an important one, but it cannot be solved in this crude and cavalier manner.

But at one point Harris does enunciate an important principle. He writes: [15] "The principle that offenders, coming as many of them do from deprived backgrounds, and failing as many of them do to adjust to society's expectations, need help is well established."

We agree with this view; and we think it significant that the word "help" rather than "treatment" is used in a passage which tried to articulate the needs of offenders. But elsewhere, Harris seems to equate "help' with "treatment," and to locate the ultimate authority for the definition of help in the social worker's professional expertise. No radical reconceptualization of traditional social work practice is envisaged. [16] But we shall argue below that once one starts talking seriously about "help" rather than "treatment," such a reconceptualization is required.

A much more lengthy and considered model for the future of the probation service has been put forward by Haxby. [17] It is difficult to characterize Haxby's position in short compass, but essentially he argues for a new "community correctional service" which will continue the recent trend of the probation service towards diversification of methods and the development of fresh alternatives to custody. Perhaps his most original suggestion is for a major shift into community work: "it must not limit its methods of social work to a casework approach; it cannot try to act *for* the community without acting *with* the community" (p. 185). To this end Haxby proposes a new statutory duty for probation and after care committees to become involved with community work with a view to the prevention of crime; and he even offers a draft for the legislation:

It shall be the duty of every probation and after-care committee to promote the welfare of persons in its area, and provide them with advice, guidance and assistance, *in such ways as seem likely to reduce the incidence of crime in the area* (italics added).[18]

But Haxby's position here is not well thought through. His statutory duty is so phrased as to make entirely possible unilateral decisions by the probation service to move into given areas. He is aware that in the Bristol Social Project of the 1950s, this kind of approach led to considerable and unexpected resistance from the residents (Spencer[19]); but he does not systematically consider the implications of this for future practice. In another passage of his book, he is aware that "unconventional or militant protest" may sometimes be part of community work;[20] but he does not consider how this squares with the statutory duty he has previously laid down. He is conscious of the need for a unified theoretical approach to the various elements of social work practice, but does not really provide this himself.[21]

Essentially, we believe, Haxby's proposal amounts to the translation of the traditional social work language of "diagnosis" and "treatment" into a more diversified and community conscious context. We believe that he is right to draw attention to the importance of community, for as we shall argue more fully below, community influences are almost certainly of great importance in producing differential crime rates between areas. But we do not think that his book asks sufficiently radical and searching questions about the nature of social workers' involvement in communities; nor that he has adequately confronted the theoretical critiques of the traditional treatment model. Nowhere is this more clear than when he speaks of a future in which there will be "a much larger *interventive repertoire practised by social workers*" (p. 237: italics added).

Two other contributions to the debate on the future of the probation service have been made by serving chief probation officers. Colin Thomas is uncompromisingly and refreshingly honest in his assertion that "critical findings about the general outcome of treatment cannot be ignored—the evidence is too strong. The certainties of our traditional knowledge base have gone."[22] His major positive contribution is, nevertheless, to argue for non-custodial sentences even without the certainties of treatment:

The Service should not feel uncertain about its overall objective because non-custodial sentences always make more sense than prison for most offenders . . . A major task lies in persuading sentencers and the public that the Service has a convincing range of alternatives to offer.

Such a case can realistically be made.[23] For example, Sinclair's research on probation hostels has shown that at least some kinds of hostels are able to "hold" some offenders in the community (for the duration of their stay in the hostel) much more effectively than others; though when offenders left the hostel and returned home, the marked difference between hostels disappeared almost entirely.[24] Similarly, there is strong evidence from the pioneering Norman House voluntary hostel for adult recidivists that men had substantially longer crime free gaps while they were at the hostel, even though their subsequent records were (though not systematically examined) by no means as favourable (Turner[25]). There is no reason to suppose that the same may not be true of day training centres, day centres, and other recent non-custodial innovations. Long term treatment effects may not be obtainable; short term "holding" effects may. This would be entirely consistent with Greenberg's inferences from the existing literature, cited above. But if this approach is taken it does mean, obviously, that the case for the use of such facilities should not be made (as currently it often is in social inquiry reports and the like) on treatment grounds.

Colin Thomas does not articulate fully the theoretical basis for his policy position, or the overall shape of the probation service in the future as he sees it. Indeed, with the collapse of the certainties of treatment he sees rather the need to "live with the uncertainties of empiricism—acting on observations and experiment, not on theory, learning as we go" (p. 30). We would agree with him about the need to move cautiously into an experimental period, checking each innovation rigorously with critical research and monitoring. But we disagree about the role of theory. In the first place, it is in fact impossible to "act on observations and experiment," as Thomas recommends, without making implicit theoretical assumptions (Popper[26]). Secondly, it is our contention that much of the reason why recent writings on the future of probation have failed to grasp the central issues is precisely that they are content to inch pragmatically forward without adequate hard reflection upon the theoretical basis of probation practice. It is for this reason that theory plays a central role in our own analysis, although we also believe that our paradigm has profound implications for everyday practice, and is itself translatable into practice.

W. R. Weston's stimulating recent analysis of the probation service is the last we shall consider here,[27] and because Weston is more concerned with a general review of probation within the penal system as a whole than with the specific issue of future probation practice, the discussion can be brief. But one point Weston makes is of cardinal importance:

> probation work is on a fairly deep foundation—that of unshakeable desire for and faith in the capacity of people to grow and improve in their personal and social functioning—and this managed to find expression before casework was thought of, and will continue when it is forgotten (p. 20).

At the base of Weston's foundation we infer that there lie the probation service's traditional values of care and respect for unique individual persons, and hope for their future potential. These values, Weston usefully reminds us, existed long before "treatment" and could therefore (at least in principle) exist if "treatment" disappeared. This is an important corrective to the view frequently held by probation officers that the death of treatment would be accompanied by the demise of hope and respect for persons. Actually, we would go further than Weston, and argue that when the concepts of "diagnosis" and "treatment" are fully embraced, a probable consequence is a reduction in respect for persons; in which case the death of treatment will allow the reassertion of this traditional value. The term "diagnosis" (as it has generally been used by casework theorists) rest upon the notion that sufficient causal explanation of human behaviour can be found; and that of "treatment" on the belief that it is possible to manipulate the causal variables to produce modifications of the behaviour (effect) which is seen as undesirable. These concepts have profound implications, for as Plant[28] points out: "if behaviour is the result of antecedent causes then it is at least plausible to suggest that the individual is not responsible for his actions." Under this model the concepts of "choice" and "client self-determination" become redundant, and that of "respect for persons" is implicitly diminished.[29]

Classical casework theorists have largely ignored the implicit conflict between the determinism of diagnosis and treatment and the frequently stressed casework principle of client self-determination. Perlman,[30] for example, in an extensive justification of "dynamic diagnosis" is constrained to argue that the essence of appraisal leading to diagnosis is the same regardless of whether the appraised "object matters" are inanimate things, animals or human beings. And although she stresses that "a human being is the most complex among the 'object matters' worked upon or with" (p. 168) the purpose of the "dynamic diagnois" is nevertheless, "to establish what the trouble is, what psychological, physical, or social factors contribute to (or cause) it" (p. 171). At a philosophical level this seems to fit very incongruously with Perlman's earlier assertion that:

> The essence of self-determination is . . . that the individual should take cognizance of what he feels and thinks, wants and does not want . . . and he should decide upon . . . a choice of action (p. 135).

Thus to us the death of diagnosis and treatment would, at least in principle, create the opportunity for the potential re-emergence of the probation service's traditional core values rather than their demise. But of course, these values cannot reappear in the same guise as for the nineteenth century police court missionaries: that social context is gone forever.[31] It is therefore a central task for theorists to consider how hope and respect for persons can be re-expressed in the modern era, and in a context where the critiques of treatment, both empirical and theoretical, can no longer be ignored.

A NEW PARADIGM FOR PROBATION PRACTICE

We argued in our introductory section that the criticisms of treatment compelled a response by probation officers in the invention of new approaches and methods. Examining recent writings suggesting such approaches, we have found ourselves unsatisfied. Many key issues have been raised—the relationship between court orders and social work practice; a possible distinction between "treatment" and "help," the importance of the wider community; the "holding" role of non-custodial sentences; the reassertion of hope and respect for persons after the death of treatment. But no sound overall response to Croft's challenge is yet discernible; various prescriptions offered often lack precision, and fit no coherent total strategy which takes really seriously the criticisms of treatment. When one looks at everyday practice in the probation service, the situation is certainly no better; all too often, officers remain committed to traditional practices without adequate reflection upon them in the light of new knowledge. As Brody has recently put it, current practice in the probation service (as in other aspects of the penal system) is taking place "with some confusion and an indistinct view of its ultimate goals."[32]

We believe there is a need for a new paradigm of probation practice which is theoretically rigourous; which takes very seriously the exposed limitations of the treatment model but which seeks to redirect the probation service's traditional aims and values in the new penal and social context. Such a paradigm must be realistic; it must take into account the present structural realities of the service (such as its separate existence from the local authority social service departments), as well as the quite severe resource limitations currently placed upon it.[33] Not without trepidation, we offer such a paradigm here for criticism and comment.

Our paradigm stems from the preliminary observation that, in relation to the criminal side of probation practice, there have been four basic aims of the service, under which all other objectives could be subsumed as second order ones. These four primary aims are and have been:

1. The provision of appropriate help for offenders
2. The statutory supervision of offenders
3. Diverting appropriate offenders from custodial sentences
4. The reduction of crime

Much current discussion has been confused by the treatment model's assumption that the first three of these aims must necessarily lead to the achievement of the fourth. We therefore repeat that on all the evidence this assumption cannot be sustained empirically. There are connections between the four aims, but they are by no means straighforward, and if we are to respond to the present situation with the inventiveness which Croft has rightly demanded, we need initially to keep a firm conception of their separateness, whilst in due course also pinpointing the connections which are vital if the somewhat diverse activities proposed are to make sense as a generally cohesive overall strategy for operation.

Aim 1: The Provision of Appropriate Help for Offenders

We have already mentioned in passing the classic official aim of probation practice: "to advise, assist and befriend." This phrase, which first appeared in the Probation of Offenders Act 1907, has remained unchanged in successive legislation, and still stands on the statute book of today.[34]

The original practice of the early probation service was probably to stress, in particular, advice and practical assistance. Within the context of a strongly moralistic relationship, the offender was steered into better paths by exhortation, the arrangement of employment, and so on. As the Handbook of the National Association of Probation Officers[35] put it as late as 1935:

> It may be necessary to try and find the probationer employment, and also to place him or her in touch with wholesome influences, either religious or social or both. Probation officers have been conspicuously successful in these good offices (p. 55).

With the advent of casework, things changed. "Advice in the form of telling a client what he should do has little place in modern casework," declared NAPO's post war handbook (King[36]). Indeed, it said, modern officers would probably want to reverse the order of the traditional trilogy, since "casework has given them so much insight into the value of befriending, and they have come to learn that advice and assistance mean little unless given in the context of a dynamic relationship." But a qualification was quickly added—friendship did not mean quite what the man in the street might think it meant; rather:

> all clients are best helped by a *special type of friendship*, viz, *the professional casework relationship* in which the probation officer's warm and sincere concern fertilizes the probationer's capacity for growth and change (italics added).

But the clients themselves have not been much impressed by this "special type of friendship." For example, a study of urban after care units by Silberman and Chapman[37] showed that over a third of the clients came for one interview only, and only one in five sustained contact with the probation service for more than three months. Fuller examination revealed the reasons for this. The "official aim" of the after care units was "to provide social casework"; and "as a casework agency the unit would have liked to help its clients by concentrating effort on the *underlying problems*" (p. 42, italics added). But, on their side, the clients most often "came to the office because they wanted material help" (p. 36). Thus, "in practice, the client and the caseworker have different views on the relative importance of material aid and longer-term measures" (p. 44).

It might be thought that this study is of an atypical group, because it took place in the context of the probation service's only major sphere of voluntary casework with offenders, and because after care units in large cities inevitably attract many vagrant recidivists. It is therefore of particular interest to find virtually identical results in a study of parolees on compulsory supervision, especially as half of the sample came from Ford open prison, with its traditionally high proportion of prisoners from higher occupational groups (Morris and Beverly[38]). As the authors summarize the position:

> Most parolees define *help* in terms of achieving a solution to practical problems; matters which relate to feelings are not usually thought to fall within the framework of a "helping" relationship and so are not expressed. Yet these are the very issues the officers themselves are often seeking to discuss. . . . The most overwhelming impressions to emerge from the interviews with parolees were of the irrelevance and superficiality of supervision. Most parolees thought that the understanding probation officers had of them as people, and of their life-style, was very limited . . . visits to the probation officer were regarded as something "apart" from all other aspects of their lives . . . the relationship was not seen to impinge upon their other social roles—as husbands, fathers, workers and so forth (pp. 131, 137: italics in original).

Any benefit that was perceived from supervision tended, ironically, to be restricted to its deterrent function as a reminder to keep away from future trouble. Rather a similar result has been recently reported in a small scale study of another, very different, client group—juvenile offenders under supervison orders (Giller and Morris[39]).

There are, nevertheless, in these studies hints about a possible way forward for future practice. These hints may be classified into two main ideas—the abandonment of "objectification" and the re-thinking of "help" as something which the client rather than the caseworker defines.

First, objectification: Morris and Beverly report that "constructive relationships developed only where parolees felt their probation officer understood them and was concerned about them *as people*" (p. 132: italics added). And this, in a very real sense, is precisely what the casework relationship, as classically conceived, fails to do—for all the lip-service it pays to this principle. Let the reader consider, for example, that NAPO definition of "a special type of friendship," and then let him try to imagine telling anyone with whom he has a real reciprocal relationship that he is going to offer him some "warm and sincere concern" which is going to "fertilize his capacity for growth." We believe, with the Oxford philosopher P. F. Strawson,[40] that there is an utterly fundamental difference between what might be termed the "objective attitude" and real interpersonal relationships:

> To adopt the objective attitude to another human being is to see him, perhaps, as an object of social policy; as a subject for what, in a wide range of sense, might be called treatment . . . to be managed or handled or cured or trained. . . . The objective attitude may be emotionally toned in many ways but not in all ways . . . *it cannot include the range of reactive feelings and attitudes which belong to involvement or participation with others in interpersonal human relationships* (p. 9: italics added).

This difference goes back to our discussion of causality and freedom (which is, indeed, the philosophical context in which Strawson's comment is placed); and it is precisely our thesis that it is the essentially causal, determinist philosophical underpinning of "casework" which has led it to espouse "the objective attitude." In the result, probation casework has at one and the same time both failed to deliver any worthwhile "treatment effects" and, by adopting the objective attitude, has engendered a considerable lack of interest by the clients. Not that one should be too harsh on casework, for, as Tim Robinson has shown in an impressive and timely essay, this is a general problem for all professionals and their clients in the modern welfare state.[41] Indeed, the issue perhaps goes wider than that, to the very roots of our society: the philsopher-novelist Iris Murdoch has complained, in a short but influential note,[42] of the denuding of vocabulary and concepts in morals, politics and literature:

> We need to turn our attention . . . away from the dry symbol, the bogus individual, the false whole, towards the real impenetrable human person, [who is] . . . substantial, individual, indefinable and valuable . . . Real people are destructive of myth.

There is, however, one more complication to be considered. Weston, contrasting the probation casework era with what went before, comments that in casework the probationer was placed "in the position of a cooperative recipient of expert treatment rather than of being a prime agent in his own rehabilitation."[43] This is undoubtedly correct, and is part of the price of the "objective attitude." But it would be as well not to over-romanticize what went before. The police court missionaries and their successors undoubtedly saw offenders as being able to make free moral choices, and thus to be "prime agents in their own rehabilitation," in a way which later caseworkers did not, or at least not always. But the strongly moralistic correctionalism of the early officers could also exact its own price in the inability of the worker to see the offender as, in Irish Murdoch's words, "a real impenetrable human person." That much has been amply demonstrated in David Matza's famous chapter on correction and appreciation—correctionalism tends to distort an adequate appreciation of the situation from the deviant subject's own point of view.[44] (There is, however, a subtle difference in logical status between this point and our earlier one: for we would argue that the "objective attitude" necessarily entails a diminution in respect for persons; but the correctional perspective, while empirically it often leads to a loss of such appreciation and respect, does not necessarily entail it.) However that may be, the lesson for the practitioner is clear: both overt moral correctionalism and the "objective attitude" are to be eschewed if the aim is an adequate understanding of clients as real people—and such an understanding may well be an essential prerequisite to offering clients adequate help.

We turn, then, to the second main idea for future practice, that of *help*. And we may usefully begin once more with a comment from Morris and Beverly:

> In establishing a relationship with their client it seems crucial for the proba-
> tion officer to begin from a point that has meaning for the parolee, yet . . . it
> seems that it is usually the officer who defines the situation (and the problem)
> and then proceeds to try and put things right (p. 132).

This seems to be an inevitable result of a situation where the probationer or parolee is cast, in Weston's words, as "a co-operative recipient of expert treatment." Of course, probation officers will say that they discuss treatment plans with clients, but the notion of professional expertise residing only in the treater runs so deep that admirable intentions are not always fulfilled, or seen as important. For example, in a small study involving probation officers attending a staff development course, it was found that in interview officers reported that they discussed plans with clients in 86% of the cases, whereas a content analysis of their case records (carried out by other trained probation officers) showed plans being recorded as discussed in only 38% of the cases: a striking and statistically significant difference ($P < 0.001$) (McWilliams[45]). A more extreme manifestation of the same officer-centred approach is to be found in Perlman's astonishing remark that "the test of the dynamic diagnosis in any case is its usefulness to the caseworker himself."[46]

The only way out of this, the only way to prevent further research results of the Silberman–Chapman and Morris–Beverly kind, is surely to begin with client himself; to begin, as Morris and Beverly put it "from a point that has meaning for the (client)." And if we reconsider the classic trinity of "advise, assist and befriend," from the client's point of view it is above all assistance which matters—though good advice and true friendship may certainly be forms of assistance.[47] For our part, though, we prefer the simpler Anglo-Saxon word _help_ rather than the Latin-derived _assistance_ to express the simplicity and straightforwardness of this notion. Clients want help from social workers; aspiring social workers apply for training because they want to help people. This simple idea should not be lost to sight in all the complexities of modern social work. Indeed, we would agree with Carol Meyer that ultimately the central business of social work is not with achieving changes defined without regard to clients' opinions of their needs; nor with effecting cures for professionally diagnosed pathologies, but with giving help; and, very importantly, that: "if we choose the helping rather than the socialising goal, then we will be freer to attend to the improvement of services—to socialise _them_, if you will."[48]

We shall return to the implications of this in a moment. At this point let us stress that the substitution of help for treatment is the central feature of our paradigm, and that by 'help' we mean help as defined ultimately by the client. We believe that the embracing of this concept, together with the abandonment of "the objective attitude" which we have already discussed, begins to allow the probation service to respond appropriately to the challenge by John Croft with which we began this paper—for it faces centrally the collapse of treatment, and yet retains in full measure the traditional values of hope for the future and respect for persons.[49] It also has implications for the other three aims to be discussed later.

What exactly are the implications of adopting a "help" rather than a "treatment" model? The treatment model, in its pure form, begins with a diagnosis by the caseworker of the client's malfunctioning; then the treater decides upon the appropriate treatment with little or no advice from the client. The client is not offered choices about the form of the appropriate treatment; he is assumed to be dependent and in need of expert attention. In the "help" model, all this is radically transformed. The caseworker does not begin with an assumption of client-malfunctioning; rather, he offers his unconditional help with client-defined tasks, this offer having certain definite and defined boundaries (we shall return to the "boundaries" later). If the offer is accepted, this leads to a collaborative effort between worker and client to define the problem requiring help, and to work out jointly a set of possible alternative strategies; the worker is also absolutely explicit about what kinds of help his agency can and cannot offer. The client is then left to make the choices for himself. Hence, schematically:

a. Treatment	*becomes*	Help
b. Diagnosis	*becomes*	Shared Assessment
c. Client's Dependent Need as the basis for social work action	*becomes*	Collaboratively Defined Task as the basis for social work action

It is not appropriate for us here to spell out the full implications for day-to-day practice of this switch of approach; but three interim comments may be made. First, nothing that we have said should be interpreted to mean that "help" means only material help. It is true that in past research studies clients have placed more stress than officers upon material assistance, and the implications of this should be taken seriously; but clients should also be offered help with relationships and other areas of feeling as part of the agency's resources—which, of course, like all other types of help, clients are free to accept or reject.

Secondly, we are aware that many probation officers currently do offer "help," in client-defined terms, in a range of situations. We have said earlier that officers do not always practise pure "treatment," and some of the other things they do may certainly be defined as within the "help" model. But at present they have no adequate conceptual apparatus with which to theorize these activities; so that the moment they begin to talk about them the language of treatment tends to be brought in and distorts what they are really offering to clients. We see it as a major task for social work theorists to provide an adequate conceptual understanding of "help" for the benefit of social workers in their daily practice. Our experience suggests that once fieldworkers really grasp the notion of "help," with its insistently client-centred emphasis, then this not only assists them to make better conceptual sense of many of their existing practices, it also enables them to revolutionize some of their practices which previously have not been adequately client-centred.

Thirdly, it is worth noting that various modern theoretical developments in social work may be interpreted as generally consistent with the switch from treatment to help—this would apply to "task-centred casework" (Reid and Epstein[50]), welfare rights work, radical social work and community work, for example, and possibly also to "systems theory."[51] Yet, as Tim Robinson has suggested,[52] all these new techniques are potentially translatable still into the old officer-centred wisdoms of traditional social work. It is therefore of prime importance to emphasize that the ultimate test of the new model is that of client help—not "task-centredness," or whatever.

There are all kinds of things which may seduce one away from this central test. Consider, for example, the following quotation:

> Students applying for courses leading to social work qualification often say that their aim is to be able to "help people," thus implying that that is what social work is about. In recent years, however, more attention has been paid to the wide range of roles which every social worker finds himself fulfilling: from correction and even punishment to community direction and social reform. Many observers have found it difficult to reconcile what appear to be sometimes incompatible objectives, and one of the attractions of systems theory is that it allows for a recognition of conflicting elements in any social situation (Davies[53]).

Now of course it is not denied that social work has manifold functions, and the probation service certainly has other functions than to help clients. But to borrow a remark heard at a seminar discussion in another context, the danger with the approach implied in the quotation above is that it may turn "the existing nonsense of day-to-day practice into systematised nonsense." By stressing the manifold nature of social work functioning it is easy to forget about the client. But whatever else social work agencies may do, they must try to help clients, or they are not *social work* agencies. The centrality of this task among the others must not be abandoned.

The wider implications of defining client help as a central task are profound. As Mayer put it in the remark we have already quoted, "we will be freer to attend to the improvement of services—to socialise *them* if you will": in other words, the modern-day bureaucracies which probation services have become will be subject to "bottom-up" monitoring from the client's eye-view, to see whether they are so organized as best to be able to deliver the services required by the clients.[54] Thus there is a considerable re-thinking of the role of the agency *vis-à-vis* the client, as well as the role the caseworker *vis-à-vis* the client, and the nature of what constitutes "professional skill." Other implications may follow: the decentralization of agency structures in order to be able to respond more closely to client requests for help, a greater use of voluntary associates, and so on. Above all, there is a need to develop specificity within the agency about exactly what kinds of help are available at the client's request, and to devote considerable care and thought to methods of ensuring that clients are informed of the range of services available.

As we have made clear, the "help" model has been adopted in this paper because it is considered more likely than "treatment" to facilitate a response to the expressed needs of clients. No expectation has been raised that the help model will be beneficial in the reduction of crime, and it is central to our argument to insist that this is not the purpose of shifting the focus from treatment to help. Nevertheless it must be pointed out that there is, ironically, at least a tiny shred of research evidence to suggest that, after all help may be more crime-reducing than treatment.[55]

The evidence comes from two sources—one indirect and one direct. The indirect source is a study of compulsory after care in a group of young adults released from a closed borstal institution (Bottoms and McClintock[56]). The application of intensive casework methods was found to have no impact on reconviction rates, even when allowance was made (through a prediction instrument) for the previous history of the offender. On the other hand, and using the same statistical control for previous history, placement in certain sorts of post-institutional social situations did have a significant impact on reconviction rates—this included marriages, jobs, and so on. It is not suggested that probation officers become marriage brokers, but an implication of this study is that if offenders are genuinely seeking to "settle down," and if probation officers are able to help them by collaborating in getting them into stable social situations, this will be more beneficial than intensive casework on the treatment model.

The more direct evidence comes from a Danish study of through-care work with short term prisoners (Berntsen and Christiansen[57]). This is one of the very few studies to produce a significantly lower reconviction rate in an experimental "treatment" group as against a control group ($P < 0.01$); and, though its favourable result is not wholly unambiguous (Brody[58]), it is worth serious attention. This is particularly so in the present context, since we are told that "normally help was only given when the prisoners themselves asked for it" (p. 53), and that the help given was overwhelmingly of a very practical kind.[59]

We repeat that we would not wish to build very much on these results. But for those who would be unwilling to adopt this part of our paradigm without at least some linked possibility of crime reduction, they are perhaps at least straws in the wind.[60]

Aim 2: The Statutory Supervision of Offenders

We have noted that the phrase "advise, assist and befriend" is used by most commentators to represent the essence of a probation officer's duties. But in the original 1907 Act, this duty was the last of four which were laid down; the first three were concerned with the surveillance or supervision of probationers, and no serious discussion of probation practice can ignore these supervisory elements.

The 1907 Act began its list of duties as follows:

to visit or receive reports from the person under supervision *at such reasonable intervals as may be specified in the probation order* or, subject thereto, as the probation officer may see fit (S.4(a): italics added).

The intended norm, therefore, was that the court would control the level of supervision. The Criminal Justice Act 1948 altered that and, with the advent of casework, opened the way for a professional assessment of response to treatment to be one of the important determinants of frequency of reporting. Soon the two components of reporting and treatment were becoming inextricably mixed:

> The necessity to report to the probation officer in accordance with his instructions may be interpreted by a client in a punitive way. It is, however, a convenient way of providing for the personal contact which is the very essence of the helping relationship, and it is for the probation officer to help his client to work through these negative feelings . . . To put a little pressure on a client, or to strengthen his resolve to continue treatment can often be helpful to him; the compulsory element in probation casework often acts here as a strength (Foren and Bailey[61]).

More recently, there have been two distinct tendencies of thought arising out of this wedding of reporting to treatment. First, in the Younger Report[62] and elsewhere we see administrators escalating the coercive role and "creating . . . an image of social work as a set of methods and techniques which can persuade, seduce or compel people into conformity with authoritative views of how they should behave" (Raynor[63]). Second, younger social workers in particular have revolted against this conception and, like Harris and Fisher whose views we have discussed earlier, have tried to dissociate themselves from the surveillance aspect of the probation officer's role.

The conception of control as but part of the general treatment package of probation has also had some unfortunate consequences in daily practice. First, as we have already pointed out, it can entail injustice by encouraging the differential enforcement of the requirements of probation orders according to rather unreliable professional judgments of response to treatment. Secondly, it has meant that taking someone back to court for breach of an order has, curiously, often come to be seen as an admission of professional failure in treatment. Thirdly, it has meant that officers have struggled valiantly with themselves for many years in efforts to work out whether "treatment" and "control" really are compatible aims, and as a consequence of this, some of them have come to minimize the enforcement side of their work, in a way which many clients have recognized as unrealistic, given that the probation officer in his current agency function, is inescapably an officer of the law.

Examples of the results of these difficulties are not hard to find. Thus Lawson,[64] in a recent study of breaches of requirements of probation orders, showed that action for breach was very rare, and that it depended to a large extent on the characteristics of officers (not of clients), with senior officers being significantly more likely to take breach action. In community service orders, breach action is much more common than in probation orders (because the treatment element is more elusive), but nevertheless there is a large amount of variation between areas on breach policies for community service, and in many places some rather curious attempts to import treatment judgments into the decision (McWilliams and Murphy[65]).

In our view nothing is gained by a refusal to face squarely the fact that probation officers are and always have been law enforcement agents, and that this part of the role cannot be shuffled off without far-reaching consequences.[66] Although (for conceptual reasons) we have dealt first with the substitution of help for treatment, we are certain that one of the "boundaries" of the help offered has to be that the help must be consistent with the agency function of law enforcement (see further below). But if we insist on surveillance and law enforcement as part of the probation officer's job, do we not align ourselves with the Younger Report's emphasis on coercion, and so make true help to clients impossible, whilst also provoking a justified revolt from the younger generation of probation officers?

We believe that a clue to the resolution of this apparent incompatibility between help and surveillance has been proposed in a recent article by Peter Raynor.[67] He correctly suggests that, in the treatment model, "the compulsory persuaders' confusion between helping and control . . . seems to rest on an underlying assumption that human behaviour can be viewed deterministically, as a simple matter of cause and effect" (p. 419). Like us, he rejects this determinism, but then draws a crucial conceptual distinction between "coercion" (as in the Younger Report) and "constraint." "Coercion" is "an assault on identity," and "any repressive, manipulative or exploitative social relations contain elements of such an assault" (p. 420). But if we accept the value of "respect for persons," coercion must be eschewed, and we must accept people's ability and right to choose—even if we do not like what they choose. Now, every society clearly tries "to influence people's choices by attaching constraints or sanctions to one alternative or rewards to another," but this does not abolish the fact of choice, for:

> Choices made under constraint . . . *are still real choices.* As in all serious
> choices, the constraint arises from the fact that choices have consequences,

and that the consequences of one alternative will be different from those of the other (p. 420: italics added).

Thus, choice under constraint is acceptable; manipulative coercion is not. Yet, in the probation context, is this a real distinction, or just juggling with words? Like Raynor, we believe it can be either, depending on the way it is applied. For it to be a real distinction a conscious effort has to be made to maximize the area of choice for the offender, since ultimately:

> the business of influencing people to change their behaviour is about choice. It has something to do with increasing people's sense of identity and responsibility by increasing the range of situations in which they have a real choice of how to behave and realise their goals[68] (p. 421).

Traditionally in the probation service there is offender consent to the making of the probation order, but this consent is largely a formal affair, not much discussed in advance with the offender, and not making it clear to him in court what the real alternative sentence is. There follows a probation order in which the offender becomes the passive recipient of compulsory treatment: "it is not mentioned on the order that probation is treatment" (Fisher[69]), yet the order is seen by officers as having a "hidden agenda" which requires compulsory treatment. In these ways, traditional probation practice comes closer to "coercion" than to "choice under constraint," in Raynor's terms.

In our paradigm, choice has to be maximized both at the court stage and subsequently. The consent to the making of the order, given to the court, has to become much more of a real consent made in a real-choice situation —we discuss this more fully under the third aim. This order, by imposing various requirements, gives authority to the officer to supervise the offender in accordance with the requirements. Within the order, the client then chooses to accept or reject social work help, any acceptance being subject to withdrawal at any time by the client, without incurring official sanctions, and without being adversely reported on in a social inquiry report in the event of a further court appearance.

Thus, offenders placed on probation or other compulsory supervision would still be obliged to submit to the formal requirements of the order, the authority-base for which derives quite clearly from the *court*; but the authority-base for the "help" would reside unambiguously in the *client*. Probation officers would have to stop operating, as they often do now, on the assumption that either the authority to treat or the authority to compel attendance derived from professional expertise. They would also have to stop setting the frequency of reporting as in part a judgment of "response"; for in our model frequncy of reporting must not and cannot be determined by officers' judgments of client response to help. The best available solution to the question of frequency of reporting would be to return to the 1907 model and have this laid down by the court.[70]

This discussion helps to clarify that both the pure treatment model and our model involve an element of pressure, but in different ways. The compulsory treatment model imposes coercion as to either "co-operating in expert treatment" or implicit rejection by the worker. The help model obliges the client to make a series of moral and behavioural choices, but the worker does not reject the client whatever choices are made. There have to be definite boundaries to the help available: probation officers cannot provide help outside the scope of their agency function; nor can they collude with the client to evade the formal requirements of the probation order; nor can they help clients in certain ways, for example in procuring drugs or housebreaking implements. But within the limits of these clear boundaries, unconditional help is offered, though the client must make the choices: this gives the client greater responsibility, and also means that in certain contexts he must carry the consequences of wrong choices—for example in further court appearances. The worker cannot help the client to avoid those consequences; but equally, the worker will not make the consequences worse for the client by an implied or actual rejection in the social inquiry report. (A fuller discussion of the implications for social inquiry reports is given under the third aim.)

Lastly, we may make two final points about this second aim of "surveillance." The first is to draw attention to some recent research which perhaps shows, in different contexts, that surveillance may (for as long as it lasts) be beneficial in "holding" clients from reconviction (Berg et al; Home Office[71]). As with the similar results in the "help" context, we do not place too much weight on such findings, but at least they may help to allay the fears of some officers that a more overt emphasis upon reporting would lead to a massive rejection by clients, and therefore more reconvictions. Secondly, we should note that this second aim provides the essential answer to the obvious question: "if we substitute help for treatment, why should any court ever put anyone on probation?" The pragmatic answer to that, we would suggest, is to look at the community service order, where the surveillance and work tasks are compulsory, and additional client assistance is voluntary—and community service orders, unlike probation orders, are a growth industry. The more careful and theoretical answer is that if courts can be persuaded to see that probation meets the community's wish for surveillance, whilst also allowing the client to select appropriate assistance if desired, then indeed there are sound reasons to make such orders. But to develop this further takes us into the themes of our third aim.

Aim 3: Diverting Appropriate Offenders from Custodial Sentences

The idea of saving appropriate offenders from going to prison where this seemed socially unnecessary has been a central part of the philosophy and practice of the probation service since its inception.

In the climate of the late 1970s, this concept received substantial support from the Home Office. A recent report of the Advisory Council on the Penal System,[72] and a Home Office review of criminal policy[73] have both stressed the need for sentences of imprisonment to become shorter, and the importance of achieving a further switch of sentences from imprisonment to non-custodial alternatives, to accelerate the post war trend in this direction.[74] One of the "main conclusions" of the Home Office review is that "the reduction of the prison population must remain a particular preoccupation."[75]

Hard on the heels of these two documents has come the publication of a study by the Home Office Research Unit of the prison population in the South East Region.[76] This study argued that, on certain given criteria.[77] some 266 out of 771 men then imprisoned in the South East Region were potentially "divertible"—a proportion of just over one-third. Given that this was a prison *population* study, and given also i) that it is the short sentence men who are the most divertible, and ii) that short sentence men make up a smaller proportion of the prison population than they do of prison *receptions*, it follows that a markedly higher proportion of receptions (i.e. persons received into prison under sentence) would be divertible than the one-third population figure. This reception-saving proportion cannot be readily calculated from the data given in the article, but a reasonable guess is that it would be in the region of one-half.

Is it really realistic to speak in terms of diverting one-half of all people sentenced to imprisonment to some non-custodial alternative? On the face of it the proposition does not sound particularly feasible. There are some technical statistical difficulties about it,[78] but of more importance are certain theoretical and practical stumbling blocks which must be given serious consideration.

To tackle these we need to consider on what grounds custodial and non-custodial sentences are currently awarded. In our view, sentencing to custody can be crudely conceptualized in the terms suggested by Figure 7.1.[79] Above a certain level of offence seriousness (which may vary in practice between different judges), custodial sentences are perceived by the judiciary as mandatory, and any other alternative as "unrealistic." Conversely, for trivial offences (with, again, some disagreement about definition), no question of custody is normally thought to arise. Within a

		Seriousness of offence		
		Low	Medium	High
Offender's social need	High	*non-custody*	*non-custody (?)*	*custody*
	Medium	*non-custody*	?	*custody*
	Low	*non-custody*	*custody (?)*	*custody*

Figure 7.1 Custodial sentencing in relation to seriousness of offence and offender's social need.

medium band of seriousness, however, prison is a real but not an inevitable possibility; and within this band, one of the main determinants of the use of custody will be the offender's perceived social need—for, up to a defined point, *the more convincingly the offender can be portrayed as a victim of his social circumstances, the more likely are probation officers to recommend, and judges to seek, non-custodial possibilities.*[80]

With this conceptual model in mind, we would like to consider four possible obstacles to the development of non-custodial disposals. First there is the question of sentencers' perceptions of alternatives. It is clearly a truism that sentencers are unlikely to divert more offenders from custody unless they perceive the alternatives as realistic and appropriate in all the circumstances. But it would be a mistake to suppose that sentencers' perceptions of what is a "realistic alternative" will always be constant. For example, judgments may alter as to what is so serious an offence that no alternative to custody is thinkable; and one of the things which might make judgments change in this way is precisely the development by probation officers of a different conceptual basis for presenting alternatives to the courts. Again, assuming it is true that the number of custodial sentences in the middle range of offence seriousness is currently determined largely by the presence or absence of perceived social need, then an alteration of that situation could obviously lead to more non-custodial sentences for offenders of low social need. In short, sentencers' perception of "realistic alternatives" whilst being a central issue to consider if this third aim is to be achieved, is not itself a fixed category but one that can be influenced by other matters, including the practice and recommendations of probation officers.

This brings us directly to our second point, which is that, ironically, the use of treatment concepts by probation officers can actually encourage a greater use of custody. For example, there is evidence from the field of community service that some officers regard this form of sentence as inappropriate for those for whom "professional casework support is needed," and therefore may be reluctant to make recommendations in such cases.[81] Given that about half of those sentenced to community service orders would probably otherwise have been given a custodial sentence,[82] this could obviously lead to certain offenders being sent to prison instead of being diverted. This curious state of affairs arises because we have grown accustomed to thinking of "alternatives to prison" in largely rehabilitative (or anyway attemptedly rehabilitative) terms. The current logic within the medium range of offence seriousness is that social and treatment needs lead to non-custodial possibilities, but ordinary offenders with few social needs go to prison.

We need to confront this logic head on. If treatment "works" in reducing crime, some kind of justification for the needs-based foundation of non-custodial recommendations can be produced (though whether this is consistent with the demands of justice is still an open question). But if we abandon assumptions of treatment effect, this whole case loses plausibility. Instead, we can certainly argue (as indicated earlier in this essay) that there are available within the probation service a number of resources—probation itself, community service, day training centres, probation hostels, day centres, and so on—which might well "hold" many offenders as successfully in the community as in prison, and more cheaply. The deliberate use of such facilities irrespective of offenders' suitability for treatment and irrespective of social need should, therefore, allow a considerable expansion of non-custodial possibilities. It would also meet sentencers' anxieties about alternatives in a responsible and realistic manner, without making any false assumptions about the treatment efficacy of such alternatives.[83]

A possible argument against this brings us to our third point. The Home Office Policy Review, while stressing the need to reduce the prison population, believed that the best hope for this lay in the use of shorter sentences of imprisonment and/or a greater use of parole, rather than in diverting more people from custody. The reason for this rather pessimistic assessment of the possibilities of further diversion was that, because of the current crisis in financial resources, "at least in the short term the development of non-custodial alternatives cannot be expected to bring great relief" (p. 10). In other words, there is no money available for further developments of such things as hostels or day training centres, so further scope for diversion is simply not available. Now certainly this point has to be given careful consideration—but it is, in our view, not as absolute a limitation as the Home Office Review suggests. For if it can be shown that existing facilities are capable of greater use, then the argument is immediately undermined to that extent; and indeed there is strong evidence of the declining use of probation orders, the scope for much greater use of community service facilities, and so on. It is our contention that if these measures were reconceptualized in non-treatment terms it would allow them to be used more fully in the middle range of seriousness because they could be considered in cases of low social need.

Even at the "bricks and mortar" end of the spectrum of alternatives to prison, there is evidence of the under-use of the four experimental day training centres and, in some regions, of adult probation hostels.[84] It might seems extraordinary that such facilities are under-used when homeless and socially inadequate men are sent to prison instead, but there appear to be two main reasons for these vacancies: wardens' and directors' natural desires to lead a quiet life, and the infusion of treatment concepts which allow them to speak of clients being "unsuitable for the kind of treatment offered in the hostel" and so on. If this kind of "initial treatment assessment" is abandoned—as, on all the evidence about the failure of treatment, it ought to be—then wardens and directors would in future be able to reject cases only on the grounds of potential disruptiveness, and this factor could be more carefully monitored than at present.

Our fourth point is a little more technical, and relates to the use of the suspended sentence of imprisonment. Although much neglected by penal analysts, this sentence is now one of the major court disposals for adult offenders in England. Forty per cent of those given this sentence commit another imprisonable offence within two years; and about three-quarters of these are given the original sentence, plus a new custodial sentence, usually to run consecutively.[85] Since there is substantial evidence also that the courts are continuing to award suspended sentences in lieu of non-custodial sentences in some cases (rather than solely in place of imprisonment as statute law now enjoins[86]), it follows that the suspended sentence is a distinctly two-edged weapon in terms of its apparent contribution as a diversionary sentence. However, it is very widely recommended by probation officers; a recent study in South Yorkshire showed that it was recommended in as many as 23% of cases (with or without an additional supervision requirement) in a representative sample of Crown Court defendants.[87] Since there is also evidence that many courts follow the recommendations of probation officers quite closely,[88] and that this is not always a question of officers "second-guessing" the magistrates' likely sentence,[89] the long term effect of making suspended sentence recommendations could well be to send an offender to prison where he might otherwise not have finished up; alternatively or additionally, it might increase the length of the ultimate sentence. These "kick-back" effects of suspended sentence are not widely appreciated by probation officers, but they are obviously of considerable importance in relation to this third aim. The only safe rule if the probation service wishes to pursue this aim seriously is, we believe, that officers should treat the suspended sentence as what it is in law—a sentence of imprisonment which has been suspended—and therefore not recommend it except where they would definitely be willing to recommend immediate imprisonment.

But that raises a further issue: should officers be in the business of recom-

mending custodial sentences in social inquiry reports? They do, of course
—the research evidence is quite clear on that,[90] and indeed the Home
Office has endorsed the practice.[91] But recommendations for custody in
social inquiry reports must either be based on the officer's view that
custody is the best available "treatment" disposal, or on the grounds that
the offence in some sense "merits" imprisonment. The research evidence
gives no support whatever to the first view, and the second ground is
surely within the court's, not the probation officer's, judgment. Hence, if
the probation service wishes to pursue its third aim, it should cease to be in
the business of recommending custody—and that must include, as we have
argued above, suspended sentences of imprisonment as well.

We have discussed four possible obstacles to a major diversionary programme as implied by the South East Population Study—sentencers'
perceptions of alternatives; the potentially anti-diversionary effects of
treatment concepts; the problem of resources; and the "kick-back" effects
of suspended sentences. It would be a reasonable summary to say that
these obstacles together are not of such weight as to suggest that a further
substantial reduction in custodial sentences cannot be achieved. We believe
it can be achieved—but only if:

   i. probation officers abandon treatment concepts in making recom-
     mendations;
   ii. they cease to recommend custodial or suspended sentence disposals;
   iii. they think imaginatively but realistically about alternatives within
     the range of existing facilities, and develop appropriate recommen-
     dations in suitable cases.

We do not consider that present practice comes near to these specifica-
tions, and we are therefore not impressed by the counter argument that
"the probation service is already doing all it can do by way of diversion." As
with the other aims we discuss, we believe that a radical reconceptualization of practice is required if this third aim of the service is to be appropriately fulfilled.

The major piece of reconceptualization required is with respect to the
social inquiry report. Fred Perry has said that "social inquiry reports . . .
are founded on the clinical treatment model of the sentencing process."[92]
He is, of course, historically wrong—social inquiry reports existed in the
probation service long before the clinical treatment model was adopted.
But certainly he is right in supposing that the major post war impetus in
developing the social inquiry report at the time of the Streatfeild Report[93]
was a "scientific view" of sentencing, based on the assumption that there
was (at least in principle) a unique "best" treatment available to prevent
the defendant from reoffending; and certainly also he is right in implying
that this model—in however attenuated a form—still constitutes the

underlying philosophy behind much current daily practice in the matter of social inquiry reports. Thus it is that two senior and very influential members of the probation service can claim, in a NAPO sponsored booklet that:

> a social inquiry is a comprehensive and objective document prepared by the professionally trained social worker of the court to assist the court in a more effective sentencing practice (Herbert and Mathieson[94]).

Two other social work writers (Pearce and Wareham) have correctly stated that "the SER has been repeatedly found wanting in relation to these criteria."[95] We shall not document this claim in full—readers are referred to the appropriate literature.[96] But Herbert and Mathieson's concept of the social inquiry report is completely antithetical to all that we have already argued about the empirical and theoretical defects of the treatment model, and about the appropriate kind of social work practice (and "professionalism") which needs to be adopted if aim 1 of the probation service is to be fulfilled. We therefore assume without further argument that this concept of the social inquiry report cannot be sustained.

But if so, what kind of social inquiry reports are to replace the existing ones? A full discussion of the point would require a paper in its own right; but three brief points can be made.

First, the purpose of the social inquiry report must be reconsidered. There is simply no real evidence that social inquiry reports have "assisted the court in a more effective sentencing practice." That being so, what is the purpose of social inquiry reports to be in the future? Bearing in mind our four aims, we suggest that the answer is that they must simultaneously aim to present appropriate social information to the court, to help offenders, and to develop appropriate diversion strategies to prevent imprisonment. This means that officers should present social information as concretely as possible (and be very careful about implied moral value judgments: see below), and in considering their recommendations they should bear in mind particularly the possibility of recommending appropriate diversion possibilities.

Second, the language of social inquiry reports will need a major overhaul. At present, these reports are replete with examples of language which embodies what Strawson has termed "the objective attitude" (phrases such as "he presents as an anxious and immature individual" give the flavour). In terms of the function of a social inquiry report in providing social information to the court, such language often singularly fails to portray the defendant as a real, living human person from a real social setting. It is also exceptionally easy to incorporate moral evaluations within the supposedly "professionally objective" assessment. As Bean has correctly noted:

The thrust towards professionalism by probation officers has meant that they now wish to slough off the evangelical image and replace it with the "professional adviser to the court" image. Once this happens they cease to be the offender's spokesman . . . they claim to have the expertise to advise the court on the most appropriate method of dealing with each case. . . . The difficulty confronting probation officers is that they believe themselves to be primarily concerned with personality assessment, when they are more likely to be involved in moral evaluations. Terms like "immature," "authority problems," "sensitive," "agreeable" and "quarrelsome" *are* moral evaluations delineating moral character.[97]

A much more direct, less "professional" and "objective" language is called for if the new purposes of the social inquiry report are to be achieved; and moral assessments, if made, must be explicitly recognized as such. This will require a considerable amount of detailed rethinking of daily practice.

Third, there are considerable implications for the practice of recommending sentences. It is implicit in this third aim that probation officers will continue to make recommendations in order to be able to present diversionary alternatives to courts otherwise contemplating custodial sentences; and we think that this is a sufficient justification for the making of recommendations in cases of this sort. But in other cases, once one has abandoned Streatfeild thinking, the justification for recommendations is not strong: therefore we might expect to see some reduction in the overall number of recommendations made if our paradigm were put into practice.

But even the making of recommendations for "diversionary packages" in pursuit of aim 3 does raise one major difficulty which must be faced squarely. For at least in some cases, what is recommended may constitute a fairly extensive amount of social control being taken over the offender in the community: as would be the case with recommendations for a hostel or DTC placement, for example. Given that we know that courts often follow recommendations in social inquiry reports, this means that the officer cannot evade a part of the responsibility for the social control element in the eventual order made. How can this be equated with what we have said in respect to aim 1 about the probation service offering only voluntary help to offenders, with the client making the choices?

In part, this issue was discussed in relation to aim 2, when we suggested that the authority for control elements in the order flowed from the court, and authority for help must flow from the client. But, at that stage, we deliberately left on one side the implications of this for social inquiry reports; and in fact, the existence of the recommendation within the social inquiry report does tend to drive a coach and horses through the neat court/client distinction, since obviously the probation officer is in a position where control may flow from his recommendations.

Given what we have argued about "choice under constraint" in relation to aim 2, we believe there is only one way out of this dilemma. This is to rule that all recommendations made by a probation officer in a social inquiry report must carry the consent of the client. In that way, the client shares the moral responsibility for the social control elements in the subsequent order: it is part of the series of moral and behavioural choices with which he is confronted in our paradigm (see the discussion under aim 2). It may be, for example, that the defendant would ideally prefer a less controlling situation to that suggested by the probation officer as an alternative to imprisonment: but if the officer's judgment is that the proposed recommendation is the likely price of obtaining a non-custodial sentence from the court, and if that judgment is made in good faith, then this is simply one among many choices under constraint which have to be made in daily life. Ultimately, however, we stress that if the defendant and the officer cannot agree, a recommendation would not be made. In Raynor's terms (as discussed under aim 2), choice under constraint must not be allowed to slide into coercion.

Indeed, we would go further and argue that to maximize the defendant's choice at the sentencing stage, the legal requirements for consent to be given by the defendant to probation orders and community service orders[98] should be treated much more seriously by courts than at present. Courts should put to defendants what the real alternative sentence is, and be prepared to abide by it if the defendant declines probation. Only in this way can the maximization of choice by offenders, argued for throughout this paper, be achieved.

These necessary considerations have led us far afield into a number of complex areas. So we end by reiterating the main argument of this section of the paper: that there is considerable scope for the further diversion of offenders from custodial sentences; that this can be achieved, at least to a considerable extent, without additional resources for "alternatives"; that it can be achieved consistently with the other aims of the service as defined in this paper; but that for this to occur, there must be a complete reconceptualization of practice in social inquiry work.

Aim 4: The Reduction of Crime

Our first three aims have between them covered the traditional work of the probation service in relation to offenders. In discussing them, we have argued that short term effects in "holding" people from crime may be available, but we have made no assumption that any of the activities will reduce recidivism in any permanent way.

Some would probably be content to leave the matter there, and to abandon any continued pretence that the probation service can reduce crime. On this argument, our first three aims would be held to be worth pursuing in their own right, and this would be a sufficient justification for the continuance of the work of the agency.

We do not share this view, for two reasons. First, the traditional expectation of the probation service by the public at large has been that it helps to reduce crime. In a situation where poor people are often the victims of crime,[99] and where there is some evidence of their increasing anxiety about such victimization, we do not think that such expectations can be abandoned lightly;[100] and if traditional methods have failed, there is an obligation at least to consider other methods. Secondly, we shall argue below that the kind of crime reduction strategy most worth attempting would in any case have other desirable side efects for the community, and also for the work of the probation service as we have reconceptualized it under the first three aims.

If treatment or "help" will not reduce crime, what will? There is only one realistic answer: crime prevention. But "prevention" can mean many different things to different people—it can mean, for example, applying extraversion tests to small children, picking out those "difficult to condition," and giving them "a much more rigorous and efficient system of conditioning than the normal person" (Eysenck[101]); it can mean the redesigning of urban architecture, especially in residential buildings (Newman[102]); it can mean advice to the public about locking houses and cars, and buying burglar alarms (any police crime prevention department); or it can mean a complete revolution in society, since "it must be possible via social transformations to create social and productive arrangements that would abolish crime" (Taylor, Walton and Young[103]).

We do not propose to discuss such prescriptions here, though all of them can be heavily criticized in different ways. The point simply is that none of the skills required to construct these alleged Utopias exist within the probation service, so they are not worth considering in depth in this context.

Rather, we shall argue here that crime is predominantly social, so that any serious crime reduction strategy must be of a socially (rather than an individually) based character; that "treatment" strategies as applied to communities are as inappropriate for crime prevention as they are for individual "help" for offenders; that nevertheless there are some plausible clues which might be followed in a crime reduction strategy by the probation service; that these clues essentially consist of possible micro-structural and socially integrative ameliorations within communities; but that these ameliorations can take place only if significant power in their implementation is given to the residents of high crime rate communities, with the professional probation officer restricting his role to that of helper and catalyst. We shall consider these points *seriatim*.

One of the most striking facts about, at any rate, recorded crime is its social regularity. Males are convicted much more often than females; persons in the adolescent age range are much more often convicted than older persons; urban centres have much higher rates of known crimes and offenders than rural ones, even when account is taken of different population levels. It is difficult in the extreme to believe that all these constant patternings of crime can be "explained" convincingly on any kind of individual theory of crime; it is also difficult to believe that the differences are simply the result of differential police activity (Mawby[104]).

Similarly, there is evidence from current research work in Sheffield of areas with markedly similar demographic characteristics, but very different rates of offending. For example, two pre-war council housing estates, separated only by a main road, have a very similar social composition (in terms of age, sex, social class and so on); but they have official crime and offender rates three to four times different, and these differences were maintained (but at a reduced level) when crime in the areas was measured by adult and juvenile victimization and self-report studies.[105] It is highly implausible to suggest that these differences are simply the result of individual personality factors or childrearing patterns; it is equally implausible to suppose that the differences could be permanently altered by intensive casework with individuals on the high rate estate.

Work with *communities*, rather than individuals, therefore seems to be called for. Yet community work with the aim of crime reduction can be done in many different ways.[106] Which way is appropriate?

One possible method is a treatment-orientated one, in which the social work team in effect diagnoses the ills of the community and tries to put them right. Such an approach was, in essence, attempted in the Bristol Social Project of the 1950s (Spencer[107]). The difficulties with the approach are exactly the same as those of the individual treatment model—first, there is no strong evidence that it works;[108] and second, the recipients of the treatment do not see the approach as meeting their real needs. This second point was vividly illustrated in the Bristol Project, where the decision to focus on a particular "problem" council estate (Upfield) produced widespread resentment which was never overcome:

> To many citizens in the selected area, the very fact of selection was a threat to their already troubled state of mind. The articulate residents of Upfield were certainly sceptical about our choice: "Why choose us" . . . "Why must we endure the stigma of yet another group of outsiders? Why not leave us alone?" (p. 25).

That the project team persisted in Upfield in the face of such criticism says much for their commitment to the view that they knew better than the residents what was good for them.

Throughout this paradigm, we have tried to stress the client's eye-view; to maximize the delivery of "help" as seen from the client's perspective, and to maximize his choice (albeit under necessary constraints) in respect of law enforcement situations. In the area of attempted crime reduction, we think there is a strong case for retaining these theoretical presuppositions; and this is precisely because, since crime is predominantly social, nothing less than the strong involvement of lay people from ordinary communities is likely to have much effect in reducing it. As the celebrated Chicago Area Project had it (in rather dated sociological language):

> It is a commonplace of sociological observation that the source of control of conduct for the person lies in his natural social world. The rules and values having validity for the person are those which affect his daily nurturance, his place in primary groups, and his self-development. He is responsive as a person within the web of relationships in which his daily existence as a human being is embedded . . . [Hence] a *delinquency prevention program could hardly hope to be effective unless and until the aims of such a program became the aims of the local populations* (Kobrin: italics added[109]).

Hence we believe that the probation service should not engage in crime prevention work except in communities which actively wish it, and that, throughout the work, the authority base for the social workers' actions should remain with the residents and their wish for assistance. This is, of course, fully congruent with the "help" concept which has flowed throughout this paper, and is radically different from Haxby's more correctionalist approach to community crime reduction.[110]

If a particular group of probation officers is invited into an area in this way, they will still need to have some ideas as to how, within this "help" framework, crime could be reduced in practice. The residents themselves will no doubt produce many worthwhile ideas which could be acted upon, but they will probably also expect some theoretical input from the probation team. In the nature of the case, it is not possible to specify in advance exactly what could be done, but two broad tactics seem worth pursuing, and these we have described as relating to the micro-structural and the integrative aspects of the area. In outlining these, we have to stress that the suggestions made are tentative, and not certain to produce the required result. Nevertheless there seems to be about them sufficient evidence to make them worth pursuing on an experimental basis.

By *micro-structural* aspects we mean those features of the local situation which appear to be crime producing, and on which local residents might have some influence. Three examples would be the school, the housing market and the employment situation. There is some (not wholly unambiguous) evidence that different schools "produce" differential amounts of juvenile delinquency, even when catchment areas are controlled for (Phillipson[111]); work by local residents with the local school may have a desirable impact in producing the kind of structure and atmosphere in the school which is more likely to reduce the juvenile offending rate. There is also now some quite strong evidence that the council housing allocation system can have a central influence upon the development of "good" and "bad" areas; and as Gill[112] puts it in his compelling book on a Merseyside estate:

> The individually orientated "social work" approach which is basic to our orientation to adolescent delinquency is virtually useless in dealing with a situation such as exists in Luke Street. Indeed it may well be counter-productive. . . . It is necessary to change our emphasis from the individual and to counteract the processes that are involved in the creation of the delinquent area (pp. 186–7).

This change of emphasis which Gill advocates might involve extensive and detailed representations having to be made to the housing authority, and certainly a much greater sensitivity and awareness on the part of probation officers about the role of the housing market in the production of crime.

A third area of structural concern is unemployment, and this indicates both possibilities and limitations. There is not much doubt, for example, that a high unemployment rate amongst school-leavers can escalate the crime rate within that group; and the structural creation of employment opportunities within a local area can therefore be well worth pressing for by residents on crime prevention as well as general social grounds. At the same time it has to be borne in mind that there are quite severe limitations on what can be done in such a context (as also to an extent in the housing and school contexts) within the existing social and economic structure. As Gill puts it in what he describes as "a final note of pessimism."[113]

> Sensitive [housing] allocation procedures have their uses. But in the end they are partially neutralised by the more basic arrangements of power in society. . . . Like it or not, when we are trying to understand what happens on [the street] corner, we are forced back into wide-scale issues of housing, unemployment, and the distribution of social power.

Ultimately this is correct, and even a massively funded crime prevention programme will not be allowed to change the overall distribution of power in society, as the well-known American project "Mobilisation for Youth" discovered (Moynihan[114]). From this it does not follow, however, that nothing worthwhile in the way of crime reduction can be pursued in the absence of major social change. Different areas of the same social type *do* have differential crime rates, and there are clues available as to ways in which some of these rates might be reduced. In Gill's own phrase, "sensitive allocation procedures have their uses," and so do other kinds of micro-structural amelioration.

The second kind of possible tactic for crime reduction by residents lies in the idea of *social integration*; and this is based on the proposition that, other things being equal, societies with strongly cohesive social bonds tend to produce less crime. There is a variety of evidence to this effect: the low crime rates of villages as compared with towns; a famous rsearch study in Cambridge, Massachusetts, in two structually similar districts with massively different crime rates, which concluded that "lack of social integration appears to have certain direct effects in a lowered level of social control of delinquent activities" (Maccoby, Johnson and Church[115]); and recent studies of two industrialized urban countries with little or declining crime, both of which attribute this, in the main, to the strength of "community" (Clifford; Clinard[116]).

But we must not be optimistic too readily about the possibilities of increasing social integration. In a recent and most important paper, Abrams[117] makes a sharp and relevant distinction between community care and community treatment. The former he defines as "the provision of help, support and protection to others by lay members of societies acting in everyday domestic and occupational settings," whilst the latter is the provision of services through the placement of professional and specialist personnel in local communities. Abrams believes—and cites considerable research evidence in support—that "community care," in this lay sense, is uncommon and improbable in our kind of advanced welfare state-capitalist society, and that community care will decline as professional social care increases. But against this realistically gloomy background, he nevertheless asserts as a possibility that there are:

> certain ambiguities in the normative context of community life which could conceivably be exploited for the purposes of procuring care. First, there is the evidence of latent community involvement. And secondly there is the realisation that altruism is self-centred. Taken together these findings suggest that *although we cannot hope to build on spontaneity as a basis for community care we may well be able to build on reciprocity*; and that a closer understanding of the nature of social reciprocity and the conditions governing it might well be the most important general research task in this whole field (pp. 84–5: italics added).

Abrams is speaking largely, of course, about community care in the sense of caring for the elderly or the handicapped. But the "decline of community" background against which his paper is written is exactly the same as that which has led criminologists such as Christie[118] to press for a return to a more neighbourhood-centred mode of life, in the explicit expectation that this would lead to an improved quality of social living, and an implicit belief that it would reduce crime.[119] Between them, Abrams and Christie provide some useful insights as to how social cohesion might be strengthened. Abrams' central notion (derived from exchange theory) is that of reciprocity: that people give care when they are in relationships which also have meaning and value for themselves, and that it is a practical possibility to build on this insight in various different contexts to see "how care can be *procured* in a largely uncaring milieu" (p. 84: italics in original).[120] The suggestions offered for improving reciprocity are largely of an individualized character (p. 91f), but well worth pursuing for all that.

Christie proposes an idealized model for a conflict-based, victim-orientated, non-professional neighbourhood court. Such an institution can exist only where there is a certain level of community, yet the relationship is reciprocal: the neighbourhood court is also explicitly intended to revitalize the social bonds in neighbourhoods, and the weaker neighbourhood bonds are, the more the court is considered essential by Christie as a means to strengthen them (p. 12). Regardless of one's views about Christie's specific model for court procedure, the important point here is that a given structural change (the creation of a neighbourhood court) is seen as a catalyst for promoting social cohesion and social care. One could obviously therefore expand this notion to consider ways of structurally altering other local institutions (such as the school) in order to revivify neighbourhoods.

It ought to be possible to build on these two notions of reciprocal exchange and structural change to promote better social cohesion, and therefore better community care, in a given area. By definition, the social work professional cannot create these things by his own strength (see Abrams' "inverse relationship"); he can only act as a catalyst for action and development by local residents. Thus these ideas fit extremely well into the client-centred community model proposed in this paper.

Two theoretical issues remain to be considered: the meaning of "community," and the link with crime. "Community" is something of a vogue-word, a catch-all which if one is not careful can lose any meaning. And Abrams makes clear that the search for community care, in a strictly neighbourhood sense, may be a misplaced one:

> The really striking thing about those few contexts in which community care is provided to a degree which might obviate the need for public intervention in contemporary Britain is that in almost every well-documented case the decisive context of care is not in fact a *community* context—at least not in

any territorial, localistic sense of community. Rather, the effective social bases for community care are kinship, religion, and race (pp. 86–7).

There are, therefore, social networks of caring, not neighbourhoods in the strict sense. Similarly, Jacqueline Scherer[121] in her analysis of contemporary community rejects a geographical base for conceptualizing community, and finds it most helpful to think in terms of social networks. Whilst these rejections of geography may be overstated,[122] the "network" conceptualization is of considerable assistance in thinking through the ways of strengthening neighbourhood ties and social cohesion, and it suggests that those who travel this road will need an acquaintance with social network theory.[123]

But what about crime? Even if community care can be enhanced on the Abrams–Christie suggestions, does this necesarily mean that crime rates will be reduced? The answer must be negative. We have seen that there is a general relationship between social cohesion and crime; but the explanation for varying crime rates within urban communities is certainly more complex than a simple correlation with levels of reciprocality in relationships (Hackler, Ho and Urquhart-Ross[124]). For example, there are some communities with highly cohesive relationships but with very high official crime rates: socialized into a criminal subculture which has arisen for complex social reasons, residents will usually refrain from intra-group crime, but crimes against outsiders will be regarded as perfectly fair game.[125] Again, we know from other research that processes such as the housing market; schools; differential arrangement and perception of social space, and so on, are powerfully important matters in the production of differential urban crime levels,[126] and this is why the structual aspect of crime prevention will also have to be developed in any crime reduction programme along the lines recommended under this aim. Despite these caveats, it remains reasonably clear that the "integrative" possibility for crime reduction also carries prima-facie plausibility in many social areas, notably those where i) there is a fairly high crime rate in the area and the residents have become actively worried about this; ii) there is independent evidence that many of the residents do not feel particularly happy or settled in the area, and that there is a high degree of social isolation and lack of "community care" in Abrams' sense; and iii) there is no strong evidence of a cohesive criminal subculture in the area.

We recognize, of course, that what we have suggested under this fourth aim is extremely difficult; that it will require considerable reorientation by and retraining of probation staff; and that there is no guarantee of success in crime reduction at the end of the day. Despite the difficulties, we believe that something along these lines needs to be attempted if the probation service is to take seriously the aim of crime reduction. And even if crime reduction is not achieved, the pushing of the "help" model onto a community base should enable communities to develop in what residents regard as desirable ways; whilst for the probation service it should strengthen the client-centred focus we have developed under the other three aims, as well as giving officers a clearer view of the real social worlds from which their probation clients come.

Finally, for those for whom this section has been altogether too theoretical and/or too idealistic, let us bring it down to earth with a practical example. The NACRO project on a high crime rate estate in Widnes, still incomplete, is a promising example of the kind of project we have in mind.[127] The focus was vandalism, and the starting point was Oscar Newman's theory of defensible space; but environmental improvements were not forced upon the residents. Rather, the project team consulted groups of residents selected on a random sample basis, and arising from their suggestions various environmental improvements were proposed:

> Environmental improvement is not new, nor is public consultation. What is new is combining the two to combat vandalism on estates. We have also used new methods to consult people and involve them more closely.[128]

After two years, impressionistic reports were optimistic.[129] The physical environment looked vastly improved, residents had more confidence and less sense of being under perpetual siege, "social activity on the estate is increasing and friendship networks are widening." Perhaps most interestingly there was also evidence of an increase in informal social controls, of the kind that had characterized the low delinquency estate in Maccoby's Cambridge study.[130] As the NACRO team put it:

> Two years ago when teenagers were causing a nuisance or smashing things, nobody dared to go out and tell them to stop. Now they are not afraid to, and the reasons they give are that they know the teenagers individually and they can rely on their neighbours to come out and support them.[131]

Thus the project has apparently combined micro-structural amelioration (environmental improvement), a strong resident-centred focus, and the development of greater community cohesion. As such, it clearly illustrates some of the possibilities that we have outlined. At the same time we would not wish to build too much upon these results, for the final report of the project is not yet completed, and recorded crime has apparently not decreased, despite the fact that "the tenants canvassed seem to feel that crime is abating on the estate."[132] Despite these caveats, we do think this project is worth careful study as an example of the kind of crime reduction project which probation officers could consider developing.

CONCLUSIONS

We began this paper with a quotation from the present Head of the Home Office Research Unit in which he raised the possibility of the demise of the probation service. We have argued that this possibility, remote though it might seem, must now be taken seriously. We have therefore attempted to specify some of the central issues which confront the service and to create a new paradigm for practice which tries to meet and overcome them in the inevitable confusion which must follow the death of treatment. Clearly, what we suggest is not intended to be a fully detailed prescription for action, but a theoretical model which might inform practice; and we reiterate that it is presented here for criticism and comment. If taken seriously, it has considerable implications for many organizational aspects of the service, such as staff training, but space precludes the development of such issues.

Of the many criticisms which can no doubt be levelled at our paradigm, there is just one which we should like to anticipate. Stanley Cohen has recently argued that our society is now spreading its control net wider and wider, with increasing numbers of people under correctional surveillance: "we can predict new levels of scrutiny and administrative disposition in the 'community'; overtly or covertly, more of our lives will be under central surveillance and control."[133] Aim 3 of our paradigm does propose having more people under supervision, but we are most anxious to avoid the insidious escalation of central control which Cohen predicts: hence we would stress that the client-centred focus of our model is a vital feature, and one that logically should lead to the reduction of centralized bureaucratic control in the probation service, not its increase.

We would also emphasize that we are concerned here only with what is immediately practicable, not with fundamental social change. We too have ideals about social justice towards which we would like our society and our criminal justice system to move. But we agree with Cohen[134] that:

> it should be possible . . . to develop middle-range policy alternatives which do not compromise any overall design for fundamental social change. This does not mean simply employing this overall design to develop a theoretical critique . . . but actually being brave enough to speculate on some policy alternatives, however unfinished and unworkable they might appear.

It is exactly this belief which has guided the development of this paradigm.

Acknowledgments

This paper arose out of joint discussions extending over several months, and has benefited considerably from the interim comments and criticisms received from colleagues and students in the South Yorkshire Probation and After Care Service and the University of Sheffield. We are also grateful to several friends who took the trouble to offer constructive criticisms of a previous draft. Our particular thanks to Professor Eric Sainsbury, who provided, and allowed us to use, some of the key analytical ideas developed under aim 1.

REFERENCES

1. Radzinowicz, L. (1958) in Preface to *The Results of Probation*, a Report of the Cambridge Department of Criminal Science, Macmillan, pp. x–xii.
2. Croft, J. (1978) *Research in Criminal Justice*. Home Office Research Study No. 44, HMSO, p. 4.
3. Lipton, D., Martinson, R. and Wilks, J. (1975) *The Effectiveness of Correctional Treatment*, New York, Praeger; Greenberg, D. F. (1977) "The Correctional Effects of Corrections: A Survey of Evaluations," in Greenberg, D. F. (ed.), *Corrections and Punishment*, Sage Criminal Justice System Annuals, Vol. 8, Beverly Hills, Sage; Brody, S. R. (1976) *The Effectiveness of Sentencing: A Review of the Literature*, Home Office Research Study No. 35, HMSO.
4. Folkard, M. S. et al. (1974) *Intensive Matched Probation and After-Care Treatment*, Vol. 1, The Design of the Probation Experiment and an Interim Evaluation, Home Office Research Study No. 24, HMSO; and Folkard, M. S. et al. (1976) *Intensive Matched Probation and After-Care Treatment*, Vol. 2. The Results of the Experiment, Home Office Research Study No. 36, HMSO.
5. American Friends Service Committee (1971) *Struggle for Justice*, New York, Hill and Wang, p. 21. This volume contains a sustained and influential theoretical critique of "treatment" in criminal justice sytems.
6. Durkheim, E. (1895) (Eng. trans. 1964) *The Rules of Sociological Method*, New York, Free Press (Ch. 3); Taylor, I., Walton, P. and Young, J. (1973) *The New Criminology*, Routledge and Kegan Paul.
7. Greenberg, op. cit., p. 141.
8. Allen, F. A. (1959) "Legal Values and the Rehabilitative Ideal," *J. of Crim. Law, Criminology and Police Science*, Vol. 50. pp. 226–32; reprinted in Allen, F. A. (1964) *The Borderland of Criminal Justice: Essays in Law and Criminology*, Chicago, University of Chicago Press.
9. Principal Probation Officers' Conference (1968) *The Place of the Probation and After-Care Service in Judicial Administration*. Leicester.
10. See, for example, Davies, M. (1974) *Social Work in the Environment*, Home Office Research Study No. 21, HMSO.
11. Recent evidence for this is provided in McWilliams, W. (1979) "Selection Policies for Community Service: Practice and Theory," in Pease, K. and McWilliams, W. (eds.) *Community Service by Order*, Edinburgh, Scottish Academic Press; and Hardiker, P. (1977) "Social Work Ideologies in the Probation Service." *Br. J. of Social Wk*, Vol. 7, No. 2.
12. "Social workers are apt to write in somewhat pompous and complex language

about the transactions between themselves and their clients. . . . Hence descriptions of social work activities are often somewhat partial and misleading and many people believe that the majority of caseworkers are immersed in long-term intensive casework dealing with their clients' intra-psychic and unconscious conflicts, discussing and interpreting childhood experiences and so on," in Goldberg, E. M. (1970) *Helping the Aged*, Allen and Unwin, p. 23.

13. Fisher, A. (1978) "Probation Service Exists on 'Elaborate Systems of Pretence,' " *Soc. Wk. Today*, Vol. 9, No. 37.
14. Harris, R. J. (1977) "The Probation Officer as Social Worker." *Br. J. of Social Wk*, Vol. 7, No. 4.
15. Harris, ibid., p. 441.
16. This makes all the more odd an amazing volte-face in Harris' argument. At pp. 435–6 he asserts categorically that "whatever social work training does do, it does not give any expertise whatever in stopping people getting into trouble"; six pages later, he declares that his proposed new structure will give social workers' "skills a chance to blossom, and who knows, *those skills may even . . . start reducing crime*" (p. 442: italics added) No reason whatever is given for the later assertion.
17. Haxby, D. (1978) *Probation: A Changing Service*. Constable.
18. Haxby, ibid., p. 201.
19. Spencer, J. C. (1964) *Stress and Release on an Urban Estate*, Tavistock Publications; and see Haxby, op. cit., p. 197.
20. Haxby, op. cit., p. 234.
21. Haxby, ibid., pp. 235–7.
22. Thomas, C. (1978) "Supervision in the Community." *Howard J.*, Vol. 17, No. 1.
23. "Alternatives to custody" schemes have not always been cheaper, or even less custodial, than their traditional counterparts: see the devastating analysis of California's Community Treatment Project and its Probation Subsidy Scheme in Lerman, P. (1975) *Community Treatment and Social Control*, Chicago, University of Chicago Press. Nevertheless, in principle and with careful planning, non-custodial alternatives should normally be less expensive, more humane, and just as effective as custodial penalties.
24. Sinclair, I. (1971) *Hostels for Probationers*, Home Office Research Study No. 6, HMSO.
25. Turner, M. (1972) "Norman House" in Whiteley, S., Briggs, D. and Turner, M. (eds.), *Dealing with Deviants*, Hogarth Press, pp. 212–13.
26. "Observations . . . are always *interpretations* of the facts observed: . . . they are *interpretations in the light of theories*. . . . Theory dominates the experimental work from initial planning up to the finishing touches," in Popper, K. R. (1959) *The Logic of Scientific Discovery*, Hutchinson, p. 107.
27. Weston, W. R. (1978) "Probation in Penal Philosophy: Evolutionary Perspectives." *Howard J.*, Vol. 17, No. 1.
28. Plant, R. (1979) "The Justice Model and Respect for Persons," in Bottoms, A. E. and Preston, R. H. (eds.), *The Coming Penal Crisis*, Edinburgh, Scottish Academic Press.
29. For a sustained discussion of this latter point, see Plant, R. (1970) *Social and Moral Theory in Casework*, Routledge and Kegan Paul, Ch 2.

30. Perlman, H. H. (1957) *Social Casework: A Problem-solving Process*, Chicago, University of Chicago Press.
31. Arguably, too, there were limitations in the police court missionaries' commitment to the concept of respect for persons, imposed by their correctional moral stance. We discuss this point more fully later in this paper.
32. Brody, S. R. (1978) "Research into the Aims and Effectivenss of Sentencing," *Howard J.*, Vol. 17, No. 3.
33. See for example Home Office (1977) *A Review of Criminal Justice Policy 1976*, HMSO, paras. 7 and 8.
34. See *Criminal Justice Act 1948*, Schedule V, para. 3(5); and, now, the *Powers of Criminal Courts Act 1973*, Schedule III, para. 8(1).
35. Le Mesurier, L. (ed.) (1935) *A Handbook of Probation and Social Work of the Courts*, National Association of Probation Officers.
36. King, J. F. S. (ed.) (1958) *The Probation Service*, first edition, Butterworths, pp. 73–6.
37. Silberman, M. and Chapman, B. (1971) "After-Care Units in London, Liverpool and Manchester," in *Explorations in After-Care*, Home Office Research Study No. 9, HMSO.
38. Morris, P. and Beverly, F. (1975) *On Licence: A Study of Parole*, Wiley, Ch. 9.
39. Giller, H. and Morris, A. (1978) "Supervision Orders—the Routinization of Treatment," *Howard J.*, Vol. 17, No. 3.
40. Strawson, P. F. (1974) *Freedom and Resentment*, Methuen.
41. Robinson, T. (1978) *In Worlds Apart: Professionals and their Clients in the Welfare State*, Bedford Square Press.
42. Murdoch, I. (1961) "Against Dryness: a Polemical Sketch," *Encounter*, No. 88, January, reprinted in Bradbury, M. (ed.), (1977) *The Novel Today*, Fontana/Collins.
43. Weston, op. cit., p. 11.
44. Matza, D. (1969) *Becoming Deviant*, Englewod Cliffs, N.J., Prentice-Hall, Ch. 2.
45. McWiliams, W. (1977) *Planning and Practice in Probation*, Leeds, Probation and After-Care Service Northern Region: Regional Committee for Staff Development.
46. Perlman, op. cit., p. 172.
47. It is perhaps not too far-fetched to suggest that the early probation officers laid most stress on *advice* in the form of moral exhortation; that the caseworkers stressed their particular version of the concept of *befriending*; and that only now is the probation service free at last to place primary stress on *assistance*.
48. Meyer, C. (1972) "Practice on Microsystem Level," in Mullen, E. T. and Dumpson, J. R. (eds.), *Evaluation of Social Intervention*, San Francisco, Jossey-Bass.
49. However, though it is a *necessary base* for meeting Croft's challenge, it is not sufficient in itself as an answer to the challenge—as the rest of this paper implicitly argues.
50. Reid, W. J. and Epstein, L. (1972) *Task-Centred Casework*, New York, Columbia University Press.

51. For a lucid introduction see Davies, M. (1977) *Support Systems in Social Work*, Routledge and Kegan Paul, Part Three.

52. Robinson, op. cit., pp. 26–31.

53. Davies, op. cit., p. 94.

54. On "rank-ascending monitoring" in probation see McWilliams, W. (1979) "Research, Monitoring and Bureaucracy," in King, J. F. S. (ed.), *Pressure and Change in the Probation Service*, Cambridge, Institute of Criminology, Cropwood Series No. 11.

55. This is not to commit the same volte-face as Harris (see above, note 16), because in this case a definitely different style of social work approach is involved, which is not the case in Harris' argument.

56. Bottoms, A. E. and McClintock, F. H. (1973) *Criminals Coming of Age*, Heinemann, Ch. 13.

57. Berntsen, K. and Christiansen, K. O. (1965) "A Resocialisation Experiment with Short-Term Offenders," in Christiansen, K. O. (ed.), *Scandinavian Studies in Criminology, Vol. 1*, Tavistock.

58. Brody, op. cit., p. 23.

59. As Berntsen and Christiansen themselves describe it (N = 126): "The social work consisted in finding work (54 cases), in finding accommodation (24 cases), clothing (30 cases), and in helping the prisoner with trade union and health insurance membership formalities (47 cases). Sometimes very modest financial help was given on the prisoner's release (31 cases), and sometimes it was necessary to help the prisoners in negotiations with tax authorities (15), with public assistance officers (22), and other public authorities and institutions as well as private creditors (60). Often assistance was needed to straighten out difficulties with wives or husbands, parents or other relatives (58). Twelve prisoners began an anti-alcoholic treatment during or after their imprisonment. . . . Through talks with particularly unbalanced prisoners the psychologist tried to cure depressions and to ward off conflicts." (p. 43).

60. The extension of this first aim to include the provision of appropriate help for *victims* would be entirely congruent with our theoretical framework and with recent developments in some probation areas. The subject is large, however, and space does not permit its inclusion here.

61. Foren, R. and Bailey, R. (1968) *Authority in Social Casework*, Pergamon Press, p. 99.

62. Advisory Council on the Penal System (1974) *Young Adult Offenders*, HMSO.

63. Raynor, P. (1978) "Compulsory Persuasion: A Problem for Correctional Social Work, *Br. J. of Social Wk.*, Vol. 8, No. 4.

64. Lawson, C. (1978) *The Probation Officer as Prosecutor: A Study of Proceedings for Breach of Requirement in Probation*, Cambridge, Institute of Criminology, Ch. 6.

65. McWilliams, B. C. and Murphy, N. (1979) "Breach of Community Service," in Pease, K. and McWilliams, W. (eds.), *Community Service by Order*, Edinburgh, Scottish Academic Press.

66. By this we mean *first*, that an abandonment of the probation officer's role as an officer of the court would lead to a major loss of credibility for the probation service in the eyes of magistrates, administrators, and others, with various

important consequential effects; *second*, that such an abandonment would essentially destroy any case for the continued existence of the probation service as a separate agency; and *third*, that within the existing agency structure even quite radical practice developments (such as the detached worker project in Sheffield reported in Hugman, B. (1978) *Act Natural*, Bedford Square Press) find that the law enforcement role ultimately cannot be evaded, not least because clients are well aware that it exists as an agency function.

67. Raynor, op. cit.

68. One qualification we would make is that in certain contexts both of the choices offered respect the individual so little as to amount to a form of coercion: an example would be the so-called choice offered to sex offenders in some countries, between continued imprisonment on the one hand, or parole and castration on the other. However, within the probation context we do not believe that any choices offered to offenders are or could be of this opressive character.

69. Fisher, op. cit.

70. It is of interest to note that senior practitioners have recently produced a discussion paper (Bryant, M. et al. (1978) "Sentenced to Social Work," *Probation Journal*, Vol. 25, No. 4) which suggests a model with some features in common with that proposed under this second aim. Although the paper in part still subtly evades the law enforcement role and appears to be based on a pragmatic desire to halt the present decline in the use of probation, it does, we think, give some indication that our model could be translated into practice.

71. A study in Leeds showed that, on a random allocation design, constant adjournments by the juvenile court led to less truancy and less offending than did conventional social work supervision: Berg, I. et al. (1978) "The Effect of Two Randomly Allocated Court Procedures on Truancy," *Br. J. of Criminology*, Vol. 18, No. 3. A study of parole showed that male offenders serving terms of over four years were more likely to avoid reconviction if paroled than if held in prison; for methodological reasons it is not clear that this is a true result, but if it is, it is more likely to be the result of surveillance than of "treatment" since no similar effect was found for short term men, who were presumably dealt with in similar ways by probation officers, but had less time under supervision and less to lose—see Home Office, *Prison Statistics 1977*, HMSO, Ch. 8.

72. Advisory Council on the Penal System (1977) *The Length of Prison Sentences*, HMSO.

73. Home Office (1977) *A Review of Criminal Justice Policy 1976* (Home Office Working Paper), HMSO.

74. In 1938, 33% of adult indictable offenders found guilty in England and Wales were sentenced to immediate imprisonment. By 1975, this proportion had fallen to 13%, although the prison population rose considerably over the same period mostly due to the very large increase in the annual number of persons convicted.

75. Home Office, op. cit., p. 10.

76. Home Office Research Unit (1978) "A Survey of the South East Prison Population," *Home Office Research Bulletin No. 5*, pp. 12–24.

77. The main criteria used were: no serious offences against the person; no crime ever for considerable gain; no large sums earned from crime over the length of a criminal career; no obvious competence in planning of crime.
78. Notably (i) that the survey was carried out in 1972, while by 1977 the South East Region appeared to have experienced "an increase in the proportion of longer sentences and of serious offences," and would thus have less potential divertibles (p. 23); (ii) there is some limited evidence of a higher imprisonment rate in the South East, which might produce a smaller proportion of divertibles in other regions.
79. In the figure the dimensions are trichotomized to aid clarity; they are, of course, continua.
80. Beyond a certain point in the conceptualization of the offender as "victim" the process which we outline can be reversed and the offender rejected as a "hopeless case." This can apply particularly to vagrants and lead to a custodial recommendation: see McWilliams, W. (1975) "Homeless Offenders in Liverpool," in *Some Male Offenders' Problems*, Home Office Research Study No. 28, HMSO.
81. Pease, K. et al. (1975) *Community Service Orders*. Home Office Rsearch Study No. 29, HMSO, p. 10.
82. Pease, K. et al. (1977) *Community Service Assessed in 1976*. Home Office Research Study No. 39, HMSO.
83. The abandonment of treatment concepts might also prevent some custodial sentences in a different way. There is strong impressionistic evidence to the effect that custody is sometimes recommended by probation officers because the offenders have "failed to respond" to the previous probation treatment offered—whereas had the offender originally been fined, a custodial recommendation would not always follow. If the probation service is to take this aim more seriously, this kind of thinking will have to be eschewed.
84. Based on current research by Stuart Palmer of the South Yorkshire Probation and After Care Service for a Cropwood Fellowship at the Institute of Criminology, Cambridge University.
85. For this and other evidence on the suspended sentence, see Bottoms, A. E. (1979) *The Suspended Sentence after Ten Years*, University of Leeds (Frank Dawtry Memorial Seminar).
86. Powers of Criminal Courts Act 1973, s.22(2) (replacing similar powers first enacted in the Criminal Justice Act 1972)
87. South Yorkshire Probation Service Diversion Project, 1977: the sample consisted of 273 defendants at the Sheffield Crown Court who were not current cases of the probation service at the time of committal. Some results of the project are reported by Harman, J. (1978) "Crisis Intervention (a form of diversion)," *Probation J.*, Vol. 25, No. 4.
88. White, S. (1972) "The Effect of Social Inquiry Reports on Sentencing Decisions." *Br. J. of Criminol.*, Vol. 12, No. 3.
89. Hine, J., McWilliams, W. and Pease, K. (1978) "Recommendations, Social Information, and Sentencing," *Howard J.*, Vol. 17, No. 2.
90. E.g. Ford, P. (1972) *Advising Sentencers*, Oxford, Blackwell.
91. Home Office Circular 195/1974.

92. Perry, F. G. (1974) *Information for the Court: A New Look at Social Inquiry Reports*, Cambridge, Institute of Criminology, p. 93.
93. Home Office and Lord Chancellor's Department (1971) *Report of the Inter-departmental Committee on the Business of the Criminal Courts*, (chairman: Mr. Justice Streatfeild), Cmnd. 1289.
94. Herbert, W. L. and Mathieson, D. (1975) *Reports for the Courts*. National Association of Probation Officers, p. 11.
95. Pearce, I. and Wareham, A. (1977) "The Questionable Relevance of Research into Social Enquiry Reports." *Howard J.*, Vol. 16, No. 2.
96. See especially Bean, P. (1976) *Rehabilitation and Deviance*, Routledge and Kegan Paul.
97. Ibid., pp. 104–5.
98. *Powers of Criminal Courts Act* 1973, s.2(6) and 14(2).
99. That is, to support crime reduction is not necesssarily to support the socially powerful. For the evidence of victimization amongst the poor see the various victimization studies, e.g. Sparks, R., Genn, H. G., and Dodd, D. J. (1977) *Survey Victims*. Chichester, Wiley.
100. "The reality of crime in the streets can be the reality of human suffering and personal disaster. We have to argue therefore for the exercise of social control, but also to argue that such control must be exercised within the working-class community": Young, J. (1975) "Working Class Criminology," in Taylor, I., Walton, P. and Young, J. (eds.), *Critical Criminology*, Routledge and Kegan Paul. Young's prescription, however, goes to the extreme of excluding all non-working-class agencies from the area; for vigorous critiques of this position see the essays by Downes and Cohen in Downes, D. and Rock, P. (eds.), (1979) *Deviant Interpretations*, Martin Robertson.
101. Eysenck, H. J. (1977) *Crime and Personality*, (third edition) St. Albans, Paladin, p. 184.
102. Newman, O. (1973) *Defensible Space*, Architectural Press.
103. Taylor, I., Walton, P. and Young, J. (1975) "Critical Criminology in Britain" in Taylor, Walton & Young (eds.), op. cit., p. 20.
104. Mawby, R. (1979) *Policing the City*, Farnborough, Saxon House.
105. For a short report see Bottoms, A. E. (1976) "Crime in a City," *New Society*, 8 April.
106. For classical sociological projects see, e.g. Kobrin, S. (1959) "The Chicago Area Project: A Twenty-five Year Assessment," *Annals of the American Academy of Political and Social Science*, Vol. 322; Mobilization for Youth Inc. (1961) *A Proposal for the Prevention and Control of Delinquency by Expanding Opportunities*, New York, Mobilization for Youth.
107. Spencer, op. cit.
108. See Christie, N. (1976) "Research into Methods of Crime Prevention." *Collected Studies in Criminological Research*, Vol. 1. For a partial exception see Smith, C. S., Farrant, M. R. & Marchant, H. J. (1972) *The Wincroft Youth Project*, Tavistock.
109. Kobrin, op. cit., p. 22.
110. Haxby, op. cit.

111. Phillipson, C. M. (1971) "Juvenile Delinquency and the School," in Carson, W. G. and Wiles, P. (eds.), *Crime and Delinquency in Britain*, Martin Robertson.
112. Gill, O. (1977) *Luke Street*, Macmillan.
113. Ibid., p. 189.
114. Moynihan, D. P. (1969) *Maximum Feasible Misunderstanding*. New York, Free Press, Chs. 3 and 6.
115. Maccoby, E. E., Johnson, J. P. and Church, R. M. (1958) "Community Integration and the Social Control of Juvenile Delinquency," *J. of Soc. Issues*, Vol. 14, No. 3.
116. Clifford, W. (1976) *Crime Control in Japan*, Lexington, Mass., D.C. Heath: Clinard, M. B. (1978) *Cities with Little Crime*, Cambridge University Press.
117. Abrams, P. (1978) "Community Care," in Barnes, J. and Connelly, N. (eds.), *Social Care Research*, Bedford Square Press.
118. Christie, N. (1977) "Conflicts as Property," *Br. J. of Criminol.*, Vol. 17, No. 1.
119. Christie states (p. 9) that he thinks the neighbourhood court he proposes would reduce recidivism, but that he does not advocate it for that reason. It would appear to follow that the general revivification of neighbourhoods which he also proposes should lead to crime reduction, although this is not explicity stated.
120. Abrams perhaps understates the extent to which care may be given in a non-reciprocal relationship; but this is not important for present purposes.
121. Scherer, J. (1972) *Contemporary Community*. Tavistock.
122. Current unpublished work in Sheffield on council house preferences among working-class tenants often shows a strong attachment to particular segments of the city.
123. Mitchell, J. C. (ed.) (1969) *Social Networks in Urban Situations*, Manchester University Press; Leinhardt, S. (ed) (1977) *Social Networks: A Developing Paradigm*, New York, Academic Press.
124. Hackler, J. C., Ho, K-Y and Urquhart-Ross, C. (1974) "The Willingness to Intervene: Differing Community Characteristics," *Soc. Problems*, Vol. 21, No. 3.
125. Kerr, M. (1958) *The People of Ship Street*, Routledge and Kegan Paul; Parker, H. (1974) *View from the Boys*, Newton Abbott, David and Charles. Both studies are of the Merseyside urban area.
126. See Baldwin, J. and Bottoms, A. E. (1976) *The Urban Criminal*. Tavistock.
127. For a full interim report see Spence, J. and Hedges, A. (1976) *Community Planning Project: Cunningham Road Improvement Scheme*, Social and Community Planning Research.
128. NACRO and SCPR (1976) *Vandalism: An Approach Through Consultation*, p. i.
129. NACRO and SCPR (1978) *Vandalism, a Pilot Project: Impressions After Two Years*.
130. Maccoby, Johnson & Church, op. cit.
131. NACRO and SCPR (1978) op. cit. p. 3.
132. Ibid., p. 2. The fact that recorded crime had not altered is not conclusive given the other social changes on the estate: one American study found that recorded

burglary rates *increased* during a period when residents in victim surveys reported a *decrease* in burglaries (Schneider, A. (1976) "Victimization Surveys and Criminal Justice System Evaluation," in Skogan, W. E. (ed.), *Sample Surveys of the Victims of Crime*, Cambridge, Mass, Ballinger). The NACRO/SCPR team is conducting a follow-up victimization study in Widnes, but results are not yet available.

133. Cohen, S. (1977) "Prisons and the Future of Control Systems," in Fitzgerald, M. et al. (eds.), *Welfare in Action*, Routledge and Kegan Paul, p. 227.

134. Cohen, S. (1979) "Guilt, Justice and Tolerance." in Downes, D. and Rock, P. (eds.), *Deviant Interpretations*, Martin Robertson, p. 49.

Chapter 8

The Redefinition of Probation: Drastic Prosposals to Solve an Urgent Problem

John P. Conrad*

INTRODUCTION

Practitioners, informed observers, and the general public all agree that there is a crisis in corrections. Differences of opinion arise in assigning causes, defining the true nature of the crisis, and proposing remedies. To review and account for all these differences would be an intolerable prelude to the proposals advanced in this essay. The necessary preliminary to the practical analysis on which I base these proposals is a statement of my own perceptions of the crisis. In formulating this description, I shall ignore other points of view. This is a set of proposals, not an argument or a review of ideologies.

While some writers assert that the criminal justice system is a "non-system," the important point is that the principal elements of this non-system interact, albeit clumsily, and each is affected by the condition of the others and by the social and economic context that turns men and women to crime and sets strict limits on what can be done with them.

All elements of criminal justice are affected by the persisting prevalence of crime and by the public demand that it must be curbed. Rightly or

*National Institute of Justice

wrongly—wrongly, in my opinion—it is supposed that the criminal justice system can and should reduce the volume of crime. That this end cannot be accomplished by the criminal justice system has been demonstrated for years by the continuing increase in the rates at which nearly all crimes are committed. That conclusion is irrelevant here. So far as the anxious public is concerned, more criminals must be apprehended, prosecuted, sentenced, and placed under some form of strict control, which usually means extended incarceration and subsequent surveillance. This demand has led to a serious overloading of the system. In this chapter, I shall propose a redistribution of correctional services that will improve the efficiency of the system and thereby provide some relief of the crisis. My proposals will focus on probation—the special concern of the Probation Mission Project—and their intent will be to enhance control of the serious offenders in the community while assuring that the services they need are really made available to them. Obviously the goals of my proposals are not inconsistent with the conventional practice of probation. But the organization of practice I have in mind is radically different from that which now prevails.

I shall take a task-oriented approach to the problems of probation, disregarding the conventional organizational structures that we now think of as "probation." Throughout this discussion, I shall use the term probation to denote a *status*. Specifically, I mean that when convicted offenders are placed on probation, they are in a status that allows them to remain at liberty in the community subject to certain defined requirements imposed by the court. If the probationer fails to meet these requirements, he or she will be subject to severe sanctions, usually incarceration for the term set by the penal code section defining the original offense.

In this definition of probation as a status, I have excluded the investigation, treatment, and surveillance functions served by probation today. By limiting the definition of the term probation we are now free to consider all the functions that have in the past been associated with this term in accordance with their most efficient performance and not with regard to present organizational design of conventional criminal justice operations. Rather than asking how "probation" agencies should be reorganized for more effective operations we begin with the question: What organizational auspices will most facilitate the effective discharge of the functions associated with the *status* of probation? The distinction between these two questions is crucial to an understanding of the contention advanced in this paper. I am arguing from the propositions that "probation" agencies cannot be organized to perform their conventional functions with the effectiveness that is desired. These functions must be considered independently and reassigned.

The changes proposed here are not ideological in nature. I hold that all the functions that "probation" agencies have been supposed to do should be done and done as well as possible. Increasing effectiveness can only partly relieve the crisis in criminal justice, but by making the proposed reassignments, we shall have done all that we can in this sector of criminal justice.

THE PRINCIPAL ELEMENTS OF THE CRISIS

There are six principal elements of the criminal justice crisis, each with implications for the functions associated with the status of probation. To define these elements is to lay the firmest possible foundation for the reorganization of criminal justice.

The Volume of Crime is Increasing and Exceeds the Capacity of the System to Respond. This imbalance has been evident for many years, and it affects the entire administration of criminal justice. There are not enough police to investigate and clear more than a fraction of the offenses reported. The courts have virtually abandoned the adversarial system for the determination of guilt. Negotiation is the rule. The traditional trial by jury has become an infrequent exception. One can argue about whether this change is beneficial, and whom it benefits. But there is no question of the absolute necessity of plea and charge bargaining if the courts are not to grow in number and costs, far beyond the dimensions to which we are accustomed.

With regard to the uses of probation status for offenders, the most important consequence of the increasing volume of crime is the stress it places on the nation's correctional capacity—our prisons and youth training schools, and our probation and parole agencies. Except in the predominantly rural states, prisons are overcrowded. It seems to be an accepted principle that prisons should be used for the confinement of only the most serious offenders, men and women whose violence or threat to the integrity of the community calls for that level of sentencing severity. It is doubtful that in most states this principle is applied in practice by the courts. According to the recent authoritative survey of American prisons and jails by Abt Associates, about half of all prisoners had been convicted of violent offenses; one-third were property offenders, and one-sixth had been convicted of other offenses (Smith et al., 1980). The survey also found that the number of property offenders was rising faster than the number of violent offenders. The survey did not collect data in sufficient detail to permit a definite assignment of causes. It appears that the violent crime is not increasing as rapidly as in the mid-seventies. It also appears that penalties for these offenses are increasing in severity. We may be receiving fewer violent offenders, but statutory requirements may force us to keep them much longer, with obvious consequences for prison over-crowding.

At first glance the data are not alarming. According to figures collected by the American Correctional Association, there were 282,398 men and women confined in state prisons on July 1, 1980, an increase of 6.9 percent over the corresponding figure for July 1, 1979 (American Correctional Association 1981:16). Thirty-five of the fifty states had an increase in prison population. The consolidated capacity of the nation's prisons was cautiously estimated at 262,788 on June 30, 1977; on that date the total prison population was 283,433. Removing the capacity and population of the federal prisons, the remaining totals of 238,378 and 251,557 represent the capacity and population of the state prisons on the date of the survey when prisons were overcrowded by about 5.5 percent. No data are available for 1979 or 1980, but there can be little doubt that the numbers of sentenced prisoners continue to outstrip the increases of space available to lock them up.

Presented as consolidated national figures, these data mask much more serious imbalances. In such large industrial states as Michigan and New Jersey, population exceeded rated capacity by 27.9 percent and 38.1 percent respectively (Flanagan et al., 1980:630). The situation has certainly not improved since 1977, and there is no reason to expect that a dramatic change for the better is in the offing.[1]

No one can estimate the extent to which community-based corrections can relieve prison congestion. Ideological debates focus on sentencing policy, and those who favor longer sentences for more offenders seem to be winning. Ardent reformers urge that large numbers of incarcerated felons could be released without undue hazard to the public, but neither legislatures nor judges seem inclined to adopt the policies proposed.

One thing is certain. For each man or woman committed to prison, some judge thought that such a commitment was the most appropriate sanction. If we are to curb the growth in the number of offenders sent to prison, these judges must gain sufficient confidence in community sanctions to accept them as satisfactory alternatives to prison. For whatever reasons offenders are committed to prison—intimidation, incapacitation, or retribution—the court did not think that a lesser penalty would serve those purposes.

In the eyes of most judges and most of the general public, probation is synonymous with leniency. It is to be meted out to persons whose careers in crime are in early stages, or not so threatening as to require incarceration for the safety of the public, or as an adequate response to the gravity of the offense committed. The status of probation will always be a more lenient punishment than commitment to prison. I believe, however, that the requirements of probation status can be made sufficiently rigorous to increase its acceptability as the sanction for more serious offenders. Because the prospects for an increased pressure on the nation's prison systems are so ominous, it is urgent that such changes in the rigor of probation be put into effect as soon as possible.

The Use of Incarceration Cannot be Significantly Expanded. The costs of building and maintaining prisons have been steadily rising, and not merely as the result of the inflation that affects the whole economy. A new maximum custody prison, if built on land that the state already owns, will cost at least $40,000 a cell, and sometimes double that amount. To keep prisoners secure in a regime of strict austerity—that is, providing only for basic needs, personal safety, and perimeter security—will cost between $10,000 and $20,000 per prisoner, depending on the location of the prison and prevailing salary scales for the staff.

In spite of these costs, new prisons are still being planned and built, but the major expansion that would make possible the incarceration of more classes of offenders will not be feasible. It follows that incarceration in the future will perforce follow the policy so widely recommended by reformers; it will be limited to the most serious offenders. Probation and other community-based sanctions must be used for more persons convicted of more serious crimes than in current practice—sometimes crimes for which a prison term would now be routinely imposed.

The General Public Regards Community-Based Sanctions as Nominal Punishments for Offenders Who Deserve Severity. Since 1972, the National Opinion Research Council has annually sampled public attitudes towards the courts' disposition of criminals. The central question in the enquiry is "In general, do you think the courts in this area deal too harshly or not harshly enough with criminals?" In 1972, 66 percent of the respondents thought that the courts did not deal with criminals harshly enough. Only 6 percent thought that the courts were too harsh. In subsequent years, the gap widened, until in 1978, the last year for which data are available, 85 percent responded "not harshly enough" and 3 percent "too harshly" (National Opinion Research Center, 1981:196–197).

These data are open to only one interpretation with respect to the use of probation. It is generally believed that too many offenders are getting off with too mild a punishment. Assignment to probation is not really punishment, and it does not sufficiently protect the public. The respondents were not asked whether heavy public investments should be made to add to existing penal facilities. But there is only one way to increase the harshness of criminal justice, given the present structure of the system, and that is to increase the use of incarceration. Until a system of community-based corrections is instituted that is seen as credibly severe, the apparent leniency of the courts—the willingness to place offenders on probation—contributes to the crisis in corrections.

Black and Hispanic Minorities Are Overrepresented in the Offender Population. In 1978, there were 9,687,995 arrests for all crimes reportable to the Federal Bureau of Investigation. Of this total, 2,562,434 arrests, or 26.4 percent of the total involved a black suspect (Hindelang et al., 1981:345). No accounting is made of Hispanic offenders, who were included in the total for whites. The percentage of blacks in the total offender population does not seem extremely far out of line with national demographics. But that percentage rises to 46.2 percent when only violent crimes are considered. These are the offenses for which the most stringent sanctions are imposed and concerning which public apprehension is greatest. Consistent with these data, 47 percent of those confined in prisons are black (Hindelang et al., 1981:496).

Some see this overrepresentation of blacks in prison as evidence of discrimination practiced by the criminal justice system. This oversimplification is not difficult to refute, but its implications are serious and intractable. In the large states with major metropolitan centers, the prison population consists predominantly of black and Hispanic offenders, but it is evident that minority group members represent a much smaller share of those on probation. The criminal justice system seems to be disproportionately harsh toward members of minority groups. In the prisons, the ugly pageant of white oppressors exploiting and dominating black and brown men and women is enacted daily—while white offenders go free on probation.

It is not surprising that poor people commit the most serious crimes, nor is it unreasonable that those who commit these crimes should be most severely punished. Informed people can show that members of minorities are the most frequently victimized. They can show that the crimes they commit are serious and that these serious crimes are committed far more frequently by blacks than by whites. Nevertheless, there is an appearance of social injustice that appears to be impossible to eradicate. It contributes to the unrest in our prisons and to a hostility toward the system as a whole by members of the minority groups.

There is no reliable way of estimating the extent to which the proportion of blacks in prison populations could be reduced by making more use of a credibly severe set of controls associated with the probation status. But it is hard to believe that probation could not be used for many black offenders who are now packed off to prison. Such a change, however, would require innovations in the organization and support of community controls that are not now in sight.

The Majority of the Most Serious Offenders Are Persons Who Are Unskilled, Irregularly Employed, and Conditioned by the Expectations Prevailing in the Lowest Socioeconomic Class. Data available on educational and socioeconomic status are so old and so difficult to interpret that I prefer not to cite them in support of this proposition (Hindeland et al., 1981:500; these data were collected in 1974 and are based on a "stratified probability sample" of all state correctional authorities). But anyone familiar with the offender population soon gets the impression that the more serious the offense, the lower on the socioeconomic scale the offender is likely to be. This condition is open to the interpretation that the system is intended for the regulation of the poor as much as for the punishment of the offender.

The polemic arising from this interpretation conceals the tragic underlying problem. By and large, the most serious crimes are committed by people who are redundant to the economic system. That condition is lifelong. Opportunities for career employment for these people have been rare. If it is true that employment at secure work with reasonable prospects for improving one's lot is a significant factor in the prevention of crime and recidivism, there is nothing in the economic prospects of these individuals to offset the attractions of a criminal career. The culture of redundancy encourages crime.

Data on the socioeconomic antecedents of offenders have not been systematically collected; what little we have consists of the results of ad hoc surveys that are never systematically replicated. We know that much crime is committed in the secure middle classes for reasons that cannot generally be traced to economic causes. Little of that crime is violent or sufficiently serious to call for a severe sanction. The major crimes against the person call for no special skills or worldly knowledge. They are the offenses that will be committed by the redundant, the men and women and youths for whom society has indicated it has no use.

This is the most ominous element of the criminal justice crisis. Some problems can be alleviated by adjustments to this justice system as a whole, or to the correctional apparatus within the system. But no amount of tinkering with any part of the criminal justice system can change the unfavorable structure of the economy. Correctional institutions and agencies face the virtually impossible task of preventing poor and unemployable men and women, people who have nothing at all to lose if caught committing a crime, from proceeding with offenses that are defined by the law as especially dangerous and punishable with the greatest severity. Once such people are in the custody of correctional authorities, the problem is to motivate them to improve their prospects for the future by education and training. It is a problem without a convincing solution for very many offenders.

It is also a problem more likely to be solved in the community than in prison. Unreality permeates the work and training programs of even the most progressive prisons; in the average prison, productivity is not a consideration, incentives to perform well are insignificant if they exist at all, and training is usually obsolete. Much more could be done by agencies working with offenders in the community, where work must be done to serious standards of production and the chances of a better job at better pay depend on performance. That conventional probation officers have not been able to do more to help the redundant find more hopeful economic situations attests only to the difficulty of the task, not to its impossibility. The task is impossible in prison as prisons are now administered. Work-release programs typically bridge the gap between prison and the community for a few favorable prospects. Little has been done to develop a probation-administered analogue to these programs, probably because those who are now placed on probation are ordinarily those whose social and economic resources are considerably above the redundancy level.

Major Changes in the Structure of Criminal Justice Are Needed, But the Tradition and the Inertia of Legislature and Criminal Justice Officials Act Against Any But the Most Gradual Changes. The weight of precedent, the requirements of fairness, and the inertia of the system have always combined to deter change. The organizational structure of criminal justice has not been significantly altered for the last century or more. Prisons are managed by the state for the punishment of the most serious offenders. Probation and other community controls are managed under the supervision of the courts, and these controls tend to be nominal because little is feared from those on whom they are imposed. In short, prisons now exist for the symbolic punishment of a few; community corrections, (including probation), allows leniency for the many. This division is seen as unfair by some, ineffectual by most, and satisfactory by none. The changes I have to propose in the next section of this essay are moderate and, at least in the beginning, mostly structural. They will not greatly reduce the nation's immense burden of crime until major social changes take place. They will, however, create a system of realistic sanctions that should increase confidence in the idea of community corrections and may assist many unfortunate men and women to extricate themselves from their hopeless criminal careers.

THE REDISTRIBUTION OF COMMUNITY CORRECTIONAL FUNCTIONS

If there is to be significant improvement in correctional services, it will take place in the community. The concept of the prison is not open to great change, although nearly everywhere a great deal must be done soon to improve administration and practice.

The critical problem in community corrections is to provide for maximum efficiency in the administration of those functions assigned to conventional probation agencies: investigation and recommendations to the sentencing court, surveillance and control of the offender, and various kinds of assistance that I will designate as services to the offender or in his behalf. These functions are almost always grouped in one agency, and ordinarily none of them is done well. As discussed below, one reason for deficiencies of performance is probably the incompatibility of these functions.

As the criminal population grows and changes in composition, it can be expected that performance will deteriorate still further. Because investigations are crucial to the courts' decisions about sentences, the performance of this task usually takes unquestioned priority on the resources of probation agencies. These reports are often required by law, and in any event they are seen as necessary to the courts' determination of the proper disposition of convicted offenders. It is not unreasonable that the requirements of surveillance and service must take a subsidiary place in the management of conventional agencies.

As to the responsibility for surveillance, probation officers can seldom claim more than an indirect role. If they are diligent and alert, they will know enough of what is going on in their caseloads to convey an intimidating awareness to probationers. The officer's approval or disapproval of probationers' requests will be based on some knowledge of their activities and the degree to which they have met the expectations of the court. But no probation officer can conduct such intensive surveillance that the probationers will be reliably deterred from illegal conduct by fear of discovery. Indeed, in the future climate of criminal justice, it is doubtful that the technical violations of probation will often result in a major change in the probationer's status. Further, the process of constantly checking the activities of the probationer seriously interferes with the remedial services that the probationer needs and the agency is committed to provide.

Empirical evidence of the ineffectual quality of probation surveillance is not readily at hand. So far as I know, the most impressive demonstration of the futility of probation agency surveillance is that of Studt's (1973) landmark study of parole services in California. She examined ninety consecutive parole revocation recommendations submitted to the Adult Authority, as the California parole board was then known, from one parole district. Only in fourteen cases did the parole officer contribute the information on which the parole revocation was based, and in ten of these cases the information was that the parolee could not be located. In seventy-five cases, the information was produced by other agencies, mostly in the form of an arrest by the police (Studt, 1973:89). Studt points out that the emphasis on surveillance results in a "context of suspicion" surrounding all interactions between the parole officer and the parolee. It is not easy to shift from a searching interrogation about the parolee's movements and associations to a helpful session of counseling, and it is not likely that many officers try. While Studt's data were based on the parole situation, the similarity between probation and parole is so close that her conclusions seem fully applicable to the probation status.

From the time of John Augustus, probation and parole officers have been committed to the ideal of service. Most probably chose their profession in the expectation that they would be providing services for unfortunate men and women in desperate need of help. Such professional training as they have had has stressed the skills that make up the practice of social casework.

Few probationers get much help from the officers to whom they are assigned. Responsibilities for meeting emergencies, negotiating with the police about reported violations, and appearances in court interfere with the systematic relationships that a service role requires. Even if some of these conflicts could be reduced in significance, it is hard to see how probation officers, playing the opposing roles of surveillance and service, could succeed at the latter. In the helping professions generally, it is believed that volition is essential to a successful service. Some correctional authorities stubbornly insist that this principle is an exaggeration, but no data have been assembled to provide statistical support for the effectiveness of programs in which participation is compulsory. So long as the probation officer must deal with the probationer in the "context of suspicion," there is a constraint on the helping relationship that must limit effective casework for any but the most resourceful probation officer.

In any human service, a conflict of interest is to be avoided. Physicians expect to give absolute priority to the interest of their patients; the ethics of the medical profession call for this precedence as the essence of the physician-patient relationship. But if a physician is employed by the state for the purposes of assuring public health and safety, his or her priority is the public interest. In such cases, no one should be deceived as to the physician's primary loyalty, and few people are. Similarly, probation officers who intend to provide services to their caseload should be in a position to give priority to the interests of the probationer. They should not be double agents, acting on behalf of the state (as they must, when playing a surveillance role), and attempting to reconcile this function with fidelity to the client's interests.

The importance of this principle in corrections seems so fundamental that I believe every possible measure should be taken to separate the functions of surveillance and service. For the correctional client, distrust of the state and its agents is basic. Information and confidences will be withheld from anyone who appears likely to pass them on to anyone— especially to functionaries who may have responsibilities to interfere with the offender's freedom. It is clear that no one person should attempt to combine surveillance and service. I think the separation must go farther;

these two functions must not be assigned to the same agency. From this point of departure follow the radical proposals presented below.

Throughout the history of probation it has been assumed that control and service could be combined. The result is that the conventional probation agency does not perform either function well. The probation officer is forced into the false position of the double agent; the probation department, his employer, compounds this extraordinary obstacle to effectiveness by attempting to be a double agency. The notion of the double agent has its origin in the field of espionage. Readers of the literature of this recondite field will recall that neither employer can trust the double agent. Loyalties are never certain, even in the mind of the agents themselves, and distrust contaminates all their relationships. The parallel with the probation agency is not exact, but I believe it offers a suggestive metaphor.

The principle upon which the redistribution of functions rests, then, is that incompatible responsibilities should not be assigned to the same agency. Neither the agency nor its employees should be affected by actual or potential conflicts of interest. It is vitally important that probationers be recognized as people in serious trouble, often needing a great deal of counsel, concern, and service. In effect, probation officers—if that is what we continue to call them—must maintain the interests of thir clients as their sole responsibility. They are advocates, charged with assuring that their clients get whatever they need to restore themselves to citizenship. If the probation officer becomes aware that his client has committed a new crime, he or she must, of course, take steps to assure that the proper authorities are informed—peferably with the cooperation of the client. Such situations will be so unusual that the resolution of the situation must be sought within its particular elements, not in a specific rule of the agency.

To sum up, the redistribution of the functions of investigation, surveillance, and service is an overdue reform of community corrections that will make possible the improved performance of each function. Investigation will be under the direct control of the court, which has the first and most important interest in assembling information about the offender that may be relevant to sentencing decisions. Probation officers will no longer be responsible for surveillance of probationers, partly because it is impossible for them to perform this function well, and partly because it compromises their effectivenss in the needed casework and advocacy functions. It now remains to suggest a reorganization of community correctional services that will carry out the principles I have proposed in this section.

THE REORGANIZATION OF CORRECTIONS

The reorganization of corrections proposed in this section is only a structure. Human services are performed by human beings and the standards for their performance cannot be prescribed in an organization chart. In corrections, more than ordinary human beings are needed to resolve the difficulties presented by a despised and refractory clientele. They must be blessed with tolerance and firmness, with professional skills and experience in the community, with empathy and objectivity. Men and women with such potential resources are rare. They are hard to find, hard to train, and hard to keep. A structure that favors their commitment to the difficult, and often unrewarding, tasks of community corrections will make possible service by such extraordinary people. The structure is only the beginning.

The reorganization that I have in mind touches all the existing correctional agencies and creates some new units. I shall describe the changes as they affect each.

The State Department of Corrections

The main task of the department of corrections is the operation of the state's prison system. Under the proposed reorganization, it will assume responsibility for setting, maintaining, and enforcing the minimum standards of performance in the management of the county department of corrections. Leverage on the counties to assure compliance will be created by a system of state subsidies for the provision of community-based controls and services for felony offenders on probation status.

Legislation like the Minnesota Community Corrections Act should be the basic support for such standards. Under the provisions of this Act, the state establishes a fund to be distributed by formula to the counties for the support of local corrections. To qualify for this subvention, a county must submit a plan that is consistent with the promulgated state standards. Considerable latitude is allowed for innovation, local preference, and the special situations of each community with respect to the volume of crime, the availability of services from other agencies, and the existing condition of correctional agencies as to the need for improvement. The requirements for compliance are intended to establish a floor beneath which operations cannot be allowed to fall. There is no ceiling except that the state subsidy cannot exceed the amount specified by the formula for distribution; counties are free to spend as much from local funds as they choose. Special disincentives are provided to discourage commitment to prison in cases where a community-based penalty is permitted by law, but these disincentives do not apply to an offender who has committed a major crime against the person.

In addition to its responsibility for standard setting, the state department of corrections will assist the counties with the recruitment and qualification of personnel. It will organize and conduct training for personnel at all levels of county corrections; expenses for this training will be borne by the department. The costs of civil service examination and certification should also be a charge on the state, and employees of county departments should also be eligible to participate in the state pension system.

The Court Investigation Service

The presentence investigation is conducted primarily for the benefit of the court. The findings contained in this crucial document must also be made available to the prison, if the offender is sentenced to prison, or to the county department of corrections. Because the first obligation of the officer who prepares this report is to the court to which it is submitted, the court should control this service. The wishes of the court concerning its organization, its content, and other requirements should determine its source of control. In this reorganization of service, the investigators who are responsible for these reports should be officers of the court.

In large courts, many investigators will be required. Inevitably, small bureaucracies will be created, with directors, assistant directors, and supervisors—as well as the personnel who are doing the investigations. Judges should do what they can to limit the number of echelons in the interest of both economy and efficiency.

The focus should be on the competence of the investigators. They should have comprehensive training in criminal law, criminology, and community organization; they should have a clear idea of the scope of the system and of the resources of the community. Although judges should have the final decision on the hiring and firing of investigators, they should be encouraged to accept and support professional standards for this sensitive occupation. Where there is a state administrative office of the courts, it should provide some supporting services for the recruitment, training, and professional development of investigators, as well the maintenance of statistics and information services.

The duties of the court investigation service are limited to the investigation of the social and criminal histories and circumstances of convicted offenders on whom the court must make a sentencing decision. Ordinarily, these investigations will be ordered only when a decision as to sentence must be made or when a revocation of probation appears to be indicated. The court investigation service will prepare presentence investigations on all convicted felony offenders. When a probationer violates the terms of probation or commits a new offense, the service will conduct a supplementary investigation with recommendations for disposition. When good cause is shown for early termination of probation, the service will prepare a report to the court with recommendations.

The service will never engage in surveillance or in remedial services. Its officers should have access to information in the files of the police and to the nonconfidential files of the county department of corrections.

Large counties will employ a considerable number of career investigators. In counties where the workload is irregular or requires less than full-time service, coordination through the administrative office of the courts (if there is one) or through the department of corrections should provide for trained personnel to serve the court as needed.

The Police Bureau of Supervision

All persons placed on probation will be required to accept surveillance by police. To manage this function, the police will establish a bureau of supervision that will receive reports from probationers on terms and at intervals prescribed by the court. The bureau of supervision will have no responsibilities other than receiving and recording reports submitted by probationer and verifying them as required by the circumstances of the probationer. When there are irregularities or violations of the conditions of probation, or when a new offense has been committed, the bureau will transmit an emergency report to the court investigation service for such action as the service may consider appropriate under the policies established by the court.

Assigning surveillance to the police makes final the separation of the traditional probation functions of surveillance and service. Surveillance is a natural function of the police. The collection and evaluation of information about criminal activities in the community is a necessary and routine task for the bureau of identification and investigation in large police departments. Close liaison with the bureau of supervision will assure that complete information on the probationer is available to the information bank of the police department. It is a new function for the police, but surely not an unwelcome responsibility, since it completes an information circuit. Already, most information about serious probation violations comes first to the attention of the police. It makes little sense for probation agencies to perform the "supervision" tasks separately. As matters stand in the conventional probation agency, the attempt to conduct surveillance risks giving the impression that officers condone acts that in fact they simply did not see.

The assignment of probation surveillance to the police serves the purpose of increasing the severity of the sanction. It is one thing to accept an occasional home call from a harassed and overworked probation officer or to appear in his office on a Saturday morning. It is quite another to make a regular trip to a police station for a report to a uniformed officer, and to be subject to periodic visitation and investigation by that officer. In their recent report on the effectiveness of parole services, Sacks and Logan argue that the intimidating effect of police supervision of parolees may well increase the effectiveness of parole operations (Sacks and Logan, 1979:74). This is a reasonable supposition. Both the intimidating effect of required reports to the police and the coordination of investigations and surveillance should assure better control of offenders on probation. It should follow that courts will place more confidence in community-based corrections and allow offenders who now are sent to prison to remain in the community.

Some will object that this system accentuates the stigma suffered by the probationer. To that the answer is that stigma is the lot of the law violator. It is a deception to suppose that it can be avoided or, indeed, that it should be avoided. Stigma is inescapable, and it can only be removed by actions inconsistent with the stigmatized status—the conduct of a law-abiding life. Reputations need not be permanently spoiled, nor are they in the case of most offenders. Surveillance by the police will be more unpleasant than casual checks by the probation officer, but need not be destructive to probationers who are leading innocuous lives.

The County Department of Corrections

Each county will establish a department of corrections for the administration of all local correctional programs. The department will consist of five operational units, in addition to an administrative services unit responsible for fiscal and personnel administration: the jail, the office of collections, the division of service and liaison, the correctional center, and the office of victim services.

The county jail will be assigned to professional correctional administrators responsible to an accountable department rather than to an independent elected sheriff. The jail will incorporate its own service elements as well as a competent custodial control. The jail superintendent will be responsible to the director of the county department of corrections, who will have the power of appointment and discharge.

The office of collections will be responsible for the collection of fines and restitution payments and, where authorized by court decree, for disbursements from these receipts.

The division of service and liaison will carry out all contact services with probationers, with the aim of helping them toward a satisfactory completion of probation. Personnel assigned to the division will be qualified as counselors. They must be prepared to assume an advocate role to assure that probationers needing special services will receive them. Division personnel will not be responsible for surveillance or control and will not attempt to assume these functions. Complaints against probationers will be referred to the police bureau of supervision. The division's counselors will be qualified and seen as helping professionals, available for any kind of assistance needed by a probationer in his attempt to lead a law-abiding life. Many probationers will need no assistance, in which case they will have no contact with this division.

In metropolitan centers, probationers will often be referred to public or private service agencies outside the criminal justice system. The division of service and liaison will make referrals and, when the service provided requires payments, the division's funds should be available and sufficient to support necessary arrangements.

In small counties, where service resources are meager or nonexistent, the division may have to provide most or all of the service the probationer gets. Sometimes it will be possible to coordinate services with agencies in nearby large communities outside the county. Usually, however, the division will have to rely on the versatility and resourcefulness of its personnel to compensate for the lack of services in a small community.

I have used the term services without a clear operational definition. Many probationers will need only a periodic reassuring interview at their own initiative. But some will need much more: assistance in finding employment; arrangements for vocational training; arrangements for remedial adult education; referral to a mental health agency; assistance with family welfare problems; placement of children for temporary periods while the family makes major readjustments in its circumstances; or arrangements for financial advice and orderly payment of accumulated debts. In addition to these varied tasks and no doubt many more not listed, probation officers will often find themselves involved in the emergencies of probationers under arrest or suspicion of a new offense. Crisis management has always been a special responsibility of probation and parole officers, and it is here that the division's value as an advocate for the probationer will be most critically apparent. The probation officer's knowledge of the probationer's situation will make it possible for him or her to forward to the court investigation service a plan for reinstatement on probation and support it with whatever positive information may be available.

A county correctional center may be established by metropolitan counties. Such a center will serve a number of functions. Usually it will be the headquarters of the department of corrections. The offices of administrative and service personnel will be located at the center, except where district offices are necessary for the convenience of personnel and probationers. If group and adult education functions are needed for the client population, these activities can take place at the center. There may be a residential halfway house to accommodate some probationers, work-release jail inmates, and perhaps parolees in need of a fixed abode. When community service orders are applied to a probationer, arrangements should be made at the center, but compliance must be enforced by the police bureau of supervision.

The Office of Victim Services will provide facilities for making application for victim compensation in states where such payments are authorized by law. It will make any authorized victim compensation and restitution disbursements. Personnel will be available for counseling and referral of victims for needed financial, medical, and psychological assistance.

The County Correctional Council

Responsibility for overseeing the county department of corrections will be vested in a county correctional council, whose members will be nominated by the presiding judge of the criminal court and confirmed by the board of county commissioners. The presiding judge of the criminal court will be the ex officio chairman of the council. The council will appoint the county director of corrections, who will be directly responsible to it, and will act as its executive officer.

This organ of the new correctional structure should not become a ceremonial appendage to the court or to the director. Its responsibilities will be real. In addition to choosing the director and reviewing his work, it will be responsible for the county correctional plan, submitted annually to the state department of corrections to support the application for the correctional subsidy. Where grants are made to private agencies for correctional services, the council will be the responsible granting authority. Finally, and perhaps most important, it will interpret the department to the community and thereby build a constituency for its support. The annual reports of the council will be the benchmark data by which citizens can judge the progress being made toward sufficient control of crime and the nature of the problem facing the community in effecting better control.

Real and occasionally burdensome duties will be associated with membership on the council. Appointment is far from honorific. Responsibility for the integrity and efficiency of the department rests directly with the council.

IMPLEMENTATION

The Hard Part

I have proposed a general basis for the redistribution of correctional functions. It is a general pattern, the frame for a mosaic of particulars.

Before that mosaic can be put together, extensive planning will be needed to enable practitioners to open offices, hire personnel, initiate procedures, and establish lines of liaison and communication. Some new legislation will probably be necessary in most states; attention must be given to the draft of model code sections. Standards of service must be prescribed and written. We must set minimum qualifications for employment in the various occupations and classifications needed. Dozens of administrative regulations must be specified and written. The reconstruction of the whole system of community corrections must not be undertaken in a haphazard manner, as though played by ear.

The plan must be developed with the full participation of all the administrative and professionl people whose experience and support will be needed if the plan is to succeed. Courts, state correctional officials, local probation chiefs, police commanders, reprsentatives of the professional organizations affected, and representative state and county officials should be urged to participate in the work of task forces to develop details of the model and to select sites in which it can be tested.

This phase, the preparations for a pilot test, will be time consuming and will require extended concentrated effort by a fulltime staff. There will be differences of opinion to reconcile and heated opposition to placate. The development of such a model will require federal funds, preferably from the National Institute of Corrections (NIC), whch will have a crucial role in support of the pilot implementation.

Site Selection

Pilot implementation should take place in several different communities. Care should be taken to choose sites in which economic pressures of unemployment and a declining tax base will not adversely affect this early trial of the model. The volume of crime should not be beyond the real control of the existing system. It will be time enough to test the plan in cities with overloaded correctional services once it has had a successful test in three or four metropolitan areas in comparatively favorable locations.

Support

Thére is no reason why the operations under the new plan should be significantly more costly than the existing system. Support should come from the existing funding by the community with such supplemental state support as has been available under the old system. No federal support for service should be required. The federal government is simply not needed on the local correctional scene.

Where Federal Support Can Help

The original development of the model is an important federal contribution, and it is unlikely that any other support for this necessary phase can be found. Thereafter, the remaining federal role should consist of funding pilot training programs needed to complete the conversion. This is a function for which NIC is ideally suited. Finally, the pilot demonstration must be documented and assessed, using systematic research methods. Monitoring and evaluation of the demonstration phase should be the responsibility of NIC.

Reasonable Expectations

No one should entertain any notion that this plan for the reconstruction of corrections will resolve the crime problem or even noticeably reduce it in the short term. The central problem in crime control is economic, beyond the reach of the criminal justice system no matter how it is structured. Chronic unemployment among minority youth in the inner cities will not respond to improvements in the criminal justice system, nor are the criminals created by these unfavorable conditions likely to be reformed merely because they get more systematic and more regular attention. No form of correctional service can be successfully administered to a workload of redundant and unemployable offenders.

What this system can do is to make the functions of community corrections realistic and consistent with what we know about offenders and their control. If an offender knows that the system will deliver exactly what it says it will deliver, he will have a better reason to desist from further criminal activity. That reason may or may not be enough to determine particular offender's future course of conduct. But I suggest that this system is better prepared to deliver predictable sanctions to those whose punishment must take place in the community.

Some Objections to the Plan and Their Resolution

An earlier draft of this essay was circulated among colleagues, who raised a variety of questions about the proposed reorganization. Some of these concerns are addressed here.

Does probation, administered as a status, fit the "justice model?" My argument throughout this paper has been that probation becomes a sanction within the requirements of retributive justice only if it is defined as a status. In assigning a convicted offender to the status of probation, the court requires him or her to submit to reporting and surveillance, and in addition threatens the imposition of additional sanction (e.g., commitment to prison, a jail term, or extension of the period of probation) if the terms of probation are violated. Thus the offender is clearly being punished and is subject to further punishment in the event of noncompliance with the court's directives. The service element of probation, with which we have so long and so unsuccessfully attempted to combine control functions, now becomes entirely separate. It is no longer required, it is *offered*. Service is not of the essence of probation, but it is an accompanying element, always available to those who want it.

What is the Mission of Probation?   I am not certain that probation has a mission in the strict sense of that word. As I see it, as a sanction imposed by the court, it is a process available to the criminal justice system as the consequence of committing a crime. Just as the prison should not be thought of as having some particular mission in the justice model, so the status of probation has no overall mission to perform except to provide a punishment milder than the prison. But just as the prison is a place in which various remedial programs may be provided to particular criminals, so too the status of probation may provide life-changing opportunities to many individual offenders.

The Role of the Probation Officer.   One critic asked for a detailed description of what the probation officer would actually do in the new setting of the division of liaison and service. (There is no role for the probation officer in the police bureau of supervision. The function of receiving reports and conducting surveillance should be left to police officers— with some training and command supervision.) In the division of liaison and service, probation officers will come into their own. First, they will be brokers and providers of services—primarily brokers where community services are sufficient, but capable of provision in other cases.

Second, probation officers will be advocates. The lives of probationers are filled with emergencies that are more than they can cope with. Some are general troubles with the social and economic environment to which we are all subject, but which some people find too overwhelming to deal with alone. Some are special troubles with the law. Probation officers would spend a lot of their time just helping probationers to cope. When a man is down to his last dollar, kicked out of the house by his wife, and suspected of a new crime by the police, the probation officer must create the new plan for his survival—if a new plan can be created. He or she will have to help the client sell the plan to the police, the prosecutor, and the court. This is probably the most useful work a probation officer can do.

Some probation officers will move from the conventional agencies to the new court investigative service. In this capacity, they become the fact-gathering arm of the court, and usually will draft proposed recommendations for the terms of the sentence to be imposed by the court. Usually, too, they will make the specific referral to the division of liaison and service.

Would the Institutional Arm of the Department of Corrections Dominate the Agency? Problems of dominance are usually problems of individual personalities. It seems unlikely to me that the chief of the division of liaison and service, if a well qualified and secure person, will lose many battles to his peers. An incompetent person, on the other hand, cannot be saved by even a firm superior in the director of corrections.

Is the Control/Assistance Problem Real or Fictitious? Some have argued that control and assistance are not as incompatible as they are presumed to be by critics of my stripe. I will not contest the conclusions from the data, but I contend that none of these examples fit the peculiar context of probation. I follow Amitai Etzioni's elegant discussion of compliance structures, which seems both logical and persuasive as a theory and, as far as I know, has yet to be successfully attacked (Etzioni, 1968: 356–359). If we agree that the punitive functions of surveillance (i.e., the requirements of reporting, the surveillance by a state official, and the transmission of reports of violation to the court) are coercive in nature, it follows from Etzioni that the response to compliance will be alienating. If we assume that the helping elements are *normative*, then to the extent that the help is authentically persuasive it can result in commitment to new values. Coercion is of the essence of the punitive status of probation, and cannot be hidden or disguised. As Etzioni says, "most prison systems are not very effective agents of resocialization, for the resocialization goal is secondary and partially incompatible with the primary goal of keeping the inmates confined" (Etzioni, 1968:372). At another point, Etzioni stresses that "force and influence seem to be incompatible in the same control relation." I submit that what applies to the obvious coercion of the prison must apply no less to the coercion exerted by the probation agency. Therefore, I will continue to hold that the separation of service from control should be organizational and not merely occupational.

Is the Police Bureau of Supervision Really an Improvement Over the Existing Distribution of Functions? This general question covers three specific issues. First, *police officers may not be good at surveillance.* I can only say that they could hardly be worse than probation officers. I do not believe that the activities of a probation officer constitute systematic and credible surveillance. But the pretense of surveillance hinders probation from performing really useful service because of the context of suspicion. Moreover, needed surveillance is not provided, and probationers know it. As to the notion advanced by one critic that the probation officer can buffer the probationer in arrest situations, I have provided for that function in arguing for an advocate role for the probation officer working in the division of liaison and service.

A second doubt is that *police officers may not want to take on this activity*. I think that they will, if they are funded to do it, and if they are charged with carrying it out. The advantages from the information point of view are vast; and not many police chiefs are likely to miss that point.

Finally, some have questioned whether *the police might be prevented from taking on such a function becuse of a constitutional bar arising from the doctrine of separation of powers*. But the execution of sanctions is a function of the executive branch of government, of which both the police and corrections agencies are a part.

A Final Note

The organization of the criminal justice system to perform functions other than those strictly required by retributive justice is less than two hundred years old. The organizational forms to carry out a variety of functions, including those required for control and services, have evolved haphazardly, most of them originating in an age that was innocent of the arts of administrative analysis. The model that I have proposed is grounded in a good deal of experience, more familiarity with the literature, and the adoption of a few general principles about which I have tried to be fully explicit. I think our current structure is ineffective, and attempts to preserve it are misguided. The model I propose will certainly be found deficient at many points in practice. But if its implementation is preceded by detailed planning of the administrative requirements and if a pilot demonstration is carried out over a reasonable number of years, the deficiencies can be ironed out, and the model can and should develop into a probation system in which the courts, the police, and the general public can have confidence. The gain from the decreased use of incarceration as a major sanction for major offenses will be well worth the effort. But there will be many other gains too—some of them in the unusual direction of public economy.

NOTE

1. By December 31, 1982, the prison population rose to over 412,000 and the U.S. Department of Justice predicted 500,000 by the end of 1984.

REFERENCES

American Correctional Association (1981). *Directory of Juvenile and Adult Correctional Departments, Institutions and Paroling Authorities*. College Park, MD: ACA.

Etzioni, Amitai (1968). *The Active Society: A Theory of Societal and Political Processes*. New York: The Free Press.

Flanagan, Timothy J., Michael J. Hindeland, and Michael R. Gottfredson, eds. (1980). *Sourcebook of Criminal Justice Statistics—1979*. Washington, D.C.: U.S. Government Printing Office.

Hindelang, Michael J., Michael R. Gottfredson, and Timothy J. Flanagan, eds. (1981). *Sourcebook of Criminal Justice Statistics—1980*. Washington, D.C.: U.S. Government Printing Office.

National Opinion Research Center (1982). National Sourcebook for Criminal Justice Statistics. Washington, D.C.: United States Department of Justice.

Sacks, Howard R., and Charles H. Logan (1979). *Does Parole Make a Difference?* Storrs, CT: The University of Connecticut Law School Press.

Smith, Bradford Mann, Joan Mullen, and Ken Carlson (1980). *American Prisons and Jails: Summary and Policy Implications of a National Survey*. Washington, D.C.: Government Printing Office.

Studt, Elliot (1973). *Surveillance and Service: A Report of the Parole Action Study*. Washington, D.C.: United States Department of Justice.

Chapter 9

The Professionalization of Probation: An Analysis of the Diffusion of Ideas

James T. Carey

INTRODUCTION

Studies of the diffusion of innovations in a wide variety of areas from medicine to agriculture have underlined the unexpectedly important role played by professional journals and other formal communication channels (Coleman, et al., 1966; Katz, 1960). Thus analyses of journals can provide an important source of information on the diffusion and acceptance of work-related perspectives.

This inquiry focuses on the diffusion and acceptance of particular explanations of crime and delinquency among probation practitioners as they relate to the issue of professionalization. The journal selected for examination was *Federal Probation*, the one Gross (1966) names as most frequently read by juvenile probation officers. (Over 80 percent of his modest sample reported that they read it regularly.) *Federal Probation* constitutes a rich source of data on practitioner outlooks. More importantly from the perspective of this inquiry, it reflects the absorption of social science explanations that seem to bear on practice and professional legitimation.

Grateful acknowledgement is made to Benedict J. Carey and Mary DeSloover for their technical assistance in the preparation of this paper.

This investigation assumes that the pattern of introduction, diffusion, and adoption of perspectives follows the pattern described by Crane (1972) for the diffusion of knowledge in scientific communities. Perspectives are first introduced in book reviews by academic gatekeepers, usually in relationship to some external event (economic crisis, dislocation caused by war, report of a presidential commission), then appear in articles espousing the perspective at a fairly abstract level by academics or high-status practitioners, then in lower-status authors, and finally in the how-to literature as unexamined assumptions—the "adoption" stage.

This study examined a sample of *Federal Probation* over its more than forty-year history with an eye to the following questions:

What are the social and professional conditions that seem decisive in the initial introduction of a perspective?

How important are models developed in academic settings as against other settings? What other sources provide perspectives for practitioners?

To what extent do these models provide guides for day-to-day practice?

How long does it take from the time a model is first systematically stated until it appears in practitioner literature?

Characteristically, how are ideas introduced and by whom? What is their pattern of diffusion?

What generalizations can one make about the appeal of various perspectives or parts of them?

Carey and McAnany (1980) concluded that delinquency theory has had relatively little influence on the juvenile court because there are no institutional arrangements for communicating ideas from the academy to the field. The supervised field placements used by social workers represent one such institutional arrangement, but they are conspicuous by their absence in the probation field. This may strike the casual observer as curious, since many probation officers have taken social work courses in college and read social-work-related journals as part of their professional development (Gross, 1966). The profession of social work constitutes one of the key reference groups for probation officers.

Social work's impact on probation—more so in its early days than today, more so in juvenile than adult probation—is undeniable. Some of probation's early leaders saw the professionalization of their field as part of social work. They argued that just as there were school and hospital social workers, so too were there court social workers. But in fact MSWs were not drawn in great numbers to the field of probation. The rewards were too meagre when compared with those of working in a private agency or private practice.

The core skill that social work delineated as unique—case work on a one-to-one basis—has had strong appeal to probation officers who see their role as essentially a treatment one (Lubove, 1965). Even those probation spokespersons who reluctantly concluded that there would be no profession of "court social worker" continued to emphasize case work on a one-to-one basis. It was this core skill linked to a theory of personality development and adapted to an authoritarian setting that they hoped would be recognized as professional by the general public and the executive and judicial branches of government. The solution of the core skill problem in social work led to the establishment of university-based programs across the nation, and similar development was projected for probation in its thrust to professionalize.

Professional status in our society brings both economic and psychological benefits. It can only be attained, so the reasoning goes, when we have developed a defensible theory of probation and a core skill that can only be taught by those who have been certified academically. So far this has not happened, and there is some question whether it ever will. Some critics have even suggested that the professionalization of everyone is not a desirable social goal (Wilensky, 1965), and that an alternative model of development might be unionization to solve the problem of occupational identity. Public Aid caseworkers have already moved in this direction. But no one in the probation field to date seriously questions the struggle for professional recognition.

One part of this struggle is the diffusion and modification of a variety of perspectives that hold promise of academic legitimation. Through the years since the founding of the National Probation and Parole Association, a number of theoretical perspectives have found their way into probation literature. These models were primarily developed in academic settings and gradually trickled down into probation circles and thinking. The frequency of their appearance in practitioner literature like *Federal Probation* is one measure of their acceptance.

SCOPE AND METHOD

This inquiry consists of a content analysis of the journal *Federal Probation*, which was launched as a newsletter in 1937 to speak to the concerns of probation and parole personnel. It provides a complex source of information about practitioner preoccupations. Included are articles, book reviews, abstracts of relevant articles from other journals, letters, reports of meetings, gossip of interest to those familiar with probation and parole, and finally what might be characterized as "fillers": quotations, cartoons, and jokes. Our hope was that a systematic analysis of this material, or parts of it, might reveal which perspectives characterized the

the field at various times and provide some clues as to how, if at all, they relate to the issue of probation and professionalization.

We selected the articles included in *Federal Probation* as our fundamental unit of analysis. Time and resource considerations dictated that we devote most of our attention to probation-oriented articles (excluding prison and parole material), looking at their focus (adults, juveniles, other) and information on authors (sex, occupation, relative prestige, location and the perspective represented). Our universe consisted of issues of *Federal Probation* (beginning with 1937 and 1938 and including every other year through 1978), which included 787 articles; 563 (72 percent) of those articles were probation-related. This sample of 563 articles was analyzed quantitatively (see Table 9.1). Classification by main focus and author characteristics was relatively straightforward. Categorizing articles by perspective was more complicated, since many included more than one perspective. In such cases, we counted lines of text to determine which perspective predominated.

PERSPECTIVES

Six academic perspectives were reflected in probation circles and thinking in the forty-two-year period beginning in 1937 and ending in 1979: social pathology, social disorganization, differential association, opportunity theory, labeling, and the justice model. Each springs from a unique set of theoretical concerns, speaks to a different set of social conditions, suggests a specific research agenda, and implies particular policies on treatment and prevention; the perspectives also vary in their appeal to probation practitioners. Almost half (47 percent) of the content analyzed in *Federal Probation* for this inquiry reflected distinctive academic perspectives. Another 45 percent reflected operational concerns and 8 percent reflected other professional/occupational outlooks. Each academic perspective is discussed in more detail below, and summarized in Table 9.1. Fuller descriptions are available in Davis (1980) and Fogel (1975).

Social Pathology

This outlook developed in the latter part of the nineteenth century among philanthropists and charity workers interested in problem children. It confidently assumed that the social sciences could solve social problems and could be used by the juvenile court to help delinquent, dependent, and neglected children. It further assumed that children in difficulty represent problems of personal maladjustment and that with the right kind of treatment they could be adjusted to the demand of social living. The key metaphor

Table 9.1. Components of Six Academic Perspectives on Probation

	Social Pathology	Disorganization	Differential Association	Opportunity	Labeling	Justice
1. Social and professional conditions	Industrialism triumphant; emergence of social science to "solve" social problems; sociology as social reform	Urbanism as way of life; academically based discipline; city as soc. lab; applied sociology	Recognition of normative pluralism and conflict as related to criminality	Rise of welfare state; gov't financing of social science research; "professionalization" of sociologists as control oriented	Liberal reaction to bureaucratic state; identification with underdog; debunking of established institutions	Disillusionment of professionals and practitioners with rehab.; concern of policy makers about costs
2. Theoretical concerns	Social Darwinism; social selection demands adjustment to institutional sector; deviance as personal maladjustment	Behavior as product of physical location and inst'l membership. Acceptance of diversity deviance as "natural" phase of disorg. urban life	Diff'l ass'n and diff'l org. as sources of crim. behavior; deviance as shared cultural traditions learned in face-to-face groups	Strain generated by disjunction between aspirations and expectations	Secondary deviation; social control leads to deviant identity	Rejection of "theories" of Causation. Cost benefit analysis of rule-breaking
3. Metaphor	"Health-illness" referent for social order-disorder	"Web of life," naturalism, interconnectedness of urban organizations	"Crime behavior system," career concept emphasizes systematic pattern of criminal motives and acts	Differential opportunity structure	"Stigma" defines and isolates rule breaker, perpetuates deviant identity	Person as rational and calculating
4. Themes	Social correction and amelioration	Sites and situations; social worlds, life cycle, or career crisis	Criminal behavior types	Delinquency as individual adaptation; delinquent subculture	Social reaction deviant careers collective rule making	Swiftness, certainty and severity of punishment as they affect compliance
5. Method	Casework	Ethnography; rates and distribution	Typologies; analytical summary	Use of official data; analysis of etiological factors	Ethnography, participant observation	Use of crime rates to discover deterrent effects of punishment
6. Policy Implications	Individual change; rejection of social planning of social services	Community reorganization	Various patchwork remedies, use of peer pressure to change individuals	Expand legitimate opportunities for low-income people	Decriminalization, deinstitutionalization, due process, diversion	Proportional sentences based on seriousness; reduce reach of criminal law

used by proponents of this perspective was that of health and illness. Court personnel were viewed as diagnosticians or quasi-medical experts who could "cure" the disease of delinquency. Cure was best effected, in this view, through the casework method.

The social pathological perspective was articulated further by the psychiatrist William Healy, who was strategically well situated to shape practitioner perceptions of their task. He established the first child guidance clinic in the nation, attached to the Cook County Juvenile Court. He and his colleagues gave physical examinations and a series of diagnostic tests to children processed by the court. Social workers interviewed each child and got together with Healy for a conference (later this "case conference" became one of the distinguishing features of social work) to synthesize all the relevant information and devise a treatment plan. His child guidance clinic, the Juvenile Psychopathic Institute, was an institutional arrangement that systematically communicated the social pathology perspective and was further developed and institutionalized in an academic setting through the work of Robinson (1930) and others. Probation officers' training in social work developed their notions of treatment from Robinson's classic text.

Social Disorganization

Another perspective saw crime and delinquency as a product of social disorganization, rejecting the notion of individual pathology as cause. This model was first systematically stated by Shaw and McKay in a series of publications emanating from Chicago. Both were sociologists in the Institute of Juvenile Research, a state-supported child guidance clinic and successor to Healy's organization. The most influential statement of this perspective was made in 1931 as part of the report of the Wickersham Commission on the causes and prevention of crime (Shaw and McKay, 1931). By 1937 this perspective found its way into practitioner literature as a challenge to the dominant pathological view. It assumed that crime and delinquency were products of the breakdown of social control and could best be understood in terms of physical location. Crime and delinquency were natural features of some urban areas. The metaphor that summarized the approach of disorganiztion theory was "the web of life"—stressing the interconnectedness of urban social worlds. The best solution to the problem of crime was community organization, since the absence of effective local organization gave rise to problem behavior. A well-worked-out research agenda was part of this perspective and to the extent that it was implemented by the criminal or juvenile justice system, it led to an official collection of indicators of community cohesion and to case studies of individuals who ran afoul of the law.

Differential Association—Value Conflict

This perspective originated with Edwin Sutherland, the leading American criminologist from the mid-1920s until his death in the early 1950s. He assumed that crime was a product of "culture conflict." Criminality is part of a shared cultural tradition that condones or enjoins it; it is learned in intimate face-to-face groups. The principle of differential association—that crime is a product of the excessive ratio of attitudes favoring law violation as against those opposing them—was elaborated into nine propositions that appeared in Sutherland's 1939 editon of *Principles of Criminology*. His principle metaphor was the "Criminal Behavior System"—crime was organized much like any conventional occupational system.

The differential association perspective did not completely displace the dominant social pathology emphasis, though its influence was greater than that of the social disorganization scheme. The perspective seemed to coincide with common sense views about "bad companions," and led to some in-house research in several juvenile courts on the influence of delinquent companions. The social implications of differential association at a global level suggest that a recognition and legitimation of normative pluralism may lead to the reduction of criminality by increasing societal tolerance. More specifically, the approach has encourged juvenile and adult corrections to accept peer pressure strategies to resocialize offenders.

Opportunity Theory

In this view, delinquency and crime are generated by strain—the discrepancy between what one aspires to and what one realistically expects to achieve. Where the discrepancy is high, we can expect high rates of crime. This position was described early in the sociological literature in 1938, but it only became influential in the early 1960s with the development of federal funding to combat poverty-related delinquency. The most influential statement of opportunity theory appeared in Cloward and Ohlin's *Delinquency and Opportunity* (1960). Its influence was significantly amplified when it was espoused by the 1967 Presidential Commission on Law Enforcement and the Administration of Justice.

The key metaphor used by opportunity theorists is "differential opportunity structures"—every community, or neighborhood, consists of a set of legitimate and illegitimate opportunity routes. Conformity to the law is characteristic of communities in which licit opportunities are plentiful and open to all, and illicit channels are practically nonexistent. Delinquency is generated in settings where illegitimate opportunities are present, and access to conventional routes to success is blocked. Delinquent subcultures inevitably arise in such contexts and socialize youths into a variety of delinquent values and traditions.

Opportunity theory has generated a strong research agenda but it has had little impact on the criminal or juvenile justice system for reasons to be discussed below. The policy implications of opportunity theory suggest expanding legitimate employment and educational opportunities for low-income people as the key crime prevention strategy.

The Labeling Perspective

The labeling perspective was first outlined in Edwin Lemert's *Social Pathology* (1951). It was restated for a wider audience in the task force report on juvenile delinquency of the President's Commission on Law Enforcement and Administration of Justice (1967). It constituted a liberal criticism of the unintended side effects of processing. The perspective underlined the role played by control agencies in isolating rule breakers and creating deviant identities. The term "secondary deviation" was coined to refer to the kind of deviance that grows out of the adaptations that the labeled prson makes to the problems created by official and conventional reactions to the primary violations: "when a person begins to employ his deviant behavior as a role based upon it as a means of defense, attack or adjustment to the overt and covert problems created by the consequent societal reactions to him, his deviation is secondary" (Lemert, 1951:76).

The key metaphor used by labeling theorists was "stigma," which suggested the power of official labeling to spoil an offender's identity. The perspective led to investigations of how individuals become deviant, the varied social reactions to rule breaking, and how rules are made in the first instance. Especially as it related to how individuals move into delinquent or criminal worlds, the labeling perspective dictated an ethnographic approach that involved a close and continuous monitoring of individuals in their local milieus. Participant observation became the key method employed by those who embraced this perspective.

The policy implications of labeling suggest that societal tolerance for minor violations be increased, that victimless crimes be taken off the books, that due process safeguards be scrupulously observed to protect those who become enmeshed in the criminal or juvenile justice network, and that institutions be shut down and a more widespread diversion policy be initiated.

The Justice Model

Over the years a number of scholars have pointed to the need to protect those accused or convicted of crimes. In 1967 a constitutionalist revision of the juvenile court was undertaken to protect the due process rights of adolescents in the criminal justice system. this move coincided with a deep disillusionment among professionals and practitioners about the effectiveness of rehabilitation at either the juvenile or adult level. Tappan (1946) and Allen (1964), in their attacks on the rehabilitative ideal of the juvenile court, foreshadowed what has come to be known as the justice perspective. The American Friends Service Committee (1971) anticipated the same set of concerns in their discussion of the "treatment" of adults who are accused, convicted, and confined. The latter statement was widely reviewed and discussed and can be considered the first official statement of the justice model. Fogel (1975) has summarized the various strands of the justice model and elaborated them further in the corrections area.

The justice view is much more explicitly policy oriented than any of the others discussed above. It rejects the search for theories of causation as unproductive and instead focuses on how volitional human beings weigh the costs and benefits of rule breaking. Presumably if we know that, we can arrange social rewards and punishments in such a fashion that most of us will remain law abiding. The model's key metaphor is that humans are rational and calculating beings, not victims of their emotions or environment. Justice theorists have revived interest in the investigation of the swiftness, certainty, and severity of punishment as they affect compliance. The favored research method is the mathematical analysis of crime rates to determine those punishments that most effectively deter. The implications for policy suggest proportional sentences based on the seriousness of the offense so as to communicate society's even-handedness, and the reduction of the reach of the criminal law.

CONTRIBUTORS TO FEDERAL PROBATION

Authors from a variety of backgrounds contributed articles to *Federal Probation*. Professionals such as agency-based social workers, psychiatrists, lawyers, and the like were the largest single group (26 percent of the total). They were followed closely by university personnel, mostly social science related (25 percent). The third largest group of contributors comprised political officials or appointees (19 percent), followed by probation personnel (15 percent) and the judiciary (12 percent). (See Table 9.2.)

There was a sharp decline in the proportion of professional contributors from the 1930s–1940s to the 1970s (24 percent versus 18 percent) and a sharp increase in the proportion of university contributors (from 17 percent to 37 percent). There were also fewer political contributors in the 1970s than in the 1930s–1940s (28 percent versus 45 percent). Political officials and executive appointees constituted the largest single group of

Table 9.2. Proportion of Contributors by Year

	1930s–1940s		1950s		1960s		1970s		Total	
Professional	(36)	24%	(39)	29%	(50)	33%	(23)	18%	(148)	26%
University personnel	(26)	17	(36)	26	(26)	18	(48)	37	(136)	25
Political	(40)	27	(28)	20	(23)	16	(15)	12	(106)	19
Probation	(27)	18	(10)	8	(27)	18	(30)	23	(94)	15
Judiciary	(17)	11	(22)	16	(20)	13	(6)	5	(65)	12
Parole	(4)	3	(1)	1	(3)	2	(6)	5	(14)	2
Total	(151)	100%	(136)	100%	(148)	100%	(128)	100%	(563)	100%

contributors in the early period, but their proportion dropped to 16 percent in the 1960s and to 12 percent in the 1970s. There were also proportionally fewer judicial contributors in the most recent period than in the early days (5 percent versus 11 percent).

Superficially, the declining contribution of political officials/appointees and the judiciary might suggest that probation was becoming less concerned about changes in the law, policy, or judicial opinion than it had been in the early days. However, a thematic analysis of articles does not support this conclusion. Rather, the concerns and viewpoints expressed in the early period by the political officials/appointees and judges are now being expressed by probation officers. A check of probation officer qualifications in the 1930s–1940s and in the 1970s shows the more recent contributors to be better educated and more comfortable discussing legal issues, social policies, and crime causation. While political and judicial contributors were declining, the proportion of better-educated probation contributors gradually increased from a mere 8 percent in the 1950s (down from 18 percent in the 1930s–1940s) to 23 percent in the 1970s.

Examination of contributors' geographical locations shows the relative influence of the nation's capital in the 1930s–1940s (30 percent as well as the Northeast and the North Central regions (25 percent and 23 percent respectively). By the 1970s the influence of all three of these regions had

Table 9.3. Location of Contributors by Year

	1930s–1940s		1950s		1960s		1970s		Total	
Northeast	(38)	25%	(43)	24%	(32)	22%	(24)	19%	(137)	24%
North Central	(34)	23	(31)	23	(35)	23.5	(25)	20	(25)	22
South	(21)	14	(6)	4	(16)	11	(19)	15	(62)	11
Washington, D.C.	(46)	30	(19)	14	(35)	23.5	(16)	12	(116)	20
West	(3)	2	(3)	2	(6)	4	(11)	8	(23)	4
California	(8)	5	(17)	11.5	(18)	12	(25)	20	(68)	12
Outside U.S.	(1)	1	(17)	11.5	(6)	4	(8)	6	(32)	7
Total	(151)	100%	(136)	100%	(148)	100%	(128)	100%	(562)	100%

declined: Washington, D.C. down to 12 percent, the Northeast to 19 percent, and the North Central region to 20 percent. The most striking change was the emergence of California as an important center of influence (28 percent; the West constituted only 7 percent of contributors in the 1930s and 1940s. (See Table 9.3.)

VARIOUS PERSPECTIVES REPRESENTED

Besides the six theoretical schemes identified above, several other perspectives were also reflected in the literature. When we noted a distinctive viewpoint of some field close or relevant to probation (e.g., police or statistician), we classified it as "other occupational or professional." More frequently observed was an operational perspective found in almost half of all the articles analyzed. Articles that were categorized as operational either expressed probation's raison d'etre (cheaper, more humane) or spoke to some central concerns of practitioners: how to get the probation story across, suggestions on technique, strategies to improve efficiency, and the importance of upgrading the field. Table 9.4 shows the prevalence of the three major kinds of perspectives—those academically generated; those focusing on operational problems unrelated to causation of crime and delinquency; and those coming from other parallel occupational sources.

If frequency of academic perspectives is an indicator of concerns about professional legitimation, then these concerns were most strongly expressed in the 1930–1940s and again in the 1960s (when academic perspectives represented 55 percent and 54 percent respectively, of the total). The 1950s and 1970s were characterized by strong operational preoccupations (47 percent and 53 percent respectively). Other occupation/professional perspectives were seen in only 8 percent of contributions. No detailed analysis of other occupational perspectives was possible because of the limited number of cases.

Table 9.4. Perspective Types by Year

	1930s–1940s		1950s		1960s		1970s		Total	
Academic	(83)	55%	(56)	41%	(80)	54%	(43)	34%	(262)	47%
Operational	(60)	39	(64)	47	(65)	44	(68)	53	(257)	45
Other Occupational	(8)	6	(16)	12	(3)	2	(17)	13	(44)	8
Total	(151)	100%	(136)	100%	(148)	100%	(128)	100%	(563)	100%

CONTRIBUTORS AND THEIR PERSPECTIVES

One would expect university personnel to embrace academic perspectives and those most concerned with probation (political officials/appointees, the judiciary, probation and parole) to reflect operational perspectives. But the reality is somewhat more complex. (See Table 9.5.)

Professionals are more likely to reflect academic perspectives than are their university-based colleagues or practitioners. One unexpected finding was the large number of university-based personnel who addressed the practical concerns of probation. Less surprising was the proportion of probation-related contributors who reflected academic perspectives.

Probation personnel and judges were most likely to discuss occupational techniques—how to do it, how it was done in the past, how it was done elsewhere, or how it was likely to be done in the future. Political officials/appointees were more concerned about upgrading probation. The five parole officers included in this category spoke to the problems of coordinating the various components of the criminal justice system.

Among university-based contributors to operational perspectives, twelve social workers represented the largest subgroup; they provided information on how to do it, or suggested various strategies to improve efficiency and upgrade probation. Eleven sociologists were concerned with efficiency or upgrading; ten professors of criminal justice focused primarily on how-to problems.

The largest group of professional contributors was sixteen lawyers, who spoke mainly to ways of modifying practice so as to bring it into compliance with judicial decisions, legislative actions, or commission reports. They were followed by nine agency-based social workers, eight psychiatrists and other medical doctors, and five psychologists urging a variety of proposals to improve practice.

THE DIFFUSION OF ACADEMIC PERSPECTIVES

The remainder of this paper deals with the diffusion of the six academic perspectives described above and tries to document their changing appeal ovr the years, the extent to which they have been accepted, the

Table 9.5. Perspective by Contributor

	Political/Judicial Probation/Parole		Professional		University Personnel		Total	
Academic	(113)	40%	(85)	57%	(64)	47%	(262)	47%
Operational	(150)	54	(53)	36	(54)	40	(257)	45
Other	(16)	6	(10)	7	(18)	13	(44)	8
Total	(279)	100%	(148)	100%	(136)	100%	(563)	100%

Table 9.6. Academic Perspective by Year

	1930s–1940s		1950s		1960s		1970s		Total	
Social Pathology	(57)	68%	(22)	39%	(16)	20%	(8)	19%	(103)	39%
Social Disorganization	(17)	21	(9)	16	(10)	13	(4)	9	(40)	15
Differential Association	(6)	7	(19)	34	(33)	41	(9)	21	(67)	26
Opportunity	(0)	0	(1)	2	(5)	6	(1)	2	(7)	3
Labeling	(2)	3	(1)	2	(0)	0	(10)	23	(13)	5
Justice	(1)	1	(4)	7	(16)	20	(11)	26	(32)	12
Total	(83)	100%	(56)	100%	(80)	100%	(43)	100%	(262)	100%

reasons for their acceptance, and their success. Originally the dominant academic perspective, social pathology, yielded to social disorganization and differential association views; they were superseded by opportunity theory; and the disillusionment of the 1960s led to labeling and justice concerns. The state of crime and delinquency theory is still developing and no one scheme commands widespread allegiance. Rather, there are a series of competing views, each with its own supporters, centers of influence, and research agendas. We expected to find roughly the same situation reflected in practitioner literature. Table 9.6 summarizes the dominant academic paradigms during the four-decade period under study.

The dominant paradigm in the 1930s–1940s was the social pathology model, though a minority of contributions reflected the competing perspectives of social disorganization and differential association. By the 1950s, the social pathology perspective had lost considerable ground. It was embraced by only 39 percent of the contributors, while differential association views followed a close second. When combined with social disorganization schemes, the two constituted 50 percent of views reflected during the decade. A crisis seems to have occurred during World War II, when contributors lost confidence in the pathology perspective's ability to account for increasing crime rates due to disruptive social changes.

Though social disorganization and differential association explanations rest on different theoretical assumptions, practitioners often combined them. Social disorganization pointed to the overall problem of the breakdown of social control, and differential association explained how one became a criminal or delinquent through natural learning processes. But the social disorganization perspective was difficult to translate into practical suggestions. Its policy implications—community reorganization—did not suggest an important role for the probation officer in crime prevention or treatment. In sum, the disorganization model was used as a "sensitizing" framework. Probation officers were enjoined to include characteristics of the neighborhood in their presentence reports or occasionally urged to recommend conditions for probation that were compatible with disorganization theory—e.g., that offenders be placed on informal probation, reporting to a person influential in the community or be required to participate in some community activity. Suggestions about mobilizing volunteers in probation or recommendations that probation officers play a more active community role were also compatible with the disorganization theory. But eventually the disorganization explanation was rejected (only 9 percent reflected this view in 1970, down from 21 percent in the 1930s and 1940s because it did not provide a core skill that probation officers could identify as distinctively their own or a research agenda that made sense to criminal or juvenile justice agencies. Table 9.7 provides some insight into the sources of support for the social disorganization perspective.

No one group of contributors selected social disorganization as its first-choice explanation, not even academic sociologists. It is a second-choice explanation for only three of twenty-three contributing groups: political officials/appointees, professional psychologists, and academic sociologists.

Table 9.7. Perspective Most Preferred by Contributor

Political/Judicial Probation/Parole	First Choice	Second Choice
Political	Pathology	Disorganization
Judicial	Justice	Pathology
Probation	Pathology	Differential Association
Parole	Justice	Pathology
Professional Group		
Lawyers	Pathology	Justice
M.D.s	Differential Association	Pathology
Psychiatrists	Pathology	Differential Association
Psychologists	Pathology	Disorganization
Clergymen	Differential Association	None
Social Workers	Pathology	Differential Association
Police	Disorganization	Labeling/Differential Association
Criminal Justice Consultants	Differential Association	Pathology
Academics		
Law	Justice	Differential Association
Medicine	Pathology	Differential Association
Psychiatry	Pathology	None
Psychology	Pathology	Differential Association
Social Work	Pathology	Differential Association
Police Administration	Differential Association	None
Criminal Justice	Differential Association	Justice
Political Science	Differential Association	Pathology
Education	Differential Association	Justice
Sociology	Differential Association	Disorganization
Other	Differential Association	Pathology

To affect practice decisively, a perspective must have a much broader-based appeal and must be accepted by probation personnel and the allied professions and occupations that influence their day-to-day operations.

Differential association theory is another story. Table 9.6 documents the increasing popularity of this perspective, which accounted for 7 percent of contributions in the 1930s and 1940s, but by the 1960s had become the dominant paradigm (41 percent). Table 9.7 indicates its widespread appeal. It is the second choice of probation officers, the first choice of professionally based physicians, clergymen, and criminal justice consultants. It is the first choice of university-based sociologists, and political and other social scientists, educationists, and criminal justice professors. Differential association theory lent itself to common-sense interpretations about bad companions that were easy for practitioners to accept. It even led to some in-house research on the effect of delinquent associations and suggestions on how to include this factor in presentence reports. The appeal of differential association lay in its promise to identify a core skill for probation. The rash of articles on peer therapy in the 1950s and 1960s suggested that group counseling rather than case work (the social worker's preserve), might be probation's core skill, and differential association theory could undergird it. This hope did not materialize. Group counseling proved to be too narrow a focus, and differential association could not compete with Skinner's learning theory in providing a foundation for behavior modification programs that involved a broader array of incentives to change than intimate personal relationship. By the 1970s, the articles reflecting differential association reprsented only 21 percent of contributions, while the popularity of labeling and justice models increased.

Opportunity theory seems to have little appeal for practitioners, probably because it has few obvious implications for probation. If crime and delinquency rates are reflections of structural problems, then probation personnel can do little to affect them. Discussions of opportunity theory become more noticeable in *Federal Probation* in the late 1960s after the report of the President's Commission on Law Enforcement and the Administration of Justice. (See Table 9.7.) That report embraced what some observers have called a "heroic theme"—the way to control crime was to change society, to eliminate poverty, to promote equality of opportunity, and thereby to eliminate the need for crime. That effort spurred the development of other professionals but had little impact on probation. Like disorganization theory, opportunity theory seemed to suggest a role for probation—that of creating employment for probationers. But probation personnel seemed to have dismissed that function early in probation's history. Diana's analysis of probation literature (1960) indicates that by 1935 this function, included under "probation as an administrative process," had been discredited. As Table 9.8 shows, most of the contributors

Table 9.8 Academic Perspective by Location

	Northeast	North Central	South	Washington, D.C.	West	California	Outside	Total
Pathology	(29) 37.5%	(32) 48%	(13) 43%	(17) 40%	(1) 14%	(6) 20%	(5) 62.5%	(103) 39%
Disorganization	(12) 15.5	(8) 11	(3) 10	(7) 16	(2) 29	(7) 23.5	(1) 12.5	(40) 15
Differential Association	(26) 34	(15) 22	(7) 23	(7) 16	(2) 29	(10) 33.5	(0) —	(67) 26
Opportunity	(0) —	(1) 1.5	(0) —	(5) 12	(1) 14	(0) —	(0) —	(7) 3
Labeling	(2) 3	(5) 7.5	(3) 100	(1) 2	(0) —	(1) 3	(1) 12.5	(13) 5
Justice	(8) 10	(6) 9	(4) 14	(6) 14	(1) 14	(6) 20	(1) 12.5	(32) 12
Total	(77) 100%	(67) 100%	(30) 100%	(43) 100%	(7) 100%	(30) 100%	(8) 100%	(262) 100%

writing about opportunity theory were based in Washington, D.C., where the recomendations of the 1967 commission created the most interest and activity.

Another theme included in the 1967 report advocated a hands-off policy that contradicted the heroic theme. This perspective underlined the negative consequences of official action, especially on youthful violators. By the 1970s, the labeling prspective was reflected in 23 percent of the contributions to *Federal Probation*. Only the justice model was more prevalent. (See Table 9.6.) Half of the articles reflecting this new perspective were from academics, mostly sociologists, and one-third came from high-status political officials/appointees. In terms of location, the North Central region and the South seem to be most influential. (See Table 9.8.) The labeling perspective has had a greater impact than the others on probation practice, but has done little to define a distinctive core skill for the probation officer. The call for diversion, especially of youthful offenders, has created a new welfare bureaucracy and a possible new career route for probation personnel. The impact has been greater on day-to-day practice than on professionalization attempts because legislators and judges have been persuaded that diversion, decriminalization, due process, and deinstitutionalization should be encouraged. This shift has dealt a massive blow to those who embrace a pathological perspective as the best hope for professionalization. The labeling scheme has not generated significant research within the criminal or juvenile justice system. It has encouraged some data gathering to show that there has been compliance with judicial decisions or legislative actions narrowing the scope of control agencies, but little else. The impact of the labeling perspective on the identification of a distinct probation core skill has been practically nil.

The labeling perspective does not have widespread appeal. As shown in Table 9.7, it is not the first-choice perspective of any group of contributors, and it is a second-choice perspective (along with differential association) only for the police. For this reason, and because of the increasing social criticism of labeling views within university circles, this perspective's influence on practitioner literature is likely to decline sharply during the 1980s.

More enduring seem to be the concerns expressed by those favoring the justice model. They, like the labelers, favor the four Ds (decriminalization, diversion, due process, and deinstitutionalization) but represent a more substantial group. Justice model advocates are not only the largest group of contributors in the 1970s, but they are more likely to be policy makers. If Table 9.7 had included a third-choice perspective, the justice model would even have been chosen by probation personnel. This perspective may also speak more forcefully than any of the others to the professionalization issue. The Institute of Judicial Administration and the American Bar Association's volume on the juvenile probation function (1977), which represents a justice perspective, outlines a series of tasks and guidelines for their performance that could constitute core skills related to social investigations.

SUMMARY

Our content analysis of *Federal Probation* suggests that the diffusion of perspectives roughly follows the hypothetical S-curve pattern. The key group in the introduction of a perspective was the journal's book reviewers, who were overwhelmingly based in universities. The book review editor was the decisive figure. He decided which books were worthy of review, which developments occurring outside the probation field were important enough to report, and who was to review them. All of the academic perspectives, except the social pathological one, were introduced in this way. A fuller analysis of this process would involve interviewing *Federal Probation* book review editors over the years as well as the journal editor, and possibly members of the overall advisory board, to determine how decisions were made. Within two years of a model's introduction, it appeared in the form of an article written by a high-status practitioner or academic, then trickled down within the following two years to the line officer level; thereafter the number of contributions leveled off, suggesting that the perspective had been adopted.

Almost one-half of the articles examined in the sample reflected operational perspectives. Obviously, some of these were concerned with professionalization indirectly, especially those that focused on how to get the probation story across to critical publics and discussed ways of upgrading probation or coordinating its activities with other parts of the justice system. However, the concern of this inquiry was how *academic* explanations of crime and delinquency were used to spur professionalizing efforts. No attempt was made to trace the diffusion of new work procedures through the operational literature, though we would expect it to follow the same kind of pattern as the dissemination of theories. It was the operational articles, especially how-to material, not those reflecting academic perspectives, that most decisively shaped day-to-day practice, if letters to the editor are any indication. Apart from judicial opinion and legislative action, the how-to articles were the single most important influence on practice. We assume that if any explanation of crime and delinquency is to carry the day among probation personnel it must not only win acceptance in university circles, but must have an important influence on practice. To date, none of the academic perspectives have done so.

The social and professional conditions that were decisive in the initial introduction of each academic perspective can only be inferred from this analysis. Social pathology was on the scene long before *Federal Probation* started; World War II and its impact made book reviewers and article contributors more receptive to social disorganization and diffential association views. Labeling and justice concerns seem directly related to the disenchantment with rehabilitation and the cost concerns of policy-makers. The popularity of each perspective reflected its changing appeal in academic circles and apparently had little or nothing to do with day-to-day practice, training needs, or the sophistication of the perspective's research agenda. There was nothing inherently antithetical to systematic data collection in any of the schemes. All of them could justify a strong research program conducted by practitioners.

We originally expected that a perspective with a well-developed research agenda, like opportunity theory, would be attractive because it could create a strong presence in the juvenile and criminal justice system; and that a scheme that was not sufficiently developed to generate testable hypotheses, like the labeling perspective, would be rejected. But the reverse happened—labeling was accepted for reasons other than its research implications. While a perspective's appeal is partly a function of its potential data-gathering strategies, it is more crucially related to its potential for legitimation. Perspectives that delineate a distinctive role for probation workers and can lead to university-based certification programs will be accepted; those that do not will be rejectd. The spate of articles about the content of university programs in criminal justice during the 1970s suggests that the locus of probation's professionalization efforts during the 1980s will be justice-related academic programs. Academicians who collaborate in this development will be required to subscribe to a defensible perspective and be prepared to demonstrate how it can be implemented in a work setting. The research done for instance on adoption of new farm practices suggests that a trial state is crucial to eventual acceptance. For probation, such a trial will require a more detailed development of institutional arrangements to communicate ideas from the academy to the field.

BIBLIOGRAPHY

Allen, Francis A. (1964). "The Juvenile Court and the Limits of Juvenile Justice," in *The Borderland of Criminal Justice*. Chicago: University of Chicago.

American Friends Service Committee (1971). *Struggle for Justice*. New York: Hill and Wang.

Carey, James T., and Patrick McAnany (1980). *Delinquency Theory and the Juvenile Court*. Paper presented to the Law and Society Association, June 6, Madison, WI.

Cloward, Richard, and Lloyd Ohlin (1960). *Delinquency and Opportunity*. New York: Free Press.

Coleman, James, et al. (1966). *Medical Innovation: A Diffusion Study*. Indianapolis: Bobbs Merrill.

Crane, D. (1972). *Invisible Colleges: Diffusion of Knowledge in Scientific Communities*. Chicago: University of Chicago Press.

Davis, Nanette J. (1980). *Sociological Constructions of Deviance*, 2nd ed. Dubuque: William C. Brown.

Diana, Lewis (1960). "What is Probation?" *Journal of Criminal Law, Criminology and Police Science* 51:189–204.

Fogel, David (1975). *We are the Living Proof*. Cincinnati: Anderson.

Gross, Seymour Z. (1966). "Biographical Characteristics of Juvenile Probation Officers." *Crime and Delinquency* 12:109–116.

Institute of Judicial Administration and The American Bar Association Juvenile Justice Standards Project (1977). *Standards for Juvenile Justice: A Summary and Analysis*, ed. Barbara Danziger Flicker, Cambridge, MA: Ballinger.

Katz, Elihu, "The Two Step Flow of Communication" (1960). In W. Schramm (ed.), *Mass Communications*. Urbana: University of Illinois Press.

Lemert, Edwin (1951). *Social Pathology*. New York: McGraw Hill.

———— (1967). "The Juvenile Court—Quest and Realities." In President's Commission on Law Enforcement and Administration of Justice, *Task Force Report: Juvenile Delinquency*. Washington, D.C.: U.S. Government and Printing Office.

Lubove, Richard (1965). *The Professional Altruist*. Cambridge, MA: Harvard University Press.

Robinson, Virginia (1930). *A Changing Psychology in Social Case Work*. Chapel Hill: University of North Carolina Press.

Shaw, Clifford R., and Henry D. McKay (1931). *Social Factors in Juvenile Delinquency*, Vol. 2 of National Commission of Law Observance and Enforcement, *Report on the Causes of Crime*. Washington, D.C.: Government Printing Office.

Sutherland, Edwin (1939). *Principles of Criminology* 3rd ed. Philadelphia: J. B. Lippincott.

Tappan, Paul (1946). "Treatment Without Trial." *Social Forces* 24:306–311.

Wilensky, Harold L. (1965). "The Professionalization of Everyone?" *American Journal of Sociology* 70:137–158.

Chapter 10

Client Biography and Probation Organization

*David E. Duffee**

The last ten years have seen a great deal of criticism directed to organizations whose primary task is processing or changing clients. Some of these organizations are public, some private. Some serve voluntary clients, others an involuntary population. In some cases, such as probation, the organization may serve more than one client or be responsible to more than one constituency. Probation, for example, serves the general public interest by meting out punishment or controlling crime or both; yet at the same time the probation organization engages particular people in rather durable and significant personal relationships as clients. Complaints about lack of effectiveness in the "human services area" have fallen heaviest on public organizations such as probation, prisons, and antipoverty, welfare, and mental health agencies, where the interests of the public and those of the specific service client apparently collide (Martinson, 1974; Lipton et al., 1975; Marris and Rein, 1967; Rose, 1974; Warren et al., 1974).

In many of these public, multiple-client organizations, the timpani of accusations have been followed by a litany of reforms. We have seen significant structural alterations proposed to make programs more effective in welfare (Hoshino, 1972), juvenile delinquency (Miller and Ohlin, 1976), mental health (Fairweather et al., 1969), mental retardation (Segal,

*Department of Criminal Justice and Public Policy, State University of New York at Albany

1977), and penology (Fogel, 1975; Morris, 1974; American Friends Service Committee, 1971). Probation is not exempt from either the claims of problems (General Accounting Office Reports, 1975 and 1976) or of pressures for structural change (see, for example, Chapter 8 in this volume).

In many, if not all, of the critical examinations of effectiveness, a central theme has been goal conflict, goal ambiguity, and goal displacement (see, for example, Nokes (1960), Cressey (1960), and Hall et al. (1966), as well as the material cited above). Consequently, many of the structural reforms, proposed or actually implemented, have been generated on the premise that the classification and modification of goals will reduce conflict and render programs more effective. For instance, Conrad (1983) proposes to separate the functions now performed by one probation officer into three separately conducted operations of investigation, service, and surveillance. Similarly, Hoshino's welfare reform resulted in separating the duties of income maintenance and social service. Miller's deinstitutionalization strategy seemed based on a belief that service to juveniles could be made effective by minimizing custodial concerns or minimizing custody-treatment conflicts (by eliminating dual-purpose institutions and dual-goal staff).

This paper is not an attempt to minimize the importance of such structural innovation and attempts at goal clarification. But it does propose another point of view in examining how *one* of these organizations, probation, and one set of clients, probationers, interact. The starting point is an assumption: that provision to the client of organizational membership—that is, requiring the probationer to perform a role in the organization—is an essential, irreducible constraint on the behavior of such organizations. By extension, the kind of role the probationer is required to perform will be a fundamental determinant of how staff are organized and how staff and clients interact. This determinant, in fact, may have greater influence on achievement, or on ineffectiveness, than changing the manifest goals of the organization or realigning staff so that the new goals are "embedded" in the operating reality of the organization.

The perspective on clients and organizations presented below does not necessarily *contradict* the standard goal-conflict/structural-reform approach to these organizations. It is quite possible that the structural reform will significantly alter the roles required of clients. If so, the client-staff interactions may be significantly changed. But many goal and structure changes may leave certain conflicts intact and may leave problematic staff-client interactions undisturbed. In this case, the structural change may be followed by new discoveries of the same old ineffectiveness.

The critical distinction between the client model of organization presented here and the goal models we frequently practice can be briefly stated. The goal model assumes that substantive changes, such as from punishment to treatment or from counseling to surveillance, have major effects on the interaction of client and organization. In contrast, the client model assumes that the substance or content of the role asked of clients is at least incomplete in describing what is asked of the client. The client model is an attempt to specify how much of the client's life is devoted to his or her organizational role. And the model assumes that the questions about extent and degree of interaction may be the most important factors to consider when we try to predict how clients and probation agencies may interact.

THE CLIENT BIOGRAPHY MODEL

Lefton and Rosengren (1974) have provided a foundation for a model of how clients and organizations interact. Their theoretical foundation seems to be primarily that of Parsons (1961), who raised the issue of the impact on organizational structure of bringing clients into the organization. It is assumed that organizations that have to process clients as members and participants within organizational boundaries face fundamentally different division of labor and control problems than organizations processing objects, or even organizations that deal with clients as external others. A major determinant of structure in these people-processing organizations is the reactivity and self-initiative of the human material being processed. Since the client can, in fact, resist the expected organizational role, these service organizations require greater discretion at their lower levels than is true of organizations with nonreactive material (Perrow, 1970), and the organizations must interact with the client to gain at least a minimum of consent (Etzioni, 1961, Katz and Kahn, 1966).

Lefton and Rosengren elaborate these initiating organizational problems by suggesting modal types of organizational response to client membership. Their Client Biography Model is built upon two key dimensions: 1) the variety of client behavior that the organization is interested in influencing, and 2) the duration of influence on that behavior. On the first dimension, organizational interest can vary from being confined to a very specific aspect of the client or a very narrow range of his behaviors, to covering many aspects of the client. Lefton and Rosengren refer to the variety of interest as the lateral dimension. On the dimension of duration, organizational interest in a client can vary from a short span of time to the client's entire future biography. Lefton and Rosengren refer to this interest as the longitudinal dimension.

Theoretically, lateral and longitudinal interest can vary independently, so that a typology of client organizations can be established by dichotomizing the dimensions. The typology designates four types of organizational responses to clients: 1) those with a high lateral interest and low longitudinal interest; 2) those with a low lateral interest and a high longitudinal interest, 3) those with a low interest on both dimensions, and 4) those with a high interest on both dimensions.

Some examples of how service organizations would be classified within this scheme may be helpful. An organization that is high lateral and low longitudinal is concerned with the client in a variety of aspects, and therefore will have technologies that can engage the client from a number of different perspectives, address a number of different client problems, or have some impact on a number of roles the client can conceivably play. Such an organization, however, is structured to affect only a short segment of the client's life career. Lefton and Rosengren's example is a short-term therapeutic psychiatric hospital, which may have a variety of diferent staff groups and helping techniques that are supposed to impinge on a variety of client psychological and social dimensions, but in which the client has no enduring interaction with the organization.

An organization that is low lateral and high longitudinal has an extremely narrow interest in the client, or a small range of client characteristics is relevant to the way in which the organization and client interact. Nevetheless, this specialized interest in the client carries over for some time, often extending beyond the client's immediate contact with organizational participants. Rosengren and Lefton's example is the tuberculosis hospital, which is structured to have immediate impact on a particular disease as well as to follow up on remission. But the organizational interest in other aspects of the client is quite limited.

A low lateral, low longitudinal organization is structured to engage the client on a very specific set of behaviors or presenting problems for a short period of time. Such organizations usually have a well-defined, advanced, but narrow technology and accord high status to a single profession that is seen as most competent to affect immediate and short-range change. Rosengren and Lefton's example is the acute general hospital.

Finally, a high lateral, high longitudinal organization is one in which the organization is interested in a broad and varied engagement of the client over a long period of time. This organization usually has a diverse technology, several equally prestigious staff divisions, and complex mechanisms for monitoring client careers. Lefton and Rosengren suggest that both long-term therapeutic hospitals and liberal arts colleges fall into this category.

Lefton and Rosengren have applied this model in several research efforts concerning mental hospitals (Rosengren, 1967; Rosengren and Lefton, 1970; Rosengren, 1968). In these investigations, they had considerable success in relating variations in organizational client interest to structural variables such as size, age, administrative or professional orientation, and organizational interaction with other agencies. Not only did variation in the two client interest dimensions permit successful predictions of a variety of other organizational characteristics, but tracing variation in these interests over time seemed particularly relevant to the issue of service organization reforms. For example, during the 1960s, federal policy in a number of social service areas stressed the development of agencies that would have high lateral, high longitudinal interests. This policy orientation seemed to reformers a palliative for fragmentation among service programs and a response to the common complaint that service organizations were impersonal and bureaucratic. But Lefton and Rosengren found that this organizational type seemed to be inherently unstable. As these high lateral, high longitudinal organizations grew older, they tended to become low lateral, high longitudinal. In other words, the general service organizations tended over time to specialize in a narrower range of client behaviors. Hence, it might have made more sense, they thought, to devise strategies for coordination of specialized agencies, rather than to establish service organizations that would care for the "whole client" (Rosengren and Lefton, 1970:190).

The problems with the model are basically those of vagueness in the definition of lateral and longitudinal interest and the resulting lack of independence in particular indicators of those dimensions. For example, Rosengren (1968) operationalized the lateral dimension in mental health facilities by counting the number of treatment modalities in each agency. His measure of longitudinal interest was the utilization of outside vocational and educational programs. There are several problems here. First, the use of the number of treatment modalities to indicate a variety of interest in the client assumes that the various modalities are independent of each other (as Rosengren acknowledges, 1968:3). Second, restriction of the measure of lateral interest to treatment modalities ignores many other ways in which organizations can engage clients, such as by regimentation of daily routine, isolation of clients from family and occupation, and using clients in nontreatment roles, as in upkeep of the institution (see King and Raynes, 1968).

Another problem is that incorporating the presence or absence of certain treatment modalities (e.g., outside education and vocational training) in the measure of the longitudinal dimension would seem to damage the independence of the two variables. Rosengren argues that the use of *outside* programs indicates organizational interest in reintegration of the patients. But it may indicate nothing more than fiscal frugality, agency size, or something about the richness and tolerance of the agency environment, rather than duration of organizational impact.

To maintain the independence of lateral and longitudinal interests, both from each other and from other useful organizational concepts, it is necessary to narrow the definitions of both terms. Lefton and Rosengren have defined lateral as the number of "aspects of the client" that are seen as relevant to the organization. In contrast, variety may be defined *as the extent to which the organization activity engages the client in organizational roles to the exclusion of nonorganizational roles.* The difference between definitions is apparent in the following example. Lefton and Rosengren might classify an outpatient mental health unit as high lateral if it used various treatment modalities, and a large inpatient hospital as low lateral because it had few modalities of treatment. Emphasizing extent of engagement instead, we would argue that the outpatient clinic has a limited lateral interest vis-à-vis the client, since the client continues to engage in many nonorganizational roles during the course of clienthood. The inpatient facility, regardless of limited psychiatric or psychological technology, engulfs the client in several organizational roles, or has a high lateral interest. In other words, the organization controls a large variety of roles for the client. Thus refined, the dimension of laterality is relatively similar to the institutionalization-normalization continuum described by Coates et al. (1978:11–20).

Lefton and Rosengren define longitudinal interest as the length of time that the client behavior remains salient for the organization. We have less difficulty with this definition but think it important to specify how "salience" is indicated. First, indications of duration of interest should not be confounded with indications of the client's scope of current involvement. Thus, in the example from Rosengren, the indicator "use of outside programs" is at least insufficient. Rosengren was attempting to measure organizational concern for an enduring change in client behavior. But to examine this concern independently of the lateral interest would entail controlling for whether the same programs were also available inside the organization. Moreover, an indicator such as inside/outside is useless in the examination of organizations in which the engagement of the client involves no penetration of the physical boundary. For example, both welfare and probation organizations have been observed to vary in their concern for eventual client self-governance (Wyman and Timmins, 1973; Studt, 1972; Stanley, 1976) but neither type of organization has the option of sending some clients "out" and keeping other clients "in." Finally, the in-out distinction is likely to become confusing if one wants to analyze complex service networks in which the boundaries of the separate organizational units are diffuse and the client flow paths circular. For example, Sarason (1974:188) claims that community mental health centers and mental health institutions are complementary units of a larger system. The existence of the former may mean the average length of stay in the latter is shorter, but it also seems to mean that short-term returns to institutions will occur more frequently. Lerman (1975:150) has noted the same relationship between detention facilities and parole in the California Youth Authority system.

To avoid such problems, we would define longitudinal interest as the degree to which the organization is concerned with the future autonomy of client from organizational intervention. The following example demonstrates the difference between our definition and the original. Lefton and Rosengren would define as high longitudinal interest an organization that has a complete monitoring system for maintaining client conformity with organizational norms once the client has left the organization. Hence, a prison with complex ties to parole and police is thought to have a long-term interest in the client. In contrast, we would identify as high longitudinal those organizations that are concerned with decreasing future client engagement with the organization. Longitudinality is concerned with future independence or self-governance, not the extent of interorganizational linkage. As Wilkins (1969:19) has pointed out, correctional systems that repeatedly treat recidivists to the same regimen are not concerned with altering the offender's future behavior. Hence many correctional agencies have rather *low* longitudinal interest, because they are not designed to produce change. In the noncorrectional area, our definition of longitudinal seems reminiscent of Scott's (1967) discovery that certain agencies for the blind constructed programs that were antithetical to the client interest in gaining autonomy.

THE BIOGRAPHY MODEL AND PROBATION

There are two ways in which we can use the biography model in the analysis of probation. First, it may be used to compare probation in general with other forms of penal sanction. That is, we can contrast the *relative* stress on variety and duration in sanctions as different as suspended sentence, restitution, probation, halfway house placement, and maximum security incarceration. This approach may also be useful in examining how probation as a sanctioning organization relates systematically to other options. A second way to use the model is in making distinctions among kinds of probation experiences. For example, even if all probation agencies intervene in the lives of offenders to a lesser extent than do prisons, we can expect the thoroughness of probation supervision will vary considerably from office to office, and probably from officer to officer. Likewise, there should be a good deal of variation in the duration of probation impact on clients. In some instances, probation officers may interact with their clients in a way that is geared only to close the case without revocation. In other instances, probation may be organized in an attempt to keep the offender from returning to the probation system, or to other forms of penal supervision. These probation agencies would rank relatively high on the duration dimension.

Probation and the Sanctioning Continuum

Many models of probation provide a means of comparing one form of probation supervision with another. This focus on alternative forms of probation can be extremely helpful in managerial decisions concerning the best way to deploy available resources. One shortfall of this type of modeling, particularly if it is the only sort of comparison being made, is that it may deemphasize the relationship between any form of probation and other aspects of the criminal process. For most offenders facing sentence, the crucial decision is between probation and incarceration, not between types of probation. In other words, we can assume that one significant aspect of probation for the offender is how probation compares with other possible sentencing alternatives. The client biography model can be used to explore the relationship of the offender to the range of sanctioning alternatives.

In the preconviction stages of the criminal process, much of the negotiation between a defendant and officials of criminal justice concerns the variety dimension—or how extensively the criminal justice system will affect the defendant, how many client roles will be influenced by membership in the organization. Throughout the preconviction process, extent of engagement is a prime concern.

Packer (1968) presents one version of this concern as the ideological tension between due process and crime control models of the criminal process. The due process model urges extreme caution in invoking the criminal sanction, which is seen as an extremely negative and powerful disruption of civil rights. Therefore it should be used sparingly and only to the extent that can be justified by the level of harm inflicted by the defendant. The crime control model, in contrast, proceeds on the assumption that the threat to social order posed by criminal wrongdoers is so severe as to justify quick and final control over the lives of offenders.

The choice of how extensive criminal justice intervention should be is apparent in many preconviction stages of the criminal process. In both *Terry* v. *Ohio*, 392 U.S. 1 (1968), and *Chimel* v. *California*, 395 U.S. 752 (1969), the Supreme Court of the United States issued important statements concerning the scope of searches. In *Terry*, the Warren Court made it clear that it would not countenance any distinction between frisks and searches that would keep frisks from being governed by the Fourth Amendment. In *Chimel*, the scope of search incident to arrest was significantly restricted.

Limiting the extent to which criminal justice intervention will curtail a defendant's noncriminal roles would also seem important in the selection of citation rather than arrest for minor crimes (Zimring, 1974).

Interestingly, one of the most significant decisions concerning extent of impact on the defendant has received a minimum of appellate court attention. With the ambiguous exception of *Stack* v. *Boyle*, 342 U.S. 1 (1951), the Supreme Court has not spoken on the issue of release pending trial, although considerable data have been amassed demonstrating the effects of pretrial detention on later decisions affecting extent of intervention. Presently, lack of bail appears to affect both the likelihood of being convicted and the likelihood of receiving a more severe sentence (Bing and Rosenfeld, 1970; New York Legal Aid Society, 1972).

In addition to these points, perhaps the most significant preconviction consideration of extent of criminal justice involvement is the negotiation about the type of sentence the offender will face if convicted. Duffee et al. (1978) have argued that the crucial item in plea negotiation concerns the offender's degree of membership in the postconviction system. Whether the specifics of negotiation involve dropping charges, reducing charges, or seeking a prosecutor's recommendation at sentencing, the usual object of negotiation, from the offender's perspective, is to reduce the scope of membership, or to constrict the extent of intervention as much as possible. Jail terms are seen as preferable to state prison terms, and probation is seen as preferable to either. Probation is the only punishment available for most serious offenses during which the offender can engage in many other social roles while being punished.

Much of the current innovation in sentencing patterns and conditions of sentence may be seen as attempts to implement punishments that do not interfere with all of an offender's other social roles. While this separation will be difficult to achieve in incarcerative settings, even here we have seen recent recommendations that purport to separate an offender's moral liabilities as a lawbreaker from his rights to choose a life style or engage in self-improvement programs (Fogel, 1975; Morris, 1974; von Hirsch, 1976). In other words, even in prison settings, reformers are seeking to narrow the extensiveness of the criminal sanction—to find some way to focus its impact on the offender as lawbreaker and to leave the other roles of the offender alone. To those who favor this trend, the advantage of probation is its relatively narrow scope compared with almost any incarcerative options.

But, of course, not all probation conditions are the same. Probation is a flexible sanction, which can offer a relatively wide range of extensiveness. It can be structured to engage the offender in a large number of probation-related activities or to engage him barely at all. We should expect that an offender's reaction to probation will be partially determined by the extensiveness of probation supervision. How much of the offender's life space will be influenced by the conditions of probation?

A particularly important aspect of this inquiry may be the offender's perception of equity in the distribution of probation conditions. Are the conditions to which he is assigned narrower or broader, or more or less controlling in his choice of roles, than the alternative conditions he could reasonably expect to receive? For example, the equity perceived in assigning a probationer to reside in a "halfway-in" house may depend on whether the offender sees the halfway placement as more restrictive than straight probation or as less restrictive than a state prison sentence. In states where halfway houses are run by the state prison service, offenders sent there in lieu of full incarceration may feel their punishment is less restrictive than the most likely alternative. Such differences may explain the relatively high absconding and failure-to-complete-program rates in Minnesota probation hostels and the relatively low absconding and program failure rates in Pennsylvania Community Service Centers (Minnesota Governor's Commission on Crime Prevention, 1976; Duffee et al., 1977).

Other rather new types of probation conditions might be evaluated in the same light. Split sentences, or jail time as a condition of probation, are being ordered by judges with increasing frequency. Some judges appear to favor the split sentence because it increases the social restrictiveness of the sentence, or is more extensive than straight probation, presumably thereby increasing the retributiveness of the sentence. One would suspect the impact of split sentences on offenders to vary depending on whether those sent to jail and then probation believe they have avoided state prison or immediate probation.

While the data available are inconclusive, there is some reason to suspect that, in general, recent probation innovations have increased rather than decreased the extensiveness of probation as a sanction. This conclusion is based on data suggesting that many new sentencing options, most of which involve some use of probation, involve greater intervention in the offender's life than the normal sanction before the innovation. This would seem particularly true of juvenile diversion programs (Klein, 1979) but may also be true in adult probation programs that add restitution or community service to normal probation supervision.

As judges and probation departments consider what kinds of probation programs to employ, one hypothesis worthy of testing is that probation results may be more related to the level of extensiveness than to the type of intervention. For example, a rather old but still provocative English study evaluated the effects of types of probation conditions on juveniles. Bottoms and McClintock (1958) discovered that juveniles required to provide work service and those required to undergo traditional probation counseling performed about equally, while another group ordered to work and undergo counseling did worse than either of the other groups. This study has normally been interpreted to mean that some treatments do not mix. However, such findings would also support an interpretation that the less extensive single roles (work or counseling) were effective while the more extensive double roles (work and counseling) were less effective.

The notion of extent of intervention can also be usefully employed in examining probation revocation. As far as we have progressed in (or is it now retreated from?) the "due process revolution," it is remarkable how the extensiveness or sanctioning scope of probation is ignored at revocation. In many jurisdictions, the length of prison sentence to be served upon revocation of probation is unaffected by the length of sentence served on probation before revocation. This practice would seem to imply that probation has no sanctioning value at all, or that probation supervision has not restricted the probationer's freedom of choice whatsoever. Perhaps at the point when probation is being revoked, judges and probation officials feel it has had little impact. But the practice of ignoring probation time served before revocation would seem to violate the principles of retribution altogether. As Packer (1968:45–50) argues, the saving grace of retribution as the basis for punishment is that it does not allow punishment without a crime, or out of proportion to the crime. And with the exception of bench probation and suspended sentences, most of probation periods are constructed as if punishment is being served, or as if an intervention is being made. Ignoring that premise at revocation is analogous to requiring an offender to serve the original prison sentence again if he commits a new crime after the first one.

In comparing probation with other sanctioning alternatives, the dimension of duration of impact is probably less important than the dimension of extent of impact. However, there are several ways in which the duration of intervention, or the degree to which the sanction leads to future self-governance of the offender, is important to understanding the sanctioning continuum.

Lefton and Rosengren (1974) remark that while the variety dimension concerns the amount of client life-space to be affected, duration refers to the amount of client life-time to be affected by an intervention. In this paper, we have spoken of variety as a determination of the number of social roles that will be influenced by (or seen as relevant to) the intervention technology. The duration dimension, in contrast, concerns the length of time for which client behavior is to be affected by the intervention.

In penology, perhaps the most visible concern with duration is the decision on length of sentence. But the length of the intervention, measured chronologically, may not be the only aspect of social time. From a social perspective, we may also consider whether the intervention is presumed to have lasting effects, or whether it will be evaluated on the basis of how the offender behaves once the intervention is completed.

We could argue, for example, that two prison sentences of equal length may vary considerably on the duration dimension. If the objective of a two-year prison sentence were retribution for an offense, the technology of intervention might be relatively simple, amounting to little more than guarding the offender for two years to prevent escapes, misbehavior during sentence, and mistreatment of the offender by others. Logically the prison experience need include nothing else, and the intended objectives of the punishment would be completed when the offender was released. If the purpose of the sentence were rehabilitation, on the other hand, the content of the punishment would be significantly different. Rehabilitative intents are not achieved during a prison sentence, but after the offender is released. They are said to have failed if the offender commits another crime. Such a criterion would be irrelevant to a retributive sentence. Rehabilitative sentences are therefore longer on the duration dimension because the intervention is designed to have an impact beyond the correctional organization's immediate contact with the offender. The results of this greater interest in duration are evident in the structure of rehabilitative prisons— they have treatment staffs and treatment programs designed to influence the future behavior of the offender (Cressey, 1960; Street et al., 1966). The move toward determinate sentencing, and particularly the attempt to decouple treatment or self-improvement from length of sentence, may be seen in part as attempts to reduce the duration dimension of correctional organizations.

What actual effects the reduction of duration will have on the future behavior of offenders is another matter. It is important to emphasize that the duration dimension is a *structural characteristic* of the intervention, not a prediction about how the offender will actually behave in the future. Many people now criticize the rehabilitative, or high-duration, prison because its expensive technology is apparently not very successful in influencing future offender behavior (Martinson, 1974; Lipton et al. 1975). At least some spokesmen for the low-duration prison imply, if not explicitly promise, that prisons concentrating on retribution alone may have a greater beneficial impact on the offender's future behavior than prisons designed explicitly to affect that behavior (see Fogel, 1975). Whether such an effect actually occurs remains to be seen, but there is nothing inherently illogical in the suggestion that a prison with here-and-now technology might have longer-lasting advantages, or at least fewer long-lasting disadvantages, than a prison with a future-oriented technology.

The duration dimension in probation is relatively similar. Perhaps since the religiously oriented philanthropy of John Augustus, but certainly since the advent of social case work in probation, probation technology has been structured to have long-lasting effects, or has been relatively high on the duration dimension.[1] That is, at least as a long-standing probation ideal, probation officers were to bring to bear in each case a planned sequence of interventions that were intended to have a long-range impact on the behavior of the probationer. This ideal was reflected in the organization of probation, in the ideals of probation officer training and education, and in the criteria against which probation has been evaluated.

This does not mean that probation has often been successful in altering offender behavior, or that the ideals of probation have ever been fully implemented. It does suggest, however, that probation officers felt justified in broaching topics with their clients related to character, personality, or entire career expectations that were hypothetically related to future behavior, rather than the behavior leading to conviction. In fact, many critics of probation and parole supervision practices perceived that undesirable goal-displacement had taken place if probation officers were more concerned with routine monitoring of cases than with implementing long-term client reintegration (see O'Leary and Duffee, 1971; Studt, 1972). Speaking specifically of parole, but using terminology that would apply equally to probation, Studt characterized the style of supervision preferred by officers as a "guardian-ward" relationship—one in which officers saw it as their legitimate interest to be concerned with the entire care and nurturance of the offender. This characterization suggests not only that officers prefer to see their legitimate sphere of influence as a very broad one, concerned with a great deal of the client's life-space, but that the interest covers an extremely long term with the officer seeking signs that the offender is committed not simply to completing probation but to being a new person long after probation is completed.

Lefton and Rosengren's original treatment of the biography model suggests that a chief problem with high-duration interest in clients is that there will be frequent disagreements between what officials and clients see as legitimate intervention. To the extent that offenders justify legal intervention in terms of what they have done rather than what they are to become, they may see a probation sanction with a long-duration interest as illegitimate, no matter how helpful the officials intend that punishment to be.

In some respects probation is used to reduce the durability of the relationship between the offender and the sanctioning system, primarily by avoiding the alleged long-term disadvantage of incarceration. For example, probation can be used to keep the offender from the social contamination of other prisoners, or to reduce chances of greater criminality in the future. Criminal socializations were recognized as a crucial problem in our earliest penitentiaries (Beaumont and de Toqueville, 1960) and were seen as a major problem in rehabilitation at least through the 1960s (Clemmer, 1958; Sykes, 1958; Cloward, 1960). More recent writing has cast some doubt on the dynamics of the prison subculture (Irwin and Cressey, 1962; Hawkins, 1974; Martin and Webster, 1971). Nevertheless, few would argue that the long-term negative impact of prison on the socialization of offenders is either negligible or preferable to that of probation settings.

A second, less debatable concern is the use of probation to reduce the stigma of incarceration. Such stigma may be real, even if negative socializazation is not, since even a "pro-social" inmate may discover that prejudice and licensing blockades hamper reintegration after a prison sentence. The desire to avoid stigma may also be a major justification of informal, voluntary or preconviction probation, in which a defendant's successful completion of a probation period will result in the dropping of prosecution and avoidance of a conviction record.

Finally, some have proposed that a restructuring of probation supervision could increase the offender's autonomy from the criminal justice system in the future. Most of these proposals involve *reducing* the duration dimension of probation either by cutting the entire supervision period (Bennett, 1973) or by having probation officers focus on meeting specific current needs of offenders through advocacy and brokerage (Dell'Apa, 1976; Sigurdson, 1973; Clear, 1977). Like similar trends in incarceration content, these proposals imply that a probation sanction with a narrower and shorter-range interest in the offender may produce more successful client outcomes than one built on larger promises.

Probation Variations and Client Careers

In addition to examining how probation compares with other sanctions, the client biography model may be useful in explicating variations among probation supervision strategies. Certainly it is important to consider how probation compares with incarceration. But we will gain greater insights into the administration of probation itself by determining the variety of ways in which probation organizations may interact with probationers. It is in this area that the biography model can be particularly useful. Many other models of probation-probationer interactions, such as those reviewed in Chapter 6, are useful, but they share the disadvantage of employing value-laden terms. For example, it is frequently found that Studt's "insider-outsider" relationship and O'Leary and Duffee's "reintegration policy" are preferred over the other strategies in those respective models because those styles manifest certain cultural cues concerning voluntarism, democratic decision making, and client-officer collaboration.

In other models, the polarization of terms such as treatment and punishment or assistance and control tends to make probation analysts focus on the abstract ideals of probation rather than on the way in which probation may actually engage the client. For example, many analysts prefer "treatment" or "assistance" to "punishment" or "control," ignoring the problem that these labels have a highly variable and ambiguous content. Some treatments may be far harsher and more rigorous than some punishments. Moreover, such dichotomies make some false or at least misleading distinctions. All treatments imply some form of control—some insistence that the offender comply with the role expectations for treatment recipients.

In contrast, the biography model focuses on the role-space and durability of role-space restrictions on persons who, willingly or unwillingly, are recruited to organizations as clients. While this model too may have its problems, it does have the advantage of being normatively neutral. It allows us, for example, to see that certain treatments and certain punishments may be relatively equal in terms of what they require from the offender. Different combinations of variety and duration of interest in clients will present different advantages and disadvantages. But this model is less likely to present one mix of costs and benefits that is preferred simply because it is popular.

Regardless of how probation in general compares with other sanctions, we can assume that probation practices can differ from each other in terms of 1) the extent to which probation engages the offender, and 2) the duration of the impact that engagement will have on the offender. Variations in extensiveness and duration will be correlated with different organizational structures; probation administrators and probation officers will interact with offenders in significantly different ways to have short-term or long-term impact, or narrow or broad influence.

Correlates of the Variety Dimension. The extensiveness of organizational interest will be manifest in a variety of ways. We have space here only to hypothesize a few of the logical correlates. We will consider type of technology, division of labor, evaluation criteria, external relations, management pattern, and interaction with clients.

Type of Technology. The more extensive the organization's interest in its clients, the more diverse and diffuse its means of intervention. Since any number of client roles are seen as legitimate targets for intervention, the organization must either devise a broad and encompassing technology, or invest in a series of separate technologies that can be coordinated (Lefton and Rosengren, 1974). Probation includes two versions of an extensive technology. One is traditional social casework, in which one practitioner is responsible for any number of interventions, as illustrated, for example, in the manifold sections of a typical presentence investigation (Hussey and Duffee, 1980). The second is a specialized approach in which probation officers focus on distinct problem areas and a team leader coordinates the separate interventions (Clear, 1977; Dell'Apa et al., 1976).

Less extensive interest in clients permits focus on one intervention strategy with a relatively narrow focus. As Lefton and Rosengren suggest, organizations with a narrow interest in clients usually have highly developed and specialized intervention skills designed to impinge on only a small part of the client's life-space. Probation organizations with a narrow interest in clients can be expected to have developed a highly standardized routine applied to all offenders and focusing on specific aspects of offender behavior without regard to the whole person. Probation departments with a policy of concentrating only on questions of legality or criminality have less extensive concern with probationers than departments committed to a wide-ranging social diagnosis. Probation departments that deliberately limit the types of problem areas on which officers are to concentrate also have a relatively narrow focus. For example, a current probation experiment in New York State has followed the recommendations of Waller (1979:176–180) to concentrate on five specific problem areas, rather than cover any and all areas the officer, or offender, may consider appropriate.

Division of Labor. Perrow (1967, 1970) has long insisted that organizational division of labor is heavily determined by the tasks faced by the organization, or its technology. Within broad limits this may be true, but, as is implied in the above discussions of probation technology, division of labor is not determined solely by decisions on the breadth of intervention. Lefton and Rosengren (1974) suggest that narrow interest in clients will be associated with a highly developed single technology, and division of labor will be organized around the one profession in charge of that technology. In contrast, broad interest in clients, according to Lefton and Rosengren, leads to several competing technologies and several specialists with equal standing in the organization.

This hypothesis also seems too simplistic to capture the possible variation in division of probation labor. An extensive interest in probationers can lead to either a single diffuse technology, such as casework, or to multiple technologies, such as community resource management teams. In the first instance, the division of labor is relatively simple. The officer in charge of the case is seen as the principal worker, and other probation staff are his or her aides. These aides include secretaries, managers, and perhaps paraprofessionals and volunteers, all of whose work is organized around the front-line discretion of the casework professional (Smith, 1967). On the other hand, another extensive probation organization may adopt a highly specialized division of labor in which different probation officers focus on particular offender needs and problems. This division is far more complex, and to be effective must include the elevation of team managers to coordinate the work of narrowly focused officers. This version of extensiveness is likely to lead to greater competition among the various specialists, and to ambiguity in status positions among those who concentrate on mental health, employment, marital relations, and so on.

Narrowly focused probation departments will also have a simple division of labor, but there is likely to be less question than in the broad casework model about who is in charge. With a narrow focus, probation administrators are likely to gain power over front-line professionals, who will lose status in the organization as their intervention responsibilities become narrower and call for less discretion and less integration of tasks.

Evaluation Criteria. The more extensive an organization's interest in its clients, the more areas of client behavior are relevant to the organization and the more diffuse and various are the legitimate evaluation criteria. The less extensive the interest in clients, the more singular and specific evaluation criteria can become. Extensive criteria are more likely to require complex information systems and a variety of information sources, and the probation department will probably have to develop procedures to deal with contradictory information. Whether or to what degree extensive criteria of success have been met may often become a decision left to professional discretion, while the assessment of success against narrow criteria is more likely to be an exercise of rule application.

External Relations. Extensive departments are designed to influence clients in any number of separate activities. In a probation department, unlike a prison, bringing this extensive interest to fruition will probably require a large number of contacts with other units in the community. In a casework approach, many of these contacts may be the responsibility of the single probation agent in charge of any particular case. Some casework departments however, may employ investigators, paraprofessionals, and other probation officer aides to extend the agents' reach. The choice of community units to be contacted will remain the judgment of the agent responsible for the case, who is likely to seek and maintain contact on a case-by-case basis. External relations with any specific unit of the community are likely to remain informal and nonroutine, and there may be few occasions in which probation managers seek to establish policy and formal relations independent of what the caseworker sees as supportive for a particular case.

Extensive relations will also be sought in a department with specialization of labor and team case loads. But in this version of extensiveness, probation agents have greater opportunity for routine and continual contact with many community units across a large number of cases. Specialized agents are not only responsible, for instance, for obtaining mental health services for offender X, but for developing and maintaining access to mental health services for all probationers who need such services. Hence external relations in these departments are much more likely to be made formal and to involve policy-level coordination by managers in probation and other community organizations.

Probation organizations with a narrower interest in clients will perceive many parts of the community as irrelevant to their operation because many of the probationers' roles in the community will be seen as irrelevant.

Two types of narrow focus seem most likely: a concentration on monitoring the legality of offender behavior and a concentration on offender needs that have been shown to relate to recidivism (Waller, 1979). Hence, narrowly focused departments may be expected to have well-devloped relationships with police, employment agencies, or both, but will go little further in developing relations with external community units.

Management Pattern. The management of probation departments will depend on the variety of influence probation is to exert on probationers. Some of these differences have already been implied in the discussions of technology and division of labor. There is more to management than we can discuss here. Arbitrarily, we will limit discussion to the amount of discretion managers have, the number of probation staff performing distinctly administrative rather than supervisory roles, and whether management tends to be democratic/participatory or autocratic.

The variety of interest in clients widens the scope of potential probation activities, makes evaluation criteria more diffuse, and requires greater effort to determine which intervention is appropriate and how the diverse interventions are to be coordinated. In a casework department, however, many of managerial decisions fall within the professional purview of the caseworker. There is a great deal of discretion on the front line, and less discretion required at administrative levels. In addition, the professional caseworker, much like a physician, is in charge of determining when and how other probation staff are to be involved in particular cases.

The extensive casework department will generally have a small administrative cadre which exercises less discretion than the case supervisory staff. Managers act as resource coordinators, responsible for ascertaining that the caseworkers have needed supplies, support staff, and information when they require it. Managers in this type of system play a role like that of the administrator in a hospital or a dean in an academic department. They may have considerable power, but their ability to affect supervision practice is relatively indirect. Because they remain administratively and politically accountable for what happens in the department, but have little direct influence on particular cases, they are unlikely to share power in the administrative decisions that remain to them. They are likely to exert control by formulating policy unilaterally and demanding compliance in those areas they do control. They may set a number of constraints, in terms of enumerating particular behaviors by offenders that officers may *not* countenance. They are also likely to exert heavy pressure for standardization and routinization of information processing, since it is through reports alone that such administrators maintain control over their staffs.

In extensive team-organized departments, the level of administrative discretion increases considerably. For example, managers not only maintain control by coordinating the activities of staff for any particular case, but are also likely to be highly involved in setting policies concerning contacts with external community units. In such departments, more managerial tasks can be performed by distinctly administrative staff and the management/supervisory staff ratio is likely to be higher than in casework departments. With more administrative discretion and a larger administrative cadre, managers will be more directly involved in day-to-day supervision and more effective in decision making to the extent that they work closely with front-line staff. In these departments there may be a greater likelihood of democratic/participatory management because feedback about clients and external community service units becomes more important than establishing constraints on caseworker discretion.

In probation departments with a narrower concern for clients, managers will have a smaller number of discretionary decisions to make, but so will front-line officers. With fewer external community units seen as relevant to the probation task and fewer internal activities to evaluate, the administrative cadre may be quite small. It is probably less significant in such departments whether the managerial style is autocratic or democratic, since there are fewer goal-oriented questions to deliberate. However, the narrowing of probation influence is most likely a reflection of demands from either external constituencies or central offices for accountability in probation supervision. In other words, the narrowing of interest in clients, with the consequent reduction in discretion at both front-line and administrative levels, is probably a retrenchment maneuver forced upon the probation department by higher or external forces who are concerned with economy or effectiveness. If so, such departments are probably facing a survival crisis. Whether probation management in such circumstances tends to be autocratic or democratic is probably determined more by managerial preference in negotiating turbulent waters than by the nature of probation supervision. Some managers may choose to open up in such circumstances, believing that the best way to survive is to have front-line staff participate in the decisions of retrenchment. Other managers faced with stern external demands may decide to restrict the decision-making power and influence of their staff to a minimum, believing that circumstances dictate such tight control. In general, however, we might assume that as managerial power is removed up the line of command, the power of front-line professionals is also thereby reduced (Ritti, 1971).

Interaction With Clients. The more extensive a probation department's interest in its clients, the more areas of the client's life will be subject to supervision, and the more the client will be granted concessions of membership in the department. The department will need to obtain a minimum level of cooperation from clients across a wider span of behavior.

The department, but particularly the front-line staff, will be faced with a large number of instances in which tradeoffs need to be made between acceptable client behavior on one dimension and questionable or unacceptable behavior on another. For instance, probation with a concern for both economic stability and educational progress among clients may need to relax a demand that offenders maintain jobs if they are also seen to need training or education. Clients may frequently press for concessions against one behavioral objective by agreeing to comply with demands for another objective. The more extensive the interest, the greater the need to evaluate total client progress against a subjective gestalt evaluation in which a client's problems with one role are seen to be mitigated, neutralized, or even justified by progress in the performance of another role.

These tradeoffs may be termed the concessions of membership because the greater the attempt to be cognizant of and influence the whole person, the more the organization has opened itself to claims of value or belonging on grounds of primary, face-to-face, or familial membership rather than on grounds of achievement against specific role expectations (Vickers, 1973).

In such departments, the rejection of the offender, either by refusing to recommend probation or by revoking probation, is likely to be seen as a failure of the department. In departments with narrower interest in clients, the rejection of the offender is likely to be seen as a failure of the offender to perform appropriately (Robison and Takagi, 1976). The narrower the interest in the client, the less the department will be concerned about conflicts among roles the offenders must play in the community. Being a probationer will be restrictively defined in terms of specific role expectations that are to be met regardless of the other demands and objectives in the probationer's life. From the probationer's perspective, the extensive department causes problems by meddling in all of his or her affairs, while the narrow department causes problems by being insensitive to the legitimacy of those affairs.

Correlates of Duration. In looking at the influences of concern with the endurance of the intervention, we will focus on the same six variables that were discussed in relation to variety.

Technology. How will the varying interest in duration of influence be related to the technology of probation organization? The longer the duration dimension, the more likely that the technology will be intensive (Thompson, 1967) rather than planned. According to Thompson, an intensive technology is one in which each step or application is guided by feedback from the object of the application. A planned technology, in contrast, relies upon preexisting knowledge about the material to be processed. In people-changing organizations, preexisting "knowledge" often turns out to be belief or ideology rather than empirically verified information (Perrow, 1970). But in any case, an intensive technology, with a heavy reliance on feedback, assumes that little is or can be known about the object of intervention before actual engagement, and that human beings, as objects of intervention, are highly self-starting and self-defining. A planned technology assumes that those aspects of the object relevant to the intervention are well known and have little variability. It is most likely the intensity of a long-duration technology that make it participative and collaborative. A short-duration technology is more likely to be character-ized by standardized rules and procedures—and in this case by more widespread and strongly held beliefs by staff about what probationers need or how they behave.

In additon to intensity, however, the technology of long-duration proba-tion seeks closure, or the decreased interaction over time of the probationer and the probation department. That is, the longer the duration of proba-tion interest, the greater the concern that probation status not limit the kinds of roles open to the probationer at the end of sentence. The inten-siveness of the intervention would be aimed at obtaining continually up-dated information on the degree to which the probationer is committed not to behaving properly as a probationer, but to behaving satisfactorily in his or her roles in the community. Unlike some high-participation programs, then, long-duration probation is concerned with increasing the proba-tioner's access to and participation in interactions that are to be maintained after probation. A short-duration technology, in contrast, is not concerned so much with the independence of the probationer over time. It would be less likely to build in transitions from probation to nonprobation status. Thus, a probation department with short-term interest in the client is more likely to establish special services for probationers, while a depart-ment with long-term interest is likely to insist that probationers gain access to services and resources that do not include probation status as an eligibility requirement. Some departments may mistake high degrees of participation and collaboration among probationers, or between proba-tioners and staff, for a concern with reintegration, when in fact such participation may lead nowhere except to continued reliance on the sup-portive climate of the probation department.

Division of Labor. The longer the duration of interest in the probationer, the more specialized will division of labor become. The greater the concern for future client autonomy, the more the organization will seek to multiply the kinds of controls or services available, to meet the variety presented by probation clients. In contrast to the relationship between variety and division of labor, it would seem unlikely that a long-duration interest can be met by both a single caseworker and team model of probation. The greater the concern that probation intervention be guided by feedback from the client, the greater will be the concern that the probationer's interaction with the department *not* be limited by the capacities of individual officers. In comparison, departments with a short-term interest in the probationer will be more likely to require the probationer to adapt his behavior to the limitations of the department and its staff. Hence, departments with short-term interest may be more likely to revoke probation, or not recommend probation, when it is believed the client is not behaving in accordance with rules and regulations, or is not amenable to the programs offered by the department.

Evaluation Criteria. The shorter the duration of interest in the probationer, the more likely that evaluation criteria will be explicit and internal to the department. The longer the duration of interest, the more likely that evaluation criteria will be diffuse and ambiguous as well as external to the department. The success of an intensive technology will be determined by how probationers perform roles established in the free community. That is, success will be judged in terms of outcomes. Short-duration departments will be more able to assess success on the basis of plans—as in whether an intervention was carried out as specified. Feedback from the client, and particularly feedback concerning whether the client is progressing, from his or her own point of view, will be less relevant.

The problem with short-term evaluation criteria is that they tend to be compilations of outputs, or computations of energy or resource expenditure, not assessments of probationer adjustment. When probationer adjustment is evaluated, it will be in terms relevant to the department rather than the probationer. The department may be more concerned with whether the probationer is adjusting to probation than with whether the probation interaction reduces the probationer's contact with the criminal justice system, or increases his or her capacity to manipulate the environment.

The problem with long-term evaluation criteria is that they often fail to demonstrate the connection between the identified outcome and the influence of the probation intervention. If probation departments have a long-duration interest in clients, they will often emphasize the probationer's immediate engagement in social activities and supports other than probation. Determining what, if any, effect probation itself had on the probationer's community interactions will be difficult and highly judgmental.

External Relations. The greater the duration of interest in the client, the greater will be the interaction of the probation department with other community units on the managerial or institutional level. The shorter the duration of interest in the client, the more likely that probation interaction with external community units will be limited to front-line contact during the supervision of specific cases. Probation departments with a long-term interest—that is, those seeking to increase the autonomy of the probationer—may be reluctant to intervene directly between the probationer and other persons or groups in the community. Such departments may seek to prevent the probationer from becoming dependent on interactions with others that are motivated or controlled by the probation department. Such departments may also be sensitive to probationer complaints that the visibility of their probation status interferes with their ability to cope with their other responsibilities, or meet their own objectives. However, probation departments with a long-duration interest may actively engage other community organizations and groups on a policy level, in the effort to increase the probationer's access to resources and to improve the quality of life support services available in the community.

Long-duration departments may frequently act to change community resource distribution and community attitudes, out of a broad concern for general quality of life in the community. Short-duration departments are more likely to limit their interactions with the community to ones with immediate impact on specific probationers under supervision. For instance, a short-duration department may allow or encourage its staff to engage directly in family counseling, while a long-duration department would work toward increasing the quality and quantity of family services available to all citizens in the area. For the short-duration department, the objective will be to manage family difficulties while the probationer is serving his sentence. For the long-duration department, the objective will be to improve services for families so that probationers (and others) can use them during and after the probation period.

Management Pattern. The greater the intensity of the probation technology, the greater the need for a complex and sensitive communication system. The greater the specialization of labor, the greater the need for coordination and integration of activities. These two characteristics of long-duration departments are likely to be associated with relatively large administrative cadres, in comparison with short-duration departments. Moreover, in long-duration departments, the drive toward integration of probation with other community units on a general policy level is likely to increase the demand for managerial personnel, although many of these community interactions can be delegated to front-line probation officers.

The importance of feedback from probationers to the probation department in high-duration departments is likely to mean probation administration will be heavily concerned with research activities. Even if feedback concerning probationer behavior is collected by the front-line officer, the task of collating and interpreting such feedback will probably fall to probation management, since the manager will be in a better position than the front-line officer to discern patterns in data collected by many agents. In addition, a highly intensive department that is concerned not only with probationer behavior but also with altering probation officer responses will press for the empirical investigation of officer behaviors—and their relationship to probationer actions. Long-duration departments will be structured and restructured on the basis of information about activities of probationers in the community. Introducing this kind of flexibility in probation operations usually requires a large number of people concerned specifically with management rather than probation supervision.

Discretion, or decision-making space, is probably more available to managers in a long-duration department than in a short-duration department. In probation agencies with a short-term interest in clients, both managers and front-line staff are more likely to be guided by set procedures from which neither group will deviate very much.

Probation managers in a long-duration department may be more democratic, or at least seek greater feedback and participation from their subordinates than will managers in a short-term department. The rationale for this hypothesis is that departments are likely to promote continual feedback and collaboration with clients only to the extent that front-line staff have the same ability to influence their own management (O'Leary and Duffee, 1971b). However, it is important to qualify the nature of participation between staff and management. Management, in a long-duration department, will eagerly accept feedback from staff concerning changes in probationers, changes in the quantity and quality of community resources, and the degree to which managerial activities support the officers in the task of increasing client autonomy. Managers in such a department are also likely, however, to limit the aspects of the probation operation that are open to debate. They are likely to stress empirical data concerning offender behavior and the interaction of the probation department with other units of community, and they may not be willing to formulate policy or change operations on the basis of personal judgments of their staff, regardless of how democratic the mutual negotiation of judgments may be. In highly uncertain or controversial matters they may place more reliance on the opinion of their own research staff than on the opinion of front-line staff.

Interaction with Clients. High-duration departments may seek intense and complex relations with clients, even though they are concerned with the eventual termination of interaction between the client and the department. Short-duration departments require less information from clients, and have less concern for the impact of the department on the probationer.

Interactions between probationers and short-term departments are more apt to be superficial, even if they are frequent.

Long-duration departments, which are concerned with improving the quality of life in a community rather than simply with the supervision of the probationer, are also likely to use probationers in different capacities. For the short-term agency, the probationer is limited to his or her role as client. In long-duration departments, probationers may sit on advisory councils or serve as probationer aides. A long-duration department will try to develop mechanisms by which probationers can alter the structure of probation, and will seek their expertise in determining the most effective interactions between probation office and its clients.

THE BIOGRAPHY MODEL AND THE MISSION OF PROBATION

In the future, probation as a class of organizations must handle a variety of problems, such as inefficiency, decreasing resources, and weak political base (see Chapters 8 and 14). The issues discussed in this chapter are not controlling concerns in all the difficult problems that probation must face. But some of the issues posed here, and perhaps the model itself, are important considerations to be included in at least some of the problem analysis and planning for change that probation will undergo.

Deciding how the client will be engaged by probation should probably be incorporated in two separate levels of analysis. The first level takes probation as a sanction and compares probation sanctions with other possible sanctions. The second level takes probation as an organized supervision system and compares probationer-agency interactions across varying mixes of the longitudinal and lateral dimensions.

On the first level, if judges and others influential in sanctioning selection are to see probation as a viable alternative to prison, the perceived severity of the probation sanction must increase. Whether it is good for probation or probationers, probation may have to toughen up. Hence we can expect to see probation increasing the variety of ways in which it intervenes in the lives of probationers. The greater variety may raise a new set of legal and ethical qustions revolving around the core question of what, as a punishment, probation can legitimately ask offenders to do.

The possibility of increasing the variety or extensiveness of the probation sanction may seem ironic at a time when the general trend is toward decreasing the extensiveness of punishments, making them more specialized or narrower in scope. In some ways, however, increasing the variety dimension of probation and decreasing the overall level of variety are complementary parts of the same sanctioning trend, if increasing the impact of probation can limit the use of incarceration.

Moreover, even if the total range of probation sanctioning variety increases (e.g., community service, restitution, and jail time are added to the intervention repertoire), it may be possible to limit the variety of intervention with any one probationer. And indeed we may be able, through more research, to focus on those roles that appear most closely related to reductions in crime by probationers. For example, if Waller (1979) is correct that only certain probationer activities are related to recidivism, then we could direct probation staff to focus on only that narrow range of probationer behavior (if indeed, we were interested only in controlling crime by probationers).

On the level of probation organization, we should be attuned to the possibility that some forms of organizational restructuring may significantly alter what is expected of probationers while others may not have much impact at all. For example, separating surveillance and service functions of probation staff into separate specialities may not have the intended effects on probationer-probation officer interaction. Certain forms of service, in their own right, will make heavy demands on probationer time and life-space while other forms of service may make few. Many forms of counseling or servicing implicitly require certain types of client monitoring and feedback (or call it surveillance) even if the point of such monitoring is not revocation warrants. Thus, even important structural reforms may leave many problems of probationer-agency interaction unresolved. Even if separation of functions cuts down on some conflicts, other problems, will remain such as the specification and development of the client interaction technology to be employed by the specializing service agents. By questioning how much of client behavior is to be changed and how enduring that change is to be, the client biography model can help us address some of those leftover questions.

NOTE

1. Elliot Studt is probably the most noted authority who would take exception to this characterization of correctional field work. She argues in *Surveillance and Service in Parole* (1972) that parole has a rather well developed surveillance technology, but only a rudimentary service technology. However, she also writes that parole agents tend to favor a "guardian-ward" relationship with parolees, suggesting a long-term interest in client behavior.

REFERENCES

American Friends Service Committee (1971). *Struggle for Justice*. New York: Hill and Wang.

Beaumont, Gustave and Alexis de Toqueville (1960). *On the Penitentiary System in the United States*. Carbondale, IL: Southern Illinois University Press.

Bennett, L. (1973). "Should We Change the Offender or the System?" *Crime and Delinquency* 19 (3):332–343.

Bing, Stephen and S. Stephen Rosenfeld (1970). *The Quality of Justice in the Lower Criminal Courts of Metropolitan Boston*. Boston: Governor's Committee on Law Enforcement and the Administration of Justice.

Bottoms, A. E. and F. H. McClintock (1958). *Attendance Centers*. London: Her Majesty's Stationery Office.

Clear, Todd (1977). "The Specifying of Behavioral Objectives in Probation Supervision." Doctoral dissertation, State University of New York at Albany.

Clemmer, Donald (1958). *The Prison Community*. New York: Holt, Rinehart and Winston.

Cloward, Richard (1960). "Social Control in the Prison" in Cloward et al., *Theoretical Studies in Social Organization of the Prison*. New York: Social Science Research Council.

Coates, Robert, A. Miller, and L. Ohlin (1978). *Diversity in A Youth Correctional System*. Cambridge, MA: Ballinger.

Conrad, John (1984). "The Redefinition of Probation: Drastic Proposals to Solve an Urgent Problem." Chapter 8 in this volume.

Cressey, Donald (1960). "Achievement of an Unstated Organizational Goal: An Observation of Prisons." *Pacific Sociological Review* 1 (Fall):43–49.

Dell'Apa, Frank, W. Adams, J. Jorgensen, and R. Sigurdson (1976). "Advocacy, Brokerage, Community: The ABC's of Probation and Parole." *Federal Probation* XXXX (4):37–45.

Duffee, David, F. Hussey, and J. Kramer (1978). *Criminal Justice*. Englewood Cliffs, NJ: Prentice Hall.

Duffee, David, P. Meyer, and B. Warner (1977). *Offender Needs, Parole Outcome and Program Structure in the Bureau of Corrections Community Services Division*. Harrisburg, PA: Governor's Justice Commission.

Etzioni, Amitai (1961). *Complex Organizations*. New York: Free Press.

Fairweather, George, David Sanders, Hugo Maynard, and David Cressler (1969). *Community Life for the Mentally Ill*. Chicago: Aldine.

Fitzharris, Timothy L. (1984). "The Federal Role in Probation Reform." Chapter 14 in this volume.

Fogel, David (1975). ". . . We are the Living Proof . . . " Cincinnati: Anderson.

General Accounting Office of the United States (1976). *State and County Probation: Systems in Crisis*. Washington, D.C.: General Accounting Office.

Hall, Jan, Martha Williams, and Louis Tomaino (1966). "The Challenge of Correctional Change: The Interface of Conformity and Commitment." *The Journal of Criminal Law, Criminology and Police Science* 57:493–503.

Hawkins, Gordon (1974). *The Prison*. Chicago: University of Chicago Press.

Hoshino, G. (1972). "Separating Maintenance From Social Service." *Public Welfare* 30:54–61.

Hussey, Frederick I. and David Duffee (1980). *Probation, Parole and Community Field Services*. New York: Harper and Row.

Irwin, John and Donald Cressey (1962). "Thieves, Convicts, and the Inmate Culture." *Social Problems* 10 (2):142–155.

Katz, Daniel and Robert Kahn (1966). *The Social Psychology of Organizations.* New York: Wiley.

King, Roy and Norma Raynes (1968). "An Operational Measure of Inmate Management in Residential Institutions." *Social Science and Medicine* 2:41–53.

Klein, M. (1979). "Deinstitutionalization and Diversion of Juvenile Offenders: A Litany of Impediments." In N. Morris and M. Tonry (eds.), *Crime and Justice: An Annual Review of Research.* Chicago: University of Chicago Press.

Lefton, Mark and William Rosengren (1974). "Organizations and Clients: Lateral and Longitudinal Dimensions." In Y. Hasenfeld and R. English (eds.), *Human Service Organizations.* Ann Arbor: University of Michigan Press: 472–485.

Lerman, Paul (1975). *Community Treatment and Social Control.* Chicago: University of Chicago Press.

Lipton, Douglas, Robert Martinson, Judith Wilks (1975). *The Effectiveness of Correctional Treatment.* New York: Praeger.

Marris, Peter and Martin Rein (1967). *The Dilemmas of Social Reform.* New York: Basic Books.

Martin, John P. and D. Webster (1971). *The Social Consequences of Conviction.* London: Heinemann.

Martinson, Robert (1974). "What Works? Questions and Answers About Prison Reform." *The Public Interest* 35:22–54.

Miller, Jerome and Lloyd Ohlin (1976). "The New Corrections: The Case of Massachusetts." In M. Rosenheim (ed.), *Pursuing Justice for the Child.* Chicago: University of Chicago Press.

Minnesota Governor's Commission on Crime Prevention (1976). *Residential Community Corrections Programs in Minnesota: An Evaluation Report.* St. Paul: Governor's Commission.

Morris, Norval (1974). *The Future of Imprisonment.* Chicago: University of Chicago Press.

New York Legal Aid Society (1972). "The Unconstitutional Administration of Bail: Bellamy v. The Judges of New York City." *Criminal Law Bulletin* 8 (6):459–506.

Nokes, Peter (1960). "Purpose and Efficiency in Humane Social Institutions." *Human Relations* XIII (2):141–155.

O'Leary, Vincent and David Duffee (1971a). "Correctional Policy—A Classification of Goals Designed for Change." *Crime and Delinquency* 17 (4):373–386.

O'Leary, Vincent and David Duffee (1971b). "Managerial Behavior and Correctional Policy." *Public Administration Review* XXXI (6):603–616.

Packer, Herbert (1968). *Limits of the Criminal Sanction.* Stanford: Stanford University Press.

Parsons, Talcott (1961). "Suggestions for a Sociological Approach to the Theory of Organizations." In A. Etzioni (ed.), *Complex Organizations: A Sociological Reader.* New York: Holt, Rinehart and Winston.

Perrow, Charles (1967). "A Framework for the Comparative Analysis of Organizations." *American Sociological Review* (32):194–208.

Perrow, Charles (1970). *Organizational Analysis: A Sociological View.* Belmont, CA: Brooks/Cole.

Robison, James and Paul Takagi (1976). "The Parole Violator as an Organizational Reject." In R. Carter and L. Wilkins (eds.), *Probation, Parole and Community Corrections*, 2nd ed. New York: Wiley.

Ritti, Richard R. (1971). *The Engineer in the Industrial Corporation*. New York: Columbia University Press.

Ritti, Richard R. (1978). "The Administration of Poverty: Lessons from the Welfare Explosion 1967–73." *Social Problems* 35:157–175.

Rose, Stephen (1974). *Betrayal of the Poor*. Cambridge, MA: Schenkman.

Rosengren, William (1968). "Organizational Age, Structure and Orientations Towards Clients." *Social Forces* 47:1–11.

Rosengren, William, and Mark Lefton (1970). *Organizations and Clients*. Columbus, OH: Merrill.

Rosengren, William (1967). "Structure, Policy and Style: Strategies of Organizational Control." *Administrative Science Quarterly* 12:140–165.

Sarason, Seymour B. (1974). *The Psychological Sense of Community: Prospects for a Community Psychology*. San Francisco: Jossey Bass.

Scott, Robert (1967). "The Selection of Clients by Social Welfare Agencies: The Case of the Blind." *Social Problems* 14 (Winter):248–257.

Segal, Stanley (1977). "Residential Care of the Mentally Handicapped." *Educational Research* 19:199–216.

Sigurdson, Herbert, A. McEachern, and R. Carter (1973). "Administrative Innovations in Probation Services." *Crime and Delinquency* 19 (3):353–366.

Smith, George (1967). *Social Work and the Sociology of Organizations*. Boston: Rutledge and Keegan Paul.

Stanley, David, (1976). *Prisoners Among Us*. Washington, D.C.: Brookings Institution.

Street, David, Robert Vinter, and Charles Perrow (1966). *Organization for Treatment*. New York: Free Press.

Studt, Elliot (1972). *Surveillance and Service in Parole*. Los Angeles: Institute of Government and Public Affairs, UCLA.

Sykes, Gresham (1958). *The Society of Captives*. Princton: Princeton University Press.

Thompson, J. (1967). *Organizations in Action*. New York: McGraw Hill.

Vickers, Geoffrey (1973). *Making Institutions Work*. New York: Halsted.

von Hirsch, Andrew (1976). *Doing Justice*. New York: Hill and Wang.

Waller, Irvin (1979). *Men Released from Prison*. Toronto: University of Toronto Press.

Warren, Robert, S. Rosen, and A. Bergunder (1974). *The Structure of Urban Reform*. Lexington, MA: Lexington Books.

Wilkins, Leslie (1969). *Evaluation of Penal Measures*. New York: Random House.

Wyman, F. Paul, and S. Timmins (1973). *A Comparison of Factors Associated with Successful Organizational Change: A Study of the Pennsylvania Department of Public Welfare*. University Park, PA: Pennsylvania State University Center for Human Services Development Report 31.

Zimring, Franklin (1974). "Measuring the Impact of Pretrial Diversion from the Criminal Justice System." *University of Chicago Law Review* 41:224–244.

PART III

Prospects for Probation Reform

Chapter 11

Probation in the 1980s— A Public Administration Viewpoint

Robert C. Cushman*

THE SEARCH FOR NORMATIVE UNDERPINNINGS

Like all other correctional services in the 1980s, probation is in trouble. Goals are confused, philosophy is in doubt, financial support has been sharply curtailed, and related resources are shrinking. Probation workers express feelings of powerlessness, complacency, or resignation, as if "no one cares." Anomie characterizes many probation agencies; others operate as embattled organizations. A form of negativism/cynicism dysfunction pervades probation work. The dissatisfactions are obvious, the solutions elusive. The critic's job is an easy one, but leaders who can unite key actors and galvanize action around promising new directions are few and far between. In many respects probation is a system "out of service," but still burdened with two-thirds of America's correctional load. Clearly, probation is in trouble.

The search for solutions, at least from the viewpoint of public administration, must begin with a redefinition and clearer understanding of the purposes of probation. We need to explore what we want to accomplish and why. These normative underpinnings are what gives the probation organization, or profession, its character; they constitute a driving force toward

*President, American Justice Institute, Sacramento, California.

unity, a guide to mold organizational effort. So we must start with an explanation of very fundamental questions: What kind of business should we be in? What should we do and why? This policy development and planning process must *precede* the identification of strategies, programs, and activities for achieving our purposes; and, if form is to follow function, it must *precede* organizational restructuring.

Policy formulation is needed at a very fundamental level. Until this is done, and done well, probation will meander. It will remain subject to myopic, piecemeal trial-and-error tinkering. Though well intended, much of the current advice concerning probation is not aimed at resolving the crucial normative issues. Without such resolution, the tremendous amount of energy being expended on patchwork solutions will continue to produce inefficient, ineffective, and unintended side effects resulting only in disillusionment. There is ample evidence that many criminal justice innovations turn out to make matters worse, not better. What at first seems to be an appropriate response later turns out to be totally the wrong thing to do. In too many cases, changes cause imbalances in workloads, force other agencies to increase costs, create inequities, and so forth. Much time is spent substituting one set of biases for another, only to find that the change has not really improved probation practice.

The difficulty of arriving at a unifying normative framework for probation is well documented. Western society has not yet chosen an acceptable theory of crime causation, nor are we clear as to how governments should respond to violations of laws prohibiting specific criminal acts. We have gone through numerous theories, remedies, and models ony to find each one lacking in effectiveness, practicality, or political acceptability. Torture, exorcism, and banishment have lost all public approval. The death penalty has been virtually abandoned as a practical measure though not yet abolished. Imprisonment has become the penalty of last resort. Its effectiveness is being challenged by many, and its costs grow more exorbitant as the years pass. As the perceived efficacy of imprisonment declines and as costs increase, we find ourselves in a situation where the public appears to want offenders locked up but is unwilling to pay the freight. The courts have increasingly moved in to stop abuse, caused mostly by overcrowding. This may be a signal that our reliance on long-term incarceration, at least for many offenders, is also passing.

THE GROWING WORKLOAD AND RESPONSIBILITIES OF PROBATION

The evolution of Western criminal justice theory and practice has followed a definite pattern. The Council of State Governments, in its 1977 report *The Reorganization of State Correctional Agencies: A Decade of Experience*, says:

The steady expansion of corrections services is the result of a series of reform efforts, each one aimed at a perceived deficiency in its predecessor. For example, incarceration was introduced out of a distaste for the practice of physical punishment; probation was in turn an effort to mitigate the inhumanness of incarceration. As each reform was introduced, it became institutionalized with its own bureaucratic structure distinct from its predecessors.

Today, most offenders who are sentenced to incarceration spend short terms in local jails and youth detention facilities. They do not go to prison, *and the bulk of the corrections workload is attended to by probation.* Reliable figures are still not available, but it is safe to say that in most urban jurisdictions in essentially industrialized states in the United States, about two-thirds of those convicted after being charged with a felony at time of arrest are placed on some form of probation. To put this in sharper perspective, it is revealing to look at the total correctional caseload on a given day. In California, for example, the State Bureau of Criminal Justice Statistics reported that a total of 275,000 juveniles and adults were under community supervision or institutions in 1978. Of these, 20 percent were juveniles and 80 percent adults. Those under the supervision of probation departments numbered 153,000 or 85 percent of the local load if the jails are included, and 56 percent of all those under local and state correctional control, including jails, prisons, youth correctional institutions, and parolees from them. National statistics in September 1978 indicated that 65.2 percent of the country's corrections caseload was on probation. The United States Departments of Justice Sourcebook reports that about 1,500,000 adults and juveniles were under probation supervision in the United States on December 31, 1982.

The growing rejection of long prison terms, except for a very few, has already put most of the workload in the hands of probation departments. When we add to this the processing duties involved in presentence investigations, intake procedures, collections, and numerous other related matters, there can be little doubt that probation services have become the major part of the country's miscellaneous aggregation of correctional programs and services. Yet probation is undersupported, weakly organized, and politically impotent.

THE STATURE OF PROBATION

Despite their importance, probation departments have become the most vulnerable part of the criminal justice system and certainly the least visible part of the correctional system. They are vulnerable for many reasons, not the least of which is the current tax revolt and pressures to cut public budgets. Among such services as police, fire protection, courts, prosecutors, schools, and hospitals, probation is low on the priority list. Probation is certainly less visible, less understood, and less appreciated than almost any of the other public services that compete for scarce public funds.

It seems useful in this context to list in summary form some of the reasons for probation's low estate. First, the services provided by probation departments are the *newest* part of the Anglo-American system of criminal jurisprudence. They are still growing toward a mature and established role in the administration of justice. It was not until 1967 that the last of our states and territories (Puerto Rico) adopted probation laws. And the first probation law was enacted as recently as 1878, barely 100 years ago.

Second, probation suffers from the "soft on crime" image. Probation officers are seen as advocates of leniency during a current popular trend toward more severity. We have not done a good job of informing the public that probation *is* more than a suspended sentence, that three-fourths of the adults placed on probation complete their terms without further convictions, and that most of the other fourth do in fact go to prison. The alternative of sending them all to prison is not only unthinkable in terms of human and dollar costs, it is just simply impossible, given the availability of space.

Third, probation agencies have no effective constituency among the citizenry. They have no PTA, no health association, no bar association, no medical association. To a large extent probation workers in the system are their own constituency. And because of their placement in the system, they are a very timid lot of advocates.

Fourth, probation has no powerful national constitutency or spokesman, either political or professional. What senator or congressman takes a special interest in probation professionals or their mission? Where is the American Correctional Association when their interests or their professional concerns are being eroded in county political chambers or in state capitals?

Fifth, probation departments are submerged (in most jurisdictions) by the judiciary; they need strong and politically effective advocates. But judges, by the very nature of their role in the system, are and must be *judges*—not advocates.

Sixth, probation services, among all similar community services, are the most vulnerable to the effects of the current tax revolt. Proposition 13, passed by California voters in June 1978, significantly reduced revenues obtained from local property taxes. It also triggered similar movements in other locations, and by spring 1979 more than half of the states either had enacted or were considering major tax and expenditure limitation proposals.

In California, the tax reform movement was not limited to the local level.

Proposition 4 (known as the McGann Amendment) placed expenditure limits on state as well as local agencies. Proposition 9, which would have significantly reduced state income taxes, did not pass until June 1980, but most observers agreed that the taxpayer revolt was not over. A study undertaken for the National Institute of Corrections by the California Probation, Parole and Correctional Association found that the immediate effects of Proposition 13 on probation were largely negative—cuts in manpower, loss of programs, workload increases, lowered staff morale, and elimination of research and training functions. Other county agencies are experiencing similar budgetary problems resulting from fiscal restraints at the local level, but in many jurisdictions probation has fared worse than any other component of the criminal justice and human services system. Politicians are reluctant to cut back on police, fire protection, or health services. Lacking a strong, vocal constituency, probation services are vulnerable to budget cuts since decision makers apparently are not convinced that these services make their communities any safer or better places to live.

Seventh, probation functions and services are weakened as a political subdivision of government by jurisdictional fragmentation within a criminal justice "system" which itself suffers from parochialism, isolation, and paranoia.

Eighth, probation workers lack professional identity. There are few, if any, recognized professional schools to prepare for this profession. Currently, practitioners come from a wide variety of educational and occupational backgrounds.

Finally, there are no nationally recognized scholars, practitioners, or administrators who can truly be called eminent leaders in the probation profession. The potential is there, but the sytem stifles it.

Certain current trends make it particularly difficult for probation to realize its full potential. Crime rates seem to grow in spite of increased expenditures on the total criminal justice system. Many legislative bodies have seized upon the lack correctional leadership and the public anger at crime and violence to pass increasingly punitive laws without supplying the funds to deal with the consequences of such measures. Probation administrators and directors of corrections have become easy targets for political attack. The controversial firing of Los Angeles County's chief probation officer, now over five years ago, is a clear case of the killing the messenger who brought bad news.

Moreover, the continuing controversy about sentencing and rehabilitation has had a negative effect on all correctional programs except those focused on simplistic concepts of punishment and retribution—in part because of a confusion of roles in the criminal justice system.

The confusion between the roles of the judge and the correctional professional is especialy worth noting. The judge should not, and probably never did, sentence defendants to programs or institutions for "rehabilitation." How would that be possible when at least 80 percent of defendants plead guilty, usually under plea bargains, actual or inferred? It is (and always was) the severity of the penalty that is bargained, not the opportunity for rehabilitation. Beyond this marketplace feature of sentencing, who could honestly argue that judges are qualified as diagnosticians and prescribers of measures for the social reform of the diversity of clients who pass before the bench?

It seems to us that correctional workers, in probation or in an institution, could maintain little respect for their profession if they did not do what they could do to help their wards to establish themselves as self-supporting and law-abiding citizens. The judges' business is to impose penalties according to law and their own concepts of justice. It is then that correctional practitioners assume their special role—to control, to manage, to counsel, and to help the client. Rehabilitation has been abandoned as a *reason for a sentence—not as an objective of corrections.*

A final difficulty is that research on the effectiveness of correctional programs has often obscured rather than revealed the truth. Probation services intended to encourage noncriminal conduct are so variable in kind and quality that systematic efforts to measure their effectiveness often have resulted in more confusion than enlightenment. Doubts have often been exacerbated, not resolved. On the other hand, the fact that three-fourths of adults placed on probation successfully complete their terms, and that half of the highly selected few who go to state prison do not show up again within five years after discharge, should be ample evidence that the system is not a total failure, even if we do not always know why.

The difficulty of predicting the likely outcomes of alternative dispositions of a defendants's case is one of the great frustrations for thoughtful probation leaders. Some research suggests that the effectiveness of probation supervision bears no relation to its intensity or quality. This is not the place for a technical discussion of this subject, but it may be useful to mention some obvious points.

First, because caseloads are extremely heavy, it is probably unreasonable to expect "intensive" supervision to differ very much from conventional supervision. Moreover, it is possible that the mere fact of being on probation, even with minimal supervision, is a powerful deterrent to some offenders because of the imminent threat of revocation and imprisonment. At the same time, short periods of supervision, especially for adults with extensive criminal experience, may be just "too little too late."

Finally, it is common knowledge to most practitioners that many probationers and parolees need no help and may do better just being left alone. Another group regards the probation officer as the enemy and will not respond positively to any officially oriented intervention. There are also some who can be reached and helped. Every agent has his or her success stories. These are what keep them going. But leaders and policy makers may be expecting too much. Rehabilitation is one of the goals of probation but not necessarily its primary one.

These are some of the many factors that add up to a poor image and low estate for probation. If probation is to develop its full potential as a vital community and human service, it is time for probation administrators to get their professional houses in order. As things stand today, probation does not have the confidence of the public or of policy makers. Probation departments now run the risk of seeing some of their functions absorbed into the routines of court management while others are preempted by the police or other politically potent agencies. In spite of reactionary laws and public frustration with crime, great changes are possible in the future. Probation can be at center stage, but only if policy makers and management can rise to the occasion.

Probation managers are presently in the paradoxical position of attempting to be responsive both to the public's demands for less governmental spending and to client and system demands for more services, which require greater spending. Greater accountability and improved performance are being demanded. The moment calls for calm, confident leadership, and a drive to discover the essentials within probation. The enormous challenge created by the Proposition 13 tax reform movement is to maintain organizational balance and strength during cutbacks. Concisely stated goals must be developed and communicated to the public and legislators, new strategies must be formulated, citizen involvement must be facilitated, and probation managers must develop a willingness to use the political process if probation is to respond successfully to these challenges. Probation leaders must learn to accept responsibility, not hedge behind the prosaic promise to do a better job if given the needed manpower. Today, a skeptical public is likely to reject the contention that more staff means more effectiveness, since past increases in department size have not brought the promised results.

A RECOMMENDED COURSE OF ACTION

Where do we go from here? First, a reappraisal of probation's goals and purposes is clearly needed. One way to begin would be to ask what has been learned from California's experience with Proposition 13. A recent study supported by The National Institute of Corrections found hopeful signs that, in the long run, budget limitations may serve as a catalyst to long overdue changes in probation. Nelson and Harlow (1980) argue that "a role may be in the making for probation, one in which the predominant doctrine will differ from traditional 'offender control' or 'offender service' models." They contend that the mission of probation may be defined differently in the future because the role of government in general is changing. In the wake of Proposition 13, "the pressures of budget cuts have caused local decision makers to question previously 'reserved' functional domains. Related human services in some counties in California, for example, are now considering combining agency resources in order to effect economies in their respective operations. Should probation and parole be integrated as one service? Can probation develop effective ways of combining its services with other community agencies? Can the private sector play a larger role?" Nelson and Harlow concluded that "agencies may be expected to do less and facilitate more, to find their strongest role in defining value choices rather than in attempting to respond directly to all societal needs."

In applying public administration knowledge to probation, however, we must avoid the tendency to perpetuate an endless cycle of exchanging one set of biases for another. We caution against the tendency to rely too much on trial-and-error substitution of some new trend or service delivery strategy that seems promising at the moment. The current California experiment with intergovernmental approaches may not be appropriate for other localities and levels of government. In looking for remedies for probation's ills, some may be all too prone to settle prematurely on a specific mission or organizational structure as the *one* model for all jurisdictions and levels of government.

For example, much has been written about the justice model for designing future probation systems. This model reflects a compliance orientation as opposed to an enforcement or treatment philosophy, and implies a commitment to the rule of law rather than the more abstract ideal associated with client services. While obviously worth serious consideration and evaluation by policymakers as a possible model for organizing and managing future probation systems in some jurisdictions, one should be extremely cautious about advocating the justice model as the single best national paradigm for probation in the 1980s. Environmental and departmental settings vary from state to state, and from county to county within any given state. It seems highly unlikely that all county jurisdictions would support the same model of probation services. It would be more realistic to assume that local values and goals would produce a diversity of appropriate structures and strategies for different probation missions in different jurisdictions, rather than supporting one model over all others.

In summary then, from a public administration viewpoint, the need to establish a clear mission for probation is paramount. Exactly what definition is adapted may not be crucial; the more important concern is that the mission be developed through a thoughtful, participative process that reflects, reconciles, and brings increased rational expression to the day-to-day operation of probation at the community level.

Whether one agrees or disagrees with the mission and values associated with a particular model, such as the compliance or justice model, it seems quite clear that in an era of limited resources, probation leaders at both state and local levels must now decide upon probation's mission and goals at their own organizational levels, articulate that mission to the public and policy makers more effectively than ever before, and explain what they do and, more importantly, why they do it.

In deciding on an action plan for probation systems in the 1980s, the second step is to develop major probation strategies that lead to action based on knowledge. We should use what we know, and do more to build a cumulative knowledge base that will eventually convince the public that the probation profession rests its service upon a definable and perhaps unique body of knowledge.

During the last few decades there have been numerous studies of probation programs and services. They include assessments of different probation service delivery systems, offender classification methods, levels and types of offender supervision, restitution programs, and a wide range of other areas of interest to probation professionals. Other evaluative research has been pursued for years by independent researchers, task forces, and ad hoc commissions. The research issues are broad and varied: Should probation be administered by the judiciary or the executive branch? At the state or the local level? Despite the cumulative body of research reports that have been produced, we still seem to be asking the same question: "What works?" The answers will probably continue to elude us until we admit that "it all depends" and begin to isolate the factors that influence success or failure, as well as the reasons those conditions exist in some settings and not in others. Only then will we be able to offer the kind of empirically derived administrative knowledge needed to guide probation leaders and policy makers toward a clear definition of mission and the management knowledge needed to accomplish that mission.

Third, probation professionals should be required to meet and maintain specific personal and professional qualifications. These standards should be known and supported by the public and probation clients. They should be accompanied by a professional code of ethics and sanctioning of professional membership organizations.

Once these three steps are accomplished, probation will be guided by a clearer, understandable and more unifying philosophy. It will employ more effective strategies and implement them through more competent people and organizations. These first three items must be sold to the public and policy makers in terms of what probation *can* do—not on unrealistic and idealistic promises. Probation should not depict itself as a kind of inexpensive substitute for prison. But—as a sanction—it can and should be such a substitute for many of those presently incarcerated.

These actions must build on the pervasive force of political power and influence in the criminal justice system. Professionalism should not mean isolation or insularity. To solve the "probation problem" one must go far beyond the bounds of the probation service to engage the police, the courts, and generally elected officials of state and local governments.

Finally, thought must be given to reorganizing probation. Probation leaders need to examine their role and their position in the total structure of public services. Are they social caseworkers? Are they truly agents of the courts? What is their position in relation to police, prosecutor, public services, and other public and private agencies? Should they be running institutions as well as court services and case analysis and supervision? What should their relationship be with the executive branch of local and state government?

It is time to reexamine the question of who should pay for probation services: county government, special tax districts, state government, or some rational mix of all of these? What are the consequences of shifting sources of fiscal support?

So, although organizational change does not guarantee improved effectiveness, alternative organizational patterns should be examined. But none of the many alternatives existing or imagined should be considered unless it would seem to support the following objectives:

1. Better leadership.
2. Stronger and more consistent public support.
3. Improved public image.
4. More realistic and effective programs.
5. Less destructive fragmentation.
6. More support for increased professionalism.
7. Reasonable insulation from unjustified, politically motivated interference.

PRAGMATIC BEGINNINGS

With the above objectives in mind and taking the pragmatic view of the public administrator, what is to be done? Probation administrators must necessarily work uphill to improve the current state of affairs. The existing situation, created by statutes and tradition, needs to be carefully assessed, for it represents the starting point for reform in each jurisdiction. First some basic assumptions must be made:

1. Probation is a sanction and a part of the criminal justice system that is here to stay.
2. Probation's share of the correctional load will not decrease, given the growing costs of institutionalization and the strong advocacy of alternative community-based correctional programs.
3. It is possible to interpret probation services to the public in a positive manner.
4. Consistent with the movements to reorganize correctional services, attempts will continue to seek better ways to finance probation services, however organized.
5. There will be continuing pressures for more consistent and rational ways of organizing correctional services, including probation. The Uniform Law Commissioner's *Model Sentencing and Corrections Act* (1979) is a case in point.
6. There is probably no one best organizational structure for all states. Structure is only important if it contributes to the achievement of the organization's goals and purposes.

There are probably other basic assumptions on which wide agreement could be reached. Beginning with only these basic premises, however, certain courses of action seem clearly reasonable. First, attempts need to be made to improve the image of probation; second, better fiscal support for probation needs to be secured; and third, the organization of probation services needs to be improved.

IMPROVING THE IMAGE OF PROBATION

The Public Climate

Just as certain plants grow better in some climates than in others, social and political institutions prosper according to the social climate in which they exist.

It is characteristic of the American culture to feel sorry for the underdog, to want to help the downtrodden and disadvantaged; at the same time, the popular American mind is outraged at continuous misbehavior on the part of some of the members of our society. We are patient up to a point, and beyond that point we want punishment, certain punishment, severe punishment, immediate punishment. Then after the punishment is imposed, we begin to feel sorry for the miscreant. This attitude may be immature, even irrational, but it is the way we are. But because of our desire to help, to be tolerant, to recognize the right of an individual to liberty bordering on license, decisionmakers usually examine the lenient alternatives first and reject or accept them on the basis of subjective criteria that vary from time to time, from place to place, and from judge to judge.

Americans are not sadistic or bloodthirsty, in spite of the rhetoric of some politicians or even the popular votes on such emotional issues as capital punishment. Most take a fairly forgiving view of human frailty ("There, but for the grace of God, go I"). For this reason probationary dispositions are acceptable to the public for most offenses, and especially for the young and the nonviolent.

Most law violators are both young and poor; only about 4 percent of the arrests made in the United States each year are for violent crimes such as homicide, armed robbery, assault, and forcible rape. American crime consists primarily of stealing and offenses against public order. Listening carefully to legislative debate, one finds little opposition to probation in general but rather to apparent leniency toward those who commit certain abhorrent crimes or who persist in living a life of crime.

Probation's Real and Potential Constituencies

Just as the general political climate is relevant for probation, so its potential constituencies. Probation's leaders generally have not made much effort to catalyze support. Unlike services for the deaf, the blind, and the aged, or even welfare services, probation has no readily mobilized constitutency of clients, former clients, and families of clients. There is no alumni association. But there are in every community former probationers who are doing well. Gaining their support in a public way is usually a delicate matter, but some will help publicly and others anonymously.

Support might also be drawn from labor unions. While their members, who work for a living, have little sympathy for the idle and parasitical, they do identify with the poor and the young, if given serious causes to promote, such as vocational training and job placement.

Minority groups are convinced that the criminal justice system discriminates against their members. They can be encouraged to help probation if it is seen as a way to decrease the inequitable and disproportionate numbers of their members who go to jail or prison. There are thousands of responsible people in every jurisdiction who for a wide variety of reasons can be recruited to help probation if asked and given feasible tasks to perform.

If one is to influence the public and affect the judgment of legislative bodies, the press, and other decision makers and opinion molders, the constituency must command respect. A constituency exists, but it is not organized and it is not verbal. The profession needs to locate and organize it. Think for a moment—where do delinquents come from? First of all, they come from families, very often families that are very much concerned, and a few of them have influence where they can make themselves felt.

Then there are the 40–50 million adult Americans who at one time or another have been arrested for a criminal act. They will not wish to come forward and boast about that experience. But a night or two in the county jail is likely to give anyone a different notion about how the system works or does not work. Many such persons would not wish to becme involved and would be ineffective if they did. But to find a few who will attract others is entirely possible.

Defense attorneys know something about the human aspects of the system as well as its legalistic side. Employers are another possible source of support. Many young offenders have never had a job for any length of time or are relatively unemployable; but in the end, as juvenile delinquents mature, they must beome employed. If they become regularly employed in our urbanized and industrialized society, they must often become members of unions. Many probationers are veterans. The Veterans Administration and the American Legion have lately become quite active in prison work through the GI bill and other veteran benefits programs. The AFL-CIO has developed community-based public information programs for its membership. Probation leaders need to link up with these continuing but little-noticed efforts.

Finally, other organizations of the helping professions—the county medical societies, the local bar association, the welfare council, the ministerial association—all have a role if they can be shown it and given an opportunity to perform.

Local police have often been critical of the use of probation. They need to be shown that they are part of the same system and are paid by the same employer, the taxpayer. The police constituencies overlap with those of probation, the courts, and prosecution. Their more perceptive leaders usually are able to see their commonality of purpose with probation. For example, when probation caseloads reach 150–190 cases per probation officer, police officials can be helpful allies to support improved probation staffing. They can be and should be supportive partners in the more indirect effort to control crime.

We should also note here the growing conviction that many probation services can be brokered out to other public and private agencies and to citizen volunteers. These too can be powerful supporters of probation.

The Public Image of Probation

Space prohibits a thorough discussion of the ingredients of an organized and continuing program for interpreting to the general public and numerous special publics the worth and quality of a public service such as probation. We should emphasize, however, that every probation department, and probation as an essential part of the criminal justice system, needs to explain itself to its ultimate employers, the people. It is fatal to try to convince the public that you are doing more or better than you are. Probation must face up to its inability to predict with any reasonable degree of certainty what the outcome will be in any individual case. We do know from empirical studies that at least three-fourths of those placed on probation successfully complete their terms, and we know that two-thirds to three-fourths of paroled prisoners complete their terms without new convictions (NCCD:1978). We need to emphasize the positive side of this equation, not the negative. Nevertheless, our ability to predict is actuarial and not precise in an engineering sense. The system as presently functioning is probably better than we think. Our problem is that we do not usually know why any one remedy works or fails in an individual case. We might note in passing (although we have abandoned the disease theory of crime causation) that even medical science owes much of its capacity to predict human longevity to the actuarial laws of probability.

Lacking specific remedies, we must do what we can about crime as a social and political problem, letting theory grow out of practice instead of the reverse. We do have a criminal justice apparatus, if not a "system," and we do have crime. We are compelled to act within the constraints of our limited knowledge and of the value systems of our culture.

Probation should not be seen as leniency. The judicial act of granting probation as an alternative to a prison term may fairly be regarded as leniency by comparison, but the role of the probation service is to do what it can to see to it that the defendant lives up to the conditions of his or her probation. If the probationer fails, it is the duty of the probation officer to take him or her back to court to determine whether probation is to be revoked and the more severe penalty imposed. That this occurs in about one-fourth of the cases is evidence of a real concern for the public's interest. Conversely, the fact that three-fourths of the probationers do not commit further crimes is evidence that the probation is a more appropriate gamble than the prison alternative for that particular group of offenders.

It is appropriate here to say a word about the professional communicators—newspapers, magazines, television, radio and all that goes with them. These people need you as you need them. If probation administrators wait to speak with the press until they attract attention because of something going wrong, they will probably want to blame the media for reporting only the negative. Journalists too are human beings and some of them will be more supportive than others. One must remember, too, that many practicing journalists got their initial training in the penal and correctional field when they were cub reporters assigned to hang around the courthouse and the police station to pick up crime news. The resulting view of the problem and of criminals in general is inevitably a limited and biased one. Correctional workers need to reorient that viewpoint by planned public exposure to their own part of the system.

One common image of probation sees its mission as "client oriented," with the implication that probation workers' crucial concern is the welfare of their probationers. But their real client is the employer who hires them and pays them—the taxpayer. It is because probation officers act as if the probationer were indeed a paying client, as in the case of a defense attorney, that it is possible to lose track of the real probation mission. Because of the inherent difficulties of the probation officer's dual role, some professional social workers have always questioned whether effective casework is possible if the professional is both caseworker and policeman. Such analogous relationships as those between parent and child or teacher and student encourage us to believe that it may be possible to fulfill both roles adequately.

IMPROVING FISCAL SUPPORT

Aside from problems stemming from public misconceptions of its role and related organizational issues, probation's greatest vulnerability is its lack of a firm and dependable source of financial support. America's dedication to local control of public affairs is an ideal that has been eroding steadily for over a hundred years. With the increasing growth of vast metropolitan governments like New York City, Los Angeles County, and Cook County, Illinois, the idea of the town meeting or even of a local council of freeholders providing local government has long since gone the way of the wild turkey as the centerpiece of Thanksgiving dinner. At the same time, the importance of property taxes as a source of revenue for local government has diminished.

Local governments have sought aid from other sources such as income tax and sales taxes, which have been largely preempted by the states and federal government. Consequently, in desperation, the cities, counties, and special districts have been forced to take one or both of two courses. They may seek subsidies from state and federal sources, almost always with strings attached, or they may relinquish certain functions altogether to the management control, and support, of a higher level of government. State and federal aid for public welfare, public health, public education, and a myriad other services has become commonplace.

The criminal justice agencies of local government present a very different picture. The cities in particular have clung tenaciously to complete control of the municipal police. The county sheriff and the prosecuting attorney continue to be chosen by popular vote in most jurisdictions.

The judges, excepting members of the U.S. judiciary, tend to operate the municipal and trial courts very much as if they were officers of local government, although they are supported in part by state funds. It is noteworthy that, in jurisdictions where such judges are elected, the election takes place in the geographical districts they serve. In spite of the state appellate court system, most of the effective load of the criminal court is local, and because of local governments' control of their budgets, these courts are subject to more local control and influence than might be supposed. Federal judicial intervention in the operation of state and local courts stems not from the power of the purse, but from constitutional issues principally involving enforcement of the Bill of Rights.

Correctional services present quite a different set of problems and circumstances. The corrections load is distributed in a wide and seemingly irrational variety of ways among federal, state, and county/city levels. After the adoption of the Eighteenth Amendment and the Volstead Act in 1920, the U.S. government began prosecuting thousands of cases formerly handled almost exclusively by the states and their political subdivisions. Soon the federal government was preempting the states in cases related to stolen cars driven across state lines, bank robberies, narcotic offenses, and scores of less publicized areas. Local police and prosecutors have been happy to relinquish jurisdiction of a car thief or a bank robber to the federal authorities even though most such arrests are made by local police. This is often a conscious fiscal decision.

The volume of cases shifted from the states to the federal government for fiscal reasons is a mere dribble compared with the analogous flow from local to state levels. Much has been made in recent years of the unjustifiable disparity in the sentencing practices of trial court judges, and especially among offenders sent to prison from different courts and different regions. These disparities are all too apparent when the prisoners from many local settings arrive in a central prison. Less readily noticed are the disparities in the judicial choice of probation as an alternative to a state prison term.

For example, if 30,000 persons are convicted of felonies in a given year, and if the judges send 10,000 of them to prison, they are collectively selecting the prison disposition in one-third of the cases. But individual county commitment rates may range from 10 percent to 50 percent. A study made twenty years ago by the California Board of Corrections first brought this issue to public attention there. The probation subsidy act of 1963 was an indirect effort to correct these inequities. Later, in 1978, it was argued, especially by some misinformed police executives, that the state was "bribing" the counties not to send felons to prison. The law was repealed and a new subsidy provided in which the police and prosecutors could participate, but which changed the provisions requiring enforceable performance standards. This has become one of the factors underlying the increase in commitment rates to California state prisons.

Many argue that local trial judges do not make their discretionary choices between prison and local dispositions on budgetary bases. Perhaps not, but the probation department whose employees make the presentence reports may well be consider whether the department is overloaded and unable to provide adequate supervision. Likewise, if the sheriff's jail is overcrowded and a federal suit is pending charging unconstitutional conditions in the jail, and at the same time the county government is faced with a reduction in revenues—who is so naive as to think that a local trial judge whose antecedents are in the community political environment can ignore the fiscal impact of these kinds of decisions?

Offenders without ties to the community are particularly likely to be sent to state prison. The presence in any jurisdiction of large numbers of itinerant workers, such as seasonal farm laborers or nonresident workers on large construction jobs like dams or pipelines, will tend to increase local crime simply because these workers change the demography of the area. These workers and their families are strangers in rural or semirural communities, and are much more likely, if convicted of a crime, to be sent off to state prison than would a local resident who had committed an identical crime. The rational is usually that the projects that attract itinerant workers have statewide or national reasons for existence and that the negative side effects, such as an increase in crime, ought to be financed by the higher level of government.

Amid all this shifting of costs, we have tended to overlook the fact that shipping bodies around to equalize or avoid costs is a fundamentally immoral practice that must eventually encounter either more rational systems for distributing the costs or law suits charging unequal protection under the law.

It seems inevitable that some of the cost of local criminal justice agencies must be shared by state governments, and perhaps to lesser extent by the federal government. In nineteen states adult probation is supported and operated by state government. In Connecticut, the state operates local jails. In others states, such as New York, Illinois, and California, probation services are locally operated but the state provides some financial support and some regulatory controls.

The real crunch between these two general solutions lies in 1) the resistance of governors and state legislators to taking on more of the burdens of local government, and 2) the reluctance of local governments to accept needed financial help if strings are atached. The entire history of subsidies and grants-in-aid speaks eloquently to this issue. That there will be some controls, standard setting, and accounting attached to subsidies is inevitable. Even if a virtual blank check is provided the first time around, it is inevitable that some loal authority will be accused of misusing its money. The certain political reaction to that charge will be new legislation, either withdrawing the money or imposing state regulation and standards more rigid than those that would have been enacted originally.

Hence standards, monitoring, and accountability should be carefully structured at the start of any new program. Space does not permit an extensive discussion of the subject here but this much guidance seems appropriate: First, a statement of the obvious—each jurisdiction with a unique set of laws, practices, and needs must start from where it is. Ideas and principles can be adapted from elsewhere but rarely can someone else's system be transplanted and superimposed on another without modification. Second, in looking for appropriate models, one should not limit the field to other criminal justice or correctional systems. There are far more mature experiences in parallel systems such as the public school systems in our fifty states and thousands of local districts. It might also be useful to examine the manner in which the British Home Office helps to support and maintain quality in its local and metropolitan police districts. There are other parallels, though not precise analogues, in mental health, public welfare, water districts, and so on.

It is a political axiom that those who give money will exercise some control over how it is used in any field. At the same time, local management must also have a strong voice in policy formulation and program management. The question is how to strike the balance that best supports the basic goals of the service involved.

IMPROVING THE ORGANIZATION OF PROBATION SERVICE

Rarely is there one best way to organize a group of related services. But one can define general ideas and purposes that an organizational structure should promote and protect. For correctional services and probation, we should first consider the need for effective national and statewide leadership. At the national level there should be two kinds of efforts, both of which now are either weak or effectively nonexistent. One should be a strong professional organization equivalent to the National Education Association or the American Bar Association. There is an embryonic American Probation and Parole Association affiliated with the American Correctional Association. It needs better support and broader membership including some judges, strong administrators, and a few good academicians.

The second kind of national leadership should be a permanent professional partner in the framework of the federal government itself. Since there is no unified federal correctional service, the choice lies between the National Institute of Corrections and the Office of the U.S. Courts. Probation chiefs might not feel comfortable in either quarter. The federal judges have always been adamant that the federal probation services should not be controlled by the attorney general, who represents the prosecution side of the adversary system. Thus it is not obvious where such an office should be located in the federal bureaucracy. Clearly, however, a strong federal advocate and a source of technical assistance for probation is desirable. Since the present U.S. Probation Office is only a rather weak entity under the domination of the federal judiciary, whom propriety prohibits from political advocacy, it may be necessary to create a separate office under the board that now oversees the National Institute of Corrections. This, of course, would place probation indirectly under the attorney general, but appropriate statutory language might provide the necessary political insulation.

There should be a relatively independent office or board in each state to administer any subsidies to local government correctional services. In addition, this body would be responsible for standard setting, technical assistance, an information center, and the promotion and development of personnel training. Whether such an office with a strong executive head reports to a board or the head of a state department of corrections, the appointing power and lines of authority should run to the governor of the state and not to some lesser elective officer such as the state attorney general. Because the governor controls the executive budget, and because other constitutional powers are inherent in the governor's office, he or she has far more influence with both the state legislature and the cities and counties than any of the other state elective executives. Placement under the attorney general would be especially unfortunate because of the direct and indirect relationships with the investigative and prosecutorial parts of the criminal justice systems.

One other caveat regarding the state probation office is important. This should be essentially a regulatory rather than an operational office. Officials responsible for the direct operation of major public agencies like prisons, youth correctional facilities, and parole services are faced with continuous threats of emergencies and crises. Their day-to-day calendar of activities is so demanding that they can give little attention to regulative functions dealing with services not under their direct command. Even if the office of director or commissioner of community correctional services is placed in the state department of corrections for general administrative purposes, the position should be established by law and the executive given as much independence as is normally possible under such circumstances. It should be noted also that no matter how local probation is administered, the state office will be obliged to maintain a close, ongoing relationship with the judiciary as well as with local administrators and elective officers who have a potential impact on probation.

Placing the correctional functions of state government under so-called umbrella agencies such as Health and Welfare or Human Services is a questionable practice. Of the thirteen states that have done so, at least three (Florida, California, and Delaware) have gone back to separate agencies. Adding a major unit of state government to oversee and assist local corrections could reinforce the separateness of state corrections from their vaguely related state agencies.

Whether local probation services are made executive departments of county government or are attached administratively to court services is obviously an unsettled question in this country. The recent movement in metropolitan areas has been to place these services in the executive branch, but this trend encounters strong resistance in many quarters.

SUMMARY

It is now obvious that most of the correctional load, in terms of human subjects, is in the hands of some 4,000 probation departments and about 40,000 employees.

Probation is clearly in trouble. Problems with probation are easy to identify and discussion of them consumes the literature. Many proposed solutions, however, are piecemeal or subject to a particular bias. It would be a serious error to encourage one organizational form over another since we must allow for variety and experimentation at state, local, and federal levels of government. No voice or level of government is in a position to articulate one "best" set of goals and purposes for probation since these are more appropriately developed by the jurisdictions that have primary responsibility for probation services.

Reassessment of the normative premises of probation is needed, followed by action based upon knowledge, and the development of a professional cadre of skilled probation workers.

A major reorganization of these scattered, largely leaderless groups of public servants is long overdue. Leadership needs to be developed that will enable probation to rise to the challenge of its growing and increasingly diverse responsibilities.

The stature of probation must be enhanced. Real and potential constituencies must be better developed; fiscal support needs to be improved, and we must settle the issue of who pays for what. Unjustifiable disparities in the granting of probation must be reduced. Sound organization models should be developed, tested, and implemented.

REFERENCES

Council of State Governments (1977). *The Reorganization of State Correctional Agencies: A Decade of Experience*. Kentucky: Council of State Governments.

Nelson, E. Kim, and Nora Harlow (1980). "Responses to Diminishing Resources in Probation. The California Experience." Report to the National Institute of Corrections.

National Council on Crime and Delinquency (1978). *Uniform Parole Reports*. Ft. Lee, NJ.

Chapter 12

The Community Context
of Probation

David E. Duffee*

The impact of community on crime is a topic with a long history
(Fischer,1976; Angell, 1951; Park et al., 1925). In contrast, the impact of
community on the agencies of correction has received increasing but sporadic attention (Coates and Miller, 1974; Jacobs 1976; Duffee, 1980). It is
true that the community context of the convicted offender has received
some consideration. Studies have sought to explain parole performance in
terms of dynamic parole experience variables such as quality of family
contact or time employed after release (Waller, 1979:176–180) or the
amount of environmental deprivation while on parole (Jenkins et al., 1973;
McKee, 1973). In a similar vein, the General Accounting Office (1976) has
examined the relationship between numbers of services received by probationers and their successful completion of the probation period. While
the data may be of varying quality and the conclusions of varying degrees
of certainty, we do know something about the effects on offenders of their
personal situation and the richness of human services in their environment. We do not, however, have similar information concerning the community context of the agencies that supervise offenders in the community.

Some way of conceptualizing the varying contexts in which probation

*Department of Criminal Justice and Public Policy, State University of New York and
Albany

operates would seem potentially highly useful for several reasons. For instance, the growth in prison populations is creating tremendous pressure for alternatives to incarceration. But the alternative of "community corrections" remains disturbingly enigmatic, because we have little ability to specify the salient dimensions of community and thereby to determine what kinds of programs may be most effectively established in what communities. Moreover, in planning halfway house, parole, probation, and other community ventures, we need to determine what administrative forms and what supervisory practices would mesh best and make the most use of the varying realities of particular communities. Dell'Apa et al. (1976) wave the flag for "advocacy, brokerage, and community" without much attention to the efficacy of the advocate's position, or to whether there is anything to broker, or to why probation represents "community" corrections any more than does the dilapidated county jail or a lynching by vigilantes. To know which advocates are seen as legitimate, to know when brokering services is more desirable than direct delivery, and to know how probation is a part of community, it would be useful to know more about community.

WARREN'S MODEL OF COMMUNITY

Of the various definitions and models of community, probably none is held in higher regard than the interaction field model presented by Roland Warren. Warren (1978:9) defines community as the arrangement of groups, organizations, and larger systems that provide locality-relevant functions. The functions that Warren suggests must be performed with some degree of effectiveness if a locality is to sustain group life are:

1. Production, distribution, and consumption.
2. Socialization.
3. Social control.
4. Social participation.
5. Mutual support.

The production function is primarily the economic one of local participation in the processes by which goods and services are made and delivered, and the structure of work that these processes entail.

Socialization is the processes by which members of society take on the knowledge, skills, values, and norms of their own society. Socialization in the earlier part of the life cycle is perhaps the most significant type, and consequently the contributions of families and schools to socialization have been most frequently stressed. But at least in American society, socialization is becoming increasingly problematic, because the knowledge, values, and behavior patterns that are most useful at one stage of the life cycle may not be appropriate at another stage. Hence, resocialization processes are increasingly observed as important, whether we are speaking of an unemployed executive learning new skills in mid-career, the aged learning how to cope with retirement and separation from family, or the delinquent learning to cope with demands of incarceration or release on parole. Social control "involves the process through which a group influences the behavior of its members toward conformity with its norms" (Warren, 1978:10).

Warren suggests that social control has traditionally been considered the province of formal government, since government has ultimate coercive power over its citizens. This may imply that criminal justice agencies are to some extent involved in control activities. Warren makes no assumption, however, that criminal justice agencies, or any other organizations of formal government, are the only or the most effective auspice of social control.

The fourth locality-relevant function is social participation: that function by which members of a locality obtain a sense of membership or identity with other persons in their area, irrespective of their roles in secondary or formal organizations. That is, social participation is probably most important factor in developing a sense of belonging to an area, and the strength of this function should have a major influence on people's ability to cut across their ethnic, occupational, or class differences, and act as a group.

The fifth community function, mutual support, refers to the provision of care or help under conditions of crisis—when the usual means of resource distribution are not functioning effectively. "Crisis," as the term is used by Warren, has several different levels. There may be individual or family-level crisis in which a particular person cannot obtain adequate life support, despite the availability of such supports to others in the same area. There may also be wide-scale disasters that acutely affect a wide range of persons in the same area, regardless of class. Warren's primary examples of mutual support agencies are public health and welfare systems. While he accepts the proposition that such agencies may also function to control certain groups and persons, he simply states that help in times of trouble is also manifestly provided.

In the model, an equally important consideration in identifying community functions is the particular structural arrangement for performing those functions. Just as complex bureaucratic organizations may have different decision and control networks and different production technologies, communities differ markedly in the way that production, socialization, social control, social participation, and mutual support activities are carried out.

Warren (1978:13) suggests four separate dimensions upon which communities may differ: 1) Local autonomy, or the independence of the local area from outside sources, may range from independent to dependent. 2) Local services areas or functional delivery areas may coincide or differ. 3) Psychological identification with the local area may be strong or weak. 4) Horizontal articulation or integration across functional units may be strong or weak.

While these four dimensions may all be important and logically separate, this presentation will concentrate on autonomy and horizontal articulation. These two dimensions are stressed for the following reasons. It would seem that the lack of autonomy of a local area may lead to lack of coincidence of service systems in that area. School districts, health catchment areas, judicial districts, and so on, may doubtless diverge rather than converge for many reasons. But divergence would seem particularly likely when such services are the responsibility of separate, hierarchically arranged service systems that are independent of each other and isolated from the local groups that could bring them together. In other words, Warren's second dimension, coincidence of service areas, seems dependent on the separation or interdependence of the local area and centralized government and specialized service bureaucracies. Psychological identification with a locality would seem to be partially dependent on the extent to which the various units of locality are integrated, or the group mobilized to a common purpose. Hence the third dimension, psychological identification, would seem to follow from the strengthening of the fourth dimension, horizontal articulation. Thus, the two most essential structural dimensions of community would appear to be the vertical dimension and the horizontal dimension.

The vertical dimension of community structure refers to the degree to which a local social unit is linked with a nonlocal system for the performance of its locality-relevant functions. The horizontal dimension of community refers to the degree to which various groups, organizations, and systems within a community are interrelated, for the performance of one function or the performance across functions. In slightly different terminology, Spergel (1976) refers to the same community structural dimensions. He suggests that communities differ in terms of both access to central authorities (vertical interaction) and mobilization of the local population (horizontal interaction). Access to central authority is roughly similar to Warren's vertical dimension, and mobilization of the local population is fairly similar to what Warren meant by horizontal articulation.

All community social functions are influenced in some degree by both horizontal and vertical structures. City and town governments, no matter how powerful in their own right, are chartered and constrained by state governments. Local school boards are dependent in some degree upon state departments of education. County prosecutors and local police enforce state laws and are constrained by federal constitutional standards. On the horizontal dimension, even communities with fairly fragmented and dispersed participatory and support organizations may be integrated to some extent by local political mechanisms, chambers of commerce, community chests, and other coordinating agencies.

As a general trend, the horizontal dimension of American communities has tended to weaken and the vertical dimension has tended to strengthen dramatically in the twentieth century. Industrialization, urbanization, and bureaucratization have tended to make communities dependent on various vertical linkages for the performance of social functions. Corporations of national and international scope, with diversified interests, have largely assumed the production/distribution/consumption functions that were once the province of individual and local entrepreneurs. State and federal governments have taken increasing responsibility for support and operation of local schools and have simultaneously become more insistent that state and national standards be met at the local level. Social control functions are increasingly state and federal concerns, as are many social participation and mutual support activities.

This trend has tended to mean that various local units charged with the delivery stages of different functional activities have less in common with each other and less loyalty to each other or to local citizenry, than to the superstructures at the state and national levels to which they belong. Health, welfare, and justice activities that may once have been performed locally, and policy decisions about each, are often made at central headquarters far removed from local incidents and local problems, and in a manner that reduces interaction among the various separate systems. There are some signs that this trend toward fragmentation has peaked, and that we shall move toward decentralization and/or return to local decision making in the last part of this century. A recent monograph (Nelson, et al., 1980) attempts to draw out the implications of that trend reversal for local corrections, including probation.

THE VERTICAL AND HORIZONTAL AXES AND CRIMINAL JUSTICE

The elaboration of community functions might enable us to understand better why the outputs of criminal justice agencies may depend on the particular community matrix in which they participate. Hence, this aspect of the model might be useful in discussions of criminal justice goal selection. Only in communities with the same functional needs would we expect criminal justice to function in the same way, everything else being equal. In other words, it would not be surprising to find that criminal justice agencies provide more mutual support in one area and more social control in another.

But the situation is even more complex. Not only may criminal justice agencies and systems vary in the extent to which they contribute to one community function rather than another, but different structural arrangements may be required to achieve the same function in different communities. For example, it is a long-standing problem, as yet unanalyzed, that programmatic structures accepted in one community simply cannot be grafted onto another. Attempts to transfer the Des Moines, Iowa, community correction model to other communities are just one example of the perplexing problems in attempting to replicate a community corrections program. A program that works well in one community will turn out not to work in another, or the community units that can make it work are surprisingly different from one community to another (Boorkman et al., 1976).

In relationship to this problem, the community structural axes seem to offer the most powerful explanations of community differences. As an example, let us isolate just one locality-relevant function and attempt to trace how differences in criminal justice administration might be related to community structure.

In Figure 12.1, the two axes, vertical relations and horizontal articulation, are treated as orthogonal dimensions. Thus we can consider localities that differ on the values of these two dimensions—or, in other words, that differ on the type of structure by which a locality-relevant function is achieved. Theoretically, there would seem to be four paradigmatic types of community structure. We can imagine 1) localities with strong horizontal patterns and strong vertical patterns, 2) localities with strong horizontal patterns and weak vertical patterns, 3) localities with weak horizontal patterns and strong vertical patterns, and 4) localities that are weak on both dimensions. The last type might be termed a community only in the geographical sense; one would expect the performance of community functions to be ineffective, so that this category represents a loss or lack of community. In the other three types, all functions are probably performed to some degree, although perhaps in quite different ways and probably with very different ancillary products. That is, in the localities that are relatively high on at least one dimension, one might argue that group life is adequately supported. Yet because these different structures imply very different auspices for the performance of functions, different constraints will be operating, and therefore the quality of services and the amount of resources may vary considerably. We will consider how these ideal communities may differ on the function of social control.

The Disorganized Community

Where both the vertical and horizontal patterns of community are weak, we would hypothesize that the community itself is weak. We would expect

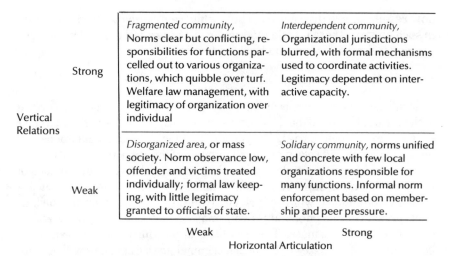

Vertical Relations	**Strong**	*Fragmented community,* Norms clear but conflicting, responsibilities for functions parcelled out to various organizations, which quibble over turf. Welfare law management, with legitimacy of organization over individual	*Interdependent community,* Organizational jurisdictions blurred, with formal mechanisms used to coordinate activities. Legitimacy dependent on interactive capacity.
	Weak	*Disorganized area,* or mass society. Norm observance low, offender and victims treated individually; formal law keeping, with little legitimacy granted to officials of state.	*Solidary community,* norms unified and concrete with few local organizations responsible for many functions. Informal norm enforcement based on membership and peer pressure.
		Weak	**Strong**
		Horizontal Articulation	

Figure 12.1. Community structural axes and the social control function.

in such instances that norms are not clearly defined and that many behaviors that would bring about some sort of reaction in other areas will not receive any organized sanction. If there is no local group commitment either to socialization or to building and maintaining a sense of group identity, social control activity will not be organized or effective. There will be few group boundaries against which to define deviant action, and few processes by which groups inculcate mutually shared standards in individuals.

Any criminal justice activity in such communities is likely to involve responses to major crimes or major group crises. Since these localities will fall within the jurisdiction of some centralized authority, there will continue to be *some* observance of law enforcement in these areas, but the officials of the state agencies are likely to be seen as outsiders, who must rely on the formal authority of the law and on coercive sanctions to rationalize their intervention. That is, criminal justice is likely to be seen as the activity of a distant authority having little legitimacy to the people of the area. Criminal justice officials may conceive of themselves in this situation as ministerial agents. Without a local group concern for criminal justice outcomes or processes, criminal justice agents are likely to contain disorder rather than to prevent it. When they feel they must act, the officials' "boundary spanning repertoire" is likely to be corrupt or brutal. (See Chambliss and Seidman, 1971, and Banton, 1964.)

Spergel (1976) calls such a community "a controlled area." This term is meant to suggest that while such areas may get considerable attention from central authorities, local residents have relatively little chance to affect the policy and program decisions of those authorities, or to influence how resources are distributed. Thus, while centralized authority is *active* in such an area, there is little *interaction* on the vertical dimension between the centralized outsiders and local groups.

The Solidary Community

In localities where there is strong horizontal articulation and low vertical articulation, there will be a strong, predominating "we feeling" and a clear sense of group boundaries. Responsibilities for community functions will be the province of a relatively small number of informal and formal organizations, all of which are closely interlocked and relatively autonomous of external financial support or policy influence. Social control in such a solidary community will rely primarily on informal mechanisms, such as peer pressure and public approval, and the fact that everybody knows everyone else's business. There is little opportunity for norm-violating behavior. In such places even formal criminal justice agencies will operate in ways consonant with local definitions of propriety. Agency processes are likely to be informal, and the criminal sanction will seldom be invoked. When it is used, sanctioning decisions are likely to center on whether the offender is perceived as an outsider or an insider. If the offender is a member of the local community, a decision to keep the punishment local is really a signal that the community considers itself to be confronting a local problem. If such a community transfers its punishment to a state agency, it is in effect ostracizing, defining that offender as no longer belonging to the group.

Such communities will not generally resort to harsh penalties, such as lengthy prison sentences. Social control is more likely to be of the remedial, negotiative, restitutive kind. However, retribution, in the form of ostracism to prison, may become an issue in one of two ways. Transient offenders would probably be more likely to be treated harshly, since they do not have claim on community membership. One might also expect these communities to become retributively oriented when they feel the present sense of order is threatened. This may occur particularly when such communities are waning, as when a predominant life style and set of norms is being displaced by the entrance of significant groups of others, or by the ascension to power of previously dispossessed minorities. In this instance, one may see "political law enforcement" rather than negotiation, with the austerity of the formal criminal justice system called upon to defend old norms against new incursions. Spergel (1976) refers to this type of structure as the "communal community."

The Fragmented Community

In some communities, locality-relevant functions are heavily dependent upon vertically organized specialty organizations, among which there is little interdependence. Such communities are likely to be highly diversi-fied, with multiple and conflicting power bases, and different organizations meeting the disparate functional needs of the area. This situation we might call the fragmented or pluralistic community, where norms are multiple and perhaps conflicting, and responsibilities for functions are parceled out to separate organizations. These organizations may battle over turf or have significant domain disputes. Or, as Warren et al., (1974) have sug-gested, these organizations may come to a relatively well understood agreement on organizational missions and therefore have very little inter-action with each other.

Because of the reliance on hierarchically organized units, each with relatively narrow specialities, there is often an emphasis on professional management and client-centered programming within the various organi-zations, whether we are dealing with mental health, municipal planning, or police and correctional services. We would see in this type of locality something we might call "welfare law management," in which organiza-tions are concerned with the organizational posture toward specified indi-vidual clients, without great regard for the community or group identity of the individuals involved. For the criminal justice system the aim is likely to be the reduction of future crime, rather than the maintenance of an existing normative pattern. Such systems might become concerned with specific deterrence, incapacitation, or rehabilitation, but it is less likely that they will be judged effectively against criteria of retribution or pre-vention of anomie for any of the many conflicting and diverse groups that form their constituency. In other words, because groups are diverse and conflicting, criminal justice agencies in pluralistic situations are likely to focus in a "professional manner" on individual offenders.

Spergel (1976) labels the fragmented community "pluralistic," while others see such areas as "interorganizational fields" (Warren et al., 1974), in which community structure is an ever-shifting rearrangement of markets and resource domains. Most commentators agree that the frag-mented community is, if not the most common, the type of community that best characterizes modern, urban life. It is the type of community that is often most troublesome in terms of the design of public human services, including probation.

Understanding the problems of social control and social service agencies in such fragmented areas is extremely problematic. Perhaps the best brief account is that of Mills (1959), although Long's seminal work (1958) and the study of community decision organizations by Warren and his colleagues (1974) are also extremely important. In brief, Mills's basic argument is that fragmented communities are heavily dependent on specialized, bureaucra-tized organizations for the carrying out of community functions. However, the organizations (and particularly public ones) operating in such areas usually find their political and economic environments so "turbulent"

(Emery and Trist, 1970) that they tend to develop elaborate systems to buffer their internal operations from the vagaries and conflicts of their plural constituencies. As a consequence, organizations in such areas tend over time to make decisions based primarily on internal criteria of effectiveness rather than on external criteria enunciated in the community.

The Interdependent Community

Finally, we can conceive of communities in which there is both frequent exchange and interaction with units external to the community and a high degree of interaction among units at the local level. It is doubtful that there are many such communities in the United States today, and examples of the nature of social control in such areas are difficult to hypothesize. This type of community may be unstable and revert relatively quickly to one of the other forms previously described (Spergel, 1976). Hypothetically, however, such an interdependent community would seem to be one in which the auspices for community functions are blurred either by informal and personal or by formal and interorganizational mechanisms that coordinate services to meet community needs and that coordinate external resources or policy decisions with local decisions and resources. The legitimacy of agencies in such communities would depend upon their integrative capacities.

Administration of social control would seem to be a difficult balancing act in such areas. Such communities are dependent on complex organizations that are supported by outside forces in order to deliver satisfactory services—much like the situation in fragmented communities. But interdependent communities are not likely to be satisfied with public bureaucracies that operate independently of each other and concentrate on independent subparts of the total community. It is possible that criminal justice structures such as team policing (Sherman et al., 1973) or federally funded but locally determined correctional programs (Boorkman et al., 1976; Nelson et al., 1980) represent attempts to create such a balance between centralized and vertically organized resources and expertise on the one hand and local participation in need determination and coordination on the other.

While Warren's model has not been used frequently in the examination of crime, Spergel's study of community organization and delinquency rates comes close to an empirical test of the model's utility. In his study, the key community dimensions were horizontal integration and vertical integration. Spergel identified four separate communities, called "controlled," "pluralist," "transitional," and "communal." Comparing the four communities, he found markedly different auspices for need provision and relatively different delinquency rates. It is his conclusion that communities without strong horizontal ties leave a vacuum in the local control of locality-relevant functions, which is filled by vertically organized public services. These services, while they ostensibly fulfill specific functions, create low psychological identification with the community and result in high overlap (divergence) in jurisdictions of separate service authorities. Consequently delinquency rates are high (Spergel, 1976).

COMMUNITY STRUCTURE AND PROBATION ORGANIZATION

Having looked at the community model and social control in general terms, let us examine the relation of community to probation organization. How probation is funded (and how well), who makes policy or decides on program content and type of supervision, how much probation officer training is offered, and what relationship prevails between the probation agency and other units of local government—these are important, often controversial questions, and the answers will significantly influence the types and quality of services that probation can offer the community and the career experiences of probation staff. Such issues have financial, political, and social impact, regardless of the variation in probation outcomes. Indeed, to the extent that different correctional programs have the same effect on future crime, the questions concerning organization become all important. As Professor Wilkins has said to his students, "If you can't save souls, save money."

Spergel is more elaborate:

> A community structural approach . . . poses the question of direction of interorganizational relations or coordination. The critical issue becomes: should the community be organized less or more vertically or horizontally? Each type of coordination has different implications for creating and dealing with the delinquency problem. Certain policies as to coordination are therefore appropriate or inappropriate depending on type of community (Spergel, 1976:92–93).

We could go so far as to say that the community structural approach is the most useful way to define community corrections because it is the only approach to the concept that is grounded in a theory of community. Consequently, it is the only approach to community correction that provides for empirical reference in explaining and predicting the variations in correctional programming. The community theory serves to relate the correctional program dimension to variations in community.

In contrast, the traditional approach to community corrections has two basic deficiencies. First, it makes no fundamental distinctions among communities as real operating systems. If "community" is treated as a monolithic concept, we cannot make intelligent statements about the relationship between specific communities and specific correctional programs. Rather, the traditional approach leads to statements about correctional administration that are so global as to be useless, if not nonsensical, such as the remark that community corrections are those correctional programs that operate in the community (Fox, 1977:1) or that community is the external environment of the correctional system (Solomon, 1976).

Second, the traditional approach to community correction makes it harder to relate institutional and noninstitutional correctional programs. As the term community corrections is often used in introductory texts, for instance, it seems to denote any correctional supervision that takes place outside a prison, jail, or reformatory. This approach probably has ideological purposes of emphasizing an offender's relative freedom from incarceration. But it sets up a false dichotomy between institutional and community forms of supervision. It ignores, for example, that many community and institutional environments have similar impacts on offenders (Moos, 1975; McEwen, 1977; Wright, 1977). It ignores that all institutions have relationships with their own communities (Jacobs, 1976; Cressey, 1958), that most institutions are not discrete entities but part of systems whose administration depends on the ability to graduate the degree of incarceration or degree of offender contact with the community (Steele and Jacobs, 1975). Additionally, it ignores that many community programs make significant use of detention (Lerman, 1975), or control their clients and maintain their programs through revocation (Duffee, Maher, and Lagoy, 1977) or recommitment procedures (Sarason, 1974).

Furthermore, such an approach makes it hard to fit in the institutional-community linkages and the state-local government relations observable in practices such as probation subsidies (Smith, 1971) or community corrections acts (Blackmore, 1978). In short, the traditional-atheoretical approach ignores the fact that all corrections programs, whether institutional or not and whether run by states or local governments, serve community functions. If we do not use a framework that allows us to examine the community functions of jails and prisons, we will have difficulty determining whether and how noninstitutional forms of supervision can supplant them.

The most systematic attempt to use a community structural approach in the examination of community corrections is probably the recent monograph by Nelson et al. (1980). Their report addresses the relatively narrow question of how local corrections can be unified. They build three models of unification: the unified, county-administered model; the multijurisdiction local government model; and the state-administered decentralized model. In detailing each model they examine seven dimensions of the "force-field" that will retard or facilitate local unification: 1) source of initiative for change, 2) values and goals of reorganization, 3) organizational scope of unification, 4) financing, 5) linkages to related services, 6) intergovernmental relationships, and 7) service impact. With the possible exception of service impact, all these variables relate directly to the major structural dimensions of vertical and horizontal relations. Thus this study may provide a valuable starting point in identifying the specific factors that determine the type and quality of correctional services from a community structural perspective.

In the remainder of this section, we have only enough space to carry such an application one step further—to begin the task of specifying what kinds of probation organization are most likely within what kinds of community structure. Strictly speaking, the following discussion does not carry the application beyond that of Nelson and his colleagues, but instead addresses the theoretically prior question: What are the most *likely* or most *common* characteristics of probation in naturally occurring force-fields, interorganizational networks, or community matrices?

Nelson's group is not unaware of this question; indeed they periodically describe the kinds of vertical and horizontal mixes that seem to press for one form of community corrections unification over another. For example, in discussing each of their models, they suggest variations that may be most appropriate to small counties, rural counties, large urban counties and so on. However, the Nelson study is primarily concerned with *reorganization* of correctional services. Shifting the focus very little, then, that study is actually concerned with reorganizing the structure of community, since the alterations of funding, program auspice, and intergovernmental relations are alterations in the values of the vertical or horizontal dimensions of communities, at least within the segment concerned with processing and supervising offenders. But as the authors are quick to point out, reorganization of corrections often follows structural alterations that have already taken place in other aspects of community. For instance, state subvention of local corrections, such as supplanting state institutions with local probation and jail programs, most often occurs in communities with a long tradition of subvention in other functional areas such as mental health and welfare (Nelson et al., 1980:60).

It is not a new observation that probation philosophies, organizations, staffing levels, workloads, and supervision practices are highly varied. For example, the research project that spawned this book identified some of the dimensions other than size that may characterize small and rural probation agencies and make their needs and problems different from those of large urban probation departments. One finding was that urban departments generally do not lack community services and resources for probation agents to broker, while rural agencies more often report a service-lean environment in which direct service delivery or service creation makes more sense than brokering (Thomson and Fogel, 1980). Other examples of variation abound. Some probation administrations are relatively centralized, such as the Pennsylvania state probation system, which has statewide responsibility for felons, statewide standards for officers, and statewide supervision regulations. But in many local probation departments, administrative responsibility rests with a presiding judge or a county board of supervisors. Probation may be organized under judicial or executive auspices. Probation caseloads vary from hundreds of clients per officer in some jurisdictions to a relatively manageable fifty per officer in some federal districts.

Typically, some of these variations are preferred to others, often with little regard for the associated costs and generally with no regard for the particular functions that may make a particular probation type advantageous or the structural antecedents that may make it feasible.

One example may suffice to make the point. Some years ago, a number of experiments or quasi-experiments regarding caseload size were carried out in both probation and parole settings. The unexpected finding was that varying workload often made no difference in terms of supervision success. It was even found in some instances that officers with lesser caseloads were revoking more frequently, perhaps because they could give more time to surveillance (Adams et al., 1971). In any event, either smaller caseloads did not lead to provision of more help, or provision of more service was not effective in reducing revocations.

With the advantage of hindsight, of course, one might question whether changing caseload alone will have much impact on probation outcome, particularly if there are not concomitant changes in probation structure (or the relationship of probation to community). We could expect that in some communities, or for some offenders, reduced caseloads and greater contact with officers may result in some changes in outcome—for instance if a face-to-face, direct-counseling mode of supervision is the type of intervention that may reduce a probationer's propensity for crime. The San Francisco time-studies, however, suggest that greater client-officer contact will do little to change the urban offender's access to resources. Greater direct service would seem most likely to be effective with probationers in rural settings (compare Thomson and Fogel, 1980; Studt, 1972; Dell'Apa et al., 1976). Ironically, it is probable that only highly centralized probation services, such as those in large urban counties or the federal system, can muster the financial outlay to provide a great deal of direct officer/offender contact, whereas such contact would be most beneficial in rural, resource-lean environments.

The most important lesson of this example may be the disadvantages of considering probation independently of its community context, or of con-

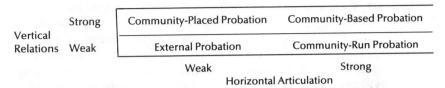

		Weak	Strong
Vertical Relations	Strong	Community-Placed Probation	Community-Based Probation
	Weak	External Probation	Community-Run Probation

Weak — Strong
Horizontal Articulation

Figure 12.2. Probation as an aspect of community structure.

sidering all communities to be alike. What probation officers and probationers may do with more time on their hands is partially dependent on the functions probation serves in particular communities and on the structures through which those functions are carried out.

The community model offers a means of making some basic distinctions about those structures and functions. Figure 12.2 reinterprets the basic categories of Figure 12.1 in terms of probation types.

External Probation

In areas that have insufficient organizational and political influence, we can expect probation organization to operate with relative independence from immediate environmental constraints, but without benefit of community support and legitimacy. We would expect probation officers to be primarily concerned with surveillance and the custodial duties of monitoring probationers' whereabouts and contacts with law enforcement officials. Probation caseloads may be high, facilities and office resources rundown and inadequate. The focus of probation supervision will be the individual offender, with little concern for marshaling community resources. Probation auspice may be either state or county government, but in either case central administrators are likely to find it difficult to keep track of actual officer activities in the disorganized area. Probation officer relationships with probationers are likely to be superficial and infrequent except after escalation episodes initiated, in most cases, by the police.

Weak articulation on the horizontal dimension means that probation officers will have difficulty establishing working relationships with non-probation organizations. The officer is likely to depend heavily on direct contact with the offender in either rendering services or attempting to control the offender's behavior. The probation office will have difficulty establishing working relationships with mental health, social service, or employment agencies or religious institutions, and those contacts that are made will often be dependent on the personality of particular officers and their informal, personal contacts in other agencies. Interorganizational relations will not be highly formalized or institutionalized.

The voice of the local area in decision-making by central authorities will be weak, whether we are examining probation itself or other organizations. We may find, for example, that probation operates from a separate central office distant from the community and that it is only individual officers themselves who ever enter the disorganized area. From the reverse perspective, probation supervisors may find it difficult to influence what actually happens in the disorganized areas, and may excuse or cover up the administrative variances that occur in such areas. They may allow officers assigned to such an area to operate informally, utilizing tactics of supervision and investigation that would not be condoned elsewhere.

Community-run Probation

In communities with a high degree of horizontal articulation (or mobilization) and relative autonomy from external authorities, probation and other correctional operations may be truly community-run. Probation organization in such communities is an integral part of community government. Officers and supervisors are likely to be long-time community residents, and their status in the community will be more dependent on that membership than on their official roles. Hence there is a high probability that probation work in such places is a reward for other kinds of contributions to the local community, not for professional training or expertise.

Community-run probation departments are likely to try to fend off efforts at standardization, and therefore may be resistant to both state-level assistance and state training or operational requirements. In solidary communities, probation and other penal sanctions are unlikely to be valued primarily for their impact on the offender. Instead, probation is more likely to be seen as a means of norm reinforcement—as a means of reinforcing community standards. Nevertheless, a community-run probation office will have easy access to other community organizations, services, and decision makers. This access, which will often be through informal channels, may present the potential for relatively quick and efficient rendering of services to probationers, should such services be deemed appropriate. Services, however, are likely to be informal and face-to-face renderings, not the ministrations of professional service agencies. It is most likely that the greatest concern is bringing the probationer back into the fold, or at least controlling excessive deviance, by relying on a strong, informal communication network.

Community-placed Probation

Probably the most typical form of probation organization combines a relatively strong reliance on centralized control of probation itself with a relatively weak association between the probation office and other units of community. This form of probation reflects a fragmented community structure: multiple sources of power governing bureaucratically organized service agents, with horizontal coordination achieved only through the exigencies of domain protection and market position. This form of community correction might be called "community-placed," because correctional agencies in such areas are relatively standardized and uniform, operate with strong dependence on central authority, and are relatively autonomous from horizontal interfaces with other organizations and groups. A good example of a community-placed probation system would be the Pennylvania Board of Probation and Parole, which has jurisdiction over all felony probation cases. Federal probation displays many of the same characteristics, except that federal district supervisors are selected by district judges rather than a central office. This unusual situation may make the federal system less vertically articulated and more dependent on local authority than the Pennsylvania state system.

A community-placed system has a number of visible advantages over other types of probation. Its concomitant problems may be less frequently observed. Because community-placed systems are financed from a central source, they are less affected by the problems and fluctuations of a local tax base. They will generally have a high pay scale and decent physical facilities, and be able to attract well-educated probation careerists. As a consequence, community-placed probation may often be well managed and be rich in traditionally respected probation expertise, such as casework training.

On the other side, community-placed systems will usually be poorly articulated with other sorts of community service or resource agencies, and there may be a consequent press toward direct service to probationers, regardless of what probationers need or desire. One would also expect that community-placed systems will frequently become rigidly bureaucratic, concentrating on the accountability demands of the central office policy makers. As a result, probation agents or entire suboffices may be unable to adapt to the characteristics of any particular community in which such probation is placed.

The central-local conflicts in community-placed probation may often be acute, and the typical administrative solution is a significant amount of decentralization, at least in matters of daily supervision.

Community-based Probation.

Finally, we find some community probation arrangements for which the term "community-based" may really be appropriate. These probation departments occur in interdependent communities—ones that combine a great deal of vertical coordination with significant mobilization of the local area into a cohesive unit. In such areas, vertically organized, professional probation is inadequate to the demands of the community for an integration of probation with other organizations.

Community-based probation exhibits some of the characteristics of the community-placed type, particularly source of financing and level of expertise. But these agencies will also share some characteristics of community-run agencies, particularly control over philosophy and policy, and the integration of probation with other units of community. However, while integration in community-run agencies may be informal, integration in community-based agencies is likely to be formal and interorganizational.

Perhaps the best-known probation operation that might serve as an example of this type is run by the unified court-services department in Des Moines (Boorkman et al., 1976). This LEAA Exemplary Project uses external financial sources and expertise but maintains local control of policy and integrates probation with other units of community. Other possible examples can be found in Nelson et al. (1980) in their discussion of the unified, county-administered model.

The establishment of community-based probation is popular now, but it remains to be seen if this form of probation is stable. Stability would seem possible to the extent that this probation form truly reflects a new form of community structure, in which federal, state, and local governments have been realigned in a new matrix of central and horizontal coordination. If, however, such probation departments are simply being forced into fragmented communities, dissolution of the central-local cooperation could be expected.

EXTERNAL CONSTRAINTS AND THE FUTURE OF PROBATION

Many changes in probation practice can probably be implemented without regard for the external environment of probation agencies. Most of the various schools of organization and management theory would agree that all organizations, both public and private, possess a significant degree of autonomy and enough insulation from external interference that many organizational practices are internally determined. As Gouldner (1959) has correctly observed, organizations as systems are "functionally autonomous." That is, many of their characteristics and behaviors cannot be accurately predicted from a knowledge of the social functions they perform, or the way they fit into society. To damage an ancient line, we must recognize today that stone walls do not all prisons the same make. The situation is no different with probation.

The external environment provides constraints that surely must be accommodated in all activities from policy making to daily supervision. But it should be recognized that many alterations, for better or worse, can be accomplished without alterations in the environment. To state otherwise is not only factually inaccurate, but probably unethical. The presumption that public administrators are powerless because of insurmountable obstacles posed by "external forces"—whether public apathy, political conflict, or lack of resources—is often merely justification of ineptitude or rigidity. To demonstrate that public organizations and their management are significantly free of external forces, one need only observe an organization resisting change imposed from the outside. Organizations can be remarkably creative and adept at resisting changes in external constraints. Changes in probation should be planned on the supposition that probation agencies usually have considerable room to maneuver and thus that the future of probation can be, in significant ways, internally defined and internally accomplished. No reader should interpret the message of this chapter differently.

Those caveats formally in mind, this chapter offers two primary contributions to the formulation of a probation mission. First, planning for changes in probation must recognize that probation is not, and will not be, the same everywhere. Even if it were decided that probation should have the same goals everywhere, the structural arrangements for accomplishing those goals would need to vary in different locations. But it is unlikely and perhaps undesirable that probation will have the same goals everywhere, since communities vary significantly in the auspices by which primary functions are accomplished. It is always possible, in other words, that in certain communities probation reforms deemed professionally efficacious will be inappropriate, unfeasible, and even contraindicated by broader criteria of community need.

The second major contribution of community theory is the recognition that some changes in probation, even if internally generated, will have external effects. Probation, no matter how organized, is a facet, albeit a minor one, of community itself. A major aspect of community structure is the interorganizational fields that influence the quality and patterns of group life in localities. To unify local corrections, as suggested by Nelson et al. (1980), is to change not only correctional agencies themselves and their interactions, but the horizontal and vertical patterns of community.

These are not new points. Criminal justice studies in general have stressed the systemic nature of the criminal process for a long time now. But there is a critical difference between the criminal justice system perspective and the community perspective. The former often stresses uniformity, standardization, and cohesiveness across discrete criminal justice systems, and disregards the structural location and functional contribution of criminal justice agencies as components of community systems. Just as the technologically superior hatchet bestowed on a backward tribe by well-intentioned missionaries can destroy a tribal order, a technically superior administrative form can destroy a community order. More probably, unlike the backward tribe, the "backward" community will reject the administrative hatchet.

But communities, like probation agencies, are not totally independent entities. Indeed, Warren (1978) has proposed that communities are not independent entities at all, but "nodes in the macrosystem." In many respects, they are local stages on which more global influences converge in such forms as crime, unemployment, and alienation—but also in neighborliness, self-help, and social order.

Thus there is room for, and need for, national-level policy in a variety of administrative sectors that would help the quality of life in communities. Improving probation may be one such area. The trick (neither to demean nor belittle the task) is to seek that mix of local and nonlocal resources, expertise, and political decision making that is most likely to be effective in particular situations. Fitzharris's (Chapter 14) broad outline for the advocacy role of the National Institute of Corrections may provide the backbone of one reasonable plan. The force field characteristics identified by Nelson et al. (1980) provide one set of community variables that may help us to determine what sort of mix is appropriate where.

REFERENCES

Adams, W., William Chandler, and M. G. Neithercutt (1971). "The San Francisco Project: Critique." *Federal Probation* 35:45–53.

Angell, R. (1951). "The Moral Integration of American Cities." *American Journal of Sociology* 57 (1):1–140.

Banton, M. (1964). *The Policeman in the Community.* New York: Basic Books.

Blackmore, J. (1978). "Minnesota's Community Corrections Act Takes Hold." *Corrections Magazine* 4 (1):46–56.

Boorkman, D., E. Fazio, Jr., N. Day, and D. Weinstein (1976). *An Exemplary Project: Community Based Corrections in Des Moines.* Washington, D.C.: Government Printing Office.

Chambliss, W., and R. Seidman (1971). *Law, Order and Power.* Reading, MA: Addison Wesley.

Coates, R., and A. Miller (1974). "Neutralization of Community Resistance to Group Homes." In Yitzhak Bakal (ed.), *Closing Correctional Institutions.* Lexington, MA: Lexington Books.

Cressey, D. (1958). "Achievement of an Unstated Organizational Goal: An Observation of Prisons." *Pacific Sociological Review* 1:43–49.

Dell'Apa, F., W. Adams, J. Jorgensen, and H. Sigurdson (1976). "Advocacy, Brokerage, Community: The ABC's of Probation and Parole." *Federal Probation* XXXX (4):37–45.

Duffee, David (1980). *Explaining Criminal Justice: Community Theory and Criminal Justice Reform.* Cambridge, MA: Oelgeschlager, Gunn & Hain.

Duffee, D., T. Maher, and S. Lagoy (1977). "Administrative Due Process in Community Preparole Programs." *Criminal Law Bulletin* 13 (5):383–400.

Emery, F., and F. Trist (1970). "The Causal Texture of Organizational Environments." In Frederick Emery (ed.), *Systems Thinking.* Baltimore: Penguin.

Fisher, C. (1976). *The Urban Experience.* New York: Harcourt, Brace, Jovanovich.

Fox, V. (1977). *Community Corrections.* Englewood Cliffs, NJ: Prentice Hall.

General Accounting Office of the United States (1976). *State and County Probation: Systems in Crisis.* Washington, D.C.: General Accounting Office.

Gouldner, A. (1959). "Organizational Dynamics." In R. Merton, L. Broom, and L. Cottrell (eds.), *Sociology Today.* New York: Basic Books.

Jacobs, J. (1976). "The Politics of Corrections: Town-Prison Relations as a Determinant of Reform." *Social Service Review* (50):623–631.

Jenkins, W. (1973). *A Longitudinal Follow-up Investigation of the Post-Release Behavior of Released Offenders.* Montgomery, AL: Rehabilitation Research Foundation.

Lerman, P. (1975). *Community Treatment and Social Control.* Chicago: University of Chicago Press.

Long, N. (1958). "The Local Community as an Ecology of Games." *American Journal of Sociology* 64 (3):251–261.

McEwen, C. (1977). "Subcultures in Community-Based Programs." In L. Ohlin, A. Miller, and R. Coates (eds.), *Juvenile Correctional Reform in Massachusetts.* Washington, D.C.: Law Enforcement Assistance Administration.

McKee, J. (1973). *Experimental Manpower Laboratory for Corrections.* Final report to Rehabilitation Research Foundation. Montgomery, AL.

Mills, T. (1959). "Equilibrium and the Processes of Deviance and Control." *American Sociological Review* XXIV (5):671–679.

Moos, R. (1975). *Evaluating Correctional and Community Settings.* New York: Wiley.

Nelson, E., R. Cushman, and N. Harlow (1980). *Program Models: Unification of Community Corrections.* Washington, D.C.: Government Printing Office.

Park, R., E. Burgess, and R. McKenzie (1925). *The City.* Chicago: University of Chicago Press.

Sarason, S. B. (1974). *The Psychological Sense of Community: Prospects for a Community Psychology.* San Francisco: Jossey Bass.

Sherman, L., C. Milton, and T. Kelly (1973). *Team Policing: Seven Case Studies.* Washington, D.C.: The Police Foundation.

Smith, R. (1971). "A Quiet Revolution: Probation Subsidy." *Delinquency Prevention* 21 (2):149–162.

Solomon, H. (1976). *Community Corrections.* Boston: Holbrook.

Spergel, I. (1976). "Interactions Between Community Structure, Delinquency and Social Policy in the Inner City." In Malcom Klein (ed.) *The Juvenile Justice System.* Beverly Hills, CA: Sage.

Steele, E., and J. Jacobs (1975). "A Theory of Prison Systems." *Crime and Delinquency* 21 (2):149–162.

Studt, E. (1972). *Surveillance and Service in Parole.* Los Angeles: Institute of Government and Public Affairs, UCLA.

Thomson, D., and D. Fogel (1980). *Probation Work in Small Agencies: A National Study of Training Provisions and Needs*, Vol. I. Chicago: Center for Research in Criminal Justice, University of Illinois at Chicago Circle.

Waller, I. (1979). *Men Released from Prison*. Toronto: University of Toronto Press.

Warren, R. (1978). *Community in America*, 2nd ed. Chicago: Rand McNally.

Warren, R., S. Rose, and A. Bergunder (1974). *The Structure of Urban Reform*. Lexington, MA: Lexington Books.

Wright, K. (1977). "Correctional Effectiveness: A Case For an Organizational Approach." Doctoral dissertation, Pennsylvania State University.

Chapter 13

Implementing the Justice Model in Probation

*Nora Harlow**

Eugene Doleschal has observed that efforts to reform the justice system generally either fail to achieve their objectives or produce consequences opposite to those intended.[1] Diversion programs, rather than reducing court caseloads or criminal convictions, have widened the net of social control.[2] Restitution programs, instead of diverting offenders to less severe penalties, have tended to increase both the degree of control over offenders and the number of people in custodial confinement.[3] Community service programs have been shown to have minimal, if any, impact on institutional overcrowding, probation caseloads, or correctional costs.[4]

These findings derive from nationwide evaluations, not studies of a few isolated reform eforts. Nor are they unique to the United States. No country that has widely adopted community alternatives to prison, Doleschal notes, has experienced substantial reductions in imprisonment rates.[5]

> In Britain, the suspended sentence . . . was introduced in 1968 as a way to reduce prison populations. As in the United States, the effect was the opposite. Courts used suspended sentences not only in place of imprisonment

*School of Public Administration, University of Southern California and The American Justice Institute

but also in place of fines and probation, sentences that in Britain carry no threat of incarceration. In addition, courts imposed longer suspended sentences than sentences of actual imprisonment. As suspendees reoffended, they had their old sentences activated and served those and their new sentences consecutively instead of concurrently. England's prison population increased as a result of this reform, *in direct contrast to what was intended.*[6]

It is not only liberalizing reforms that have been thwarted in implementation. Those designed to increase the predictability and severity of penalties also have failed to elicit the intended results. The 1973 revision of New York State's drug law is a classic example. Severely curtailed plea bargaining, mandatory prison sentences, and lifelong parole were combined in an effort to crack down on drug offenders. Yet evaluation of the nation's toughest drug law showed that it did not increase rates of conviction or prison sentences (which actually declined), and instead of speeding up the processing of drug cases, it slowed the system down.[7]

Other examples of nullified "crackdowns" on criminals and crime abound.[8] Mandatory capital punishment laws have been shown to deter not crime but convictions, as judges and juries refuse to invoke a remedy seen as excessively punitive.[9] A prosecutor's decision to rule out plea bargaining for selected offenses has been found to shift bargaining from the prosecutor to the judge, through both sentence bargaining and increased use of dismissals.[10] And both legislative and administrative attempts to force harsher treatment of drunken drivers have been followed by reductions in rates of arrest, prosecution, conviction, and sentencing.[11]

National and international experience thus demonstrates that the criminal justice system has "a life of its own, independent of and oblivious to the intent of administrative or legislative reform."[12] Reforms tend to be absorbed into the existing system and transformed by it. They are turned to the advantage of those who are charged with implementing them. They are modified by the organizational dynamics of the agency or system into which they are introduced. They fall in line with more dominant political, social, and ideological movements or trends, even if they are designed to counteract such developments.

The dismal record of criminal justice reform need not dissuade us from attempting change,[13] but surely it should make us humble. The most successful reforms are likely to be those that grow naturally within the social organism. These are not implemented in one piece by anyone's conscious effort, though well-timed action on occasion may promote decisive movement in one direction or another. Generally, reformers may be most successful when they tune in to the rhythms of change in the social system, contenting themselves with small but significant tinkerings and discarding notions of creating a whole new world.

Proponents of a "justice model" for probation thus might do well to ask not how such a model might be implemented, but whether and to what extent the model is congruent with deep undercurrents of change in society and its system of corrections and crime control. Does our understanding of the justice model describe the direction this society now seems to be taking? Are the strong trends in criminal justice compatible with the model's basic tenets? Are probation agencies today engaged in the kinds of change that will move them toward a justice model, or are they committing themselves to quite different and contradictory goals?

Because of the huge variety contained within these United States, any assessment of national trends is subject to substantial risks of overgeneralization. There are significant regional and demographic differences along any dimension one might wish to measure. National tendencies regularly are modified or even neutralized by contact with local cultures. Nonetheless, it may be useful to consider a few of the many points of possible congruence or conflict between the model known as "justice as fairness" and the world its proponents believe it should describe.

What follows will be restricted to developments in the probation field, with observations drawn primarily from two recent studies of probation in California and nationwide.[14] Related trends in the criminal justice system or in society will be touched on only in passing. To provide a basis for discussion of the implementation of justice model probation, a brief review of that model's goals and characteristics will be attempted first.

IN SEARCH OF THE JUSTICE MODEL

Because proponents of the justice model share no single perspective, it is difficult to assess the degree to which current trends are in the direction of justice as fairness. At a high level of abstraction there is a core of values that most would agree are pivotal: proportionality (punishment to fit the crime); equity (equal time for equal crime); retrospectivity (a focus on past, not future, behaviors); and predictability (as opposed to individualization). Beyond that core consensus is a diversity of perception that might seem to allow unlimited variation in implementation.

In an earlier version of Chapter 4, Doug Thomson describes four variations on the justice theme: justice as retribution; justice as remediation; justice as public protection; and justice as ritual. At least two of these—remediation and public protection—discard or downplay the core value of retrospectivity, or punishment only for past deeds. Thomson, who himself advances the justice as ritual variant, sees this as an unfortunate but probably unavoidable development as the justice model is put into practice. But if the model can survive excision of its retrospective approach (on which notions of desert would seem to depend), of what does it most essentially consist?

Some writers have implied that the essence of the justice model lies in the reduction of discretion and structuring of decision making.[15] In this view justice is served when suspects, defendants, and convicted offenders are treated fairly, when individual rights are protected, and when police, judicial, and correctional decisions are constrained by guidelines and open to review. Yet rehabilitation, deterrence, incapacitation, and other goals are served equally well by an injection of this kind of fairness. The justice model has no natural hegemony in the areas of due process and reduced discretion.

Others have stressed the reparative nature of the justice model.[16] In this view the meaning of criminal justice is found in the requirement that an offender do something to return the situation to its pre-offense state. Instead of, or in addition to, punishment for the crime, an offender makes restitution either personally to the victim or collectively to the society of which both victim and offender are a part. This does represent a distinctive approach to criminal justice and corrections, and it is one that seems eminently practicable, if not alone, at least in combination with incapacitation (e.g., surveillance) or some other preventive mode. Whether and to what extent preventive goals can be tolerated by the justice model remains an issue of much debate.

Nonutilitarian is a term commonly used to describe the justice or "just deserts" model. Sanctions are predictable, but not predictive. Discretion is controlled (increasing predictability), but prediction of future crime and its prevention through rehabilitation and/or surveillance are avoided. Efforts to deter crime, though always tempting as a means of protecting the public, are seen as punishing the innocent and undermining the law.[17] The law exists to punish the convicted; any attempt to prevent crime, at least through measures directed at individuals, punishes the suspect—an activity supposedly condemned by our system of law.

The justice model often seems most easily described in terms of what it is not. It is not a medical model, which tends to treat people as objects rather than as responsible, volitional human beings. It does not depend on experts to determine sanctions or conditions of their service. It is not based on notions of needs deprivation, with treatment plans aimed at filling gaps in the offender's life or character. As noted above, it does not seek to foretell the future, and it especially refrains from imposing sanctions based on what might be seen in the crystal ball. In some formulations, it is noncustodial in orientation, with a decided bias against incarcerative sanctions.[18] In others it rejects both service and surveillance, adopting instead a narrow focus on compliance with conditions integrally related to the punishment and the crime.[19]

Perhaps the greatest appeal of the justice model lies in its opposition to the tortuous logic of our present systems for dealing with offenders. It is simpler, at its core, than utilitarian systems, and it fits well with popular conceptions of justice as involving the righting of wrongs and the matching of punishments with crimes. At an abstract level, the justice model makes sense; but the closer it comes to real-world constraints, the more elusive and internally inconsistent it seems. This may account for the proliferation of model variants as the theory is increasingly elaborated. If so, the issues surrounding implementation are bound to be problematic. For example:

What does the justice model mean to those who would implement it? Does it mean different things to different people? If the justice model shades gradually into deterrence, incapacitation, or rehabilitation, how does one know when the line has been crossed?

Do people tend to use the model, or its language, for their own purposes, and do these purposes violate the integrity of the model? For example, can a model based on notions of desert survive the inclusion of undeserved conditions of sentence service, even in the name of protecting the public from further harm?

If proportionality means that punishment fits the crime, can it be separated from retrospectivity (which implies a focus on the offense)? If, because these goals are inseparable, one cannot be set before the other, must they both be jettisoned in a utilitarian world?

Does fairness demand a nonutilitarian approach? For example, can a predictive system be fair?

Can a model that posits a "moral community" and encourages participation of the victim and the public presume to require a bias against incarceration (or any other sanction)?

Can one phase of criminal justice (e.g., probation) be utilitarian and another (e.g., sentencing) not, as has been proposed,[20] or is sentence service an integral part of sentencing? Alternately, what happens to probation's aspirations to justice where the state mandates indeterminate sentencing, judges sentence for rehabilitation, and the public demands protection from the potential crimes of convicted offenders?

DOING JUSTICE TO THE JUSTICE MODEL[21]

Proponents of the justice model are well aware of its many implementation problems, and they have sought to adjust to real-world constraints—primarily by accommodation.[22] With some prominent exceptions, answers to the kinds of questions posed above have stressed the flexibility of the model and its ability to incorporate local preferences for such traditional objectives as community protection and even (if properly packaged as a retributive effect) rehabilitation. There seems to be a reluctance to offend or alienate anyone. Justice model probation apparently need give up neither services nor surveillance; it may even continue to predict—a focus on the offense apparently not requiring a disregard of behavioral outcomes.[23] Implementation of the model is said to involve not change, but a "rearrangement of priorities." Justice will be paramount, but other goals may be invoked "where no substantial damage to proportionality and equity takes place."[24]

To a large extent, of course, any model must accommodate the reality of multiple goals and conflicting interests as it leaves the realm of theory and works its way into the world of practice. But how far can the process of accommodation go before we have justice as rehabilitation, justice as deterrence, justice as incapacitation? It seems important at this point, with attempts at implementation being made at various locations throughout the country, to begin to draw the line somewhere. If we are to do justice to the justice model, we cannot allow it to lose its meaning in applications indistinguishable from supposedly competing paradigms.

Needless to say, this is not the place to make any pronouncements about what the justice model should and should not be. We can, however, put forth some tentative assumptions on which to base an assessment of trends in probation today. For example, we can suggest that justice model probation might require a much greater focus on the offense than many probation departments may be prepared to adopt. And it would probably disallow heavy emphasis on either "dangerousness" or "need," and avoid dispositions based on factors irrelevant to the present situation.

Justice model probation undoubtedly would involve a reparative element, with offenders directed to make good the losses of those they have harmed. It would also assume the offender to be capable of making choices and acting upon them; it would not treat people as objects to be manipulated.

A probation agency dedicated to justice certainly would limit discretion by structuring the important decision areas; it would increase accountability by monitoring all official activities; and it would provide for fair and equitable handling of all cases coming under its jurisdiction.

The justice model probation agency probably would align itself closely with the court, focusing on compliance with court orders and the conditions of probation. These conditions may require both service and surveillance kinds of activity on the part of the probation officer; but officers would refrain from extensive involvement in either the functions of law enforcement or those of social service. In most cases, participation in treatment or services would be voluntary and brokered to other agencies. Law enforcement officers would handle instances of new crime.

Under the justice model, probation would be viewed as a sanction rather than as a suspension of punishment. All involuntary conditions of that sanction would be acknowledged for what they are—restrictions on the liberty of the individual—and thus aplied with concern for fairness, equity, and proportionality. No restriction on liberty could be excused solely on the basis of its benign or helpful nature.

Finally, justice model probation probably would reach out to involve the local community in various ways. Victim and community both might be involved in the act of reparation; and, to some extent, the community-based sanction would reflect and embody community norms.

TRENDS IN PROBATION

A review of developments in the probation field, undertaken in connection with research on responses to diminishing fiscal resources,[25] provides some information on the direction or directions this diverse collection of public organizations currently seems to be taking. The research spanned the years from 1979 to 1982, tracking changes in values and orientations as much as programmatic or procedural kinds of change. The focus was on ways probation organizations were resisting or adjusting to fiscal cutbacks, but the data revealed broad trends and developments not necessarily related to the fiscal situation.

Prominent among the findings of this research were two seemingly contradictory facts. First was the tendency of probation agencies to take on the character of their settings, and thus to vary widely from one jurisdiction to another. There could be little if any resemblance between different probation departments. The most successful departments (i.e., those viewed as vital and viable both by their own members and by important outsiders) generally were those whose character (including mission and methods) was *congruent* with the expectations (including values and goals) of critical elements of the organizational environment.

A second observation was that certain practices and professional orientations were rather broadly dispersed among otherwise different departments. There were commonalities among many, though certainly not all, of those agencies coming under the rubric of probation or community corrections. At the same time that agencies were diversifying, they also were becoming more alike in important ways.

Interestingly, the changing fiscal climate seemed to be at the root of both the tendency to diversify and the tendency to converge. As resources become scarcer, there are increasing pressures on the probation department both to choose among programs and functions and to define itself more clearly to mandating constituencies (especially funding bodies). Because different environments press for different styles of probation service, departments tend to emphasize different aspects of probation's general character—those for which there is most local support and those that fit within the system of interlocking domains carved out over time by agencies and organizations involved in related work.

The tendency to coverge also seemed spurred, at least in part, by the new fiscal climate. There are growing pressures on public organizations everywhere to account for the funds they expend, and probation departments are responding by structuring and formally defining their activities, improving their record-keeping, and working on their relationships with those to whom they are accountable. The rapid spread of probation-specific management information systems is only partly due to the efforts of the National Institute of Corrections. Time studies, workload measurement, standardized case management, risk/needs assessment, integrated records, and computerized generation of management reports all help administrators both to make the difficult choices and to respond to the questions of significant outsiders.

The use of risk/needs instruments for offender classification is undoubtedly the most popular of current efforts to structure the activities of probation organizations. Classification, of course, has always been practiced by probation officers, but generally in no systematic or standardized way. Different officers in the past had their own means of distinguishing among cases and applying differential case management techniques. Contemporary classification and case management schemes attempt to routinize the decision-making process, providing for both more consistent case decisions and increased accountability. Formal classification also can produce the data needed to improve prediction capabilities (i.e., by connecting case dispositions with outcomes) and thus ultimately to make more supportable recommendations to the court.

Probation today also demonstrates a growing concern with the victim of crime, whether defined as the individual or as the community generally. This shift in focus from the offender to the offended is responsive to the increasing militancy of citizens who believe such a redirection of effort is long overdue. A "victim's bill of rights" on the ballot in California recently gained public approval with relative ease. (Wisconsin, Washington, and Oklahoma already had enacted similar legislation.) Victim/witness laws have been passed in many states; over thirty now have set aside funds to compensate victims of violent crimes and many also provide for restitution paid by the offender.[26]

Probation's entry into the victim services area most commonly has involved the monitoring of restitution payments and supervision of community service. In some jurisdictions community or victim restitution is the showpiece of the department,[27] and more and more probation agencies are rewarking their mission statements to feature such reparative services.

Restitution and community service are not the sole province of probation, however; public work programs and private nonprofit volunteer bureaus frequently handle the placement of court-referred individuals, and restitution may be monitored and collected by such entities as the county or district attorney's office or a fiscal office of the health or human services department.[28] Probation must compete for the role of restitution manager if its leadership sees this as a proper component of the probation mission.

Some probation departments are reaching out to involve the community in significant ways, but the hesitancy and vacillation of other departments in this area make it difficult to label this a national trend. There is a nationwide awareness of the growing importance of the taxpaying public, but much of the action in this area is devoted to "selling" probation and building constituencies rather than genuine involvement. Jurisdictions in which public involvement includes participation in such mission-relevant activities as planning, policy-making, and assessment of probation programs seem an exception to the rule. Where the community is meaningfully involved through such mechanisms as an active citizens' advisory board (e.g., Missouri and Minnesota), the probation department takes on a distinctive character that sets it off from organizations with other conceptions of the probation mission.

As to mission, few probation administrators today talk openly of rehabilitation, though offender aid and services still are stressed by many departments. Most mission statements now mention community protection, indicating a recognition that contemporary corrections should adopt a public-services stance and in some contexts, downplay the human-services aspects of the job. David Duffee views this as a predictable tendency in a faltering economy: as the social value of offender assistance declines in relation to other goals, corrections agencies may attempt to maintain resource levels through timely alterations in organizational mission.[29]

Those departments that continue to stress offender services, or combine public protection and client services in what has been labeled a "balanced mission,"[30] tend to describe contemporary services in terms that suggest not changing the offender but helping him or her in a practical, nonjudgmental way. Proponents of the community resource management teams (CRMT) approach describe such help as meeting "normative" or "survival" needs—jobs, education, drug treatment—and express a preference for voluntary participation in services brokered to community-based agencies.[31] Various aspects of the CRMT model (including team staffing, officer accountability devices, and brokering itself) have slowed its acceptance in the field, but the withdrawal from in-house offender treatment has proved highly compatible with current trends.

In sum, then, the typical probation department today is defining its own locally suitable organizational character, drawing from the wellspring of national trends or innovations, but rejecting those that do not help in the ongoing effort to solve its own organizational problems. Just as communities and local justice systems differ in values, goals, traditions, and personalities, so do probation departments vary in the domains they define for themselves in concert with other local actors. As a field, nonetheless, probation appears to be moving collectively in a number of directions: a much heavier reliance on risk/needs assessment, standardization of routines and decisions, more pragmatic aid to offenders, and a more balanced focus on the interests of the public as well as the needs of clients.

PROBATION AND JUSTICE

The fit between trends in probation and the justice model is close but not complete. Several current trends suggest a fertile soil for the growth and spread of justice model concepts in probation. A few run counter to the model or simultaneously support and contradict it in complex ways.

Most obvious among the supportive trends is the new and expanding focus on victim services. Probation professionals are beginning to define their work as a public service, rather than primarily as a service to offenders. One hears less today about offender advocacy, treatment, or rehabilitation, and much more about aid to victims and reparation by offenders for harm they have caused. This may be part and parcel of a community protection mode oriented to the goals of law enforcement, but it fits well with the reparative aspects of the justice model, and it seems to strike a responsive chord among public constituencies everywhere. Both victims and offenders reportedly perceive these kinds of sanction as fair.[32]

One problem with victim restitution and community service programs is that they apparently do not serve the goal of reducing the use of incarceration, nor do they rationalize the use of resources in community corrections.[33] Offenders given the sanction of restitution generally are not diverted from incarcerative sentences, and restitution commonly is applied as an add-on sanction rather than as an alternative to probation supervision or fines.[34]

Another problem with restitution as a sentencing option is that, like other "alternative" dispositions—and like determinate sentencing itself—it can serve liberal or conservative purposes with equal facility. Restitution may satisfy a demand for harsher penalties; or it may be used to expand the number of alternatives in a system of graded sanctions. It may be applied in an offense-based retrospective framework; or offender needs and characteristics may be considered in designing reparative sanctions. The danger is that restitution may come to be associated with a justice model approach, yet be used in a manner that lacks fairness, equity, and other essential traits of justice.

The trend toward greater structure and formality also supports the emergence of the justice model in probation practice. Individual discretion is reduced through the use of classification instruments, and standardized case management helps to ensure that similar offenders are handled in similar ways. Officers may override any of the instrument's suggestions that conflict with professional judgment, but the need to justify and document exceptions exerts a centripetal force on individual decision making. Formal classification and structured case management also support the development and use of graded sanctions, with "banking" of many less serious cases and differential handling of the rest.

Fairness, equity, and predictability all are enhanced by the introduction of formal instruments and the training of officers in their use. Decision making tends to be more objective, explicit, and replicable, especially where decisions are monitored and reviewed. But the more common classification instruments today contain such strong utilitarian elements that their use may be incompatible with a justice model framework for probation.

The risk/needs assessment scales promoted by the National Institute of Corrections and being adopted by probation departments nationwide serve as a prominent example. The risk scale is designed to "assess an offender's propensity for further unlawful or rule-violating behavior."[35] Originally developed in Wisconsin, where it "proved to be a valid predictor of future criminal activity," this instrument scores such items as number of address changes and percentage of time employed during the past twelve months, alcohol and drug use problems, and attitude (i.e., motivated to change, dependent, negative). To be fair, six other items deal with criminal history (though not current offense), which can be seen as compounding guilt or increasing responsibility to make amends; and a policy item (not predictive, but included to satisfy community concerns) heavily weights any conviction for an assaultive offense within the preceding five years.

The Wisconsin-based needs assessment scale asks probation officers to judge the extent and nature of offender need in such areas as academic/vocational skills; employment; financial management; marital/family relationships; companions; emotional stability; alcohol or drug use; mental ability; health; and sexual behavior. In addition, the officer is asked for his or her own overall impressions of the client's level of need. Scores in all of these categories are added to produce a total score, which is incorporated into a risk/need classification used to determine placement in one of several supervision levels.

The outright dependence of contemporary classification schemes on experts' assessment of risk and need, plus the assignment of offenders to graded levels of liberty-restriction on the basis of such utilitarian considerations, may make the practice inconsistent with justice model probation. Prediction pervades all criminal justice decisions,[36] and it probably cannot be expunged from the conditions of community supervision. Still, the heavy investment of probation resources in prevention of future crime and the inclusion of need as a factor in determining the conditions of sentence service surely run counter to the spirit and intent of probation as just deserts. Not all probation agencies have jumped on the classification bandwagon, but in those that have, the commitment to more traditional functions of surveillance and service would seem to be reaffirmed.

The trend away from therapeutic forms of offender treatment partially offsets the recommitment to need assessment, at least as far as compatibility with the justice model is concerned. Many probation departments are orienting their efforts to more practical aid to offenders (e.g., coping skills such as the managment of money or job search techniques), or limiting assistance to crisis intervention (housing, drug withdrawal, financial aid). Where possible, these services often are brokered to agencies specializing in the kind of aid sought. Some probation chiefs admit that the shift to more limited direct assistance has been forced by an unmanageable growth in workload; but the demise of the rehabilitative ideal and a gradually changing conception of justice have probably also played a part.

Despite some loss of faith in rehabilitation, the concept of voluntary services has not been widely embraced. The element of choice that would imbue probation with a nonmanipulative respect for its clientele seems to violate core values of probation as it traditionally has been practiced. The probation department, of course, is hardly the sole decision maker in this area, since judges set the conditions of probation and frequently order a probationer to participate in some kind of service. But both judges and probation professionals express the belief that involuntary treatment is effective often enough to justify its continued use. Probation is coming to be viewed as a sanction, and no one would argue that offenders should be punished in proportion to their needs. As yet, however, the affinity between involuntary help and punitive sanction is one few criminal justice officials or systems seem willing to acknowledge.

IMPLEMENTING THE JUSTICE MODEL IN PROBATION

Aggregate data are interesting for the light they shed on directions society as a whole may be taking, but national trends tell us little about implementation of a plan, concept, or model at the level at which its real effects are felt. American society is a patchwork of diverse regional and local cultures, each with its own collection of values, goals, and traditions. Common threads exist, but they often change in color or texture as they come in contact with local systems.

Studies in California and nationwide have found probation organizations to follow varying normative patterns in different localities and settings.[37] While each department can be seen as uniquely adapted to its own environment, many seem to fall into a few general categories. Some departments have forged an image that aligns them closely with law enforcement. Recruitment and training, policy and procedures, professional and working relationships, public education, and budget defense all tend to enhance the image and reality of probation as a public safety organization. These departments may share training and equipment with police departments, participate in enforcement-oriented investigations and arrests, tap into police communications systems, and in other ways actively seek to establish a capability and a reputation for policing their charges and preventing crime.

Probation has evolved quite differently in other settings. Some departments both present themselves and function as a component of the human services system. They may have few working relationships with the police or sheriff, their activities, values, and concerns placing them more often in contact with health and social service organizations. Training, policy and procedures, budgeting, and professional relationships all reflect and support this definition of mission and domain.

A third group of probation agencies is oriented almost wholly to the business of the judiciary. Perceiving themselves as court services, these agencies relate to offender assistance and surveillance primarily in terms of the conditions of probation and the expectations of judges to whom they report. Conducting presentence investigations and monitoring compliance with court-ordered conditions are the dual emphases of these organizations. Relationships with the rest of the task environment are moderated by and mediated through the primary relationship to the court.

Still other probation departments attempt to walk a line connecting the various extremes, seeing offender services, community protection, and services to the court as equally important goals. This definition of domain necessarily spreads efforts and resources thinner, but it provides what many regard as a more balanced probation mission. Image and relationships in these organizations are less clear, but what is lost in strength of ties and character may be made up in flexibility and capability for change.

How might organizations in each of these categories react to the attempt to implement justice model principles in probation? Major factors governing the success of any reform that affects character and domain include:

Distance between existing mission/methods and proposed reforms. Certain types of probation mission (e.g., court-oriented compliance and the balanced service) seem inherently more compatible with justice model precepts. Both the abstract level of values and goals and the practical level of activities and relationships are relevant here. Sometimes the current system is closer to the proposed reform than at first may be apparent (e.g., probation officers may already be functioning primarily as mediators, but think of themselves as engaged in the "collateral contacts of casework").

Strength of present identity. Type of current mission is not in itself a sufficient determinant; strength of commitment to that mission is crucial. Commitment depends on such factors as the number and power of interest groups served by the organization's present identity and the strength of agency commitment to those groups; the extent to which current mission is manifested in and supported by formal procedures and tools; and the fit between organizational identity and ideological currents of the immediate setting. To some extent, the success of a new model may depend on its ability to label things appealingly (e.g., "sanction" tends to be more acceptable than "punishment").

Current organization problems. If the agency or system currently is experiencing no serious problems, there will be little motivation to institute reform or cooperate with change initiatives. Where problems exist, acceptance of a particular reform will depend in large part on the extent to which it resolves those problems, and does so more effectively than competing options for change. The number and nature of new problems raised by the reform also will influence acceptance and success. On balance, the reform must be perceived as contributing to organizational survival. No agency can be expected to commit organizational suicide, even for a good cause.

Comprehensiveness of change effort. The plan for reform must take into account all major elements of the system in which reform will occur. A change in probation's mission or methods may be thwarted if it interferes substantially with the goals of complementary or competing organizations. This does not mean that cooperation must be universal before reforms can proceed, but that changes must be designed either to satisfy major needs or to neutralize potential opposition within social, political, economic, and ideological spheres.

Successful introduction of justice model reforms thus will depend not only on their fit with the current mission or character of the probation department, but also on the strength of that character and the relative extent to which current identity and proposed reforms serve organizational and environmental needs. What happens if reform is attempted in an organization with a strong and incompatible identity? What results, for example, are likely in an organization that has based a viable character on the law-enforcement mode? Or in an agency committed in mission and methods to offender rehabilitation?

There is little evidence as yet to answer these questions directly, but the frustrated reforms described at the outset of this chapter may provide a few clues. Reforms, it seems, have no effect or are counterproductive when they fail to engage existing systems, ignore predominant ideological themes, contradict important trends, or threaten basic needs. The moral suasion of any proposed reform is easily overpowered by the sheer logic of an existing arrangement that works.

For illustration, consider a setting in which the probation agency has gained public recognition and official support for its hard-line approach to offender control. The entire justice system probably is responsive to local demands for public safety. Arrest rates may be high, sentencing relatively harsh, and resources invested heavily in surveillance. A high degree of cooperation among police, sheriff, and probation officers may have produced in each some degree of dependence on the others. Judges also may expect and depend on the control orientation of probation as they articulate sentences.

If probation in this setting were to draw back from its surveillance role, the system around it could be expected to attempt to neutralize this change. Probationers probably would be arrested more often for new crimes and less often cited for violations of probation conditions. For many arrests, charges would be upgraded to more serious offenses in an attempt to insure more control-oriented dispositions upon conviction. More of those convicted would receive sentences involving incarceration—state prison, jail, weekend confinement, split sentences, even civil commitment—and, where probation was granted, conditions related only tenuously to the offense more often would be imposed. Ironically, the implementation of justice model probation might produce an increase in the severity of sanctions and an extension of the system of social control.

Parallel distortions probably would occur in a system committed to rehabilitation, as the prohibition against involuntary treatment led judges and probation officials to relabel services as sanctions or to exert informal pressures on offenders to accept "voluntary" aid. If we have learned anything from the history of criminal justice reform, it is that a system strongly committed to any goal will find ways of pursuing its real objectives, whether by changing labels, by shifting to underground, informal measures, or by compensatory actions at another level or in another sphere. The justice model cannot be expected to turn public vengeance into equity and justice for offenders; nor can it easily overcome the tenacious grip of a system that succeeds by serving other goals. The model must be applied where the mood is not vengeful and where justice can assume its proper place.

SUMMARY AND CONCLUSIONS

In American probation today there is strong but not universal support for the major precepts of the justice model. Some of the directions this profession is taking seem to lead naturally to greater equity, fairness, and respect for the offender as a volitional human being. The move away from treatment to less judgmental offender aid, the structuring and monitoring of decision making, and the new emphasis on the victim/community as client are some of the more supportive trends.

Other strong trends seem to lead in the opposite direction. The widespread adoption of risk/needs assessment tools and their use in determining supervision level is the most prominent of these developments. Many departments, responding to demands for public safety, are staking their reputations on the ability to predict who will and who will not commit another offense and to place on individual offenders the appropriate amounts and kinds of control. Many also insist that the ability to require participation in treatment in appropriate cases is essential to the effective management of any community-based offender population.

Individual departments vary widely in apparent receptivity to the principles of justice model probation. Some probation organizations are already working on a redefinition of mission that would place them firmly in the justice camp. Los Angeles County, with the largest probation department in the world, is now planning for implementation of a relatively pure version of justice model probation (a focus on monitoring reparations and court-ordered restrictions on liberty, with services voluntary and brokered), and other jurisdictions have expressed interest in similar kinds of change.

A broad-based commitment to a incongruous mission involving offender rehabilitation or community protection through prevention of crime seems the most serious obstacle to justice model reforms. In such a setting attempts at implementation could be expected to produce not only opposition to reform, but some unacceptable distortions of the core principles and values of the model itself. We cannot predict what mischief might be caused by the attempt to force change in values through procedural reforms, but the cooptation of determinate sentencing by control-oriented groups seeking longer terms serves as a recent historical example.

The justice model, of course, could attempt to accommodate those values and goals that appear to oppose its implementation. In varied guises the model known as justice as fairness could live more or less comfortably with preventive, deterrent, or rehabilitative goals, taking on, rather than altering, the coloration of its environment.

Alternately, the model could abandon the presumption of overarching relevance to the entire probation field, contenting itself with the more limited but far more meaningful success that will come with full implementation in those jurisdictions to which it is conspicuously suited. It is within this latter option—standing fast on core values and implementing the model selectively but well—that the most satisfying applications undoubtedly will be found.

NOTES

1. Eugene Doleschal (1982). "The Dangers of Criminal Justice Reform." *Criminal Justice Abstracts* 14(1):133–152.
2. National Institute of Justice (1981). *Diversion of Felony Arrests: An Experiment in Pretrial Intervention*. Washington, D.C.
3. University of Minnesota, School of Social Intervention (1980). *National Assessment of Adult Restitution Programs: Final Report*. Duluth, MN.
4. Glenn Cooper and Anita S. West (1981). *An Evaluation of the Community Service Restitution Program: A Cluster Analysis*. Denver, CO: University of Denver, Denver Research Institute.
5. Doleschal, 1982:137. John H. Hylton (1981). *Rhetoric and Reality: A Critical Appraisal of Community Correction Programs*. Regina, Saskatchewan: University of Regina.
6. Doleschal, 1982:138. Emphasis added.
7. Eugene Doleschal (1978). "Social Forces and Crime." *Criminal Justice Abstracts* 10(3): 395–410.
8. The following examples are drawn from Doleschal, 1978.
9. Philip E. Mackey (1974). "The Inutility of Mandatory Capital Punishment: An Historical Note." *Boston University Law Review* (Winter), pp. 32–35.
10. Thomas Church (1976). "Plea Bargains, Concessions and the Courts: An Analysis of a Quasi-Experiment." *Law and Society Review* (Spring) pp. 377–401.
11. H. Lawrence Ross (1976). "The Neutralization of Severe Penalties: Some Traffic Law Studies." *Law and Society Review* (Spring), pp. 403–413.
12. Doleschal, 1982.
13. Doleschal (1982). concludes, however, that we should leave the criminal justice system alone, intervening only when absolutely necessary.
14. These studies surveyed current developments in probation, with a focus on administative responses to resource constraints: E. Kim Nelson and Nora Harlow (1981), *Responses to Diminishing Resources in Probation: the California Experience*, Washington, D.C.: National Institute of Corrections; Nora Harlow and E. Kim Nelson (1982), *Management Strategies for Probation in an Era of Limits*, Washington, D.C.: National Institute of Corrections; E. Kim Nelson, Lenora Segal, and Nora Harlow (1982), *Probation Under Fiscal Constraints*, Washington, D.C.: National Institute of Justice.
15. Patrick D. McAnany (1981). "Justice in Search of Fairness." In David Fogel and Joe Hudson (eds.), *Justice as Fairness: Perspectives on the Justice Model*. Cincinnati, OH: Anderson.
16. David Fogel ("Probation and the Justice Model: the Constituency of the Victim" in Patrick D. McAnany, Doug Thomson, and David Fogel (eds.) *Probation and Justice: Surfacing a Hidden Mission*. Chicago: Center for Research in Law and Justice, University of Illinois at Chicago, 1982), presents one view of justice as "righting the wrong."
17. Patrick D. McAnany makes this point in Chapter 2 of this volume.
18. For example, A. von Hirsch (1976), *Doing Justice*, New York: Hill and Wang; D. Fogel (1975), *We are the Living Proof*, Cincinnati, OH: Anderson; James Q. Wilson (1975), *Thinking about Crime*, New York: Basic Books.

19. M. Kay Harris, Chapter 1 of this volume.
20. The Model Sentencing and Corrections Act, which adopts a nonutilitarian approach to sentencing, allows for early discharge from community supervision, stating that rehabilitation objectives might be used to determine length of sentence in the community. Harvey S. Perlman and Carol G. Stebbins (1979). "Implementing an Equitable Sentencing System; the Uniform Law Commissioners Model Sentencing and Corrections Act." *Virginia Law Review* 65(7):1175–1285.
21. This title was used by Patrick D. McAnany in "Doing Justice to the Justice Model: An Exorcism of Some Persistent Myths," a paper presented to the annual meeting of the American Society of Criminology, November 1980.
22. Most of the contributors to this volume address implementation problems. See, for example, Chapters 1–5.
23. Doug Thomson (1982). "Practicing Probation as a Justice Pursuit." in Patrick D. McAnany, Doug Thomson, and David Fogel (eds.), *Probation and Justice: Surfacing a Hidden Mission.* Chicago: Center for Research in Law and Justice, University of Illinois at Chicago.
24. McAnany, Chapter 2 of this volume.
25. Nelson and Harlow, 1981.
26. American Bar Association (1981). *Victim/Witness Legislation: Considerations for Policymakers.* Washington, D.C.: Victim Witness Assistance Project.
27. For example, the district court of Quincy, Massachusetts, has attained nationwide publicity for its "Earn-It" program, a restitution/community service option that absorbs a significant portion of the probation caseload. Andrew Klein (1981). *The Earn-It Story.* Quincy, MA: Citizens for Better Community Courts.
28. M. Kay Harris (1979). *Community Service by Offenders.* Washington, D.C.: National Institute of Corrections.
29. David E. Duffee (1981). "Changes in Penal Goals and Structure in a Downward Economy." In Kevin N. Wright (ed.), *Crime and Criminal Justice in a Declining Economy.* Cambridge, MA: Oelgeschlager, Gunn, and Hain.
30. Nelson and Harlow, 1981.
31. Nelson, Segal, and Harlow, 1982.
32. Joe Hudson, Burt Galaway, and Steve Novack (1980). *National Assessment of Adult Restitution Programs: Final Report.* Duluth, MN: University of Minnesota, School of Social Development.
33. Cooper and West, 1981.
34. Joe Hudson and Burt Galaway (1981). "Restitution and the Justice Model." In David Fogel and Joe Hudson (eds.), *Justice as Fairness: Perspectives on the Justice Model.* Cincinnati, OH: Anderson.
35. National Institute of Corrections, Model Probation/Parole Management Project, orientation and training packet.
36. Michael R. Gottfredson and Don M. Gottfredson (1980). *Decisionmaking in Criminal Justice: Toward the Rational Exercise of Discretion.* Cambridge, MA: Ballinger.
37. See note 14 above.

Chapter 14

The Federal Role in Probation Reform

*Timothy L. Fitzharris**

Probation today is in trouble. Though it was seen as "the brightest hope for corrections"[1] a decade ago, probation's forward momentum has been slowed in recent years by skepticism about our ability to rehabilitate offenders or predict crime, by public demands for a crackdown on criminals, and now by diminishing resources in the public sector.[2] Probation has survived occasional criticisms of its conflicting goals and "negative" results over the years, but today's assault couples these accusations with the deadly weapons of public fear of rising crime and scarce government resources.

Never before has probation been so vulnerable. The frustration and fear associated with a highly publicized growth in crime have led to an increased reliance on institutionalization.[3] At the same time, voter disenchantment with big government and with an increasing tax burden in a declining economy has resulted, in many jurisdictions, in the imposition of taxation and expenditure limitations. These restrictions in turn have placed constraints on public agency budgets, with probation among the departments receiving the largest cuts.[4]

The political climate too has been unfriendly to expanded use of a sentencing alternative some view as leniency. Although the evidence is

*California Probation, Parole and Correctional Association.

that probation cases are handled in an efective and cost-efficient manner,[5] many politicians and hard-liners have been quick to doubt the positive findings of evaluative research while turning even the cautious questionings of researchers and academics into partisan political ammunition.[6]

In such a setting probation finds itself exposed and susceptible to attack. The reasons for probation's vulnerability include:

An unclear mission.
Overstated, unspecified, and unmeasurable objectives.
Undemonstrated expertise and inadequate standards and training.
Unsubstantiated results.
A history of inadequate funding.
Isolation from the public (noninvolvement) and a lack of public awareness.
Lack of strategic planning and effective management techniques.
A weak constituency.[7]

Noting evidence of a trend away from the use of probation, the strident criticism of its premises and practices, and the controversy over its ethical and legal foundations,[8] a group of practitioners studying the subject recently concluded: "What we now have has been characterized as a 'non-system', resulting from resurgent growth, entangled jurisdictions, conflicting goals, and too little articulation and coordination. Probation may or may not add to the confusion, depending upon whether its basic objectives can be clarified, its functions defined and operationalized, and criticisms of it (valid or not) responded to constructively—and in time."

"Responded to constructively—and in time." But how? And by whom? Who speaks for probation in these tumultuous times? It is the thesis of this chapter that probation today has no advocate, at least no nationwide or field-wide "voice," and that this role could be played effectively at the federal level by the National Institute of Corrections. A brief review of the reasons for the lack of leadership in the probation field today may help to put this discussion in context.

WHY NO NATIONAL LEADERSHIP IN PROBATION?

Except for a few isolated individuals who have spoken out, there has been no national response to the critics of probation. "Nationally, professional and employee groups have been strangely silent," observes a recent report. "Little official response to the GAO studies of local and federal probation, or to Martinson, Banks and others, on the part of national correctional leaders (including federal agencies with corrections responsibilities), has been published."[10]

Whether conceived as a legal concept, an alternative to incarceration, a service delivery mechanism, or an organizational entity, probation lacks a voice, an advocate. Why is this so?

One answer lies in the fact that there is no agreed-upon definition of probation or of its primary mission. Twenty-seven states and the federal government lack a legal definition of probation. Only four states define probation as a discrete sentence; thirteen provide for the suspension of sentence execution accompanied by placement on probation.[11] A recent survey of thirty-seven California probation departments found that twelve (mostly rural) had not adopted formal purposes, goals, or objectives, but even among those that had, there was significant disagreement and divergence.[12]

The time-worn controversy over whether probation is punishment, treatment, or an amalgam of both has now been enlivened but complicated by the introduction of the justice-equity model, which seeks a focus that goes beyond the offender alone.[13] We are confused by the fact that probation is both a legal status and an organizational entity that has objectives and performs a wide range of activities—some totally unrelated to the person placed in such status. Adding further to the confusion are those circumstances in which the probationer is supervised by someone other than the probation officer (i.e., the court or court clerk, the police, the prosecutor, state agencies, private organizations, or volunteers). Is probation essentially the absence of incarceration (leniency), or is it a legitimate sentencing alternative? Is it simply the justice system's "steam valve" to relieve burdened court calendars and bulging correctional facilities? Is it the system's scapegoat for the failings of judicial decision making or the counterbalance to prison in the plea bargaining game? It is true that every national study and commission has endorsed the expansion of probation, but none has specified exactly what functions it should perform or when and how it should be used. If we are not sure of our goals, terminology, or program thrusts, we can have no coherent public policy about probation at national, state, or local levels.

Probation's organizational diversity also hampers its ability to speak as a field. A 1980 survey located approximately 2400 probation offices in 885 agencies serving adult probationers in the country.[14] An earlier, less rigorous study found 2126 juvenile probation agencies.[15] These agencies are variously operated by state, county, or city governments;[16] they also may be administered under the executive or the judicial branch of government.[17] Five states have a unified corrections system; thirty states administer probation in combination with parole by the same state agency; a small group of states operate it as a state agency separate from the parole function; four states provide for local administration in the courts with overall supervision of probation officers and services by a state agency or supreme court; and the remaining states provide for local administration.[18]

Not only does the organizational diversity of probation agencies nation-wide impede unified public advocacy, but the political and administrative position of any single probation agency militates against its leaders speaking out. Where probation is a local function, the chief probation officer usually is competing with an elected sheriff, an elected district attorney, and elected judges. Having their own political bases and forums, the latter usually speak freely, often reflect their constituencies (or their perceptions of voter sentiment), and almost always seek reelection. Probation administrators, on the other hand, are most often career professionals promoted through civil service or merit systems, or are appointed and serve at the pleasure of the judiciary. In either case, they are in a relatively weak position to compete for public support with other elements of the justice system and other public service departments. Where probation is a state function, it often takes a back seat to state institutional issues and concerns, especially at budget time. Also, the agency usually is constrained by the governor's executive policy and political preferences or, in the case of the judicial branch, by those of the judicial council or governing higher court.[19]

Evidence of the inability to speak out independently is ample. The tenure of correctional administrators is generally short, particularly for those who rock the boat or make waves.[20]

If individuals are generally muted, what about employee or professional organizations as advocates for probation? Employee groups tend to concentrate on employee issues (salaries, benefits, and working conditions) rather than organizational issues or client services. Indeed, studies have shown that unions in corrections tend to impair correctional reform, taking positions against affirmative action, prisoners' rights, and community corrections, for example.[21] Professional associations are generally less myopic, more ready to embrace change and provide leadership. But beyond the development of standards, some limited research, and idea sharing at conferences, these groups have not developed strong advocacy roles for the field they represent.[22]

Academics and leaders from the private sector have had occasional impact on the field (i.e., Lipton et al.'s initial pronouncements, the years of advocacy by the National Council on Crime and Delinquency (NCCD), the American Bar Association's sojourn in corrections, the American Friends Service Committee's *Struggle For Justice*, and a host of national commissions). For the most part, though, change from the outside is resisted and gains are temporary. The few academics who venture from the university setting to become advocates for change in the field usually wind up blackballed in the political and then in the corrections arena.[23]

As for politicians, corrections represents dangerous turf: taking any position other than pro-victim and hard line on criminals could cost an election. "It is a no win, no votes, no constituency field. Politicians can at best get headaches out of it and very often adverse coverage."[24]

The courts in the 1960s and 1970s stepped out of their traditional hands-off role to make some major decisions that shaped public policy, prticularly with regard to due process in probation and parole hearings and the constitutionality of certain prison practices.[25] Some twenty-five states, in fact, today are operating their correctional systems under complete or partial court order.[26] However, the U.S. Supreme Court has noticeably drawn the line on the progress of the prisoners' rights movement,[27] and the Chief Justice recently called for the restriction of prisoner appeals.[28] The courts may be pulling back from a policy-making role in corrections, with as yet unknown implications for the probation field.

The leadership vacuum in corrections means that developments in this area are shaped by politics, pressures, and emergencies. "These pressures," says Breed, "without any kind of framework, tend to result in fragmentation where we badly need consistency and coordination . . . vacillation around policies and principles where we need understood positions, calls for reaction to emergencies rather than a proactive stance, and . . . frustration on the part of staff and chaos in terms of organization instead of efficient and effective organizations."[29] The lack of public knowledge and agreement leads directly to public fear, he argues, and in turn to repressive measures:

> As long as correctional decision-makers remain moral neuters on criminal justice issues facing the field, as long as we expect to operate without any clear cut public policy, it is understandable that the public attitude will be shaped by fear, misunderstanding, and understandable revenge. Corrections then becomes a repressive, warehouse operation with limited resources placed in those community programs which are most hopeful but which also are potentially the most dangerous.[30]

A more discouraging picture could not be drawn. Nationally, our correctional system is in trouble and there is little confidence that the field can pull itself together. For just those reasons, however, the National Institute of Corrections (NIC) was established.

NIC IS ESTABLISHED

"There are literally thousands of separate probation departments, and thousands of jails all working in relative isolation," noted the Senate Judiciary Report that explained the addition of the NIC amendment to S.821. "The recent proliferation of community-based corrections projects and the increasing participation of private agencies in corrections, as desirable as this trend has been, has added to the general picture of fragmentation and confusion of objectives and practice." Decrying personnel deficiencies in the field, wide variations in the use of correctional alternatives, sporadic research and slow application of results, the lack of coordination and communication in the corrections field, and the absence of an accepted national policy for corrections, the Committee added the amendment:

> The provision for a National Institute of Corrections in this bill is intended to establish a center in the nation to which the multitude of correctional agencies and programs of the states and localities can look for the many kinds of assistance they require. The Institute would serve as a center for correctional knowledge. It would identify and study the many problems that beset the Correction field. With the advice and active participation of state and local correctional personnel it would develop national policies for guidance and coordination of correctional agencies.[31]

It is clear that Congress intended NIC to be the focal point for reform in corrections. "The Institute would help immeasurably in bringing organization, direction, and public and official recognition and support to such efforts," the Judiciary Committee said. "Its coordinating role would also assist in eliminating the duplication and waste of public and private funds that now often attends correctional reform, particularly in the area of research." The Committee concluded:

> The National Institute of Corrections, as conceived in this bill, can *provide the needed coordination, stimulus,* and *leadership* . . . A National Institute of Corrections fits within the sphere of Federal influence because of the total and complete recognition that the state of correctional activities in the United States amounts to a national problem of such moment that *only this course can yield the results which we hope to achieve.*[32]

Moreover, S.821 specifically pointed to the priority of community corrections (including probation), remarking that "the projected scope of activities, covering both adult and juvenile offenders and the full range of correctional problems, programs, and needs—with due emphasis on *community corrections as opposed to institutional corrections*—would establish the Institute as the focal point for a long belated national drive to bring about vitally needed improvements and reform in corrections."[33]

It is clear from the record that the Congress intended NIC to be (among other things) the national advocate for probation. Through its aggressive leadership, it was hoped, would come unification, coordination, consistent philosophy, clearly stated national corrections policy, research initiatives with attendant proliferation of the successful methodologies, and ultimately increased correctional effectiveness.

With these high hopes, and apparently without debate or dissent, NIC was created and sent into battle.

SHOULD NIC ASSUME A STRONGER LEADERSHIP ROLE?

It is the central thesis of this chapter that the National Institute of Corrections was created explicitly for the purpose of centralizing and focusing corrections reform efforts nationwide and that it provides the best hope for developing the leadership so necessary in probation today. At first blush, this position may not seem congruent with the current federal trend toward decentralization and local control. Nor does the early period of the Reagan presidency seem an encouraging time to advance such a position.

NIC staff members themselves are not certain that national leadership is the role the institute should be playing. NIC Director Allen Breed has said, "I seriously question that a Federal agency, regardless of size, should have such a strong role in developing public policy in corrections."[34] Robert L. Smith, NIC's assistant director, expressed similar skepticism: "Since the county and the state or even the professional associations can't do the job, a Federal agency is given the opportunity. I just don't see higher levels of government being able to do what the locals have not been able to do. I'm not even sure that I want a Federal intervention in corrections 'ala' LEAA."[35]

The first task, then, is to explore whether NIC has a commission to proceed in this area; the second, to determine the appropriateness of that role today, even if originally granted in 1974.

NIC's Commission

The expression of purpose by the Senate Judiciary Committee is very clear: NIC was established to overcome the problems of fragmentation in corrections and "the confusion of objectives and practice." There was an underlying expression of hope in the Committee's statements that NIC would enhance communication in the corrections field, and with "the advice and active participation of state and local correctional personnel, *develop national policies for the guidance and coordination of correctional agencies.*"[36]

Nothwithstanding the language of legislative intent, it has been argued that there is no ground swell of support for correctional reform nationally.

Smith of NIC doubts that the fedearl government recognizes corrections as a national problem: "Corrections (or at least Part E) was hammered into LEAA as an afterthought and over the protest of many. It was deleted from current legislation. NIC existed as an idea for three years without an appropriation and then it was modest. If corrections is seen as a National problem, the behavior of Congress sure makes it a well-kept secret."[37]

That there is no uniform demand for correctional reform throughout the land today is not the point. Areas of public service that are (and historically have been) unpopular, and to which the citizenry would rather not face up, will never get such recognition. There may be a moment of support and a national call to action during a perceived crisis, but it will quickly subside. This is as true with a national gun control policy or a national energy policy as it is with corrections. The fact that the administration of criminal justice is generally perceived to be a function of local government makes a national initiative even more elusive. This being the case, it is important to review the genesis of NIC's commission.

The Chief Justice of the United States proposed the creation of a national corrections training academy with a strong technical assistance capability during the National Conference on Corrections held in 1971 at Williamsburg, Virginia. The 350 delegates to the conference, including national leaders in corrections, education, and other disciplines associated with corrections, enthusiastically endorsed the proposal and recommended that federal government establish the National Institute.[38]

Its proposed functions were to include:

Service as a clearinghouse for information on crime and corrections.
Provision of consultant services to Federal, state, and local agencies on all aspects of corrections.
Development of corrections programs.
Development and presentation of seminars, workshops, and training programs for all types of criminal justice personnel associated with corrections.
Technical training teams to assist the states in the development of seminars, workshops, and training programs.
Funding of training programs.
Coordination and funding of correctional research.
Formulation and dissemination of policy, goals, and standards recommended for corrections.[39]

In April 1972, the U.S. Department of Justice convened a panel of state and local correctional administrators to develop the general concept of a national institute. Shortly thereafter, a more permanent policy-making advisory panel of correctional practitioners, educators, judges, and laypersons was formed which developed and administered several training and technical assistance projects before the passage of S.821 in 1974.[40]

The effort to establish the institute was given a boost by the prestigious National Advisory Commission on Criminal Justice Standards and Goals. In its 1973 report on corrections, the Commission made one of its major recommendations the creation of a "national institute with . . . authority and funds" to serve as "a powerful force in the coordination and implementation of a national corrections reform effort." Noting that expertise and information available to corrections was both limited and thinly dispersed, the advisory group suggested that the institute could provide a center and a pooling of resources "from which all states and correctional agencies could draw." "At present none of the [functions proposed at the Williamsburg conference] are being fulfilled effectively on a national basis," it said. The wide scope of the functions would "remedy this severe deficiency and give the institute the stature, and presumably the prestige, to gain acceptance and *a highly influential role in correctional reform.*"[41]

Finally, the Commission recommended that the proposed institute be given the responsibility for upgrading and revising the corrections standards it developed and presented in its 1973 report. Clearly, the intent underlying this recommendation was to give ongoing life and continuing consideration to the standards and goals by charging a permanent federal body with the responsibility for their care and maintenance. And for this purpose, the commission did not tap the federal judiciary, the Justice Department, the Federal Bureau of Prisons, the American Correctional Association, or any other national body; it called for a new institute.

The proposals finally came to fruition, as we have seen, in 1974 with the passage of S.821 (now Section 521, Title 18, of the United States Code). Paraphrasing the legislation, we can conclude that NIC was commissioned to:

Make grants to local governments, public and private agencies, and educational institutions.

Serve as a clearinghouse and information center.

Serve in a consultant role in the development, maintenance, and coordination of programs, facilities, services, training, treatment, and rehabilitation.

Conduct seminars, workshops, and training programs.

Conduct, encourage, and coordinate research on corrections.

Evaluate the effectiveness of new programs, techniques, or devices.

Encourage and assist efforts to develop and implement improved corrections programs.

Formulate and disseminate correctional policy goals, standards, and recommendations for federal, state and local correctional agencies, organizations, institutions and personnel.[42]

The NIC Mission

The National Institute of Corrections, now in its tenth year of operation,[43] has developed a mission statement which also suggests a broad federal role. Two fundamental assumptions upon which NIC operates are specified as follows: "1. *That an increasing need exists for federal leadership to assist state and local governments in improving correctional practice.* 2. That corrections has long been the weakest component of the criminal justice system." The statement attributes corrections' weakness to such factors as fragmentation, conflicting purposes, the lack of a commonly accepted national policy, and the need for training and assistance. "Based on these circumstances," continues the mission statement,

> *NIC has taken a leadership role to ensure that state and local corrections have an advocate at the national level* and are provided practical guidance and assistance. . . . The National Institute of Corrections will continue as *the primary national advocate for federal correctional policy affecting state and local correctional programs.* . . . To accomplish this, the Institute will co-ordinate its efforts and interest with other federal agencies. The coordination of these resources will be a primary goal for the 1980s.[44]

In its final comment in the mission statement, NIC pledges to assume leadership in the corrections field: "The National Institute of Corrections will continue to offer its services in a timely and realistic way to state and local correctional agencies and *assume a leadership role in the formation of federal policy."* [45]

The Mission's Relevance Today

NIC's commission is clear. The need and purpose have been agreed upon by the Chief Justice of the United States, the National Advisory Commission, a representative national assembly of correctional practitioners, the Congress, and the field (expressed through active participation and support). A stronger endorsement probably is not possible.

But there is a long history of opposition to intrusive federal intervention which cannot be neglected. Every U.S. president since John Kennedy has campaigned on the platform of getting the federal government "off our backs." President Reagan apparently feels that his lopsided election is a public mandate for return to local control and has acted accordingly. (This alone might suggest a more modest role for NIC in the next four years.) Any proposal to strengthen the leadership role of a federal agency thus should be examined in light of current trends and past experience relevant to domestic public policy making by the federal government.

The Federal Role in Policy-Making. Over the past fifty years, and especially since the late 1950s, the Federal government has assumed ever greater responsibility for dealing with state and local problems. Grant-in-aid programs have been a major vehicle for this expansion of federal influence, primarily because this approach very early was seen as a means of affecting local policy without resorting to the extreme measure of direct federal administration. Writing in 1937, V. O. Key, Jr., expressed a preference for a grant-in-aid system as opposed to federal assumption of responsibility for coping with national problems:

> The grant system builds on and utilizes existing institutions to cope with national problems. Under it the states are welded into a national machinery of sorts and the establishment of costly, parallel, direct Federal services is made unnecessary. A virtue of no mean importance is that the administrations in actual charge of operations remain amenable to local control. In that way, the supposed formality, the regularity, and the cold-blooded efficiency of a national hierarchy are avoided.[46]

Federal grant programs, then, are a device for achieving a national purpose short of direct federal intervention in local affairs. They can be designed to stimulate action in a field where none existed before, to guarantee minimum service levels, or to ease special hardships. Many recent project-type grants have been designed to demonstrate the feasibility of novel approaches to a public program, while others emphasize planning and coordination.[47] But it is clear that such indirect policy-influencing efforts vary widely in other important ways: they can be less centralized, more or less sensitive to local circumstances, and more or less burdensome to the communities they purport to assist.

Federal grants-in-aid programs were perhaps at their peak in the 1960s, when administrative tendencies were toward centralism and direct federal leverage to create the Great Society. (The style of this period is often referred to as Creative Federalism.)[48] Responding to local and state objections and criticism, the Johnson administration in its later years, and especially the Nixon White House, moved toward greater decentralization (the New Federalism)[49] even while pumping more federal dollars into state and local systems. By pushing decision-making to lower levels (the LEAA program, in its regional planning and required "pass-through" to local governments, was an expression of this shift)[50] the federal government turned to a more subtle form of influence: the demonstration program. Using seed money to promote desired innovations at the local level, the demonstration program became a major tool of national policy formulation and implementation.

Even these programs, however, have gone through an interesting metamorphosis, as Chelimsky points out. In the early 1960s it was said that a demonstration program "tests out a hunch or conviction based on experience or practice and *systematically builds up evidence* designed to show whether the hunch or conviction stands up to the test." Ten years later a proselytizing goal was added, defining the demonstration program as "an action planned to *prove* that an innovation is an improvement, with the additional express purpose of convincing others that the innovation should be duplicated." In contrast to experiments, which test uncertain hypotheses, "demonstrations generally proceed from the belief that the innovation will work. . . . Demonstrations have evolved because of the need to find new solutions to social problems *without extensive experimentation.*"[51]

It is clear that by 1972 the prevailing view of the demonstration program had expanded; it had, in fact, doubled to include two goals—to prove *and* convince—instead of one. By 1977 what had started out as a "test" of a "hunch" had become an innovation "operating at or near full-scale" for the purpose of "formulating national policy." There are indications, however, that the escalation expectations for the demonstration program have now begun to taper off. Chelimsky shows how the evolution in attitudes toward government intervention paralleled the changing climate of the 1960s and 1970s, "running from hopeful and confident in the early sixties, to grandiose and somewhat fuzzy in the early seventies, to analytical, cautious, and maybe a little sour today."[52] The most recent shift reflects some disillusionment and a lowering of expectations, a trend that is evident in changing attitudes toward our system of "cooperative federalism" generally.[53]

Attitudes toward federal involvement in local policy making have always been ambivalent, especially in areas such as criminal justice which traditionally have been viewed as local responsibilities. Indeed, some believe that the failure of the President's Crime Commission to specify implementation priorities for its many recommendations was a deliberate attempt to avoid giving the impression of strong federal control.[54] Currently, however, in part because of scarce public resources, but also because of growing disenchantment with federal regulation, we are witnessing a sharp downturn in expectations for federal aid to the localities, as well as a pulling back on the part of federal agencies from overt attempts to shape policy at state and local levels.

The Law Enforcement Assistance Administration, in its final years, was beginning to be more cautious in its promotion of policies and programs for the improvement of local criminal justice activities. Convinced that its role was not that of a change agent, LEAA officials urged that the agency advocate only those programs that had gone through "an appropriate process involving clear definition, careful design, intensive testing and full evaluation."[55] One reason for the shift in stance undoubtedly was local resistance to more overt pressures to assume the cost of demonstration programs once federal aid was withdrawn. And, of course, as diminishing resources hit local governments and local skepticism about the value of the programs grew, that resistance could be expected to increase.[56]

A turning away from direct federal involvement in local policy making, however, does not mean abandonment of the states and leaving localities to fend for themselves. The intergovernmental system is undergoing redefinition, not being torn down. In the process of rethinking what oversight functions ought to go with the provision of federal grants-in-aid, it is likely that the advocacy/policy-making role will remain more controversial than some others a federal agency might perform (e.g., information dissemination, training, research). But that role too is being modified, not discarded, and there are already some indications of one form it may take.

"Flexible Leadership": A New Model. In its report, *Improving Urban America*, the Advisory Commission on Intergovernmental Relations argued that success in criminal justice activities "depends on a combination of leadership and flexibility by the Federal government in providing assistance to state and local criminal justice efforts."[57] The notion of "flexible leadership" may suggest a new and different role for the federal government in domestic policy formulation and implementation. The main outlines of such a role are already being drawn. They suggest a more facilitative, flexible, and responsive role, one that the National Institute of Corrections seems eminently equipped to fulfill.

A few examples of current attempts to define a more flexible leadership role for the federal government may be helpful here. Fletcher observes that the failure of local governments to assume the costs of demonstration programs once federal aid is terminated is due to the lack of commitment to the program or policy by local decision makers. There may be some commitment on the part of the technicians who implement the program, says Fletcher, but there often is no integrated commitment at the top.[58] He suggests four ways the federal government can be more effective in demonstrating or advocating a program:

1. Efforts should be made to integrate these initiatives within the regular budgetary procedures so that commitment to them develops.
2. The federal government shuld take into account the uniqueness of such factors as community values and organization, the political system, and the type of innovation, timing, and be flexible in its application.
3. Some consideration should be given to the agricultural extension model, in which the innovations, knowledge, and technical transfer are delivered at the local level on the basis of perceived local needs.
4. The federal government must pay attention to its various parts and reduce competitive conflicts.

The way to get better diffusion of ideas, Fletcher argues, is to develop an intermediation system (or translator) that can adjust federal incentives to meet the unique needs of each user. The most effective networks for this purpose, he suggests, are the peer networks in which users have trust and confidence.[59]

A Mitre Corporation expert made the same observation in reverse concerning intergovernmental communications upward. Federal consultation with state and local levels, he remarked, "doesn't occur because there are no mechanisms in place which would allow it, or could force it to occur. Most agencies have no routine ways of channeling state and local thinking into the Federal planning process. Such channeling, if and when it occurs, is exceptional and *ad hoc* . . . It is a problem of regularized systematic mechanisms and procedures."[60]

LEAA administrators were beginning to acknowledge this problem just before the program was terminated. James M. H. Gregg said, "Systematic program development is very different from urging upon state and local governments the latest fad or the conventional wisdom of the day," and argued that scarce resources made it imperative that governments promote programs that 1) have proven potential, 2) address real needs, 3) address real concerns on the part of citizens and the field, 4) have real capacity to effectuate change, 5) provide reasonable periods of time for consensus to develop around the proposed change, and 6) contain an evaluation component.[61]

A recent study by Nelson et al. of models for unifying community corrections echoes these same themes: "Solutions to organizational problems in community corrections today must be fashioned in an intergovernmental context," the authors note, but "there must be a shared understanding of the problems, the strategies used, and the resources committed."[62] Success depends on a keen understanding of the field of forces within which the proposed change is attempted: "The ability to discern forces that support and those that oppose proposed changes, a sense of timing, and the ability to turn adversity to advantage are examples of the kind of leadership required to bring about more reasonable and cost-effective organizations for delivering community correctional services."[63]

Nelson and his colleagues provide an excellent list of initial questions to ask:

Where does the impetus for policy change originate?
What are the objectives of the policy change?
What is the scope of the policy change?
What intergovernmental relationships help to shape the policy change?
What revenue sources will be tapped to support the policy change?

What revenue sources will be tapped to support the policy change?
What linkages exist (or are being sought) between the corrections
organization and resources systems in the surrounding community?
What is the impact of the policy change on service delivery? [64]

Fletcher adds a list of factors that must be taken into account in determining the environment for innovation and transfer:

The value system of the community.
The political system of the community.
The organizational system of the community.
The type of innovation.
The legitimacy of the innovation (i.e., are others doing it? Is it unique? Is
it known to be effective?).
The timing of the innovation.
The perceived payoff at the local or state level in terms both of incentives
and disincentives). [65]

In summary, if a federal agency such as NIC is to play an advocacy/
policy-influencing role, it must be able to gain true commitment from state
and local participants (as opposed to simply providing economic motivation). We have coined the phrase "flexible leadership" to describe one
approach to engendering that type of commitment. The flexible leadership
model would contain the following elements:

1. An intermediation system, including peer networking.
2. A mechanism to channel local and state thinking to the federal level.
3. A means for developing a shared understanding of problems, strategies, payoffs, and resource comitments.
4. A vehicle for assessing the field of forces in each situation.
5. A recognition of the time needed for consensus to develop around
change.

NIC and Flexible Leadership. Because of its size, organizational
structure, commission, and congressionally mandated advisory requirement, the National Institute of Corrections is in an excellent position to
assume a strong but flexible leadership role in the probation field. Some of
its organizational and administrative characteristics, in fact, make the
NIC ideally suited to such a role.

Since its inception, NIC has been oriented to the field, in large part
because of the role played by practitioners in its historical development.
The language of S.821 also clearly expressed the intent of Congress that
NIC's activities be carried out "with the advice and active participation of
state and local correctional personnel." To institutionalize that concept

NIC established a fifteen-person advisory board made up of five federal officials (representing the FBI, LEAA, U.S. Parole Board, Federal Juvenile Center, and the Department of Health and Human Services), five correctional practitioners, and five individuals from the private sector who have demonstrated an active interest in the field. The advisory board plays a dominant role in NIC's policy decisions, including program thrusts and fiscal allocations. Every year, the board holds regional hearings across the United States to obtain input from the field on priorities, policies, and problems.

Its size and its less bureaucratic style (at least by federal standards) permit NIC to be more responsive, flexible, and adaptive. Because it has limited financial resources, it must set priorities, find "targets of opportunity," direct its efforts where potential payoff is highest, and so on.

Finally, NIC's staff is made up of experienced practitioners who seek continual feedback from governments and agencies regarding the effectiveness, practicality, and usefulness of its assistance. This feedback loop is continually utilized to keep policy and activity on track.

SOME NEW DIRECTIONS

If NIC is ideally suited to the flexible leadership role, what kinds of activities might it pursue?

During the 1979 regional "sensing" hearings conducted by the NIC Advisory Board, the California Probation, Parole, and Correctional Association (CPPCA) challenged the federal agency to assume an aggressive leadership role in correction.

> We are looking for a national body which:
> anticipates problems and issues;
> identifies core issues and develops alternative solutions;
> fosters innovation;
> sponsors futuristic peeks into tomorrow's corrections;
> plays a major role in researching, evaluating, synthesizing, summarizing, and disseminating information;
> develops ways to coordinate local, state, Federal efforts/approaches;
> determines if training is relevant to the field's current needs.[66]

Some of the vehicles suggested by the CPPCA for achieving these purposes were leadership institutes, town-hall meetings, critical-issues surveys (such as an annual survey to assess national issues and set priorities), think tanks, consortiums, resource fairs, information series, and "methodologies which encourage innovation."[67] Many of the approaches mentioned would provide the "intermediation," "thought channeling," and development of "shared understanding" identified as missing in past federal initiatives. Some additional steps that might be considered by the federal agency in the support of probation are:

Facilitating the development of public policy for various levels of government through sponsorship of sessions at national, state, and local levels.

Identification of the purpose of probation; its strengths and weaknesses; its constituencies and publics; its varying "field of forces."

Sponsorship of reviews or reaction sessions by the field (and others) to all probation standards proposals (i.e., the President's Commission, American Bar Association, Juvenile Justice, California Chief Probation Officers, etc.).

Sponsorship of studies of the criticisms of probation for purposes of strengthening "a new model."

Focusing on critical issues such as 1) dealing with diminishing fiscal resources, 2) alternative funding, 3) the cost-benefit balance of correctional programs, 4) standards, 5) the differences among probation organizational models and goals, 6) the politics and probation, and 7) the impact of inter- and intra-governmental relations on probation.

Sponsorship of think tanks on special problems in probation (i.e., probation and the violent offender or the increasing liability of the probation officer).

Sponsorship of futurist studies relative to the needs and problems of criminal justice and corrections in the 1980s and 1990s, vis-à-vis probation's role.

Development and encouragement of formal and informal communications linkages, information sharing among peers, and community participation.

Sponsorship of training sessions on such topics as "The Politics of Corrections," "Corrections and Public Finance," "Managers and the Media," "Community Relations," and "The Art of Advocacy."

Development of an active clearinghouse or information center (where information is disseminated) as well as a passive one (where agencies must seek information).

Development of a more aggressive approach to technical assistance and technology transfer (provide examples of technical assistance available, ask for identification of needs, and ways NIC can help, etc.).

Sponsorship and development of a national campaign (i.e., public television and in-studio panels, Advertising Council promotions, education of legislators, etc.).

Development of a user evaluation system, field reaction teams, consumer evaluations, and other sensing methods.

Training of corrections advocates.

Initiation of an active program of involvement in legislative deliberations affecting probation.

Emphasizing and suggesting ways and means of developing the role of probation in dealing with the problems of prison and jail overuse and crowding.

TWO EXAMPLES

Perhaps the flexible leadership role can best be clarified by some specific examples. Two that readily come to mind are the recent efforts to begin developing *a national focal point for probation* and *a national corrections policy*.

Probation Focal Point

Aware of probation's problems with organizational diversity, lack of clear purpose, and political vulnerability, several influential leaders in the field have approached NIC requesting assistance in developing a national probation "center."[68] The actual structure of the center—whether it be a training academy, a think tank located at a university, or a permanent, semiannual national probation conference—has not been specified.

The purpose, according to the probation leaders, would be to create a national focal point for probation—a forum for directing attention to and resolving probation's generic problems (as opposed to responding to specific parochial needs). Activities might include broad standards development, creation of a national public information program, specification of needed research, and development of a communication vehicle for probation executives nationwide.

The critical issue here is not whether the proposal is viable, or whether it will come to pass. The important point is the suggested function of NIC. That the approach is *a local initiative* is crucial, as is *the facilitating role* to be played by the federal agency.

NIC is not being asked to determine what the priorities of such an initiative should be, or how it would be governed. On the other hand, such an effort would probably never get off the ground without 1) recognition of its national importance, 2) NIC coordination and staff support, 3) NIC fiscal resources (at least initially), and 4) NIC leadership.

Very few probation administrators (or other interested parties) have the necessary broad perspective, the time, or the resources to develop such an effort. Although the need for better communication among probation leaders and agencies has been acknowledged at every national conference in the last thirty years, virtually no vehicle for such exchange exists in America today.[69]

Such a capacity-building role fits both NIC's legislative commission and—because of its nondirective, noncontrol aspects—the requirements of the New Federalism. It is a clear example of flexible leadership.

For several years now, NIC Director Allen Breed has been the major advocate for development of a national corrections policy that would specify "what good correctional practice requires and what failure to achieve it portends."[70]

> While we [corrections professionals] have been necessarily focusing on the details of problems we cannot ignore today, others have been casting an eye to the future. Unless we start to act now to gain the lead role in policy development, we may find that when that future arrives, it is indeed unpleasant and unmanageable. . . . Far too often . . . we have sat on the sidelines or played minor roles while decisions were being made, only to gripe when we had to administer the consequence.[71]

But Breed is not proposing that the federal government *develop* a national corrections policy. As "the operator of the largest correctional system," the federal government has "an obvious interest in what such a national policy might require or proscribe," but "neither that interest nor the investment of the federal government in state and local correctional programs should give it special standing in the policy development process."[72] Further, he suggests a national corrections policy should strive to indicate the safe navigational passage without abrogating the power of any state to sail off alone.[73]

Breed has proposed that the field itself, through the American Correctional Association, take the leadership in developing the national approach. He urges the ACA to fund at least the initial development costs by itself, as a sign of commitment and a means of getting started promptly. Self-financing would "obviate the need to compromise over the development process," and "at least for the foreseeable future, . . . is the most assured form of support."[74]

Breed strongly recommends that the ACA membership seek out the involvement and participation of its professional affiliates and state chapters through carefully planned meetings and hearings on policy development. As the policy is developed, through a special task force made up of experts representing all facets of corrections, government, and the law, the ACA should turn its attention toward a broad-based implementation program designed to take advantage of the involvement and commitment of all levels of the corrections profession and other groups.[75]

In this second example of flexible leadership, NIC plays a problem-identification and advocacy role. Director Breed is providing leadership for the field, but is not directly influencing what the policy should be. In essence, he is lighting a fire underneath professionals in the field, challenging them to take hold of their own destiny, and offering some ideas on how that might be done.

A TIME TO ACT

In a January 30, 1981, editorial in *Corrections Digest,* Charles Bailey called upon corrections officials to take a proactive stance as a new administration entered the White House. "I feel there will be a carefully constructed federal response to crime in America," he wrote. "The questions yet to be resolved are what structure that response will take, how much money the Reagan administration is willing to invest, and what part corrections professionals will play in the decision-making process that is now on-going." [76]

If our hopes are to be realized, probation needs facilitating, flexible, and unifying national leadership. The National Institute of Corrections can play that role effectively, helping state and local probation professionals to define their own mission, develop their own constituencies, and move the field toward more active participation in the decision-making process through which the future of probation will be decided.

NOTES

1. National Advisory Commission on Criminal Justice Standards and Goals (1973). *Report on Corrections.* Washington, D.C.: U.S. Government Printing Office, p. 311.
2. Two recent publications chart these developments: E. Kim Nelson and Nora Harlow (1980). *Responses to Diminishing Resources in Probation: the California Experience,* draft report to the National Institute of Corrections, Berkeley, CA: University of Southern California; and Timothy L. Fitzharris (1979), *Probation in an Era of Diminishing Resources,* Sacramento, CA: The Foundation for Continuing Education in Corrections.
3. *U.N. Paper on Deinstitutionalization and Residual Offenders,* presented at United Nations conference in Caracas, Venezuela, August, 1980, by the United States delegation.
4. In California, for example, despite the state bail-out of local governments and enactment of a new local justice subsidy (of which 68 percent or $37 million went to probation), probation departments experienced budget cuts ranging from 10 percent to 20 percent following passage of Proposition 13. These percentages were nearly twice that of the budget cuts received by courts and three to four times that of law enforcement or the prosecution. A review of probation agencies across the country found the California experience not to be atypical. See Fitzharris (1979) and Warren E. Walker et al. (1980), *The Impact of Proposition 13 on Local Criminal Justice Agencies: Emerging Patterns,* Santa Monica, CA: Rand Corporation.

5. Success rates vary between 75 percent and 90 percent in this country and in every foreign country where its use is extensive. See California Probation, Parole, and Correctional Association (1979), *The Future of Probation*, Sacramento, CA; and Harry E. Allen, Eric W. Carlson, and Evalyn C. Parks (1979), *Critical Issues in Adult Probation*, Washington, D.C.: U.S. Department of Justice. For a detailed discussion of the cost-benefit argument for probation, see Timothy L. Fitzharris (1981), *Economic Strategies in Probation: A Handbook for Managers*, Sacramento, CA: California Probation, Parole and Correctional Association.

6. For example, a large volume was synthesized in the famous summary of Robert Martinson—"With few and isolated exceptions, the remunerative efforts that have been reported so far have no appreciable effects on recidivism"—which has been shortened further in the popular vernacular to "Nothing works!" See Martinson (1974), "What Works?—Questions and Answers About Prison Reform," *The Public Interest*, No. 35.

7. Fitzharris, 1979:37.

8. For details on the criticisms and trends away from probation, as well as responses to the criticisms, see California Probation, Parole, and Correctional Association (1979).

9. CPPCA, 1979:30.

10. Fitzharris, 1979:30.

11. Ohio State University (1978). *Critical Issues in Adult Probation*, "Technical Issue Paper on Legal Issues in Adult Probation," Report No. 7, Columbus, OH, pp. 227–230.

12. The Foundation for Continuing Education in Corrections (1979). *Probation Information Series, Report #1*. Sacramento, CA: The Future of Probation Project.

13. David Fogel and Doug Thomson, remarks delivered at the American Correctional Association convention in San Diego on August 20, 1980.

14. National Council on Crime and Delinquency (1980). "National Probation Reporting Study." In *Uniform Parole Reports, Final Report*. San Francisco.

15. U.S. Department of Justice, LEAA, National Criminal Justice Information and Statistics Service (1978). *State and Local Probation and Parole Systems*. Washington, D.C.: U.S. Government Printing Service, p. 2.

16. The LEAA study found 916 juvenile agencies operated by the state, 1,167 by the county, and 43 by a city government. The NCCD data found adult agencies to be distributed as follows:

	Branch		
Level	*Executive*	*Judicial*	*TOTAL*
State	44	12	56
County	538	241	779
Municipal	30	20	50
	612	273	885

17. National Council on Crime and Delinquency, 1980:26. NCCD observes that the importance of this distinction is somewhat tempered by the fact that the judiciary often has appointive power over staff in executive branch agencies, and at the operational level all probation agencies are necessarily responsive to the judiciary.

18. Ohio State, 1978:197–200.

19. Fitzharris, 1979:19–20.

20. Allen Breed (1979). Speech to the 49th Annual CPPCA State Training Conference, June 14, 1979, as reported in *California Correctional News* 33(7-8):12.

21. American Justice Institute (1980). *The Organizational Context of The Prison: A Study of Five Maximum Security Prisons*. Sacramento, CA: AJI.

22. Nevertheless, Allen Breed (1979) has expressed the opinion that "constructive change will come to the field of corrections only to the degree that professional organizations force it to." Recent activities of the American Correctional Association and the creation of a new organization—the National Association of Probation Executives—provide some hope that professional associations may be adopting a more aggressive stance.
23. Breed, 1979:10.
24. Breed, 1979:10.
25. Sol Rubin (1973). *Law of Criminal Correction*, 2nd ed. St. Paul, MN: West Publishing Company. See also Timothy L. Fitzharris (1973), *The Desirability of a Correctional Ombudsman*, Berkeley, CA: Institute for Governmental Studies, University of California.
26. NCCD (1981). *Criminal Justice Newsletter*, 12(4):6–7.
27. See, for example, the historic case of *Bell* v. *Wolfish* #77–1829, New York, May 1979.
28. Chief Justice Warren Burger, remarks delivered at the American Bar Association, Houston, Texas, on February 8, 1981.
29. Breed, 1979:11.
30. Breed, 1979:11.
31. Senate Judiciary Committee, 93rd Congress (1974). Report on S.821, Juvenile Justice and Delinquency Prevention Act of 1974. Washington, D.C.: U.S. Government Printing Office, pp. 49–50.
32. Senate Judiciary Committee, 1974:53–54 (emphasis added).
33. Senate Judiciary Committee, 1974:53 (emphasis added).
34. Allen Breed (1980). Letter to author, October 6.
35. Robert L. Smith (1980). Letter to author, September 30.
36. Senate Judiciary Committee, 1974:25. (emphasis added).
37. Smith, 1980.
38. National Institute of Corrections (1980). *Mission for the 80's*. Washington, D.C.: Federal Prison Industries Printing Plant, p. 1.
39. National Advisory Commission, 1973:604 (emphasis added).
40. Senate Judiciary Committee, 1974:50.
41. National Advisory Commission, 1973:604.
42. Senate Judiciary Committee, 1974:33 (emphasis added).
43. Although the enabling legislation passed in 1974, it was not until fiscal year 1977 that the first congressional appropriation for the Institute was made. For two years, the Institute operated as a joint project of LEAA and the Federal Bureau of Prisons.
44. National Institute of Corrections, 1980:3 (emphasis added).
45. NIC, 1980:12 (emphasis added).
46. V.O. Key, Jr. (1937). *The Administration of Federal Grants to States*. Chicago: Public Administration Service, p. 383.
47. Diel S. Wright (1968). *Federal Grants-In-Aid: Perspectives and Alternatives*. Washington, D.C.: American Enterprise for Public Policy Research, pp. 5–6.
48. During the Johnson years, over 240 new grant programs were enacted, and the assistance dollars were more than doubled. See David Burlkes (1974). "How Fares Federalism in the Mid-Seventies?" In Joseph A. Ureges (ed.), *The Dimensions of Public Administration*. Boston: Allyn & Brown, Inc., p. 104.
49. Leigh E. Grosenick, ed. (1973). *The Administration of The New Federalism: Objectives and Issues*. Washington, D.C.: American Society for Public Administration.
50. Advisory Commission on Intergovernmental Relations (1977). *Safe Streets Reconsidered: The Block Grant Experience 1968–1975*. Washington, D.C., pp. 12–14. LEAA later modified the broader block grant approach to a categorical one, which met with serious criticism by some reviewers, including ACIR.
51. Eleanor Chelimsky, ed. (1978). *Proceedings of a Symposium on the Institutionalization of Federal Programs at the Local Level*. McLean, VA: The Mitre Corp., p. 1.

52. Chelimsky, 1978:2.
53. Carl W. Steinberg (1981). "Beyond the Days of Wine and Roses: Intergovernmental Management in a Cutback Environment." *Public Administration Review*, January/February.
54. Gerald M. Caplan (1973). "Reflections on the Nationalization of Crime, 1964–1968," *Arizona State University Law Journal* 3:594.
55. James M. H. Gregg, Administrator, LEAA, in Chelimsky, 1978:83.
56. Blair G. Ewing, Director of the National Institute of Law Enforcement and Criminal Justice, in Chelimsky, 1978:15.
57. Advisory Commission on Intergovernmental Relations (1976). *Improving Urban America: A Challenge To Federalism.* Washington, D.C., p. 24.
58. The corollary is that as long as these programs are treated as separate functions and separate departments within a local or state agency, it is very easy to sever them when they become politically or economically infeasible. See Thomas Fletcher, Stanford Research International, in Chelimsky, 1978:157.
59. Fletcher in Chelimsky, 1978:158.
60. Chelimsky, 1978:22.
61. Gregg in Chelimsky, 1978:88.
62. E. K. Nelson, Jr., Robert Cushman, and Nora Harlow (1980). *Unification of Community Corrections* Washington, D.C.: U.S. Government Printing Office. For a discussion of the importance to government of adopting an interactive role (rather than a "center-periphery" mode), see Donald A. Schon (1971), *Beyond the Stable State.* New York: W.W. Norton & Co.
63. Nelson et al. (1980).
64. Nelson et al. (1980).
65. Fletcher in Chelinsky, 1978.
66. CPPCA testimony before NIC Advisory Board, Los Angeles Hearing, November 6, 1979, Terminal Island, CA, reported in CPPCA (1979), *California Correctional News*, 33(12):5.
67. CPPCA, 1979:5.
68. Craig D. Dobson, Memorandum to Robert L. Smith, "Recommendations of the Clearinghouse Planning Seminar, October 27–28, 1980," dated November 3, 1980; Letter from author to Larry Solomon, NIC, dated January 28, 1981.
69. There is some indication that this may be changing. The same probation leaders who approached NIC concerning a national probation center have now formed a new organization called the National Association of Probation Executives. The group's goals include effecting communication linkages among probation administrators and creating a political voice for probation nationally.
70. Washington Crime News Services (1981). *Corrections Digest* 12(3):8.
71. Allen Breed (1980). "Mission Possible," remarks delivered at The American Correctional Association Congress in San Diego, CA, August 17, pp. 14–15.
72. *Corrections Digest*, 1981:8.
73. Breed, 1980:5.
74. *Corrections Digest*, 1981:9.
75. *Corrections Digest*, 1981:9.
76. *Corrections Digest*, 1981:9.

About the Editors

Patrick D. McAnany is a professor of criminal law and criminal justice at the University of Illinois at Chicago. He graduated from Harvard Law School in 1960, taught and practiced law in Missouri and Illinois, and served as Rapporteur for the Illinois Unified Code of Corrections from 1969 to 1971. His previous books and articles reflect a continuing interest in sentencing and corrections.

Doug Thomson received his Ph.D. in sociology from the University of Illinois at Chicago, where he is assistant director of the Center for Research in Law and Justice. He began his criminal justice career as a volunteer probation officer and served as research coordinator at the Cook County (Chicago, Illinois) Juvenile Court. Dr. Thomson's previous research and associated publications include studies of police social work, juvenile diversion and restitution programs, probation training, enforcement behaviors, and revocation practices. His current research focuses on criteria used in sanctioning juvenile offenders and on public perceptions of criminal sentences.

David Fogel, who received his D.Crim. from the University of California at Berkeley, is professor of criminal justice at the University of Illinois at Chicago. His previous positions include tours of service as commissioner of corrections in Minnesota and executive director of the Illinois Law Enforcement Commission. His books and articles have focused on correctional practices and policies. As a Fulbright and U.S. German Marshall Fund Fellow, Dr. Fogel recently completed a study of alternatives to incarceration in Western Europe.